A SENSE OF PLACE

HARVARD EAST ASIAN MONOGRAPHS 361

A SENSE OF PLACE

The Political Landscape in Late Medieval Japan

David Spafford

Published by the Harvard University Asia Center
and distributed by Harvard University Press
Cambridge (Massachusetts) and London, 2013

Printed in the United States of America

The Harvard University Asia Center publishes a monograph series and, in coordination with the Fairbank Center for Chinese Studies, the Korea Institute, the Reischauer Institute of Japanese Studies, and other faculties and institutes, administers research projects designed to further scholarly understanding of China, Japan, Vietnam, Korea, and other Asian countries. The Center also sponsors projects addressing multidisciplinary and regional issues in Asia.

Library of Congress Cataloging-in-Publication Data

Spafford, David.
A sense of place : the political landscape in late medieval Japan / David Spafford.
pages cm. – (Harvard East Asian monographs ; 361)
Includes bibliographical references and index.
Summary: "Examines the vast Kanto region as a locus of cultural identity and an object of familial attachment during the political and military turmoil of the late fifteenth and early sixteenth centuries in Japan"–Provided by publisher.
ISBN 978-0-674-72673-4 (hardcover : alk. paper) 1. Kanto Region (Japan)—Social conditions—To 1500. 2. Kanto Region (Japan)—Social conditions—16th century. 3. Place attachment—Japan—Kanto Region. 4. Group identity—Japan—Kanto Region. 5. Elite (Social sciences)—Japan—Kanto Region—History—To 1500. 6. Japan—History—Muromachi period, 1336-1573. 7. Japan—History—Azuchi-Momoyama period, 1568-1603 I. Title.
DS894.465.S73 2013
952'.13023–dc23

2013007729

Index by the author

♾ Printed on acid-free paper

Last figure below indicates year of this printing

22 21 20 19 18 17 16 15 14 13

For my parents, and for Viviana

Contents

Acknowledgments

Many deserve credit for anything good this book may have accomplished, while of course bearing no responsibility for its failings.

My mentor at Berkeley and since, Mary Elizabeth Berry, has been a constant source of inspiration and intellectual support, and without her fierce commitment to making this book as good as it could be everything would have turned out quite differently. My thanks also go to my other advisors at Berkeley, Irwin Scheiner and Mack Horton. Mack in particular I am indebted to for sharing unpublished translations with me, which I drew on in making my own.

Miranda Brown of the University of Michigan tirelessly read and commented on every draft I sent her (more or less the whole manuscript, in several versions). She has also been invariably patient during the time it took me to recognize the correctness of the suggestions she offered. Morgan Pitelka of the University of North Carolina, Chapel Hill, and Adam Warren, of the University of Washington, not only patiently read and thoughtfully commented on several parts of the manuscript, but were available to do so, over and over, in the frantic last days of revisions.

Adam was also part of my writing group at the University of Washington (UW), together with Elena Campbell, Purnima Dhavan, Shaun Lopez, Noam Pianko, Florian Schwartz, and Charity Urbanski; without our regular meetings and their thoughtful and mutually contradictory responses to my chapters, I would never have finished this project. Many others in Seattle read and commented on portions of the manuscript.

Paul Atkins deserves mention apart, not only for reading Chapter 1 and offering nuts-and-bolts advice about all things literature, but also for patiently reviewing and helping me improve my translations. Chapters 2 and 3 were made better by the suggestions of fellow participants in the History Research Group, in particular Pat Ebrey, Kent Guy, Benjamin Schmidt, Joel Walker, Simon Werrett, and (visiting) Todd Weir. I am thankful to members of the Society of Scholars at the Simpson Center for the Humanities who read a draft of Chapter 4 and helped me think beyond the disciplinary confines of history—especially Kathy Woodward, Kiko Benitez, Peg Laird, Matt Sparke, Amanda Swarr, and Lynn Thomas.

At the University of Pennsylvania, I received stimulating comments on the Introduction and on the project as a whole from my colleagues Linda Chance, Ayako Kano, Paul Goldin, Eugene Park, and Frederick Dickinson.

During my time at Tokyo University, Yamada Kuniaki, then at the Historiographical Institute, invited me to join the seminar on document-reading that he was guest-teaching at Keiō University, and gave generously of his time, cheerfully assisting me with obscure texts and sharing with me his extraordinary knowledge of Japanese history, for all of which I am endlessly grateful. My thanks also to Marushima Kazuhiro, then a doctoral candidate at Keiō, who made time to read medieval texts with me, and to Oka Yōichirō, at the time at Aoyama Gakuin, who spent long hours discussing ideas about castles and their archaeology with me.

Colleagues and friends at several other institutions assisted me over the years: Filippo Marsili, now at Saint Louis University, read drafts of chapters and offered valuable feedback—along with invaluable friendship. David Eason of the University at Albany repeatedly made available to me his bottomless knowledge of late medieval Japan and commented incisively on several parts of the manuscript. Together with Morgan Pitelka, David dreamed up the informal research group on "Japan's Long Sixteenth Century," which I joined from the beginning along with Peter Shapinsky and Tomoko Kitagawa. Over the last four years, the group has organized a number of conferences, where I presented early drafts of several chapters of this book. At the conferences held at the University of Southern California, Princeton, and Berkeley, I received helpful comments and questions from my fellow organizers and from several participants, including, among others, Thomas Conlan, Suzanne Gay, Harada Masatoshi, Kitagawa Hiroshi, David Neilson, Noda Taizō, Eric Rath, and Luke Roberts.

The students in the graduate seminar I taught at Berkeley in the spring of 2011 (Tyler Blalock, Andrea Horbinski, Larissa Jesanis, Shan Lin, Ti Ngo, Jonathan Tang, and Taro Tsuda) read a draft of the manuscript and offered thoughtful feedback, for which I am grateful.

I do most of my writing in library reading rooms: in Doe, at Berkeley; in Suzzallo, at the UW; and, most recently, in the Starr East Asian Library, at Columbia (for access to the last of which, I am thankful to David Lurie and Haruo Shirane). But for research, like most of my colleagues, I depend on the assistance of librarians—in particular Hisayuki Ishimatsu, then at Berkeley, and Keiko Yokota-Carter, formerly at the UW, were wonderfully helpful.

Over the course of researching this project, I have gratefully received institutional and financial support from several organizations: a fellowship from the Japan Foundation made possible a year of dissertation research at the Historiographical Institute in 2003–4. Grants from Berkeley's Institute for East Asian Studies in 2004, and Center for Japanese Studies in 2005, supported me during the writing of the dissertation that would become the starting point for this book. The History Department at the UW granted me quarters off from teaching in 2007 and again in 2008. A fellowship from the UW's Simpson Center similarly gave me relief from teaching for two quarters in 2010, which I took advantage of to complete Chapters 2 and 4. The Helen Riaboff Whiteley Center of Friday Harbor, on San Juan Island, generously offered me space and quiet to complete the first draft of the manuscript in the summer of 2010. Finally, research funds from the University of Pennsylvania allowed for a research trip to Japan in the summer of 2011, before I embarked on the final round of revisions.

At the press, I wish to thank my editors, Will Hammell and Deborah Del Gais, for being patient and flexible with me while efficiently shepherding the manuscript through production, and Melissa McCormick of Harvard University, for offering helpful suggestions late in the process, which helped me improve the final result in a variety of significant ways. For his beautiful maps, I must thank Bill Nelson.

My final and most personal thanks are to my parents, Robert and Susan Spafford, and to my wife, Viviana Mura, loving and supportive throughout. I imagine I could have written the book on my own—but, really, what would have been the point?

Figures and Maps

Figures

Maps

Abbreviations

DNK	*Dai Nihon komonjo, iewake*
GKS	Gunma Kenshi Hensan Iinkai, ed. *Gunma kenshi shiryō hen*
SKS	Saitama-ken, ed. *Shinpen Saitama kenshi shiryō hen*
KKS	Kita Kushi Hensan Chōsakai, ed. *Kita kushi shiryō hen*
NJT	Hirai Kiyoshi et al., eds. *Nihon jōkaku taikei*
TKS	Tochigi Kenshi Hensan Iinkai, ed. *Tochigi kenshi shiryō hen*

Note on Conventions

Throughout the book I have adhered to the following usage:

Ties of kinship were central to late medieval society, but various. The medieval vocabulary of kinship reflects that variety, raising potentially thorny problems of translation. My solution has been schematic and is not meant to be taken as more than an expedient device for attaining some clarity of expression.

Contemporary sources, and modern scholars, refer to two different kinds of kinship groups, the *uji*/*-shi* and *ie*/*-ke*. The word *uji* and the suffix *-shi* tend to be used for extended, multilineage groups that may or may not have lived together, or shared property or social status, by the late Middle Ages. Examples of such groups are the Ashikaga and the Uesugi. I call this level of kinship "family." I am aware that, in modern English, the word often denotes a nuclear family, but family is also the word most commonly used to refer to kinship in general so it seemed reasonable to utilize it for *uji*/*-shi*, which is often employed in a similarly nonspecific way as well.

Ie and the suffix *-ke* tend to appear in medieval sources (and in modern Japanese scholarship) to designate specific subgroups—lineages—within extended families. Members of *ie*/*-ke* typically shared residences, property, and hereditary titles. These lineages often took surnames based on their places of residence, surnames that could be used together with the family surnames or alone. Examples are the Ōgigayatsu, the Yamanouchi, and the Iwamatsu. I refer to these *ie*/*-ke* as houses or lineages.

Usage in both medieval and modern Japanese is likely to be less than completely consistent, particularly when referring to kinship groups that did not subdivide into individual lineages. Thus, the Hōjō are referred to sometimes as a family (*Hōjō-shi*), sometimes as a house (*Hōjō-ke*). Because most of the warrior elites that populate this study were part of kinship groups that *did* divide into lineages, I have tried to be consistent in differentiating between families and houses, at the risk of oversimplifying.

For personal names, in all cases I follow Japanese usage, in which surnames precede given names (e.g., in "Nagao Kageharu," "Nagao" is the surname and "Kageharu" the given name).

Toponyms function very differently in English and in Japanese. In English the word "river" in, say, "Mississippi River" is not an essential part of the name. In Japanese, the word river (*kawa*, or sometimes *gawa* in compounds), is an integral part of the name, with which it forms one word (e.g., Tonegawa). So, in general, I have maintained the original forms of place names rather than leaving half as a name and translating the other half into English. Thus, Arakawa instead of Ara River; but also Bannaji instead of Banna Temple and Hachimangū instead of Hachiman Shrine. In these cases, I have drawn on context to insure that my subject was clear.

There are two exceptions to this general rule. One is for mountains: I only mention Mount Fuji and Mount Tsukuba, and Mount Fuji in particular is so well known as just Fuji that using its full name, Fujisan, seemed counterintuitive (Mount Tsukuba followed, for consistency). The other exception is for castles. Modern Japanese scholars generally append the suffix *-jō* ("castle") to the names of fortresses. My sense is that late fifteenth- and early sixteenth-century castles were not christened, but were simply referred to by the names of the places where they were built. So I have considered *-jō* as purely descriptive and translated, say, "*Hachigata-jō*" as "the castle at Hachigata."

Names of provinces, too, present complications. Most premodern documents use the Japanese and the Sinicized names of provinces interchangeably: thus, Kōzuke often appears as Jōshū; Musashi as Bushū; Sagami as Sōshū; and so forth. For clarity, in my translations I have used the more widely known Japanese names, except when discussing naming practices themselves.

Dates and calendars in premodern Japan functioned very differently from our own. Years were not counted in one continuous era. Rather, the count of years would start anew whenever an auspicious or inauspicious event warranted the change (the accession of a new emperor, a famine). Each new era was given a name (*nengō*) so dates are translated as, for instance, "the twenty-seventh day of the twelfth month of the fifth year of Bunmei," or as "Bunmei 5.12.27," with the year preceding the month and the day.

Another problem is that the years in the lunisolar calendar used in medieval Japan did not exactly match the corresponding years in the Julian calendar used in Europe at the time. First of all, calendar years in Japan were slightly shorter than the Earth's revolution, so every thirty-three to thirty-five months or so, an extra—intercalary—month would be inserted to compensate for slippage. For example, an intercalary eighth month would follow the eighth month and precede the ninth. Second, years did not begin and end at exactly the same time as they did in Europe. Typically, the twelfth month corresponded to part of December and part of January; sometimes it could be as late as February. As a result, direct correspondences between Japanese and Julian years are not always possible. To return to the example I used above, we cannot simply render Bunmei 5.12.27 as 1473.12.27, since the last seventeen days of Bunmei 5 actually correspond to January 1474. Hence, when accuracy is not at risk and precision is not essential, I simply refer to the corresponding year in the West at the time of an event; when precise dates are required, I give them as "Bunmei 5.12.27 (1474)," where 1474 represents only the Western year to which *that particular date* corresponds.

Finally, Japanese words have been romanized according to the Hepburn system, as modified by Kenkyūsha; for Chinese, Pinyin has been used. All translations are my own, unless otherwise noted.

Introduction

A Persistent Medieval

This book analyzes the spatial and territorial imagination of various levels of eastern Japan's provincial elite during decades of intermittent but widespread armed conflict in the late fifteenth and early sixteenth centuries. The project began with questions about the shape of the land and people's attachment to the places they lived in—questions spurred by my own puzzlement over shifting boundaries and allegiances, and the ways contemporaries not only kept track of what they owned and what they ruled but also how they thought of these things. I was certainly interested in long-term shifts (because conflict lasted so long and local society looked so different in 1450 and in 1600), but my primary concern was with how people experienced (or at least wrote about) short-term adjustment and reorientation brought about by the vagaries of war. I began this study looking at a time of prolonged unrest and deep displacement for evidence of the waning of a medieval spatial consciousness and the emergence, from the turmoil of war, of a new political localism. What I found, to my initial surprise, was the tenacious survival of a spatial syntax that was centuries old, and which had generally been assumed by scholars to have had little real relevance by the fifteenth century. Its relevance—at times more narrowly political, in the organization and exercise of authority, at times more broadly emotional, shaping familial identity and dictating warriors' responses to circumstances—is everywhere expressed in our sources, if not always self-reflectively.

Silently, assumptions about landscape and territory shape every document. More volubly, contemporary sources—diaries, memoirs, chronicles, letters, and land registers—evince a strong preoccupation with upheaval itself and with family integrity, continuity, and definition. Always, attention and longing are directed at the past. The land over which families vied, the countryside through which warriors rode and marched, fade from attention, like scenery on a stage. At best, they provide the occasion for conflict—the real story to be told. In this book I attempt to invert this relationship, to foreground what so often is left in the background: the landscape, and fifteenth- and sixteenth-century Japanese's experience of it. I make no claim that this is the only story that needs telling, or that it is a deeper one, hidden below the surface of political or military events; rather, I propose that no accounting of the country's endless civil unrest can be complete without reckoning with contemporaries' attachment to the fragmented political and tenurial landscapes they inhabited. We cannot understand what families—our sources' ostensible protagonists—are about without understanding how they related to the region around them. Necessary here is an understanding that addresses the Kantō not as a passive receptacle for events but as a geographical space, whose "placeness" was constituted by (and constitutive of) the history of eastern Japan in the fifteenth and sixteenth centuries.[1] How that "placeness" was constituted in writings about place—self-conscious and less so, and more or less informed by generic conventions that directly or indirectly conditioned the representation of experiences of space—is the main subject of this book.

In this vein, I am concerned less—or less directly—with the dizzying complexities of alliances, rivalries, and wars that consumed Kantō warriors and many of our sources. No doubt, consideration of such events is essential to analysis of contemporaries' many and contradictory senses of place, but it is not, in and of itself, the end of this study. At various points in the pages that follow, I dwell on the fortunes and misfortunes of several extended families and individual lineages, such as the Yamanouchi and Ōgigayatsu lineages (houses) of the Uesugi, the Ashikaga

---

1. For help thinking through my assumptions on the subject, this book is indebted to P. Carter, *Road to Botany Bay*.

Lords of Koga, the Iwamatsu family of Nitta Estate, as well as the Nagao, Ōta, and Ōishi families. All these families are described, in their own accounts of themselves, or in sources produced by contemporaries, as natural, multigenerational organisms of sorts, whose life of decades and centuries is best told biographically, one incident at a time, one successive leader at a time (and there is an undeniable appeal in the ordering possibilities offered by a dynastic approach to the unruly, messy plot of a long civil war).

Because my main focus is on space and place, on the ways different portions and levels of the provincial elite negotiated their relationships with the Kantō region, I do not seek out an understanding of the protracted crisis of the medieval institutional and social order in the political vagaries of any one family or any one chieftain. I do not, in other words, organize my investigation chronologically, as a "biography" of families or institutions. The families and individuals I do consider I consider in terms of their positions in local warrior society and within the political order built by the shogunal house in faraway Kyoto; I do so to shed light on the ways in which social and political circumstances conditioned different kinds of families within the shifting geography of power of the late fifteenth and early sixteenth centuries.[2]

So, if attachment to place is my main concern, why choose the Kantō as that place? And, for that matter, what was the Kantō? The word, which means "east of the barriers," described the region as seen from central Japan, not as experienced by locals; it referred to a space "beyond" rather than a place, and did so with little concern for its own ambiguity. Even now "Kantō" evokes two overlapping though not coterminous areas—both a plain and a group of administrative units into which that plain and the surrounding hills and mountains are organized. As an institutional

2. In recent years, a growing body of scholarship in English has sought to tackle local history not only as a mirror of nationwide trends and developments, but also with an eye to its particularity and eccentricity. Much of this work has focused on Japan's periphery, and on the process of its assimilation, in an attempt to expose the fraught construction of a Japanese polity in the premodern and early modern periods. In particular, see Yiengpruksawan, *Hiraizumi*; Walker, *Conquest of Ainu Lands*, 17–98; and, for an extended analysis of the Japanese frontier, Batten, *To the Ends of Japan*, 19–122.

construct, the "Kantō" had acquired a degree of precision and specificity by the Muromachi period (1338–1573), for the term was applied to the eight eastern provinces of Sagami, Musashi, Kōzuke, Shimotsuke, Hitachi, Shimōsa, Kazusa, and Awa (Map 0.1). During the fourteenth century these provinces, which had once been known collectively as Bandō ("east of the passes"), were grouped together as an official unit in the territorial administration of the shogunate. A member of a junior line of the ruling Ashikaga family was charged with governing this unit in the shogun's stead.[3] At various times, a ninth province, Izu, was added to the other eight.

Beyond the sphere of governance, though, the name Kantō also conjures images of the vast plain that lay at the center of the eight provinces and made up, with its approximately 17,000 square kilometers, a little over half of their overall area. Except for Awa, which was entirely hilly, tracts of all Kantō provinces were taken up by the plain; flatland occasionally interrupted by low, mound-like hills represents the region's most characteristic and continuous landscape. Much of that flatland is constituted by a number of low plateaus covered with a thick layer of volcanic loam. The rest of the plain is made up of the shallow alluvial valleys and deltas created by several major rivers, which flow from the mountains and hills that mark the region's western, northwestern, and northern edges. To the south and east the Kantō is bounded by the Pacific Ocean, including the broad inlet now known as Tokyo Bay, which was unnamed in the Middle Ages, or simply referred to as the inland sea, and into which poured all of the region's main rivers: the Tonegawa, which at that time had yet to be diverted eastward into the Pacific, as well as the Tamagawa, Irumagawa, Arakawa, and others.

In Japan, the Kantō plain was, and is, a decidedly anomalous landscape: there are other coastal plains, to be sure, but the Kantō is by far the most expansive (though at about 40 percent of the surface of California's Central Valley, it remains unremarkable compared to plains in other countries). The plain is vast enough that most of the time, even before the air pollution of industrialization, its edges would have been lost in the hazy distance, though it is not so vast that residents or travel-

3. Koyama, "Tōgoku to saigoku," 233–37; see also Koyama, "East and West," 367–70.

Map 0.1. The Kantō provinces and Japan.

ers would long forget about the surrounding mountains and ocean. On very clear days, typically in winter, the faraway mountains appear on the horizon, reminders that the plain does, in fact, end.

This wide open yet clearly bounded panorama makes the plain appealing for a study of warrior elites' diverse experiences of their (geographic and political) place in the provinces. In most of the archipelago, local society developed and defined itself within the narrow horizons of valleys, hemmed in by mountains. In this respect, the experience of Kantō warriors living in the plain may have been atypical. To be sure, in the decentralized political system presided over by the Muromachi shogun, every region and locale was shaped by intensely particular circumstances. As seen in John Whitney Hall's explanation of his choice of Bizen Province for his now classic case study—as a region close enough to the center to reflect national trends while still retaining its distinctiveness—typical and representative in late medieval Japan are a matter of approximation.[4]

For this study, what the Kantō (whether the eight provinces or the plain) lacks in typicality, it makes up for in other ways. Whereas in other parts of Japan a certain environmental overdetermination may sneak into analyses of historical actors' senses of place, leading to the assumption that the local, the provincial (regional), and the nationwide would have rested on clearly distinct levels, in the case of the Kantō the very openness of the landscape, the very ambiguity of the distinction between those different levels in terms of daily political or cultural practice draws our attention to the analytical risk of environmental determinism. In other words, the Kantō's distinctiveness, its scale, forces us to question the very boundary between local and regional; it allows us to investigate that boundary, and the tensions it generated, within the more manageable scope of a local case study. How did a family like the Iwamatsu, for example, construct for itself those two spheres of action and identity (the local and the regional) in response to evolving circumstances produced by ongoing civil unrest?

In the Muromachi period the institutional dimension of the Kantō gave the region a particular cohesion, which now lends it value as an analytical framework. Even at its most assertive, the shogunate exercised its authority in the provinces indirectly, through the offices of military governors (*shugo*), who in turn relied heavily on their deputy governors (*shugodai*) to control the territory and carry out their political will. In the Kantō (as in Kyūshū, in western Japan) there was one more level of

4. Hall, *Government and Local Power*, 15–16. Hall, it should be noted, was less interested in local history per se than he was in using it to trace national trends in social, political, and institutional history. Interestingly Kären Wigen (*A Malleable Map*, 231, 235–38) also refers to Hall's case study in explaining her own choice to focus on Shinano, and her interest in the lessons about scale that local history can teach us.

intermediation and delegation: the governors of the eight Kantō provinces reported not to Kyoto as their counterparts did in the rest of Japan, but to the so-called Kamakura Office (*Kamakura-fu*), which took its name from the ocean-side town of the same name in Sagami. Presiding over this office were the Lords of Kamakura (*Kamakura kubō*), heads of a junior line of the Ashikaga shogunal family; day-to-day administration of the office was entrusted to the "Kantō deputy" (*Kantō kanrei*), a post monopolized by the Uesugi family. The shogunal family had its roots in the Kantō, as did many of its most powerful allies (and potential rivals), and the Kamakura Office was established to keep tabs on that volatile region after the Ashikaga removed to Kyoto, in central Japan, in the 1330s.[5] The region's distinctive chain of command was so ingrained that it was not abolished even after the collapse of the Kamakura Office, in 1455: the military governors continued to report to those who claimed its mantle, rather than to the shogun directly. Under the rule of the Lords of Kamakura (and then, later, under the Lords of Koga and the Uesugi), the Kantō functioned as a regional replica of Japan as a whole, as a microcosm of the shogunal regime established in Kyoto (with the important proviso that this small-scale representation of the archipelago had no central metropolis comparable to the capital).

But different scales also inevitably produced different types of relations to the land, and to local warriors. As in the rest of Japan, governors ruled Kantō provinces in absentia, seldom leaving the court (Kamakura), and entrusting day-to-day administration to the deputy governors in the various provincial capitals. In the Kantō, too, governors administered and distributed among their loyalists the nominally public lands that had not been converted into private estates; in the Kantō, too, the wealthiest families and temples collected vast portfolios of landholdings scattered far and wide and overseen from a distance. Still, for all its vastness, the Kantō was not the whole archipelago, and distances were not so great

5. The Kantō was not the only region far from the capital to be assigned to an especially created office: in Kyūshū, in western Japan, the Dazaifu was established to help the shogun pacify recalcitrant local warriors in the early, turbulent years of the regime. What distinguished the Kamakura Office from the Dazaifu, besides its less prominently military character, was that it was entrusted to members of the Ashikaga shogunal family.

that landholdings could not be conveniently visited. When in 1455 the Kamakura Office collapsed as a result of a fight between Ashikaga Shigeuji and the Uesugi, eastern governors did not behave as their counterparts would after the Ōnin War (1467–77) ravaged Kyoto. In the Kantō, no strong division developed between families that decided to retreat to their provincial lands and families that remained engaged in the struggle for supremacy at the center. Different strategies were adopted by warriors of different status and political aspirations, but they did not map onto the territory in ways that mirrored developments in central Japan. After 1455, the hostilities between Ashikaga Shigeuji and the Uesugi divided the region in half, but those hostilities remained, by and large, centered on that same Kantō region (Map 0.2). The more contained scope of the conflict and the ease of movement throughout the open plain presented elite families with the opportunity and the challenge of remaining engaged in the larger regional struggle while turning to the task of forging ties to villages and local warriors. The Kantō's continuing relevance as a political space meant that this crisis played out mostly within the region's confines.

To be clear: I do not argue that the region was independent or even, really, politically autonomous. But during the Muromachi period the Kantō was deemed unstable enough and distant enough from Kyoto to need its own institutions—being farther away meant having a longer chain of authority linking the plain to the center (it took nine days for news of the outbreak of hostilities in the east to reach Kyoto in 1455; under normal circumstances, the trip between the Kantō and the capital would take closer to two weeks).[6] This in turn led to a distinctive historical trajectory. Both local magnates and provincial representatives of the regime tended to look inward, to the affairs of the Kantō; the existence of the Kamakura Office meant that Kantō warriors did not have to take their demands and petitions all the way to the capital when they could not be addressed by authorities in their home provinces. The point here is not to stress that the Kamakura Office rendered the Kantō fundamentally different so much as to note that it created a coherent political space that transcended, in scope, any individual province. This coherent

6. *Yasutomi ki*, 122.

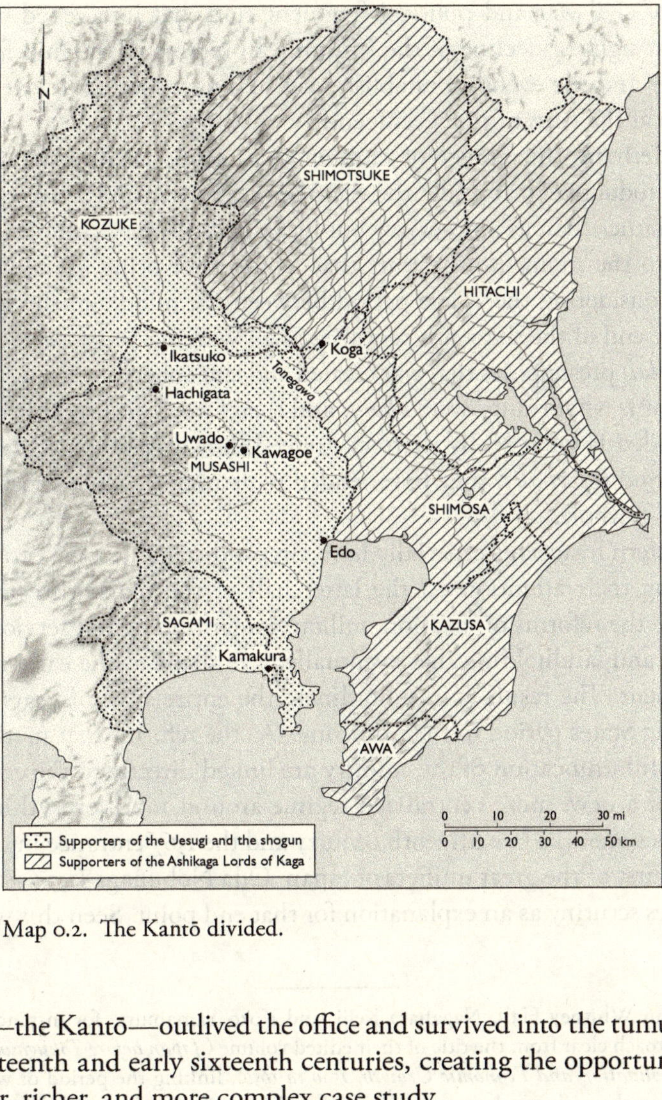

Map 0.2. The Kantō divided.

space—the Kantō—outlived the office and survived into the tumultuous late fifteenth and early sixteenth centuries, creating the opportunity for a vaster, richer, and more complex case study.

The Kantō's usefulness as a geographical framework also shapes my choices with regard to this study's chronological dimension: the main subject of the book is the years between 1455 and 1525—although I do analyze aspects of the decades after that, by way of comparison and conclusion. The period roughly corresponds to the first half of the nearly 150 years of civil war and political fragmentation that intervened between the first signs of decline of the Muromachi regime in the mid fifteenth century and the eventual establishment of a new shogunal government in Edo at the turn of the seventeenth.

Underlying this choice of chronological scope is the idea that it is more productive to consider the years between 1455 and 1525 in their own right, rather than as a necessary but bleak and not very compelling prologue to the momentous events that would later bring an end to civil war. Considering the whole period between the middle of the fifteenth and the end of the sixteenth centuries as a "Warring States period" (*Sengoku jidai*) presupposes that war created and lent coherence to an epoch—that war is what things were *about*, and therefore, logically, that how the war ended is what really matters. Indeed, however scholars subdivide the period *internally*, they have tended to assume that it is most intelligible as a whole.[7]

Western historians especially have almost disregarded the early years, focusing their attention on the latter half of the sixteenth century to analyze the reforms of taxation, military organization and service, commerce, and landholding that eventually gave shape to the early modern settlement. The result is to subordinate the entire span of years of this Warring States period to their outcome. As the reforms that marked the successful unification of the country are linked directly to the establishment of a new, more centralized regime around 1600, everything that came between the late fifteenth century and the 1567 entrance into Kyoto by the first of the great unifiers of Japan, Oda Nobunaga (1534–82), only deserves scrutiny as an explanation for that end point. Seen this way, the

---

7. John Whitney Hall, Nagahara Keiji, and Kozo Yamamura, for instance, make this approach clear from the title of their edited volume (*Japan before Tokugawa: Political Consolidation and Economic Growth, 1500 to 1650*), linking the period of war in its entirety to the early modern state that emerged from it. The Japanese edition of the book was given a title that more openly (but more narrowly) referred to the Warring States: *Sengoku jidai: 1550 nen kara 1650 nen no shakai tenkan*. In Japan, the period is more frequently subdivided two or three ways: either Muromachi and Warring States, or Muromachi, Warring States (from the rise of the Hōjō), and Unification (*tenka tōitsu*). Either way, the late fifteenth and early sixteenth centuries get short shrift. For a discussion of the problem from the perspective of Muromachi history, see Hall, "A Note on Periodization."

early years provide little of interest, whether because the plot of the civil war was still too messy, in the absence of the ultimate goal of national hegemony, or because they were graced with few personalities of any note.

Such a picture, of course, largely ignores the perspective of contemporaries. To be sure, in bemoaning the lawless spirit of the times, authors invoked grand comparisons with China's ancient warring states. Yet in retelling the prosaic particulars of recent unrest they parceled out time and events in a succession of discrete disturbances rather than in one, all-encompassing age.[8] As Mary Elizabeth Berry has observed, the sense remained strong that the peace was shattered by individual, circumscribed wars and disturbances, as if the resolution of each would bring back, as it always had in the past, a time of calm and order.[9] It was not so much the beginning of something new as a sense of the disordering of what had always been. The perspective was resolutely backward-looking; the point was to return things to their original (proper) place. But our attention to the later years has meant prizing change alone, be it "negative" change (disintegration, dysfunction, decline) or "positive" change (innovation, reform, vision). It has meant disregarding persistence, in the form of both willful conservatism and unreflective inertia (more on this shortly).

A focus on the early years also ensures that the study remains regional and local, rather than countrywide. With the rise of the Hōjō family of Odawara, which gained momentum in the 1520s, the history of the Kantō region entered—in certain respects, became—the mainstream of the history of Japan. Not only have the Hōjō rulers been hailed as the paradigmatic examples of sixteenth-century warlords because of their pioneering reforms and efficient governance (again the emphasis on change and outcomes), but their history, largely equated with the history of the Kantō as a whole, can only be told in relation to those of warlords and families far beyond the edges of the region. In this sense, the Kantō, as a place, is erased, or at least obscured, in a narrative of "dynastic change," shaped, biographically, by a succession of rulers. The transition

8. For a discussion of the appearance of the phrase "warring states" (*sengoku*) in sixteenth-century texts, see Kajihara, *Muromachi, Sengoku gunki*, 116.

9. Berry, *Culture of Civil War*, 1–10.

to Hōjō rule, which certainly had important repercussions on local warriors' experiences of the region they lived in and on their attachment to it, demands treatment. Most of that treatment, however, has been concerned with the ways in which the new lords refashioned governance in the Kantō. Here, I discuss the transition to Hōjō hegemony not merely as a way to look forward to the early modern settlement, but as a way to reflect back upon the world of the Lords of Koga, of the Uesugi, Iwamatsu, Nagao, and others who participated in the upheaval of the late fifteenth century.

Freed from this "teleology of unification," a reading of the sources that survive from the turn of the sixteenth century reveals what I call a "persistent medieval," a conservatism and an inertia that are everywhere in the texts but so often go unacknowledged. Spatial practices and the discourses that produced and perpetuated them ranged widely between reflexive and reflective, as frequent concern with immediate contingency (a dispute over a landholding here, mobilization of troops to defend a position there) combined with the inertia of spatial frames of reference and metaphors of place. Inasmuch as defending one's rightful claims to land, sometimes nearby, more often far away, came to be linked at this time with the ability to move—and move troops—across the plain, consideration of the language of space and place offers a privileged vantage point for an analysis of the tensions that shaped conduct in times of heightened uncertainty about the inherited wisdom of authority. To attempt to recover the significance of such tension, of local magnates and regional lords' anxiety about their place in the plain's social order, is to find not a new pragmatism, or a search for new solutions, but a dogged attachment to the ways of old. In this sense, this book finds meaning not so much in the abrupt shifts of an epoch of convulsive change, or in the gradual, inexorable accumulation of piecemeal adjustments—both of which have their place in fifteenth- and sixteenth-century history, to be sure—but in continuity, the perception of continuity, and the fiction of continuity.

The field of this enacted continuity was the medieval order, broadly construed. It was the medieval rather than the Muromachi order because although in institutional terms the shogunate was the wellspring of legitimacy, political authority and prestige were also handed down through personal and familial ties. These ties were of course worthy of pursuit in direct proportion to the access they provided to office and its rewards, and thus in certain respects were cultivated along with more openly institutional forms of political capital. But personal ties were also hereditary, or imagined and remembered as such, and were evoked and invoked in a spirit of continuity with the more or less distant past; thus, even when those ties were with figures higher up in the hierarchy of the regime, they were, often enough, cherished because associated with the past—the more distant the past, the better. In the late fifteenth and early sixteenth centuries, past precedent could be more appealing than whatever present loftiness was formally offered (and less and less often actually provided) by a beleaguered shogunate.

In using the word "medieval," I expose myself to the charge of wanting to have it both ways. But I use the word only as convenient shorthand for the order of things that the authors of my sources returned to over and over as a reference for claims both polemical and uncontroversial.[10] To assert that warrior elites clung to medieval practices, or at least to the memory of them, is not to suggest that they clearly saw themselves living through the waning of an age that had begun in the late twelfth century. Rather, it means that in the late fifteenth and early sixteenth centuries the practices and structures that enabled the precarious yet intentional balancing of the tenurial and political interests of a diverse and multilevel elite, although most commonly associated with the Muromachi regime, were understood to draw on older precedents. From its inception the regime founded its right to rule on its inheritance of the mantle of the previous shogunate, and Muromachi law explicitly drew upon the framework established in the thirteenth century. To elites at the turn of the sixteenth century the substantial repurposing of that original framework in the intervening years meant less than its continuing availability. Expectations surrounding land, for instance, were particularly inflected by fictions of continuity, despite the malleability of legal concepts regulating property, taxation, and management of holdings. In this sense, my use of the term

10. The word "medieval" (*chūsei* in Japanese) would not have been recognized by anyone in the fifteenth and sixteenth centuries—not in the sense we understand it now, at any rate. As with the European medieval, its Japanese counterpart was born after the fact, at a time of critical reappraisal of the recent past. From the beginning, the term was meant to denote a fundamental otherness from the present. See Keirstead, "The Romance of the Middle Ages."

medieval is less a statement about periodization than about disposition: to turn to legal precedents and judicial procedures for redress; to receive appointment to positions like governor and deputy governor, with shaky presents but prestigious histories; to hold on to ancestral lands located many days' travel from one's home, whose possession granted more distinction than income.

The changes wrought upon the landscape as a direct consequence of war and as creative responses to the opportunities and imperatives created by the faltering of the Muromachi regime did contribute to the early modern. But many of those involved were looking backward, not forward. Early modern rulers are commonly found by historians to be backward-looking, to search for solutions to novel problems in ancient texts and precedents. Less frequently acknowledged, except as an impediment to progress or a negation of the age's better instincts, is the prevalence of the same stance among the elites of the fifteenth and sixteenth centuries.

There has long been a tendency to view the unifiers as having brought to a halt much of the innovation that characterized the sixteenth century (with each of the three being viewed as more conservative than his predecessor), but only more recently have scholars begun to question not only the degree to which sixteenth-century warlords were great innovators, but also the degree to which they viewed themselves as such. The parvenu Hōjō are commonly used as poster children for a new breed of warlords, who claimed no attachments to the faltering Muromachi regime and based their authority and right to rule on their track record as administrators and their success on the battlefield. In fact, the Hōjō hardly passed on an opportunity to use the trappings of traditional legitimacy to bolster their rule: besides assuming the name Hōjō, with its associations to the virtuous warrior rule of yore, they made heavy use of titles borrowed from the old Muromachi-period government; they established family ties with the Lords of Koga; and they patronized, with great pomp and circumstance, the restoration of the Tsurugaoka Hachimangū in Kamakura, a shrine traditionally associated with the medieval warrior elite in the east.[11]

---

11. See Nagahara, *Sengoku no dōran*; Irei, "Odawara-eki"; Satō H., "Sengoku-ki kokkaron"; and, more recently, Yata, *Nihon chūsei Sengoku-ki kenryoku kōzō*, 221–32. Yata's skepticism about the judicial assertiveness and innovativeness is of sixteenth-century

Guiding the actions of the lords and rulers in the Kantō region were not only visions of reform and the future but, equally often, longings for the reestablishment of the only order they had known. Even their more imaginative solutions to the novel problems of war were hardly lauded for their novelty—"new" was seldom a term of praise, or "the future" something other than a cause for concern; the new was generally disguised as a rediscovery of something old.[12] The phrase *gekokujō* ("those below overthrowing those above"), invariably used to describe the age and its tumult, was not a celebration of new opportunities for advancement, but a lament for the loss of civility.

Below I provide a short list of the successive crises and their protagonists (the reader is referred to Appendix A for a fuller outline of these conflicts). What matters here is that none of the conflicts that took place between 1455 and 1525, from the falling-out between Ashikaga Shigeuji and the Uesugi, to the conquest of the plain by the Hōjō, were about institutions or legitimacy or ideas of governance. All were about disagreements over succession and appointment to office, and the slights and grudges that grew out of these disagreements. Each new dispute was, in effect, an outgrowth of, and a variation on, the one that preceded it:

1455–83	Kyōtoku Disturbance. War between Ashikaga Shigeuji and the shogun (represented in the Kantō by the Uesugi family).
1476–80	Rebellion of Nagao Kageharu, against the Uesugi.
1488–1505	Chōkyō Disturbance, also known as the war of the "Two Uesugi" (the Yamanouchi and Ōgigayatsu houses).
1507–12	Eishō Disturbances. The Kantō deputy dies quelling a rebellion in Echigo Province. Succession disputes erupt

warlords echoes Fujiki, *Sengoku shakaishiron*, 191–200. For an assertion of the forward-looking governance of sixteenth-century warlords that is more attentive to regional differences, see Yamamuro, "Sengoku no chiikisei."

12. Nor was this outlook exclusive to the embattled elite: Hitomi Tonomura (*Community and Commerce*, 122–24, 136–38) has demonstrated "the tenacity of traditionalism" of sixteenth-century merchants, for whom precedent (*yuisho*) was a virtue and innovation (*shingi*) something to be regarded with mistrust (even as they pushed forth an expansionist agenda that was in fact very forward-looking).

within the Yamanouchi Uesugi. The Lord of Koga, Ashikaga Masauji, is overthrown by his son.

1516– The Hōjō complete the conquest of Sagami and make inroads in Musashi, toppling the castles of Edo (1524) and eventually vanquishing the Uesugi at Kawagoe (1546).

Mostly the crises that followed one another over the decades ended with a (nominal) return to the state of affairs that had preceded them; each sapped the resources of those involved, and ended in the destruction of several once prosperous families and lineages even as it restored the main players to their original positions. With each new quarrel, divisions seeped deeper into alliances and families, until eventually they pitted against each other even members of the same lineage: wars were fought between lords and followers (Ashikaga Shigeuji vs. Uesugi; Uesugi vs. Nagao Kageharu). They were fought between different lineages of extended families (among the Nagao, Kageharu of the Shiroi house vs. his uncle Tadakage of the Sōja house; among the Uesugi, the Yamanouchi house vs. the Ōgigayatsu house). They were fought between brothers (Uesugi Akizane vs. Uesugi Norifusa), and between father and son (Ashikaga Masauji vs. Ashikaga Takamoto).

On one level, little plot can be discerned here. The inward turn of hostilities did not portend breakthroughs in, say, the rationalization of authority; these crises changed little, except for the names of the holders of various desirable titles. The violence that characterized such disagreements tells us how seriously participants felt about the stakes, but did little, alone, to produce novel outcomes. Those came about almost incidentally.

Assuredly, much did change in the Kantō during three-quarters of a century, some of it, more narrowly, as a result of war(s), some of it, more broadly, in response to opportunities and necessities presented by the emergence of competing centers of authority and sources of legitimation. Such change is hard to discern from the story of grudges, failed uprisings, and barely restored order that runs through any account of the period. Even broken down into individual crises for the sake of intelligibility, the narrative remains unconcerned with the stuff of governance, let alone reform, or policy-making. The arrival of the Hōjō at the close of the story helps explain the eventual eviction of the Uesugi from the plain, and introduces an element of direction to the plot of war. It does little for the other, hidden plot of governance—good governance—for which the Hōjō would be renowned, once they had the plain more or less to themselves. Changes, even those changes that did occur, remained curiously unconnected to the specifics of the conflicts, and to the goals of most actors in them.

The point here is not that war was not productive of change, for it certainly was, and sometimes directly; the point is that a more interesting story may be found in the ways in which war alone did not rearrange all priorities, and in the ways changes both in outlook and in practice were resisted even when they were recommended by the enticements of victory or the dread of defeat. Often enough, these changes arrived unsought and undesired, for what offered itself as an opportunity to some, per force loomed as a threat to others.

How to organize this book, then, if plotting change seems to obscure more issues than it reveals? The chapters that follow, arranged thematically, are concerned as much with how people wrote about contemporary circumstances and events as they are with what changed and what did not. They consider in particular the anxieties attendant upon the physical and social dislocation of civil war, the apprehension over the loss of self, and the efforts made to reaffirm what was perceived to be in peril. They ask: How did travelers describe the countryside ravaged by war? How did local warriors frame their petitions to regain lost lands? How did the authorities justify their rulings? How did lords talk about the rebellions of followers?

In considering not only the practical challenges of the age, but the conceptual difficulty, for members of the provincial elites, of reimagining themselves and their place, this book privileges analysis of contemporaries' perception of the options they faced. And it finds that the resilience of established ways of thinking—the persistent medieval—conditioned action, not just as an obstacle to change but as a part of change itself. In this sense, it is a story of inadequate responses—"inadequate" from the comfort of our armchairs, at least. It is, in the best of Japanese traditions, a losers' history, although, ironically, defeat would only become apparent, and inevitable, in the decades that follow the end of this study; here, the various actors (mostly families, sometimes individuals, invariably men) are caught in mid-struggle.

As the armies of the Uesugi and the Lords of Koga marched and rode through the plain, setting vast camps along roads or near river crossings; as great lords like Dōkan launched armies against castles defended by rebellious petty warriors, or set surrounding villages ablaze to goad the enemy out from behind a stronghold's wall; and as local warriors took advantage of the commotion to move in on their neighbors' untended holdings, beginning years of feuding and legal wrangling over rightful ownership—as all of this happened, simultaneously, and over and over, the warrior class's diverse relationships with the land and the landscape were brought into relief, and often tested. The Muromachi regime inherited a landscape that had long since moved away from the systematic organization of the early imperial state. In this landscape, multiple spatial frameworks coexisted, superimposed, to describe land as the foundation of production and taxation, as the currency of wealth and the measure of familial prestige; to describe territory as the jurisdiction of governance and the object of conquest.

Yet if the fragmentation of the landscape into multiple vying or simply diverse structures of production and governance made it resistant to the imposition of a single set of organizing principles, warrior elites did nevertheless agree on values that gave meaning to the land and their experience of it.

This book traces those values, in five chapters that analyze provincial elites' approaches to the landscape in the literary, legal, patrimonial, military, and governance spheres (to put it schematically). It shows that, no matter how various the approaches, they were all predicated on, and unified by, a shared understanding of the importance of the social, political, and cultural prestige of those who populated any given place. Place was experienced—or at least discussed in the different sorts of sources that have come down to us—as an expression of familial or institutional prestige, as an embodiment of history and traditions. In this sense, the landscape was made of people.

Let me outline the development of my analysis. First, the literary portrayal of the Kantō landscape, which put forth an explicitly unified and unifying view of the region (Chapter 1). The Kantō immortalized in poetry, and in travel writings (which followed the formal dictates of poetry), was untamed, unsettled, and timelessly peaceful. It was remote, programmatically so, for it was a distant land, imagined as beyond the pale of civilization by those aristocrats in Kyoto who had collectively established the rules for writing about the world beyond the capital and its environs. So binding were those rules, imposed as a matter of course through the unmatchable splendor of the court's literary tradition, that those actually living in the provinces committed to paper not their experiences of the landscape around them but inevitably derivative iterations of common places. What they did not commit to paper we shall never know, though we can imagine that they felt no special displacement at the everyday sight of a plain that was more prosaic and more lively than the melancholy grasslands travelers and pilgrims from the capital invariably chose to see. Even when armed conflict in the capital, in 1467–77 and later, encouraged poets and literati to travel the country in search of patronage among the wealthy if unpolished magnates in the provinces, no effort was made to turn the image of the Kantō on its head, to draw literary portrayal closer to experience. The newly itinerant arbiters of literary elegance were welcomed in the mansions and encampments and castles of the Kantō elite, as the economic and political straits of the Kyoto aristocracy in no way diminished its literary status in the eyes of provincials. These visitors' presence enhanced occasions for socialization among local magnates by creating the opportunity to participate in the civilized pleasures of poetic composition.

At the same time, in a war-torn landscape, travelogues written by wayfaring poets, although still organized by a well-established topography of famous poetic sites, also made room for mention of places less lofty. References to "a certain man," to the "kind hospitality of a stranger," to a night spent in a "humble hut"—repetitions of common places that erase particularity and contingency—now shared the page with lists of places visited, with the names of the patrons who offered hospitality and sometimes requested assistance. War itself could not inject history and experience into the knowledge of the Kantō landscape that poets brought with them to the east, though war and fire and carnage must have been on the minds of Kantō patrons. Interest in a more familiar and more prosaic Kantō was spurred by a new professionalization of the masters of verse, by their cultivation of the patronage of eastern magnates. The lords and petty magnates, who fêted these celebrities of the day on their tours of the provinces, desired cultural rewards that would last beyond a poetry session and a banquet. Many obtained poetic treatises, or copies of the poets' travelogues, as gifts. In these texts, predictably, the itinerant poets made sure to include references to their stays with local warriors; they described a geography of patronage that filled in the blanks left by the more rarefied geography of literary common places, and along the way made their journeys, which were still filtered through literary genres and sensibilities, into processes.

But the centuries-old image of the Kantō as a frontier region did not disappear, however complicated by the expectations of its eastern consumers (patrons) and enriched with scenes of hunting and cheerful, frank sightseeing. The ambiguous embrace of the new returns of patronage, and the tenacity of the old conventions of representation, were no doubt made easier by familiarity with the fragmentation of the landscape, which demanded little coherence or system. But this tension—a tension between the "meaningful-because-traditional" and a sort of "urgent-because-present"—went well beyond the literary: the Kantō remained in some ways caught in between, and its elites were slow to adjust to new challenges, or to come to terms with the contradictions in their relations to the region and its land.

Some of the deepest of these contradictions, and so, for contemporaries, hardest to resolve, concerned land as property, and developed in ways that were predictably different from family to family and from holding to holding. The political disorder of the late fifteenth and early sixteenth centuries often placed formal title at odds with actual control. How disputes between claimants and occupants were resolved, and how their resolution revealed the role of provincial authorities, help us understand not only the legal dimensions of landholding, but their political significance as well. Different parties viewed the stakes differently, so I take them up separately.

For the families tied institutionally to the Muromachi regime—the Ashikaga (once Lords of Kamakura, now Lords of Koga) and the Uesugi and their deputies (Nagao, Ōishi, Ōta, and others)—land rights mattered politically, both as an instrument and as a potential problem (Chapter 2). In times of war, these provincial lords could, as representatives of the shogunate, requisition holdings or incomes from holdings to punish rebellious local lords or to aid the war effort by rewarding loyal ones. The laws regulating these prerogatives were drawn up by shogunal officials in Kyoto; they both granted and limited provincial governors' power of confiscation, whose judicious use was essential to the survival of the regime. On the one hand, the authority of provincial governors as representatives of the Muromachi regime—indeed, the very legitimacy of the regime itself—rested firmly on their ability to keep the peace and enforce the lawful order of society. This mandate meant defending the rightful entitlements to landed revenue of the imperial house, the Kyoto aristocracy, the religious establishment, and the warrior elite. On the other hand, provincial governors' success in creating personal, affective ties with local magnates and petty warriors—essential to the mobilization of supporters when the provincial authority of the great lords was challenged—rested on the bestowal of favors and rewards, of titles and lands.

So provincial governors like the Uesugi found themselves in the distinctly uncomfortable position of having to mediate between two impulses, two guises of authority: the official and the lordly. Their official authority as provincial governors gave them the right to requisition lands and incomes, but dictated that they use that prerogative only when absolutely necessary; their lordly power, instead, needed to be fueled by punishments and rewards, and encouraged a more liberal use of that same prerogative. Further, in wartime disorder and distance from the capital slackened oversight and bred temptation among local warriors, who came to appropriate land in the name of the authorities, but in violation of their laws.

The official and lordly impulses had never been formally distinguished, or fully extricated—not in practice, anyway, not by those in office who distributed largesse or those without office who received that largesse in exchange for service of various sorts. The official and the lordly were distinguished in contemporary parlance, when they were, through the imperfect parallel of public and private, which were in turn treated as shorthand for selfless and selfish rule and loaded with the clarity of moral judgment—and so mostly unhelpful in sorting out the peculiar blend that made up authority under the Muromachi regime. Whether as a reality or an aspiration, the careful balance of the two impulses remained central to the structure of authority even after the regime's power began to wane.[13] Not just for years but for decades after the outbreak of hostilities

13. Cf. Imatani, "Muromachi Local Government," 231.

in the Kantō, both the Lords of Koga and the Uesugi continued to seek the backing of a progressively enfeebled shogunate. As late as the early sixteenth century, when the Yamanouchi house of the Uesugi was rent by a succession dispute, the two contenders urgently petitioned Kyoto for the title of Kantō deputy, synonymous with the position of chief of the Uesugi. The attachment was to more than titles: the judicial procedures established and overseen by the shogunate for the arbitration of disputes over land remained in place, as did the courts' claims to the broad, impersonal authority signified by office. To be sure, evidence of patrimonial lordship, of a conflation of territorial authority and landholding, was everywhere at the time, especially in the correspondence with local warriors whose support was sought in this or that disturbance; but not to the point of overshadowing the perduring reliance on the offices of the Muromachi regime.

For the many local magnates who made up the lower tiers of the region's warrior elite, who had been excluded from the operation of the Kamakura Office and, even after its demise, had no access to the posts of governor and deputy governor, disputes over landholdings were a matter of patrimony and family survival (Chapter 3). By the fifteenth century, most families of some stature had amassed portfolios of holdings; some of these were in the vicinity of the family residence, but many were scattered farther away. As turmoil spread across the Kantō region after 1455, it became harder and harder for families to keep tabs on their more distant holdings. The encroachment of others could not always be held off from afar, and the authorities could not always be counted on to enforce rightful claims (not that right and wrong were always too clear-cut, or easy to demonstrate). The great temples in Kyoto and Kamakura were more likely to stir the authorities' commitment to law and order, both before and after the outbreak of war; local warriors tended to fare better when tugging at the strings of personal attachment. Lordly rule worked best, in times of unrest especially, when it could draw on personal ties of more or less heartfelt loyalty and gratitude.

But loyalty, whatever the rhetorical fiction, was always negotiated: the greater the independent wealth and the status of a local family (or its own sense of its status), the harder the great lords of the region had to work to earn reliable loyalty. In practice, the Uesugi and the Ashikaga always led coalitions of the willing. Not all "allies" could afford to be recalcitrant, and the mobilization orders of the authorities were not lightly ignored. Nevertheless, those who could, made demands—for lands and titles, most frequently. They called on the Uesugi and the Lords of Koga to exercise their official authority—to assign lands and titles in accordance with established, quasi-bureaucratic procedures—when fulfilling the pledges made to bolster their lordly sway. Local magnates too, in other words, looked for the sanction of proper procedure, even as they demanded rewards tailored to the ostensibly affective character of the service rendered.

And demands of those who turned to the authorities were not as aggressive and aggrandizing as we may imagine—at least not always, and not necessarily. We are accustomed to the idea that from the small but contiguous holdings of local families would emerge the great warlords of the late sixteenth century, greedily expanding outward by amassing new lands and territories, with blithe disregard for all rules but those of opportunity and force. We know this picture to be exaggeratedly truculent, fostered by the period's reputation as one of incessant warring, and by the declarations left behind by a number of men of especially Machiavellian disposition. But even with the bluster stripped away, it is hard not to emphasize that consolidation and the establishment of strong local roots were crucial to survival, for only those families with complete access to, and complete control of, their land base could hope to marshal the resources necessary for the endemic warfare of the age.

When considered from the vantage point of the early modern settlement, consolidation was the most rational course of action, strategically and economically. But local magnates of the time did not consider their options and demands from the vantage point of the early modern settlement. From where they stood, lawlessness and consolidation were not obvious paths: those who appealed to the authorities wanted confirmation of titles to lands they already held; legal sanction for illegally acquired holdings, at least (with hollow formalism, but formalism nonetheless); or restitution of lands rightfully owned by them but recently appropriated by others.

Relations between the Uesugi and Iwamatsu families lend themselves to illustrate such dynamics, for they showcase both local magnates' view of their dealings with provincial authorities and the ways in which they construed their struggle to hold on to ancestral and more recently acquired holdings. As a condition for military assistance, early in the 1470s the Iwamatsu requested the restitution of eighteen holdings scattered throughout the western half of the plain, which had been taken from the family in recent years. The lands in question had been in Iwamatsu possession for generations, acquired thanks to the largesse of great shoguns long dead. Recovery of the lost lands, whose enumeration evoked by association the Iwamatsu's more glorious past, almost as a recitation of genealogy and pedigree, was seen as symbolically equivalent to restoring the family's luster. In a plight shared by many of the local magnates in the region, who had been shut out from office by the rise of the Uesugi and their deputies, the Iwamatsu looked longingly not to a future as powerful, entrenched local lords, but to a past when they had consorted with shoguns. The eighteen holdings were among the last tangible ties to the family's own history and sense of self. Families with adversarial relations to the Uesugi, families which had been marginalized politically during the Muromachi regime's heyday, still looked back to the order of society before the middle of the fifteenth century, to society as it should be and the place they imagined for themselves in it.

Disputes over land, then, bring to the surface both the diverging and the converging trajectories of adjudicators and plaintiffs. While provincial authorities (the adjudicators) turned to the precedents and procedures of the enervated Muromachi regime in search of legitimacy, local magnates invoked the same past to maintain, or reestablish, their pedigree. For both, the reaffirmation of links to the heyday of the Muromachi regime (which could and would be construed to suit the ends of each party) served to heighten prestige by confirming membership in something greater than the narrow local concerns of the moment, membership in an elite that mattered not only in the Kantō, but in the whole country.

Land, of course, was not only property, and battles far more violent than lawsuits were being fought. Local warriors could ill afford to close their eyes to the contemporary political landscape in the name of a rhetoric of place that was overtly nostalgic. Even as they appealed to occasionally inattentive authorities for enforcement of land rights, local families cultivated their own lordly pretensions to protect their patrimony: in the late fifteenth century in particular, the landscape of the

Kantō plain was dramatically redrawn as castles large and small appeared in great numbers across the region (Chapter 4). For the first time warriors used strongholds as more than ad hoc, temporary military facilities. These new structures were built to last, and to become the residences and headquarters of their builders. They were built by families of great wealth and pedigree as much as by local peasant-warriors. They served to stave off the threats posed by neighboring warriors and to check peasant communities that resisted taxation and exploitation. During this or that disturbance, they were used to garrison loyalist contingents, or to shelter insurgents chased down by the regime's armies. Even after a campaign or a disturbance came to a close, the castles were left standing, permanently militarizing the countryside and overlaying one more level of fragmentation upon the spaces of landholding and official jurisdiction.

Yet however vividly these new strongholds may tell us about new configurations of territorial power, no single, novel conception of space came to discipline the Kantō elites' experience of place; the landscape of castles and warrior lands did not overwrite the preceding organization of provinces and dispersed private holdings. The Uesugi, for instance, who as an extended family were among the busiest castle builders, resisted the new lordly organization of the plain's territory that those castles produced and denoted. Instead of settling in one of their fortresses, for over fifty years after the outbreak of war in 1455 the Uesugi divided their time among a number of residences around the region. Mostly, new archaeological evidence has shown, they ruled from military encampments, two of which lasted not weeks or months but years, even decades. With their mobility—a nominal, theoretical mobility, at least—these camps allowed the Uesugi to maintain a vigilant presence on the war-torn land they ruled. At the same time, that same mobility kept the Uesugi from settling in one particular locale and reinventing themselves as local magnates. The family's heads maintained, adamantly, their role as representatives of the Muromachi regime, embodying the authority of their office wherever they set camp.

Ruling as they campaigned, itinerantly, the Uesugi presided over a landscape where their claims to a broad spectrum of rights obtaining throughout the provinces under their jurisdiction—to adjudicate disputes, to levy taxes, to commandeer labor, to mobilize troops—had to be negotiated, case by case, in each pocket of land over which a warrior proprietor held lordly sway. That the Uesugi (and the Lords of Koga, for that matter) could only define the boundaries of their authority by consensus, no less geographically than politically, does not mean they were powerless, or invariably hard-pressed to convey the wisdom of compliance. However embattled, by surviving disturbance after disturbance the Uesugi proved the extent of their resources, and the continuing power of their office among Kantō warriors. Still, having real power and authority did not mean they were able to wield them equally throughout the region, for the landscape remained intractably discontinuous. Itinerant rule worked (for half a century, at least) for the Uesugi, who could draw on a culture and a language of authority that associated rule with people—the members of the regime—rather than with territory; it did not translate into a theory of rule that could be applied to sedentary local lords, ensconced behind castle walls.

The itinerant rule of the Uesugi would not have seemed odd to contemporaries, for at the time lordship had no obvious territorial dimension, and territorial domains still lay in the future (Chapter 5). The identification of landholdings and territorial rule had only recently taken root, as local families tried to overcome not only the parcelization of tenurial rights typical of farmland throughout the country, but also, more reluctantly, their own nostalgia for the quasi-genealogical form that wealth had taken in earlier times. The next step, the imagination of spheres of authority as territory that extended beyond a family's own landholdings, remained exclusive to those governing provinces in the name of the Muromachi regime, and even for them its implementation was in need of constant renegotiation. A vivid testament to this noncontinuous—in fact, nonterritorial—political and military landscape is in the lack of references, in contemporary documents, to boundaries other than those of individual landholdings or of the old imperial provinces.

In descriptions of campaigns, even military frontiers fail to appear (both as words and as phenomena); letters and chronicles speak instead of entranceways—of access points where travelers, or attacking armies, made their way into property and met resistance. Territorial domains, and even coherent military blocks, remained elusive so long as families held lands dispersed across a wide region, so long as a small stronghold defended each family's small main holdings, and so long as conflict took the form of transversal uprisings that erupted everywhere across the plain, simultaneously, as the rebellion of Nagao Kageharu did in the late 1470s.

A counterpoint to the situation described in this study, and a conclusion of sorts, is offered by the organization of the Kantō under the Hōjō of Odawara, beginning in the second quarter of the sixteenth century. Glimmers of a shift in (some of) the ways land and landscape were viewed by warriors became visible as the new lords gradually asserted their control over the plain, steadily moving north and east as they subjugated territories and families once under the sway of the Uesugi and the Lords of Koga. The Hōjō did not unify the plain under their direct rule—that would have been too bold politically, and too alien from the contemporary experience of territory and lordship. Many of the local magnates who had resisted the advance of the Odawara lords pledged their loyalty to them after the fall of the Uesugi, and many were allowed to hold their lands. But the Hōjō made sure to assert control over the region's main castles, building new ones and demolishing others in order to establish a capillary network over the territory of the plain.

The Kantō went from having no frontiers—or rather, from being everywhere a frontier between petty local warriors—to being carefully divided between a domainal core and multiple specially governed frontier zones. For the first time, the identity was established between a ruling house and the territory it ruled. The identity was not yet perfect, as petty lordships persisted within the Hōjō domain. Nationwide reforms would further simplify and clarify the picture of land tenure after the fall of the Hōjō (while in the process again disengaging authority from territory). Still, during their time in power, the Hōjō ushered in different ways of holding land (by recording the value of all their grants to followers, and the service they were owed in exchange for them); of traveling through the landscape (which was now structured politically according to the ruler's overarching plan); of exercising lordship (by creating a hierarchy of territorial administrators, by strategically distributing followers and especially family members throughout the plain, in castles). In many ways, it has been noted, the Hōjō remained almost nostalgically attached to the trappings of authority of the Muromachi regime, but in the remaking of the plain, in the novel distribution of authority and power, it is clear that the medieval space stubbornly kept alive by the Uesugi during nearly a century of civil unrest was, at last, being undone.

* * *

Much, though by no means all, of the momentous change initiated by the Hōjō lords belongs to the story of the mid- to late sixteenth century, past the nominal end point of this book. In the years covered here, change was acknowledged, when it was recognized, only to be resisted. This is one of the reasons for avoiding a chronological organization for the pages that follow. Still, my desire to avoid the story of incremental change that often comes with a chronological narrative does not stem from the sort of anxiety about change that suffuses the debate and the tension between historical continuity and rupture. My emphasis on continuities—on the persistence of a medieval outlook that long survived the slippages and disjunctures that everywhere tormented the certainties of the elite—is not meant to keep change at bay.[14]

Manifestly, both subtle shifts and cataclysmic displacement were part of the experience of regional elites in the fifteenth and sixteenth centuries, whether or not they chose to identify them as new departures. The appearance of castles across the land was certainly impressive enough for any observer to take notice, though its historical suddenness (it happened in about fifty years) was still hardly a brief time span for individuals, many of whom were far too engaged with the pressing demands of the present to take stock of changes over decades. So it is not surprising that we should have no meditations on the militarization of the landscape. Similarly, new relations of patronage—occasioned at least in part by the political and military instability that periodically threatened the capital from the late 1460s on—subtly inflected the compositions of the time. But the dictates of elegant composition had been recalibrated many times before, and now again generic conventions were bent but not broken. Other changes—or rather, their tangible consequences—were greeted with greater anxiety. One, for instance, was the pressure to surrender far-flung landed interests, and one's history of involvement in far-flung landed interests, in exchange for the safer but narrower horizons of local ascendancy. Another was the new challenge of governing itinerantly, across vast distances, while those governed withdrew to their

14. The two poles and the perils of their attraction are analyzed by Herman Ooms in his *Tokugawa Ideology*, 3–15. See also Keirstead, *Geography of Power*, esp. 1–24 and 98–118.

strongholds in defiance, individually far from irresistible but collectively troublesome. Yet another, of course, was the ebbing of the power of office, despite all efforts.

The certainties the elite held dear were those of meaning and precedence (and precedent).

The medieval, which may seem more deserving of a capital "m" to us than it did to those who lived in it, could, and did, tolerate fragmentation, imbalance, and disorder to a degree that has long strained our ability to understand; as a system, if we can think of it as one, it was accommodating of change not because incremental change did not matter, but because the medieval derived whatever coherence it had (invoking "days of old") from its availability to provide stability of meanings and expectations. The prizes over which so many lost their lives—the post of Kantō deputy, the restitution of ancestral lands—remained surprisingly constant over the course of decades of turmoil, for even though locally lords could override the rules of landholding, or rearrange power relations through military success, no one yet could devise a new social order, new approaches to territorial governance and landholdings, and adjudication compelling enough to be accepted by all throughout the Kantō region (let alone Japan as a whole) in place of what was discarded.

CHAPTER I

The Grasses of Musashino

Leaving Tokyo takes some trying. So vast is the sprawl of the megalopolis that it can take an hour, on a local train, to reach the less densely populated outskirts—longer yet to reach the countryside that spreads out, mostly flat and heavily built up, as Japan's largest agricultural plain. But leaving Tokyo is hard in another sense as well—imaginatively—for its bustling train stations and shopping centers, its neighborhoods crowded with single-family homes, its narrow thoroughfares choked by traffic provide such a thick layer of human settlement that it takes a leap of imagination just to picture what the plain might have looked and felt like before the twentieth century, when agrarian communities dotted the countryside, and townsfolk and villagers took to the roads in great numbers for business or for leisure.[1] In the midst of the intensely human landscape of the turn of the twenty-first century, conjuring an image of the Kantō as it was described even earlier, by medieval wayfarers—wild, sparsely populated, quiet—requires ignoring our experience of the landscape entirely.

I mention the imaginative effort required of modern travelers not to suggest that we are uniquely at a disadvantage in picturing the Kantō

---

1. The subject of leisure travel and its role in the diffusion of ideas about an early modern Japanese geography and identity has recently received considerable scholarly attention. See Yonemoto, *Mapping Early Modern Japan*; Berry, *Japan in Print*; and Nenzi, *Excursions in Identity.*

of days past. Rather, I do so because the need to imagine a landscape that has long vanished is one we share with late medieval wayfarers, and our efforts to disregard what we see in the service of what we *ought* to see help us understand some of the challenges those travelers faced in describing the region with images drawn from past literature. Just as we now struggle to imagine a plain not yet urbanized, poets in the late Middle Ages had to make an effort to evoke a plain wild and not yet settled. Even before the dramatic changes wrought on the landscape in the 1500s by the Hōjō family's conquest of the region, or by Tokugawa Ieyasu's relocation to Edo, the Kantō had been developing for centuries, slowly but steadily, and was widely if not intensively farmed. Yet the plain sung by poets, whether travelers seeing it with their own eyes or courtiers writing of a distant and exotic land in forms dictated by literary tradition, had evolved little. In its rough contours the literary image of the Kantō was established early on, and remained remarkably consistent over the centuries—as described by travelers, a distant and desolate frontier land. Perhaps because over time so many only experienced it through texts, the Kantō of fifteenth-century literature is strikingly similar to—if not indistinguishable from—its twelfth-century counterpart.

But in the late fifteenth century a change occurred in the ways the image of the region, which was codified in literary circles in Kyoto, circulated throughout the country. Civil war broke out in the streets of the capital in 1467, and even though the original conflict, known as the Ōnin War, nominally concluded in 1477, violence and destruction returned frequently in the century that followed. A side effect of the devastation visited upon the capital was the flight from the city of literati seeking refuge in their distant holdings or patronage at the residences of provincial magnates.[2] For many, what had begun as a temporary absence in the face of emergency eventually became a normal way of life,

---

2. Yogo Toshio (*Sōseki to chihō renga*, 2) quotes an entry dated 1473 in a temple register, *Daijōin jisha zōjiki* (Account of the affairs of temples and shrines of Daijōin), which lists an impressive number of aristocrats among those who had left town and taken refuge in the provinces. The immediate cause was the war, but the growing economic importance of the provinces, he notes, was also a factor.

as ties of patronage developed with provincial warriors eager to host poets and literati (and artists) of renown.[3] With them the travelers brought courtly culture, in the form of instruction and texts (from collections of verse to composition manuals). They were men of learning as well as poets, and many were Buddhist monks, and patrons expected a variety of skills and services from them. Accordingly, they served as teachers, propitiators, negotiators, and all-purpose celebrities. Even in strictly literary terms, the professionalization of itinerant poets' activities meant that they were uniquely subject to the influences of locals' tastes and interests.[4]

In the pages that follow, then, I trace some of the effects that the exodus of literati, coupled with the ongoing state of civil war, had not only on the literary self-cultivation of provincials and on the unprecedented diffusion of courtly culture to the far reaches of the archipelago, but also on the very literary traditions that were now being disseminated so broadly. In a twofold process, the connection was reaffirmed between peripheral regions and the capital, which remained the source of poetic (and more broadly literary) standards, credentials, and vogues; at the same time people living in places like the Kantō received a renewed impetus to imagine their region synoptically along the lines codified in the capital. To this impetus residents of the Kantō reacted in complex ways: the newly central dynamics of patronage did not bring about a reimagining of the region or a new perspective, for easterners, however frequently described in medieval literature as inhabitants of a world apart, seemed eager to participate in received literary traditions they did not

3. While here I have limited my focus to the discursive production and circulation of ideas about the Kantō—a Kantō image—broader studies of the visual culture of the Middle Ages have stressed the links between poets and artists, and between the poetic canon and pictorial themes. Indeed, literati and artists (not that the two categories were mutually exclusive or even sharply bounded) were often involved in the same circles of patronage. Just as the painter Tosa Mitsunobu joined in linked-verse sessions with the poet Sōgi in the capital, so too painters sought out the patronage of provincials along with poets. See McCormick, *Tosa Mitsunobu*, 92–95.

4. Kumakura Isao ("Sanjōnishi Sanetaka, Takeno Jōō") makes an interesting attempt at classifying poets in five categories on the basis of their backgrounds and relations to the practice of poetry: nobles, professionals, practitioners, skilled amateurs, warrior chieftains.

perceive as foreign; yet while embracing the image of their region as a distant frontier, Kantō residents also prompted poets and travelers to populate their accounts with the names of their patrons and to supplement the poetic geography of the east with one that acknowledged a landscape of castles and battles and violence. In trying to make sense of subtle shifts in the portrayal of the plain, I focus on one of the images most consistently associated with it: Musashino and its grasses.

Travel, Poetic Practice, Patronage

The literary characterizations of the Kantō and other regions long predate the literati's flight, though travel and travel literature played a central role in giving them shape and circulation in the fifteenth and sixteenth centuries. Underscoring the importance of the link between place and poetry, medieval poetic rule books enshrined "places of renown" (*nadokoro*) among the principal lexical categories to be used when composing verse. The poet Shōtetsu (1381–1459) famously declared, "If someone asks you in which of the provinces Yoshino may be found, you should answer this way: when I write my poems I simply remember that for blossoms one goes to Yoshino, for red leaves to Tatsuta. Whether those places are in Ise or wherever is not my concern."[5] Centuries of collectively policed poetic diction produced a literary geography that organized the space of the archipelago in a hierarchy of meaningful places—places whose poetic resonances made them central not only to the composition of verse, but also to the elites' imagination of space.

The evocative importance of places not only shaped literary production, but mediated literate travelers' experiences on the road (or at least their recollections of them), drawing would-be authors to certain sites, compelling them to add their own compositions to those of others before them. In this respect, from its inception travel literature as a genre was inseparable from poetry, for which it often acted as a vehicle; the prose in travelogues often provided little more than connective tissue between poems composed on the road, though it could, and in the later Middle Ages often would, acquire a character of its own, thanks in part to the less stringent rules of diction that regulated it.

5. Quoted in S. Carter, *Road to Komatsubara*, 148.

Travelogues could be also written in Chinese, in which case different rules of composition applied. Eastern Japan (or any other part of the country, for that matter) could be portrayed through allusions to continental literature, and authors writing in Chinese might take note of Kantō forests and rivers and lakes and villages—not only grasses. Still, even in Chinese, as we shall see, authors were mindful of the geography of famous places.

When used in literary compositions—poetry in particular—famous places were known as *utamakura* ("song pillows").[6] These were words (mostly, but not exclusively, place names) that had been given special prestige and evocative power by celebrated poems, and mention of these aesthetically and even spiritually charged places by later authors was understood to enrich their efforts by association.[7] Indeed, the desire to visit a locale given renown by poets of old is commonly offered at the beginning of a travelogue as the impetus for undertaking the trip. The nun and poet Abutsu framed her travel diary, *Izayoi nikki* (*The Journal of the Sixteenth-Night Moon*, 1279–80), as a search for *utamakura* rather than as the more pressing if more prosaic trip she was actually undertaking, to file a lawsuit at a distant court.

In the case of later authors, particularly those who took to the road in the wake of the Ōnin War, travel was made appealing by the promise of patronage offered by local warriors, who might invite a man of letters to reside at their mansions for a while, or pay him to grace with his presence the poetic gatherings they wished to sponsor. This new breed of itinerant poets, nevertheless, maintained the fiction that trips were purely literary in inspiration. Indeed, the frequency and prominence of authors' protestations of artistic intent have rendered them suspect to scholars, who

6. The word *utamakura* originally referred to booklets that contained lists of words (especially place names) for use in poetry and that were kept by one's pillow. Over time (just how much time is not clear) people came to refer to the booklets and their contents interchangeably.

7. Edward Kamens (*Utamakura, Allusion, and Intertextuality*, 28) has described *utamakura* as "those richly signifying kernels or nodes within a poem through which the maker of that poem reaches out to make contact with other poems (or poetic moments) and thereby to complicate or enrich the signifying process of that poem as a whole."

have been tempted to seek ulterior, secret motives for many journeys.[8] Yet the centrality of *utamakura* to travel is apparent even when it is not invoked explicitly; so powerful was the hold of place names on the imaginations of travelers that their accounts sometimes read more as lists of items to be ticked off than as personal experiences. (In this respect, at least, the experience of the modern traveler on a guided tour may not be so very different from its medieval counterpart after all.) To apply Paul Carter's formulation to Japan's literary tradition and to the experience of the Kantō that tradition imposed on those who wrote of it: "The uniquely spatial experience is replaced by a ritual of repetitions. Putative journeys are effaced by the cult of places."[9]

In the eastern provinces, and the Kantō plain in particular, several poetic places were prominent enough to entice artists to travel for days or weeks to catch a glimpse of literary history, to experience a brief moment of real or feigned communion with the greats of the past. The more celebrated landmarks in the eastern provinces included rivers (like

---

8. The suspicion that has typically accompanied linked-verse poets in their tours of the provinces is that they were, in fact, running errands for warrior patrons in the capital: gathering information, brokering alliances, negotiating the return of expropriated holdings. Sōchō candidly admits to conducting talks with warriors along the way, interceding on behalf of temples in the capital. More problematic is the contention that the poets were gathering intelligence for warring houses, or acting as partisan messengers for them during conflicts. The classic instance of this is represented by the near-simultaneous arrival in the east of several prominent poets (Shinkei [1406–75], Sōgi [1420–1502], Gyōjo [1405–69]) just before the outbreak of the Ōnin War. The poets, it has been suggested, were sent by the factions in Kyoto to gauge the attitudes of eastern warriors and garner their support (S. Carter, "Sōgi in the East Country," 169; Ramirez-Christensen, *Heart's Flower*, 56–57, 77, 130, 135). The argument is inspired by Kaneko Kinjirō (*Shinkei no seikatsu to sakuhin*, 116–20; *Sōgi no seikatsu to sakuhin*, 110–11). Kaneko's argument works better for some than for others. More cautiously, Tsurusaki Hiroo (*Sengoku o yuku rengashi Sōchō*, 154) has observed that in order to travel and count on a network of support poets had to have the trust of their hosts. On the road, they surely took note of what they saw and shared information. But who could hire one poet to *spy* on a neighbor and still be comfortable accompanying another poet through his own lands? See also Tsurusaki, "Rengashi." Poets who had close ties to one warlord surely gathered and relayed more sensitive information as well, but also found that well-known ties to one party could limit their ability to seek patronage from others. See Horton, "Sōchō and Imagawa Patronage," 139–42.

9. P. Carter, *Road to Botany Bay*, xxi.

the Sumidagawa), peaks (like Mounts Tsukuba and Fuji), and barriers (like the one at Shirakawa).[10] Mount Tsukuba, for instance, was venerable especially among linked-verse (*renga*) poets, seen as the fountainhead of their art.[11] The mountain was invoked by the greatest among them, Sōgi (1420–1502), at the beginning of both the travelogues he wrote, where it is called upon as a muse to propitiate the success of his travels and inspire his record of them.[12] (It is worth noting in passing that one of the two travelogues, *Tsukushi michi no ki* [An account of the road to Kyūshū, 1480] was not even about a journey to the east.) Mount Fuji had at least as much luster, known as the mountain "without equal" (*fuji*) long before its heyday as an object of artistic representation in the early modern period. In his travel diary, *Baika mujinzō* (Plum blossoms without end), the poet Banri Shūku (1428–?), who had once been a monk at Shōkokuji, in Kyoto, but had returned to lay life to devote himself to letters, began his panoramic description of the Kantō with "the snow accumulated on Mount Fuji" and concluded it at the opposite end of the plain, where "the peaks of Tsukuba pleasantly hang in the sky at dawn and dusk."[13] Yet just as in Banri's description, both mountains remained at the edges of the region: Tsukuba's appeal was tied most closely to linked verse; as for Fuji, it was visible and indeed defined and

10. Saitō ("Minami Kantō no toshi to kaidō," 176) suggests that the Sumidagawa only developed into a "famous place" after the beginning of the civil war, in the 1450s. The river became a boundary of sorts at this time, which may have helped draw attention to it, but it seems more likely that its heightened profile was part of the greater knowledge of eastern landmarks fostered by the travels of poets and literati in the region.

11. Both *Kojiki* (Record of Ancient Matters, 712) and *Nihon shoki* (*Chronicles of Japan*, 720; also known as *Nihongi*) cite what was canonically accepted as the first example of linked verses, which were composed about Tsukuba, during a military campaign to pacify the wild eastern provinces, by the legendary Prince Yamato Takeru and an old man in his retinue charged with tending the fire. In English, see Philippi, *Kojiki*, 242–43; Aston, *Nihongi*, 1:207.

12. Tsukuba's role as a muse is made clear in the very first sentence of *Shirakawa kikō*, in which Sōgi mentions his visit to the mountain even though that portion of his trip is elided from the narrative. See S. Carter, "Sōgi in the East Country," 180; Horton, *Song*, 108. Sōgi recalled his trip to Tsukuba twelve years later, in the opening lines of *Tsukushi michi no ki* (An account of a journey to Kyūshū); see Kato, "Pilgrimage to Dazaifu," 341.

13. Ichiki, *Baika mujinzō chūshaku*, 4:58–62.

delimited the plain geographically by rising at its southwestern edge, but did not require a trip to the Kantō to be seen. Although Fuji was a part of the landscape for the plain's residents, in other words, its *canonical* location was as much in the more westerly Tōkaidō region—where literate travelers from the capital caught sight of it long before arriving in the Kantō—as it was in the Kantō itself.[14]

Inasmuch as an *utamakura* mattered, it was for the poetic associations it evoked. Central geographically and embodying the defining characteristics of the Kantō in the eyes of the literate elite in the capital were Musashino (the Plain of Musashi) and its fields of tall grasses. The grasses appear as a distinctive feature of the barbarous east in Japan's earliest texts, the imperial mythohistories compiled in the early eighth century: in both *Kojiki* and *Nihon shoki*, Yamato Takeru, the heroic imperial prince sent by the emperor his father to subdue the rebellious eastern barbarians, is treacherously led into a field of tall grasses by a local chieftain, who then sets a fire to it in hopes of slaying the hero.[15] In verse, meadows of grasses taller than a man characterize the landscape of Musashino in *Man'yōshū* (Collection of ten thousand leaves), an anthology of poems compiled in the mid-eighth century, and remain its most distinctive trait thereafter.[16] The most celebrated reference to the grasses (itself indebted to the earlier Yamato Takeru myth) is probably the one in *Ise monogatari* (*The Tales of Ise*), the tenth-century tale about the amorous entanglements of the courtier poet Ariwara no Narihira (825–80): Eloping with a woman with whom he has fallen in love, Narihira ("a certain man") flees to the east, but is hounded by the governor of Musashi. Panicking, Narihira conceals the woman in the tall grass and makes a run for it. When local authorities, believing he is hiding in the grass, decide to set fire to the meadow, the woman cries,

Musashino wa	Do not burn
kyō wa na yaki zo	Musashino today!

14. That Mount Fuji "faced" the Tōkaidō in the Middle Ages is a point also made by Ambros, *Emplacing a Pilgrimage*, 240–41. See also Tyler, "A Glimpse of Mt. Fuji," 152. Kären Wigen makes a similar observation in her analysis of medieval Shinano in *A Malleable Map*, 31–55.

15. Philippi, *Kojiki*, 240; Aston, *Nihongi*, 1:205.

16. Endō, "Kodai."

wakakusa no	My husband is hidden
tsuma mo komoreri	and I am hidden
ware mo komoreri[17]	in the young grasses.

Reference to the grasses would remain a constant in writing about the region, although the types of flora most likely to make up the grasses subtly shifted over the centuries in response to evolving literary tastes. First, writers turned from okera, with its white blossoms in summer, to gromwell (*murasaki*), with similarly colored flowers but dark red roots, used to make dye; then to reeds and pampas grass. Partly under the influence of the poetics embraced by Saigyō (1118–90) and other poets in the eighth imperially sponsored poetic anthology, *Shinkokinshū* (New collection of poems old and recent, ca. 1205), with the new plants came new seasons (autumn and winter), new weather, and a new mood.[18] In *Shinkokinshū*, book 4 (Autumn poems), we find this poem by the abbot Jien (1155–1225):

Musashino ya	Travel though I may
yukedomo aki no	through the fields in Musashino
hate zo naki	there is no end to autumn.
ikanaru kaze ga	What sort of wind
sue ni fukuran[19]	might be blowing where the fields end?

And this one by then chancellor and great minister of state Kujō Yoshitsune (1169–1206):

yuku sue wa	At the end of my path,
sora mo hitotsu no	in Musashino,
Musashino ni	where the sky is one with the land,

17. *Ise monogatari*, 124–25.

18. On the influence of Saigyō and the poetics of *Shinkokinshū* on portrayals of Musashino, see Misumi, "Chūsei bungaku ni okeru Musashino to tōgoku." More generally on the attention to autumn in poetry, which began with the earliest anthologies and grew so that by the early Middle Ages the season far outstripped the other three in importance, see Shirane, *Culture of the Four Seasons*, 25–55.

19. *Shinkokinshū*, bk. 4, no. 378; see Minemura, *Shinkokin wakashū*, 121. For another translation, see McCullough, trans., *Tales of Ise*, 78.

kusa no hara yori	emerging from the grassy fields—
izuru tsukikage[20]	the moonlight.

The shift in tone was not confined to poetry. As if the mood of the plain itself had changed, travelers' memoirs, too, came to paint the fields in cooler hues. In her recollection of a pilgrimage that took her through the Kantō in the winter of 1289–90, Lady Nijō, a court lady who had taken Buddhist vows, and the author of the court diary and travelogue *Towazugatari* (A tale unrequested, completed after 1306; *The Confessions of Lady Nijō*), wrote, "The Iruma River flowed in front, and on the far bank stood the Iwabuchi Lodge, where a group of entertainers lived. There were no mountains at all in this province. Far into the distance in every direction stretched the famous Musashino Plain, its fields of reeds drooping under the bite of winter frost. I felt the loneliness of life in these desolate plains so far from the capital."[21] Again, upon crossing the region on her way back: "To get there I had to pass through vast fields so densely covered with bush clover, ominaeshi, reeds, and pampas grass that no other plants were able to grow in them. The height of the grasses was such that a man on horseback could pass through unseen. For three days I pressed on through the fields without reaching my destination. Travelling accommodations could be found on small side roads, but otherwise there was only the plain stretching far into the distance far behind and before me."[22]

The atmosphere has grown decidedly forlorn, the weather is chilly, and travel has become a lonely matter. Worse yet, the bush clover, *ominaeshi* ("golden lace"), reeds, and pampas grass block all view and annul all sense of direction and distance.[23] In the Middle Ages the trope of the wayfarer hemmed in—even submerged—by the grasses, deprived of sight, became ubiquitous in travel literature about Musashino. The desolate landscape, featureless but for its grasses, empty of almost all human presence, was confined to a curious placelessness, given purchase on the world beyond the grasses by its poetic status. The main road running through

20. *Shinkokinshū*, bk. 4, no. 422; see Minemura, *Shinkokin wakashū*, 132–33.

21. Brazell, *Confessions of Lady Nijō*, 195; Misumi, *Towazugatari*, 183–84.

22. Brazell, *Confessions of Lady Nijō*, 198; Misumi, *Towazugatari*, 186.

23. Misumi, "Chūsei bungaku ni okeru Musashino to tōgoku," 72–73; see also the entry for "Musashino" in Katagiri, *Utamakura utakotoba jiten*, 414–16.

the plain and the grasses of Musashino is not named in *Towazugatari* or in other accounts, though its presence in the journeys can easily be inferred (the "small side roads" imply the existence of a main road, of course). But that main road, the so-called Kamakura Road (*Kamakura kaidō*), is relegated to the margins of the literary experience of Musashino by remaining unnamed, lest it reveal itself as a product of the human colonization of the landscape. Without people to populate it and describe it—to make it a place—the endless, undifferentiated expanse of grassland would cease to exist culturally. The cult of place, the link it had with the capital as an *utamakura*, was all that kept Musashino, in the eyes of the literate elite, from slipping hopelessly beyond the pale—and even that link was ambivalent at best, as it enshrined the fields in the literary canon by constructing them as a bleak backwater or a distant frontier—a definitive other.

For all the changes they underwent over the years (botanically at least), the grasses remained an intrinsic part of Musashino, and were regularly evoked in poems worthy of collection in imperial anthologies.[24] Centuries after *Shinkokinshū* appeared and Nijō completed her pilgrimage, the grasses of Musashino were still part of the region's poetic panorama for another visitor from the capital, the famed linked-verse poet Shinkei (1406–75).

machiwabite	Even the tips of the grass,
kusaba no sue mo	are weary of waiting for it
yoyo naran	every night—
yūgure tōki	the dew in Musashino's
Musashino no tsuyu[25]	distant dusk.

The customary pose for the man of letters traveling in Musashino remained one of brooding nostalgia for places more civilized, but one poet, Sōchō (1448–1532), would allow himself to strike a much more cheer-

24. Poems on Musashino appear in the last three (less celebrated) imperial anthologies: *Shinshūishū* (New collection of gleanings, 1364; four poems), *Shingoshūishū* (New latter collection of gleanings, 1383; five poems), and *Shinshokukokinshū* (New continued collection of poems old and new, 1439; three poems).

25. *Shinpen kokka taikan* 8:258, no. 128.

ful note, unable to contain his enthusiasm at the sight of the storied *utamakura*:

> On the fifteenth of that month Ujimune, his son Masasada, and I [rode] off, our ponies side by side. For a full two days we made our way through the bush clover and pampas grass of Musashino, arriving at a place called Hachigata, residence of Nagao Magotarō Akikata. I extemporized this verse on horseback for Masasada.

Musashino no	On the Plain of Musashi
tsuyu no kagiri wa	I have pressed through
wake mo mitsu	the dew in full measure.
aki no kaze o ba	And now for the autumn wind
Shirakawa no seki[26]	at Shirakawa Barrier.

Sōchō's wink at his audience and at Japan's poetic tradition helps us bring into focus the function of an *utamakura* like Musashino within its literary context, as well as the function this tradition had in shaping notions of place in Japanese history at large. Confessing to the draw of *utamakura* was neither new nor unusual for a poet recording his travels. Striking here is that Sōchō steps out of the forlorn persona required of the wayfaring poet and admits to the reassurance that comes from traveling through the grasses. Everything is as it should be, he says, in effect—the poetic order is in order. Literary conceits aside, the Mita were one of the great houses of Musashi Province, so the poet was traveling in the safest possible company. He was no solitary traveler blindly making his way through the tall grasses.

Sōchō is at ease letting both us and his contemporaries (the intended readers) see the links he builds in the poem and the passage. By wading through the tall grass (and planning to visit Shirakawa) Sōchō physically locates himself within an established geography of Japanese verse and writes himself and his travelogue, *Azumaji no tsuto* (Souvenir from the Eastland, 1509), into a sort of literary genealogy; by adding his name and his particular variation on a well-worn theme, he also reaffirms and renews the place of Musashino (and other *utamakura*) within the poetic order of

26. *Azumaji no tsuto*, 488. For an equally enthusiastic discussion of the passage, see Tsurusaki, *Sengoku no kenryoku to yoriai no bungei*, 13.

Japan. But Sōchō also links this tradition to his hosts: he flatters the Mita by mentioning them in an especially salient passage in a work of lasting literary merit and by highlighting the association of their house with a local landmark of great fame; he impresses upon them the continuing thematic relevance of the fields of Musashino, to which they are now tied textually as well as geographically; and in so doing he renews the ties between the Kantō region and the distant political and cultural center of Japan, where the theme was established and canonized in the first place.[27]

The mechanisms that reinforced the ties between the center and the periphery of the poetic geography were at work in other ways as well: traveling through Musashi in 1486, Dōkō Jugō (1430–1501), author of the travelogue *Kaikoku zakki* (Miscellaneous records of provincial travels), mentions his arrival at a place called Asajigahara ("Fields of cogon grass"), where he composes a poem,

hitome sae	Even my sight
karete sabishiki	withers away
yūmagure	in the lonely dusk
asaji ga hara no	as I wade through the frost
shimo o waketsutsu[28]	of the fields of cogon grass.

Although it contains the requisite mention of grasses that block the traveler's view, the poem operates on another level as well: Asajigahara was an actual place in Musashi, but the inescapable reference is to an *utamakura* of the same name near Nara, in central Japan. In this manner, even a reference to a quintessentially "eastern" feature of the landscape like grasses becomes a link to the broader cultural tradition of which men of letters were a part. Traveling to the Kantō reinforced that tradition, as the itinerancy of poets like Sōchō and Dōkō enabled the diffusion of literary trends, practices, and standards from the capital region, but also the assimilation of a poetic geography centered on Kyoto. At the same time the spread of this Kyoto-centric poetic geography reiterated—or kept alive, for provincial elites—a meta-literary idea of the Kantō. The region's peculiar and distinctive literary attributes offered a

27. On the genesis of *Azumaji no tsuto*, see Note 81 below. Horton, "Sōchō and Imagawa Patronage," 134, 149.

28. *Kaikoku zakki*, 196.

unitary (countrywide) discourse to counter the prevailing rhetoric of political particularism, and the treatment of the fields of Musashino, as we shall see, is exemplary of this process.

Poets did not confine the links between themselves and local magnates to the pages of their travel accounts. Offering a literary treatise or a work of literature as a gift to a provincial magnate reinforced personal as well as literary bonds, and was part of the elaborate etiquette of patronage that helped ensure that local aspiring literati would be exposed to the appropriate commonplaces, and reminded of the returns of patronage. Sōchō presented a copy of his travelogue to Mita Ujimune, who had ridden across Musashino with him and, as we have seen, appears in the text. And Sōchō's was not an exceptional case. A catalog of those who received primers, treatises, and works of literature from visiting poets reads like a *Who's Who* of the Kantō elite at the time, and illustrates local notables' investment in the cultivation of such ties. After arriving in the Kantō, for instance, Shinkei wrote *Oi no kurigoto* (Old man's prattle, 1471) for the abbot at an old temple in Sagami Province where he was staying courtesy of the Uesugi family; Sōgi wrote *Chōrokubumi* (Letter to Nagao Magoroku, 1466) for Nagao Kagemune and *Azuma mondō* (Questions and answers in the Eastland, 1467) for Nagao Kageharu.[29] And the list would be longer if it included the fruits of linked-verse sessions and "poetry matches" (*utaawase*) sponsored by provincial magnates at their residences and attended by visiting literati and local enthusiasts.

Indeed, it is important to remind ourselves that poetry (and linked verse in particular, which came of age between 1450 and 1550) was not an act of quiet creation but a group activity and a performance. The circulation of poetic vocabulary and precepts was therefore a form of socialization, ensuring that the poetic geography of Japan did not remain confined to the written page.[30] The value of verse, moreover, was by no means limited to entertainment: words were understood to be efficacious in bringing about the auspicious outcome of a crisis, or at least to ingratiate gods and

29. Recent scholarship has begun to draw attention to the links between the cultural prestige derived from hosting poets and poetry sessions, and a provincial family's political stature. See Yata, *Nihon chūsei Sengoku-ki kenryoku kōzō no kenkyū*, 121–28; Morita, "Yamanouchi Uesugi-shi no kyoten ni tsuite," 111–13.

30. Horton, "Renga Unbound."

Buddhas. Warriors held propitiatory poetry sessions before battles, and skilled poets were often called upon to produce votive linked-verse sequences (*hōraku renga*) at local shrines and temples before or after campaigns. Sōchō, for instance, produced a solo one-thousand-verse sequence (*senku*) after the battle of Tachikawa, in 1504.[31] It is readily apparent that these practices translated poetry beyond the ludic and the literary (which would not have been clearly separated spheres anyway), but it is more difficult to trace the survival and influence of specific contents—the image of Musashino, or of the Kantō plain as a whole—beyond the page.

It is difficult to document what provincial consumers of literature "made of" the *utamakura* they were taught by literati from Kyoto. At the same time, recovering the ways in which local elites assimilated established literary conventions and perhaps repurposed them to suit their local perspective is essential to understanding how a synoptic image of the Kantō could emerge, and how the fruition of "metropolitan" poetry could serve a provincial agenda. If *utamakura* represented literary and geographical commonplaces, were provincials "inhabiting" them in the same way as courtiers?[32] In the highly structured literary circles of medieval Japan, recognition of practitioners of poetry as competent by legitimate authorities was necessary for those practitioners' voices to be heard,

---

31. Uzawa, *Sōchō Suruga nikki*, 6; Horton, *Journal of Sōchō*, 10, nn. 34 and 35; Sōchō did the same in 1509 (*Azumaji no tsuto*, 502) and in 1517 (Uzawa, *Sōchō Suruga nikki*, 6; Horton, *Journal of Sōchō*, 11–12); as did Sōboku just before his death in 1545 (*Tōgoku kikō*, 292b). For a discussion of Sōchō's role as provider of votive verses, see Horton, "Sōchō and Imagawa Patronage," 121–24. Traveling poets were not the only ones to write votive verses: in 1531 the courtier Sanjōnishi Sanetaka (1455–1537) collaborated with Sōboku on one such votive sequence. ("Setsuboku ryōgin Sumiyoshi hyakuin"); see also Tsurusaki, *Sengoku o yuku rengashi Sōchō*, 94–95; and Kaneko, *Rengashi Sōgi no jitsuzō*, 95–96.

32. Michel de Certeau (*Practice of Everyday Life*, xiii–xxii, 32) argues that consumers, while forced to accept texts as they are created, work within the parameters established by the producers to "make something of" them, something that ultimately repurposes the text's discourse to suit the consumers' needs, which are often in opposition to the producers'. Relying on spatial metaphors, Certeau characterizes consumers' efforts as devoid of a discursive place of their own: when "making something of" received texts, consumers manipulate them within the sites established for themselves by dominant discourses, which he describes as verbal "commonplaces"—an idea with obvious similarities with *utamakura*. In making "commonplaces" habitable for their own readings, consumers often subvert their producers' intentions.

thus reducing the opportunities for manipulation of the generic conventions of theme and diction. To be sure, Japanese poetry had a longstanding practice of creative repurposing: practitioners often used parts of existing and well-known poems to fashion their own compositions (the practice was called *honkadori*, "taking a source poem"); or, they simply alluded to a celebrated image or turn of phrase from an old poem as a way to add depth to their own. The resulting verse would stand as self-conscious variation on literary precedent. Further, the possibility of ironic manipulation was always present in the form of *haikai*, or unorthodox, verse. Yet both practices were so firmly built into the poetic system as to constitute a dubious space for reinvention, let alone subversion.[33]

In compiling linked verse's definitive canon, *Shinsen tsukubashū* (New collection of Tsukuba, 1495), Sōgi and Kensai (1452–1510) gave space and voice to provincial authors—something Sōgi had already done in an earlier, private anthology, *Wasuregusa* (Grasses of forgetfulness, completed by 1474), which is notable for the heavy representation of Kantō elites. To be sure, Sōgi and Kensai represented Kyoto's poetic authority: Sōgi was and is known for his respect for orthodoxy whereas Kensai, a poet from Mutsu Province, in the far northeast, traveled to Kyoto, where he spent over twenty years honing his craft; neither man gave any intimation in his career of wishing to subvert or even reinterpret the poetic or geographic order. Still, arduous though the attempt may be, there is a real benefit in examining whether we can, in fact, find evidence of local writers' (if not local readers') creative engagement with the literary treatment of their region, to understand whether, and how, the depiction of the plain moved beyond a sort of self-exoticism.[34]

---

33. For a reading of the potential for subverting the literary canon and of the literary canon's potential for subversion of the social order—albeit in genres formally less stringently defined than poetry—see Marra, *Representations of Power*, 136–71.

34. A similar attachment to the Kyoto perspective seems to have been characteristic of painters trained in the capital who made a living in the Kantō, such as Kenkō Shōkei (fl. late fifteenth, early sixteenth centuries). See Aizawa and Hashimoto, *Kantō suibokuga*, 49–82.

Musashino and the Plain

One starting point for addressing these issues might be to consider the relationship between the geographical Musashino and its literary counterpart. The toponym Musashino means "Plain of Musashi"—more of a description than a name. That Musashino and its fields (*Musashino no hara*) directly evoked their location in Musashi Province (*Musashi no kuni*) opened up the possibility of considerable slippage between literary and political spheres. The geographic overlap between the two, moreover, meant that potentially the grassy plains would be associated with the province as a whole (as the fields of Musashi rather than the fields of Musashino, in other words), although the prosaically political and the poetic seem to have remained distinct, largely confined to different sorts of text.[35] It was the fields of Musashino and not Musashi Province that held center stage in literature from and about the Kantō. Where Musashi was but a unit in the administration of the country, Musashino was a place name redolent of literary tradition: what the medieval wayfarer invariably saw, when he traveled through Musashi, were the grasses of Musashino.

Whether or not the grassy plains continued to dominate the area as they dominated its poetic reevocation may be beside the point. In fact, the shifting species that made up Musashino's vegetation over the course of centuries of poetic composition were coupled, as we shall see, with a certain intentional ambiguity in the area's geographical contours. This indeterminacy of the image's constituent parts lent it a flexibility that contributed to its lasting popularity. Through the years, the reeds (*yoshiashi*), miscanthus (*kaya*), pampas grass (*susuki*), bamboo (*take*, *shino*), bush clover (*hagi*), cogon grass (*asaji*), okera, gromwell, and golden lace provided the backdrop for multiple prevailing aesthetics, and the poetic and visual cue for forlorn travelers lost in the wilderness and longing for the comforts of civilization (Kyoto). The very stability of the association between the grasses and the plain—indeed, Musashino's celebrity as an *utamakura*—cautions the reader not to accept portraits of desolation like *Towazugatari*'s as unmediated descriptions of experiences, regardless of how realistic, vivid, and detailed they may be (especially when the type of plant

35. Ono Kazuyuki ("Musashino o aruku," 19) notes that the early form "the fields of Musashi province" (*Musashi no kuni no no*) did not outlast the Nara period (710–84).

tends to change over time without radically affecting the panorama).[36] Already in the thirteenth century, *Azuma kagami* (Mirror of the Eastland), the official history of the first shogunal regime, mentioned the need to develop land for paddies along the upper course of the Tamagawa, in Musashino, suggesting that by then the grasses without end might, in fact, have occupied a shrinking area, as farmland was opened up.[37]

Although Musashino's popularity as a poetic commonplace does not necessarily undermine the veracity of any passage in which it appears, the reiteration of a motif does require an acknowledgment of the literary play behind even the freshest of portrayals. When in 1486 Dōkō arrived in Kawagoe, he did not mention that it was the site of one of the region's most important castles, and a thriving town; his first reaction (on paper, at any rate) was to compose a poem observing that Kawagoe was clearly the threshold of Musashino, that beyond it grew grasses through which he had to make his way.[38] Likewise, when in his travelogue, *Azumaji no tsuto*, the linked-verse master Sōchō recalls a scene of "frost-withered reeds over more than fifty acres of fields"—to cite an example from a little further north in Musashi—his use of the stylized *yoshiashi* to indicate reeds ensures that we do not take the passage as a direct, unadorned recollection of his trip.[39]

Attention to the formulaic image of the grasses has meant that the actual location or extent of Musashino has received comparatively little scrutiny. In the early modern period, Musashino seems to have had an identifiable, if narrow, contour, extending east–west for ten kilometers or so, from Kichijōji to Koganei (Map 1.1).[40] In the fifteenth and sixteenth centuries, before the political center of the country moved to the Kantō and agricultural development transformed the plain, Musashino

36. Mizuhara, "Towazugatari no kyokōsei"; Mitamura, "Gofukakusa Nijō."

37. *Azuma kagami*, 33:287 (bk. 34, entry for Ninji 2.10.22).

38. *Kaikoku zakki*, 501a: *Kagiri areba / kyō waketsukusu / Musashino no / sakai mo shiruki / Kawagoe no sato.* "The village of Kawagoe—where clear is the boundary with the Plain of Musashi, which I shall travel through today, for it has an end."

39. *Azumaji no tsuto*, 503. *Yoshiashi* plays on the association of the more common word for "reed," *ashi* (which is a homophone of the word for "bad"), with the word *yoshi*, which means "good" (but also, because of its link to "bad," "reed")—a conceit meant to evoke the pleasantness of the grassy plain while also referring to the difficulty of proceeding on such terrain.

40. Ibi, "Edo bunjin no Musashino," 104–6.

extended much farther. Or, at least, the grassy meadows invariably referred to as Musashino did. Analyzing the road networks that crisscrossed the region around the turn of the sixteenth century, Saitō Shin'ichi has proposed that Musashino stretched north–south at least from the Kumegawa Lodge to Musashi Fuchū.[41] Literary evidence indicates that the geographical limits for legitimate invocation of Musashino and its imagery were even broader. The poetic itinerary vaguely sketched in *Towazugatari* has the grassy fields stretching as far east as the area of present-day Tokyo's urban core, its "twenty-three wards" (*nijūsanku*);[42] the paths traced by Dōkō and Sōchō in their travel diaries reveal that the meadows reached as far north as Kawagoe, on the banks of the Irumagawa, and as far west as the foothills on the edge of the plain.

In its broadest—and vaguest—sense, the literary "Plain of Musashi" covered ten districts in the area delimited by the Chichibu foothills and the courses of the Tamagawa, Sumidagawa, and Arakawa.[43] In this definition the area included the better part of Musashi Province and corresponded with the region of the Musashino plateau.[44] If this was still only a fraction of the overall area of the Kantō plain, it was nevertheless a considerable swath of land, all the more significant because it was nearly homonymous with the most central province in the region. It is evident that the precise contour of Musashino—even if we concede that there was such a thing—was not a matter of urgent concern to those who wrote about it as an *utamakura*. Yet it is equally apparent that the *utamakura* was central to travelers' imagination of the Kantō as a whole, much as Musashi Province, Musashino's political, quotidian, and prosaic alter ego, was to the region's physical and political geography (Fig. 1.1).

The basic flatness of the Kantō plain meant that an uncommonly vast area could be viewed panoramically, captured synoptically. During his

41. Saitō, "Kamakura kaidō Kamitsumichi to kita Kantō," 159–60. Saitō reaches his conclusion on the basis of another thirteenth-century travelogue, *Shinshō Hōshi nikki*. Kumegawa Lodge (Kumegawa-shuku) corresponds to a location in current Higashimurayama; Musashi Fuchū corresponds to present-day Fuchū. Both are in Tokyo Metropolitan Prefecture.

42. Misumi, "Chūsei bungaku ni okeru Musashino to tōgoku," 87.

43. Ibi, "Edo bunjin no Musashino," 104–6. The ten districts were Tama, Tachibana, Tsutsuki, Ebara, Toshima, Adachi, Niiza, Koma, Hiki, and Iruma.

44. Taniguchi, "Hakkutsu sareta Toshima-gun," 69–71.

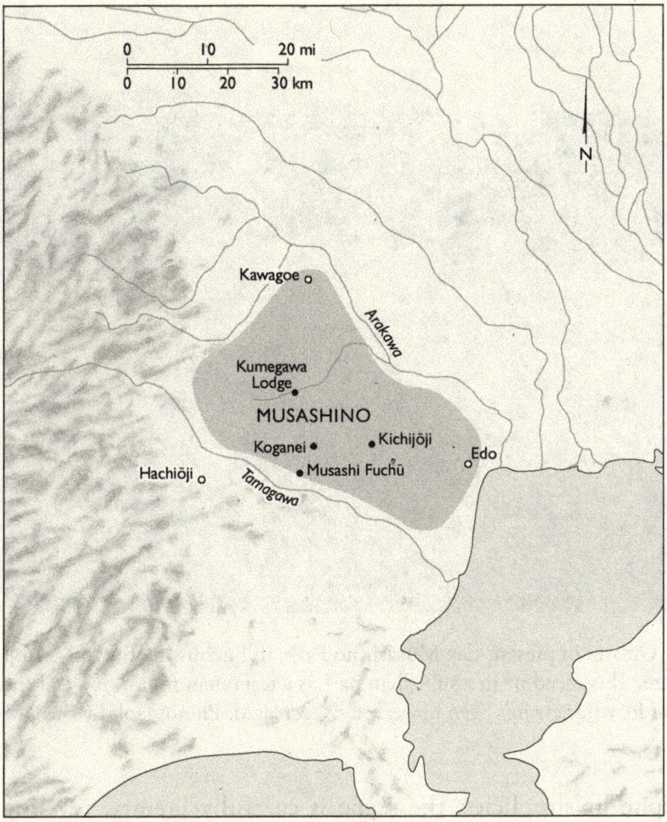

Map 1.1. Musashino.

long travels throughout the country, the poet Banri spent a number of years in Edo and Kawagoe, in Musashi, under the patronage of the warlord Ōta Dōkan. Of the view from his retreat in Edo castle—in Musashino, as he puts it—Banri writes, "To the east is the most splendid view of Tsukuba and the Sumida[gawa]; to the south are the sea of Sagami and the hills of Awa; to the west and north are thriving woods and tall bamboo groves. The peak of ten thousand *jō* [Mount Fuji] stands high above the treetops."[45]

45. Ichiki, *Baika mujinzō chūshaku*, 4:45–50. Ten thousand *jō* (about 30,000 meters) is, needless to say, an exaggeration.

Fig. 1.1. Grasses in present-day Musashino Park, in Fuchū-shi, Tokyo Metropolitan Prefecture. This meadow in a suburban park is a testament to how little of the grassy plain and its wildness has been preserved or recreated. Photograph by the author.

Despite its simplicity, the scene is carefully literary, reveling in the variety of sights, contemplating, in one 360-degree sweep, views of forests, a river, two mountains at opposite ends of the plain, the ocean. It is not, of course, generically literary, as it is punctuated by places famous in Japanese literature, even though the text is written in a Japanese version of classical Chinese. Banri returned more ornately to panoramic description upon visiting another powerful Musashi lord, Ōishi Sadashige.[46] In the passage about Fuji and Tsukuba briefly mentioned earlier in this chapter, Banri describes the surroundings of his host Sadashige's residence, in western Musashi Province:

46. The Ōishi appear in a number of accounts as hosts and patrons; around the time of Banri's visit, another traveler and literatus, Dōkō Jugō, was repeatedly welcomed at the family's residence, where he composed poetry and admired the view. *Kaikoku zakki*, 201a, 206a.

> Having assessed the location with the best view in Musashino, [Sadashige] equipped it with some ramparts and walls. After that, he built a pavilion: to the west is the snow accumulated on Mount Fuji, which will not vanish in a thousand years; to the east, mist and fog continue into the distance, unending; between that and the south are flatlands and plains of pines; as a cool wind blows over them, the song of the wind through the pines beautifully plays a tune of nature on a stringless zither; to the northeast, are a lake and two villages, and between them the peaks of Tsukuba pleasantly hang in the sky at dawn and dusk.[47]

As settings for composition, both Edo, Ōta Dōkan's fortress in the east of the province, and the Ōishi strongholds near present-day Hachiōji, in its western reaches, were well situated to behold Fuji and Tsukuba. In between were thriving pinewoods and bamboo groves—a refined quote from a Chinese classic if not necessarily a factually accurate statement—and the mists and fogs of the plain, receding in the distance.[48] Banri's panorama is evidence that different literary conventions yielded different landscapes: in its Sinitic version the plain is considerably sunnier, if not noticeably more populous.

This is the vast, empty plain where, according to Lady Nijō, "there are no mountains." The modern commuter, riding on a train through the haze of Tokyo's pollution, may be inclined to agree with her that there are no mountains, and none are visible in Musashi. Noting that the air was far cleaner and clearer in the past would be missing the point, though.[49] The mist, much like the grasses, was an obstacle to one's view only when elegantly appropriate. Obstructed or contemplated, the panorama was evoked to affirm the existence of the plain and its essential wholeness. Contemplating the view from Edo in his travelogue, *Tōgoku kikō* (Journey to the eastern provinces, 1545), the poet Sōboku (?–1545) could playfully observe, "The panorama of Musashino must all be [visible from]

---

47. Ichiki, *Baika mujinzō chūshaku*, 4:58–62.

48. "Thriving trees and tall bamboo" is a citation from *Lantingxu*, a work by the great calligrapher Wang Xizhi (307?–65?). The reference is noted by Ichiki in *Baika mujinzō chūshaku*, 4:84.

49. Horace similarly (and to similar incredulity on the part of present-day readers) extols the view he enjoys from Rome of Mount Soracte thirty kilometers north of the city: "Vides ut alta stet nive candidum / Soracte . . ." (Do you see how Soracte stands, white in deep snow . . .) (*Odes* 1.9.1–2).

here: 'the eastern turret,' or the 'Mount Tsukuba residence'; sails returning from a distant shore look like they are traveling through Musashino, on a moonlit night when the moon rises in the evening."[50] Any reader would have recognized the image of the "sails returning from a distant shore" as one of the "Eight Views of Xiao and Xiang," a celebrated subject of Chinese poetry and painting.[51]

So Banri lists *utamakura* in a travelogue in Chinese; Sōboku cites Chinese literary and pictorial motifs in a diary in classical Japanese. For both of them the actual visibility of landmarks miles away, much like the extent and flora of the meadows, is less important than its poetic reverberation. The expansive views of the plain meant that if the fields of Musashino, even in their broadest definition, corresponded with the Musashino plateau, their mood extended beyond the limits of their geographic reality, drawing areas beyond their borders into the unity of the Kantō. The thematic attributes of Musashino are echoed in descriptions of Nasuno (the Plain of Nasu) in Shimotsuke Province, at the northeastern edge of the Kantō plain, and of the marshes around Oshi castle in northern Musashi, between the Arakawa and the Tonegawa. On the way north to Shirakawa barrier in his 1468 travelogue, *Shirakawa kikō* (Journey to Shirakawa), Sōgi comes across Nasuno, which he cannot help but relate to Musashino:

> When we reached Nasu Plain, the way ahead was filled with grass so tall we could not even see the tip of the warrior's bow. I was disconsolate, thinking that but for our escort we must surely lose our lives on such a road. Though Musashi Plain is likewise of endless expanse, there one can rely on its "grasses of affinity"; here, I felt bereft of support. But then a withered scene of bamboo leaves bent under thick dew brought to mind lines by the Great Minister of the Right, and I began to be moved.[52]

50. *Tōgoku kikō*, 292b.

51. Ch. *Xiao xiang ba jing*; J. *Shōshō hakkei*.

52. Horton, *Song*, 108–9; Kaneko, *Sōgi tabi no ki shichū*, 9. The minister of the right is Minamoto no Sanetomo, who wrote a poem about a warrior traveling through the bamboo of Nasuno (now in his personal collection, *Kinkaishū*). See also S. Carter, "Sōgi in the East Country," 180–81. Carter translates Nasuno as "Nasu Moors" and Musashino as "Musashi Moors."

Reminded of the other, more celebrated meadow, Sōgi makes a point of bemoaning that he is now in the uncharted land of Nasuno and not in Musashino. When he notices one particular kind of grass, though, his connection is reestablished with the world of the Kantō as he knows it, through reference to a poem on Musashino by a thirteenth-century shogun, Minamoto no Sanetomo. Indeed even Sōgi's initial hesitation is a pose, adopted to let him allude to the poem: his initial, dejected description of Nasuno closely echoes the one offered for Musashino in the eleventh century by the author of the courtly diary *Sarashina nikki* (Sarashina diary) and reveals to the reader that the poet is already drawing comfort from the literary resonance between the two places.[53] There is some irony to Sōgi's posture: he is comforted in the midst of a desolate frontier land by memory of another place known as a desolate frontier land; the reader is tickled by the interplay of real and imagined, by the comfort drawn from the fantasy of a frontier that had long ceased to be a frontier.[54]

Shinkei followed a different path in writing his version of the Kantō, one that—in this case, at least—used not so much Musashino itself (for Shinkei describes a hilly landscape) as the poetic associations that linked that *utamakura* and the Kantō as a whole. In *Oi no kurigoto*, Shinkei describes his hermitage in the foothills of Ōyama, at the southwestern edge of the plain, in prose sprinkled with allusions to Chinese literature, and to the work of the great Tang poet Bo Juyi (772–846) in particular.[55] As Banri would in *Baika mujinzō*, Shinkei details a luxuriant natural landscape rather than one of autumnal solitude. Still, Shinkei draws an analogy between his own retreat on Ōyama and the image of the

53. The description of the grasses in *Sarashina nikki* is discussed in Misumi, "Chūsei bungaku ni okeru Musashino to tōgoku," 71. The reference is also noted in Kaneko, *Sōgi tabi no ki shichū*, 9 n. 9.

54. The history of landscape painting in Europe was strongly shaped by a similar effort to match the appearance of the countryside as actually experienced with landscapes represented artistically. See Hirsch, "Introduction," 2–3. On a similar note, Thomas Keirstead ("Gardens and Estates," 302–6) discusses the reassurance obtained from traveling into a painting instead of into unmapped territory.

55. For a translation and analysis of the passage, see Ramirez-Christensen, *Heart's Flower*, 160–65.

Chinese master, in exile on Mount Lu,[56] and in doing so, suggests that he, too, was in exile, and that the Kantō was still a region beyond the pale. (All of this in spite of the more prosaic reality that his patron's residence, in Kasuya, was a stroll away.)

A generation after Sōgi and Shinkei, Sōchō too affirmed the associative links between Musashino and the rest of the plain, though he did so neither by evoking the *utamakura* explicitly, as Sōgi had done, nor by transposing its emotional and evocative freight into a Chinese context. Rather, Sōchō built on the confusion, or conflation, of political and poetic boundaries, of Musashino and Musashi (and the Kantō).[57] In *Azumaji no tsuto*, Sōchō writes of the view from Oshi castle:

ashigamo no migiwa wa kari no tokoyo kana	Ducks in the reeds at the water's edge, the eternal land of the geese!

> This village is on the water. This refers to the scene one sees all about: Around the residence [of Sōchō's hosts] marshes upon marshes in all directions; frost-withered reeds extending for more than fifty acres of fields, and a great many water birds and geese.[58]

A few days later, he reprises the wintry image at a linked-verse session in Sugaya, some twenty kilometers further southwest:

fuyugare ya kaya ga shitaba no aki no kaze	The withering of winter; but through the lower leaves of the miscanthus, the autumn wind.

---

56. Ambros, *Emplacing a Pilgrimage*, 24.

57. Ono Kazuyuki ("Musashino o aruku," 19) makes a similar remark: "Did [poets] sing of 'Musashino' referring to Musashi, which was the name of a political administrative jurisdiction of the state's rule?"

58. *Azumaji no tsuto*, 503. My former colleague, Professor Paul Atkins, has alerted me to the possibility of additional levels of meaning in the poem: the word *kari*, which I have translated as geese (and is written with that character in the Itō Kei's annotated edition of the text) is homophonous with—and when read aloud would be indistinguishable from—two other words: the first, "hunting," would turn the poem into a joke about the area's appeal to hunters; the second, "temporary, impermanent," would create a playful oxymoron with the word "*tokoyo*," "the eternal land."

These are the conditions in the eastern fields of Musashino. It is just a frost-withered scene.[59]

There is no evidence to suggest that these somber scenes do not reflect the landscapes Sōchō saw (even if he had not explicitly vouched for the truthfulness of his portrait after the second poem). The reference to the paddies' size reads like the poet's actual estimate, and the odd spectacle of Oshi castle surrounded by marshlands jibes with what we know of that fortress, which Toyotomi Hideyoshi's (1536–98) forces famously tried to attack with a fleet in 1590. The lords of Oshi, the Narita, operated extensively on the Tonegawa, and the castle itself was built on the wetlands near the water. Still, the description is couched in fitting poetic terms: "geese" is a standard seasonal referent for autumn, the time of year when the passage takes place; the reeds are withered in the frost—another autumnal word. Regardless of what we know of the area, Sōchō's landscape is one of untamed growth, empty of human settlement beyond the village, isolated, besieged, featureless as far as the eye can see. Sōchō's description echoes the elegant melancholy of a verse by Shinkei:

yuki no oru	Snapped beneath the snow
kaya ga sueno wa	miscanthus to the edge of the fields
michi mo nashi[60]	leave no path.

Despite the passage of time and the increasing settlement and frequentation by travelers (poetically minded or not), well after the outbreak of the civil war the prevalent image of Musashino and the Kantō had remained one of remoteness, particularly in passages written in Japanese.

Yet it is around this time that we also begin to see—counterbalancing the exoticism of stock portrayals of the region—a growing attention to empirical detail. We see it in the number of locations visited and described in later travelogues, which far surpass the dictates of aesthetic effect; we see it in the more careful recording of the names of local hosts

---

59. *Azumaji no tsuto*, 504. Sōchō appears to have been disoriented here, for the area he describes is at the northwestern edge of the Musashino.

60. The first verse (*hokku*) is generally the only link that was preserved in a sequence. This particular verse opens a sequence composed in the winter of 1468 and printed in Yokoyama, *Shinkei sakuhinshū*, 443–46.

and places of little renown. Unlike Sōgi's, Sōchō's panoramas of reeds and winter appear in the midst of prosaic discussions about flooding rivers and the forwarding of rents. In this context, the reinforcement of the sense of wonder and wildness through scenes like the ones in Oshi and Nasuno may well have been designed to offset the frequency of references to delightful but mundane stops in places like the hot springs in Ikaho, which appear in several of the travelogues and threaten to complicate the associative landscape of the region.

The Eastland Seen from the Kantō

If the thematic expansion of Musashino contributed to the consolidation of an identity for the Kantō, it is nonetheless hard to escape the conclusion that the creation of an "Eastland" (Azuma) through the reiteration of themes like the grasses of Musashino still functioned primarily to reinforce the inclusion of the plain within a tradition that was firmly anchored in the capital and shared its perspective. Men like Shinkei, Sōgi, Banri, Dōkō, Sōchō, and Sōboku devoted significant portions of their time and talents to the eastern provinces, but were nevertheless visitors using literary motifs to make a foreign land intelligible, not locals reflecting on their own identity through poetic conventions. So although we might wish to interpret the surge in popularity of eastern Japan among poets and literati after 1467 as a sign of subversion of those spatial and poetic hierarchies, it is important to realize that it was such hierarchies that led these men of letters to the east in the first place. For their part, easterners would have been accustomed to the perspective their guests brought along—and were delighted by their own association with it, if the escorts they provided for poets making their way past storied landmarks are any indication.

We cannot know how literate residents of the Kantō felt about the disjuncture between experience and verse, though on a certain level this may be a false problem. For all of its depiction as beyond the pale, the Kantō was part of Japan; its portrayal, too, part of a long-established tradition. Its residents willingly and eagerly participated in the reproduction of a cultural geography created in the capital—which may have been distant and even unreachable, but was not ideologically foreign. Residents of the Kantō, we may guess, perceived the disjuncture no more and no less—and with no more or no less anxiety or consternation—than residents of the central provinces did when they traveled to famous places near the capital and wrote about them in travelogues and poems. But related to this problem is another. Who were these provincials who were invited to participate in the reproduction of a literary canon of which they were, in a sense, the subject matter? Were the multitude of provincial poets and aspiring literati—for travelogues make it abundantly clear that it was a multitude—a first order of consumers? Before the early modern period we cannot trace a clear distinction between producers and consumers of literature: all producers were, of course, consumers, but all consumers, too, were also producers, for with few exceptions the production of poetry—even if derivative, and formally and expressively mediocre—was an activity firmly rooted in the niceties of polite social interaction. No doubt these poets, amateurish to varying degrees, were viewed as distant from the cultural center by more serious practitioners. But the eagerness with which they sought to be admitted to that center is perhaps a sign that they should best be viewed as marginal producers and reproducers of the dominant discourse rather than more or less intentionally subversive consumers.[61]

The Kantō did have a number of accomplished poets and literati of the local, nonprofessional variety, warriors like Tō no Tsuneyori (1402–84), who introduced Sōgi himself to the secret transmission of poetic precepts, *Kokindenju*. But as Tsuneyori's own receipt of *Kokindenju*, the ultimate insider's distinction, attests, these highly proficient easterners are perfect examples of the need for provincials to conform to rules of poetry established in Kyoto.[62] Kido Takanori (1434–1502), another well-known denizen of Kantō poetic circles, described reeds near his residence in a preface to a poem (*kotobagaki*) that would echo a few years later in Sōchō's description of the reeds near Oshi: "I lived in a place

61. Cf. Kamens, *Utamakura, Allusion, and Intertextuality*, 19–20.

62. *Kokindenju* was made up of a series of esoteric, "true" readings of poems contained in the first imperial anthology, *Kokinshū* (Collection of poems old and recent, 905). The transmission was conceived by members of the Nijō poetic school, the most conservative of the literary lineages that emerged in the Middle Ages, although the 1471 transmission from Tsuneyori to Sōgi became a landmark in its own right. For a splendid in-depth analysis of *Kokindenju*, see Lewis Edwin Cook's dissertation, "Discipline of Poetry."

called Iriegatake, 'Bamboo by the Inlet,' in a district called Toshima in Musashi Province; before me reeds and so forth grew thick, stags always wandering about."[63]

Whatever their alienation from the Kantō of verse, locals, naturally, had their own Kantō as well, a product of personal encounters with the region's landscape. The imagery imported from the capital through assiduous literary practice dominated poetic composition but must have had a more complex relationship with these men's daily experience of their surroundings. In a 1489 letter to the new castellan of Edo—a piece of pure political correspondence, in its format and language—the warrior lord Uesugi Sadamasa (1443–94) complains of his adoptive son's predilections, of the time he wastes chatting with friends "about bird-hunting in Musashino, and bush warblers."[64] Sadamasa's scornful remark is part of a more extended lamentation on the ineptitude of his heir and the certain demise of the house upon his succession. The lament sits neatly within the long tradition of casting doubt on the aptitude and abilities of a young heir and on the moral fiber of the younger generation, and the catastrophic scenarios Sadamasa envisions for his successor-to-be are no more original than the young man's distractions.[65]

But the reference to falconry in Musashino is more interesting than a simple, timeless, heartfelt but stock rebuke of a wayward son. It is there that we may catch a glimpse of the dialectic between literary commonplace and daily life. On the one hand, the comment reinforces the picture

63. The forward is for a poem in Takanori's eponymous collection, *Takanorishū*; cited in Kaneko, *Rengashi Sōgi no jitsuzō*, 148. Poetically speaking stags, and deer generally, were animals representative of autumn. As for Takanori, he was a Kantō native (born in Kōzuke) who became part of the court of the Lord of Horigoe, in Izu.

64. *SKS* 5, no. 1019 (*Koshōmon*). At first glance it would seem that Musashino does not appear as a literary motif here, and that the accusation is of overindulgence in hunting alone. But reference to the bush warbler (*uguisu*), a popular subject for verse, makes it clear that Sadamasa's own scolding is designed to evoke both activities, which, combined, reveal his son's general lack of focus on more serious matters.

65. One famous example is *Imagawa jō* (The Imagawa letter, ca. 1412), which Imagawa Ryōshun wrote to chide his heir. It was translated and discussed in Steenstrup, "Imagawa Letter." In Sadamasa's day, Asakura Takakage wrote a set of house precepts, which concluded with an admonition to his heirs not to let their guard down, lest the family's fortunes come to an end. Ishii et al., *Chūsei seiji shakai shisō, jō*, 350–52. For an English translation, see Lu, *Japan*, 176–78.

of Musashino as a space beyond settlement: a blank space of leisure beyond engagement in the politics of intrigue and war and conquest, a space, indeed, fit for hunting. The reference to the bush warbler—not only a bird but also an important and well-worn subject for poetic composition—further suggests that the literary Musashino was on Sadamasa's mind. And in the next sentence, the association becomes explicit. In his enumeration of the frivolities enjoyed by his heir, Sadamasa describes a life filled with "tales about skilled calligraphers, linked-verses of Shinkei and Sōgi, tales of nobles high and low, young and old, and men and women in the capital . . . and the styles of noh dancing of Kanze and Konparu."[66] By linking Musashino with bush warblers and two famous masters like Shinkei and Sōgi, Sadamasa gives away his internalization of the link between Musashino's "non-place-ness" and poetry; by lumping together poetry and dance, he shows us the realm of belles lettres as it might have appeared to an outsider. At the same time, of course, for all of its derisiveness, the passage reveals how much access both Sadamasa and his heir had to some of the cultural refinements of the capital, for it is not only the verses of poets "in exile" in the east that they could debate, but also the performing styles and techniques of two celebrated theatrical troupes—interspersed, as they may be, with the latest gossip.

On the other hand, among the objects of Sadamasa's contempt the one activity directly tied to Musashino is hunting, a pastime distinctly associated with the warrior elite, and one that had many successful warlords among its enthusiasts.[67] (So, really, Sadamasa may have erred on the side of petulance in this regard.) And the association between hunting—falconry specifically—and Musashino did not begin or end with Sadamasa. Falconry had indeed been a courtier pastime before it was associated with warriors. Still, falconry, and hunting generally, while certainly practiced in Musashino well before Sadamasa's time, does not figure prominently among the poetic attributes of the grasslands. And Sadamasa's reference does not appear in verse.

---

66. *SKS* 5, no. 1019 (*Koshōmon*).

67. See for instance *Asakura Sōteki waki*, 6. One of the more avid falconers of the sixteenth century was Tokugawa Ieyasu. See Pitelka, "Empire of Things."

Half a century later, though, a hunting expedition in Musashino provided the occasion for the travelogue *Musashino no kikō* (Journey to Musashino): "In the middle of the autumn of the fifteenth year of Tenbun [1546], wishing to see Musashino, we thought this would be a good time, and when the moment came to set off we were accompanied by a great many people, and thought of enjoying some falconry."[68] "We," in this case, refers to the narrator, the warlord and literatus Hōjō Ujiyasu (1515–71), master of much of the Kantō in the sixteenth century, and the man who *did* eventually put an end to Sadamasa's line. The passage and its author's interest in Musashino as hunting grounds echo Sadamasa's characterization of Musashino, providing a perfect encapsulation of the way warriors used old literary conventions to represent and elevate their soldierly interests. Or, to put it differently, writing about a hunting party in Musashino reveals the way local warriors apprehended their surroundings even as they sought to follow courtly poetics in framing the experience as a traditional travel account.

To add some complication to this picture, doubt has been cast on the authenticity of *Musashino no kikō*, specifically on Ujiyasu's authorship; and it was inaccuracies in the text's treatment of Musashino that provided much of the evidence against its putative narrator and author's involvement.[69] Yet forgeries are documents in their own right, and the mistakes made by its author (let's call him "the pseudo-Ujiyasu") make *Musashino no kikō* no less compelling as an artifact.

Most of the factual mistakes that give *Musashino no kikō* away, it turns out, are in passages lifted from Sōchō's *Azumaji no tsuto* and placed in the newer travelogue without too much attention to context or verisimilitude. We may not be surprised to find out that what made sense in 1509 no longer did in 1546. In particular, the characterization of Musashino offered in the later work is at variance with its purported author's experience: the historical Ujiyasu would have been intimately acquainted with Musashino—particularly by the 1540s, when he spent most of his time campaigning in central Musashi in his quest to extirpate Uesugi

---

68. *Musashino no kikō*, 240.

69. Tanaka Y., "Hōjō Ujiyasu no Musashino kikō no shingi ni tsuite" (quoted in Zoku Gunsho Ruijū Kanseikai, *Gunsho kaidai* 3:383–86).

resistance. Surely, even with all due deference to the hackneyed but hallowed fiction of the grassy fields as a sort of *terra incognita*, the notion that after many delays he was about to set out to see Musashino would have seemed silly to contemporaries. There are several other oddities in the text as well, such as, for example, Ujiyasu's incongruous itinerary—which made sense in the context of Sōchō's trip of 1509 but seems unnecessarily convoluted for Ujiyasu. (It is worth repeating that there are several oddities because, alone, noting that Ujiyasu must have known Musashino quite well would hardly be enough to prevent him from feigning ignorance or pretending never to have been there.) Ultimately, that the area was fit for hunting expeditions means that it must still have been only thinly settled at best, or that, for the pseudo-Ujiyasu, writing a fictional account of a trip to the area, the prevailing image of the region was still powerful and appropriate enough to keep his narrative within the bounds of (literary) plausibility.

It is tempting to view the text's inconsistencies as manifestations of the tension between acceptable literary utterances and a slowly changing landscape, between an "outsider's" portrayal based on a Kyoto-centric, canonical literary geography and an "insider's" portrayal, still attentive to the dictates of elegant speech but increasingly receptive to the appeal of surroundings that could and did have multiple uses as circumstances evolved. After all, even while making every effort not to stray from such dictates of elegant speech—or because of those efforts—narratives of trips across the region could resemble a Grand Tour, the ironic distance between author and narrator plainly, almost lazily, in view. Such was the case of *Kaikoku zakki*, whose narrator can be followed as he travels through the region, back and forth, not on his way somewhere else, but to visit as many local temples and patrons as possible, in a profusion of references to tall grasses and loneliness absurdly belied by the multitude of settlements he encounters. Yet the increased but still very partial population of much of the region is not sufficient, alone, to explain what appear to be glimmers of a more complicated characterization of Musashino, alongside its long-lived image as a frontier land beyond the pale of civilization. That image had endured for centuries, more or less indifferent to the region's rising and ebbing political importance, to its growing political proximity to the loci of power during the course of the Middle

Ages. For Uesugi Sadamasa and, later, for the pseudo-Ujiyasu, Musashino remained wild, but was also a place of leisure and entertainment rather than a threshold to the unknown. It could be more prosaic.

To be sure, the insider/outsider dichotomy is too clean-cut and explains little. It has two obvious failures. First, provincials' reinvention of the culture they were expected to consume passively, if it occurred, was not overt or programmatic. Indeed, provincials fancied themselves participants in a courtly culture, for if geographic distance was no impediment to an aristocrat in Kyoto imagining a trip through Musashino, it could be no great impediment to a Kantō warrior borrowing other commonplaces to adorn his compositions. To make something new of a poetic language developed elsewhere was not a self-conscious assertion of local identity. Indeed, the most distinguished voices in the literary panorama of the eastern provinces—men whose compositions were included in poetic anthologies of the caliber of *Shinsen tsukubashū*—gained their status by functioning as representatives of Kyoto's culture in the east. Second, the prosaic—by which I mean the intrusion of something akin to actual experience, of registers other than the lofty and rarefied—appears not only in texts written by locals (even assuming the pseudo-Ujiyasu was a local).

Haruo Shirane has recently written about the confluence of courtly and "rustic" conventions in the literary depiction of nature and landscapes in the late Middle Ages, particularly after the onset of civil war.[70] Esperanza Ramirez-Christensen has drawn attention to Shinkei's unconventional poems on the senseless suffering of war.[71] H. Mack Horton has drawn insightfully on Mikhail Bakhtin's theory of the novel to analyze the variety and the dialogical relationships of registers and genres (heteroglossia) that the poet Sōchō adopts in his works, a variety unseen in the monoglossic, epic narratives (to borrow Bakhtin's categories) of earlier poets like Sōgi.[72] Ramirez-Christensen's and Horton's research is focused on the originality of the works of individual authors (albeit, particularly important ones), and Shirane is concerned with the theme of seasonality in poetic composition, but some of their observations could

70. Shirane, *Culture of the Four Seasons*, 113–31, esp. 113–14.
71. Ramirez-Christensen, *Heart's Flower*, 156–57.
72. Horton, *Song*, 107–46.

perhaps be applied more broadly. We can see some of the unruliness of actual experience—or at least the willingness to adopt registers other than the courtly—beginning to show up in texts composed after the Ōnin War by a variety of men. The endless conflicts that erupted all over Japan in the wake of that war intrude with particular frequency, and in a conspicuously unadorned fashion. The delicate elegies of Sōgi (and even Shinkei), early in the war, are more rarefied than the accounts of men writing only a few years later, like Sōchō, Sōboku, and Banri. In *Shirakawa kikō*, Sōgi remarks that his travel plans were almost disrupted, referring elliptically to "some disconcerting news" that for a moment appeared to frustrate his wish to see Shirakawa.[73] Faced with a similar predicament, Sōchō rather more plainly explains that the last leg of his own trip to Shirakawa had to be called off because of the double obstacle presented by ongoing war between local families on the road ahead and by the flooding of one of the major rivers in the area.[74] The incorporation of mundane details from current events was not embraced by all authors, of course, nor did individual authors necessarily or consistently shift in that direction over time. Ramirez-Christensen, for instance, has shown how Shinkei, in revisiting his relocation to the Kantō in successive works, gave progressively less detailed and more literary accounts of circumstances and motives for leaving the capital.[75]

Generic conventions played a significant role in these divergent responses: travelogues, as a genre, had shared since their inception the poetic aesthetics and aims of verse, and had often served as framing devices for collections of poems, but they were not bound by the same explicit rules by which orthodox poetry had to abide. Even as different voices made their way, or could make their way, into the prose sections of a travelogue, its portions in verse remained scrupulously anchored to precedent. And poetry in Chinese, of course, was not subject to the same restrictions that delimited the boundaries of refinement in Japanese. As the examples below demonstrate, poets and authors took advantage to

---

73. S. Carter, "Sōgi in the East Country," 181.

74. *Azumaji no tsuto*, 495.

75. Ramirez-Christensen (*Heart's Flower*, 88–91) compares passages in *Hitorigoto* (Solitary ramblings, 1468) and *Oi no kurigoto*, written three years later.

varying degrees of the opportunities for expression offered by different genres.

Nevertheless, even when it did not lead to testing of the boundaries of genre, the growing messiness and violence of the world came to be more prominently featured in literature. Poets may have continued to resort to formulaic phrasing and to borrow standardized pathos, but ongoing war increasingly provided the occasion for explicitly topical poetry. Musashino, too, became a stage for new emotions: a 1473 poem by Shinkei on the theme of evanescence veers from a delicate image of fields to a stark image of the ravages of war:

nobe ni mishi aware mo samete kuni sato no keburi to naru o kiku zo kanashiki[76]	Waking from the moving sight of the fields, to the sadness of hearing of province and village up in smoke.

A decade later—a particularly violent decade later—Dōkō, too, mourned those who had fallen, explicitly mentioning the recent fighting, its toll, and the indignities visited upon the bodies of those who had participated.

At a place where tens of thousands have perished in the recent wars of the Kantō, many are the burial tumuli, with the bones of men and horses piled together in the mounds.

naki o tou okabe no hara no furuzuka ni aki no shirushi no matsukaze zo fuku[77]	Among the old mounds in the fields by the side of the hill where we mourn the dead, wind blows through the pines, the sign of autumn.

In 1488, Banri composed a quatrain (Ch: *jueju*) bluntly assessing the fighting in the Kantō:

---

76. "Shinkei sōzu hyakushu," 915b.

77. *Kaikoku zakki*, 189a. Okabe (which I have translated as "by the side of the hill") was also a place name. Congruently with the theme of the poem, it was there that the Ōgigayatsu Uesugi established their "satellite" camp when the main camp was built at Ikatsuko. *Shōin shigo*, 791b.

武陵兵馬気如雲	Troops and horses filled the air of Musashi like clouds.
鷹鈞天哉俄敗軍	Ganchō's fate was to be quickly defeated.
乱落桃花紅雨薄	Scattering and falling peach blossoms, thin like a crimson rain.
斯詩聊爲故人云	This poem is a trifle, I composed it for the late lord.[78]

He added a gloss at the end, lest anyone think his was only an elegant divertissement on the theme of war: "As for Uesugi Sadamasa, this lord is known as Ganchō. Once, I wrote a Chinese poem for him. Further, I was in Musashino so I knew him well. For no reason at all, he assassinated Dōkan. Now, he has already been defeated in battle."[79] In this case, Banri inverts the common usages of "Musashi" and "Musashino," choosing the former, the administrative subdivision, in his poem, while reserving the latter, the poetic place name, for his more prosaic gloss.

The blurring of lines between the rarefied world of literature and the less tidy one in which literati and patrons operated was paralleled by a conspicuous blurring of lines between genres. In his longest diary/travelogue, *Sōchō shuki* (*The Journal of Sōchō*, 1522–27), Sōchō detailed a clash that had occurred two decades earlier between two of his patrons in the Kantō. For all its use of metaphor, the description of the battle is detailed enough to be used as a piece of historical evidence with few of the caveats that usually accompany quotes from travelogues:

> At the beginning of the ninth month of the first year of Eishō [1504], war broke out between the Yamanouchi and the Ōgigayatsu houses (known together as the "Two Uesugi," the Yamanouchi being the deputies in Kamakura). The Ōgigayatsu were allied with Sōun and held Kawagoe and Edo. The Yamanouchi held Uwado and Hachigata. The conflict became general, and overran the borders of Musashino. For three Kantō leagues the foe would not fall back, nor could our allies advance. When the deadlock had continued more than ten days, the Ōgigayatsu requested support from Imagawa Ujichika, who immediately set out at the head of an

78. Ichiki, *Baika mujinzō chūshaku*, 2:88–89.
79. Ichiki, *Baika mujinzō chūshaku*, 2:88–89.

> army. On the thirteenth, Asahina Yasuhiro and Fukushima Saemon no jō followed with their forces from Tōtōmi and Suruga. On the twentieth, twenty-first, and twenty-second of the same month, Sōun made camp at Masukata. The enemy appeared to have pulled back. Our allies pursued them, making camp one night in the open. The next day, at about eight in the morning, our allies and the foe caught sight of one another through the mist of Musashino, both armies thick as a mountain forest. They met with a crash of thunder. At about noon the cavalry charged and the battle raged for several hours thereafter. The foe was defeated and their main force retreated to their stronghold at Tachikawa. Contact was lost with them in the night. Two thousand and more were missing, killed, cut down and left for dead, or made prisoner, and horses and armor were taken in abundance.[80]

The fields of Musashino have become battlefields; much like solitary wayfarers, armies "made camp in the open" and opposing troops "caught sight of one another through the mist of Musashino." In Sōchō's account, not only generic but geographic boundaries turn out to be permeable. The castles and battlefields (Uwado, Hachigata, Kawagoe, Edo, Tachikawa) were indeed all in Musashino—in fact, they marked its boundaries. But Musashino here is the *utamakura*, or at least it borrows from the *utamakura*'s ever-expanding web of associations. When the text says, "The conflict became general and overran the borders of Musashino," the reader who thinks of Oshi or Nasu cannot but understand that fighting embroiled the whole of the plain, spreading beyond the borders not only of Musashino but also of Musashi Province. Not only does the literary nature of the account invite the use of Musashino to describe a battle; reference to distant Hachigata makes it clear that Sōchō conflates the province and the *utamakura*.

Continuing warfare, and poets' firsthand experience in it, certainly contributed to contemporary events' intrusion into and acceptance as literature. But it was not only war that seeped into the controlled envi-

---

80. Adapted from Horton, *Journal of Sōchō*, 9–10; Uzawa, *Sōchō Suruga nikki*, 5–6. For years Sōchō had maintained cordial relations with both contenders, even during the fighting. And although in this account the poet's sympathy is for the Ōgigayatsu because his lord, Imagawa Ujichika, sided with them, we know from *Azumaji no tsuto* that by 1509 Sōchō would be on good terms with both sides once again. It is worth noting, in passing, that Sōchō's presence at the battle in Musashino, in 1504, somewhat undermines the adventure and novelty of his 1509 ride through the grasses.

ronment of courtly literature. In *Tōgoku kikō*, Sōboku's recollection of an evening viewing Mount Fuji, loftiest of mountains, is colored with gentle but unmistakable irony: "[My host's] younger brother Seidō's drinking party was hard to avoid, [so it ended up] a perfect case of me being extremely drunk. On the way back, having been told I must take a look at a pavilion for viewing Fuji, I headed to Tominaga's place. . . . The sun had set, and even Fuji was not visible."

The dialogical process outlined by Horton for *Sōchō shuki* (and traced in other works above) is primarily one of genres. Yet, I would submit, it is possible to consider the heteroglossia of works like Sōchō's as the literary reflection of broader social processes. The tensions between genres that animate Sōchō's work, in other words, can be understood to reflect—and reveal—the elusive dialectic of production and consumption that shapes literary relations between upholders and propagators of the literary orthodoxy on the one side and provincials on the other. More concretely, one way of looking at the emergence of a prosaic world alongside the more rarefied one of court poetry is to think of this new world as the result of locals' making something new of received traditions. This opportunity was presented by the diaspora of literati, whose willingness to be patronized more than ever before helped bring provincials up to a level of proficiency adequate to exchange verses with their courtly counterparts. These local aspiring poets, under the schooling of the visiting masters, certainly learned to view their own region in accordance with the criteria established in Kyoto. The diffusion of this tradition affirmed the Kantō's ties to the central order even as that order foundered.

But itinerant poets and literati were also dependent on the largesse of their patrons, and had strong incentives to promote their own services along with literary knowledge. Sōchō's *Azumaji no tsuto*, for instance, has been shown to be a primer of sorts: copies of the travelogue at various stages of completion (some including more of the itinerary than others) were left in the keeping of the poet's patrons, along the way.[81] Accordingly, there is as much exposition as lyricism in the travelogue,

81. Both Tsurusaki Hiroo (*Sengoku o yuku rengashi Sōchō*, 91–92) and Shimazu Tadao (*Rengashi Sōgi*, 147) credit Ijichi Tetsuo with first offering this interpretation. See Ijichi, "Sōchō no *Azumaji no tsuto* shohon kō."

and the tone is often didactic rather than rarefied.[82] Pedagogy—one of the services most sought after by provincial magnates—may have been only one aim for a travelogue, but it was by far the most important aim in the composing of those treatises, mentioned above, which were donated to—or expressly written for—provincial magnates. At the same time, men like Sōchō were also hired as negotiators and were entertained in banquets designed to show off patrons' wealth, so the Kantō that emerges from travelogues like *Azumaji no tsuto* or *Tōgoku kikō* was not only made up of Musashino and the disorientation experienced amid its grasses, but also of drunken parties, amusement at "seeing the sights," and bitterness at the loss of acquaintances in the turmoil of war. The appearance of many place names and the recording of unimportant sessions were part of this new process, one in which relations of patronage inflected the contents of itinerant poets' production. To put it another way: poets now wrote for provincials—and they wrote works of literature for them, not only works of literary criticism or pedagogy. In the process, the distinction between literature and criticism, too, lost some of its sharpness.

Some, like Shinkei, remained ambivalent about their role. During his stay in the Kantō he was the leading poet in two landmark events sponsored by the powerful Ōta family, the "Kawagoe senku" (One thousand links in Kawagoe) of 1470 and a poetry match held in Edo four years later.[83] These gatherings drew other professional poets, like Sōgi and a young Kensai, and literary notables like Kido Takanori, as well as other men—Kantō warriors—whose verses would later be included in *Shinsen tsukubashū*.[84] Still, in spite of the several years he spent in the east, Shinkei never seems to have overcome the sense that he was an exile. His account of the intellectual and artistic decline of Bontō, a poet of a pre-

82. For an in-depth discussion of the ways in which poets of Sōchō's generation reinterpreted the relationship between literary convention and firsthand experience, see Horton, *Song*, 12–24, 95–105.

83. Inoue M., *Chūsei kadanshi no kenkyū*, 229. Ramirez-Christensen (*Heart's Flower*, 132) calls the event unprecedented; Okuda, *Sōgi*, 47; Saitō, "Minami Kantō no toshi to kaidō," 173–74; and S. Carter, "Three Poets at Yuyama," 131; for "Kawagoe senku," see Hanawa, *Zoku gunshō ruijū*, vol. 17, pt. 1, 432–58; for "Bushū Edo utaawase," see Hanawa, *Shinkō gunsho ruijū* 9:668–71.

84. Kaneko, *Shinsen tsukubashū no kenkyū*, 548–53.

vious generation who had wandered the east for many years before returning to the capital, reads like a reflection on his own fate:

> Bontō was a good poet and people made much of him; starting around the age of forty he fell low and entirely abandoned the path of poetry; for twenty years he hid his footsteps at the ends of Tsukushi [Kyūshū] and in the remotest corners of the Eastland. Afterward, having returned to the capital more than sixty years old, perhaps because his words' flower had lost color and fragrance, and his heart's spring had grown clouded, they say that his form faltered and that he would completely forget about the previous verse [when composing his own verse in a sequence]. Truly, having been out of use for so long, is it unexpected that [his art] should thoroughly decline?[85]

Shinkei would not be the last to decry the rusticity of poetry and aspiring poets in the provinces, yet he continued to participate in poetic gatherings, and produce literary treatises for local patrons. The very work in which he voices such complaints, his most important work of literary criticism, *Sasamegoto* (*Murmured Conversations*), also reveals his desire to keep interacting with provincials: written in 1463–64, before his departure for the Kantō, the treatise was produced in the form of questions and answers exchanged between the poet and a rustic, but eager, provincial.[86] And we know that when Shinkei was visited by Sōgi during his final years in the east, the younger master made sure to produce a copy of that treatise for himself.[87]

Directly or indirectly, then, *Sasamegoto* (and presumably many other such texts) would have been read or taught in the Kantō. Shinkei's work seems to have borne fruit: he continued to influence the Kantō poetic scene even after his death in 1475, as Uesugi Sadamasa's complaint about his heir's interest in the poet's work, in the 1489 letter discussed above, attests. As for the rusticity of provincials, even a generation later, both Sōchō and a Kyoto-trained, local poet, the warrior Nitta Shōjun (Iwamatsu Hisazumi, 1461–1511?), would take up their brushes to enumerate

---

85. Shimazu, *Oi no kurigoto*, 414.

86. For an annotated and commented English translation of the treatise see Ramirez-Christensen, *Murmured Conversations.*

87. S. Carter, "Sōgi in the East Country," 170.

the many frustrations they experienced in the Kantō poetic scene[88] (although in a more cheerful moment Sōchō could praise a session in which he participated as "indescribably elegant"[89]).

Yet despite the lack of improvement among Kantō practitioners that these lamentations suggest, literati continued to travel to the east and develop bonds with local patrons: Sōgi, who laid down the template for the wayfaring linked-verse poet, if not for a new way of writing about one's travels, visited the east no less than seven times. And younger poets, while hardly turning their backs on the capital, seem to have been less recalcitrant than Shinkei—more willing to rely on their provincial patrons. Kensai, an easterner by birth, traveled to Kyoto after receiving Shinkei's mentorship during the master's years of "exile" in the Kantō. (Kensai's move to the capital occurred well *after* the beginning of hostilities in the city, and reminds us that for all of the damage wreaked by the fighting, and all of the relocation on the part of the talents of the day, the cultural scene in Kyoto still exerted enough pull that a young and ambitious talent would choose to spend over twenty years there, becoming one of the preeminent poets of his day.) But Kensai eventually returned to the east, settling at the court of the loftiest of eastern patrons, the Lord of Koga.[90] Kensai did not establish a new, locally rooted language of place, or even a new image founded on the language of Kyoto, for his patrons were happy to have him (and others like him) celebrate the region in accordance with precedent.

The circulation of texts and the circulation of people are our best evidence of the ways in which provincial demand drove a market of literary knowledge. The poets who traveled east early—ambivalent as Shinkei was, seemingly more eager as Sōgi was—produced texts that still expressed the poetic ideals of Kyoto's literary circles unmediated, or

88. Nitta Shōjun wrote *Renga kaiseki shiki* (*Rules for Linked-Verse Sessions*, n.d.), a series of twenty-one articles instructing country poets about the proper demeanor for a day of *renga*. Sōchō wrote *Renga jūmuyaku* (*Ten Vexations of Linked Verse*, n.d.), lamenting the inadequacies of many participants in poetry sessions (Horton has translated both texts as appendices to his "Renga Unbound," 106–12).

89. *Azumaji no tsuto*, 503.

90. The Lord of Koga, at this time, was Ashikaga Masauji (1466–1531).

uncomplicated, by interaction with easterners. But the civil war continued in the capital and political unrest spread to the provinces, and soon portrayals of the Kantō grew varied in tone and contents along with poets' contact with local practitioners. Where Shinkei had endeavored to refine his earlier travel accounts in subsequent works by omitting details and elevating motives, and Sōgi had avoided topics and language that could undermine the lyrical coherence of his eastern travelogue,[91] later travelers showed fewer hesitations about revealing the mundane in their travels.

Yet we should not simply replace the insider/outsider dualism with new dualisms, between lofty and prosaic, monoglossia and heteroglossia. To do so would be to suggest that the synoptic if archetypical and ahistorical image of the Kantō was swept away by a more fragmented but historically grounded one. I have argued that the creative engagement of locals introduced some of the contingency of real experience, but several considerations are in order. Useful though it is in highlighting the dialectic between itinerant poets and local magnates that shaped literary exchange, the metaphor of the market of literary knowledge elides the persistent cultural imbalance between visitors and hosts, who interacted as masters and pupils. Linked-verse masters, the most popular among itinerant poets, were invited to the east to share the Kyoto-centric poetic geography and were rewarded lavishly for their mentorship.[92] Local magnates, however proficient in the conventions of composition, remained to the end consumers of a culture that came to them ready-made. Further, even the newly discovered variety of registers and themes seen in

91. S. Carter, "Sōgi in the East Country," 170–71; Horton, *Song*, 107–22.

92. Just how lavishly they were rewarded is hard to assess precisely: patronage was granted in several different forms, "both material and financial" (Tsurusaki, "Shōkō and the Salons of Sakai," 60), and recipients seldom disclose their earnings in their travel diaries. Sōchō occasionally refers to gifts of 100 to 1,000 *hiki* from provincial warriors; from one patron alone, he estimates receiving, over the years, some 10,000 *hiki* (Horton, *Journal of Sōchō*, 124, 130, 133, 149). One hundred *hiki* were equivalent to one measure (*koku*) of rice (roughly 180 liters of rice, or the amount necessary to support one adult for a year). Horton calculates that over the course of his lifetime the poet donated some 30,000 *hiki* to Daitokuji, a major Zen temple in Kyoto ("Sōchō and Imagawa Patronage," 140). For the sake of comparison, the aristocratic Sanjōnishi house had an annual income of about 26,000 *hiki* (Horton, "Sōchō and Imagawa Patronage," 98).

works by Sōchō and others by no means entailed a rejection of literary orthodoxy. To return to the example of *Azumaji no tsuto*: in the introductions and glosses to his poems Sōchō may have described places he saw *as he saw them*, but the poems themselves hew to a poetics of Musashino that by no means requires the author's firsthand experience of the various *utamakura* he describes. Despite the upheaval that Sōchō details elsewhere in the text, the grasses of Musashino he traverses in his poem are as timeless, and peaceful, as the pseudo-Ujiyasu's.

Where Sōchō (and Sōboku and others) help us go beyond the "ritual of repetitions" described by Carter and typified by pilgrimages to "famous places" is in their accounting of the actual processes of travel, the in-between moments that bring back the process of discovery—something akin to what Marcia Yonemoto has described, in the context of the travel literature of the seventeenth and eighteenth centuries, as "annotation": "Unlike a map, which tends to depict a space frozen in time, the travel narrative narrates space as a continuum, through time."[93] In producing and offering their patrons texts that were not meant to be perfect, closed literary statements, but primers and works in progress, these authors not only created the opportunity to cultivate literary skills, but also initiated the circulation of texts that enabled provincials to engage with the process of perpetuating a literary canon. The pseudo-Ujiyasu's *Musashino kikō*—whatever we make of its claims—can hardly be topped as an illustration of the possibilities offered by the appropriation and reimagination of a literary "commonplace."

No less than any other such commonplace, of course, Musashino survived the upheaval of Japan's long sixteenth century. The sustained contact and exchange between professional poets from the capital and literate provincial magnates helped render less forbidding the barriers dividing the fields of poetry and travelogues from those of geography and political experience. During the decades of civil war the grasses of Musashino were enriched by the possibility of functioning not only as metaphors for placelessness and longing, but also as context for some of the contemporary world. Combined with continuing poetic resonances with places throughout the plain, the thematic expansion of Musashino and

93. Yonemoto, *Mapping Early Modern Japan*, 52, 54.

other "famous places"—beyond a formalized existence as *utamakura*—may have provided the region as a whole, and its residents, with an element of continuity and shared identification, both geographic and imaginary, to juxtapose to the narrowing scope of political authority and personal attachment.

At the same time, and helping us account for the abiding power of literary tradition in a time of profound displacement, the image of the Kantō was held together in the face of particularism by literary commonplaces like the grasses of Musashino, keeping alive the connection with the capital for provincial magnates. The geographical and political distance from Kyoto had always been real, if not especially insurmountable, but ongoing turmoil made travel and communication more difficult, and the capital more remote. As I discuss in the chapters that follow, the political distance in particular became a source of anxiety for local lords. The language of *utamakura*, despite being only marginally open to reinvention, offered a way to bridge that distance. Access to courtly culture (particularly if not exclusively in the form of poetry) had always been a hallmark of social prominence; even as the success of itinerant poets' efforts to cultivate the sensibilities of provincials made that culture less exclusively courtly, literary patronage and the acceptance of longstanding poetic practice reassured provincial lords of their proximity to the political center and of their membership in Japan's elite.

CHAPTER 2

Disputes over Land

The Kantō, of course, was more than a backdrop for song or a stage for hunts; it was a vast expanse of arable and potentially arable land, parceled out into discrete holdings for the extraction of revenue. Beyond the poetic allure of a plain that remained recalcitrant to settlement lay the self-evident economic reality that land, with its bounty, was the currency of the realm. On land (or on disputes over land) the differing interests of four groups converged: first, absentee proprietors, mostly aristocrats in the capital and powerful temples and shrines, but also high-ranking warriors; second, local warriors, frequently entrusted with managing the absentee proprietors' land and often accused of misappropriating it or failing to forward the goods and rents it produced; third, villagers, tasked with farming the land, and exploited no less by local managers than by distant proprietors; and finally the shoguns and the high-ranking warriors allied with them, who tried to appease the other three groups and mediate among their mutually incompatible desires.[1] By the middle of the fifteenth century, hundreds of years of unlawful encroachments and lawsuits, hundreds of years of legal accretions, exceptions, redefinitions, and compromises had yielded a tenurial landscape of intractable complexity.

---

1. Membership in one or the other group was not always clear-cut, of course, with high-ranking warriors often sharing interests with the capital nobility, and local warriors and village communities inhabiting a social spectrum in the provinces, rather than entirely distinct classes.

Indeed, the Muromachi regime—from the shogun and his magistrates and functionaries in the capital, to the military governors (*shugo*) and deputy governors (*shugodai*) in the provinces—could not avoid mediating disputes over land, however hopeless the task might appear. Because so much conflict stemmed from competing claims of entitlement to land, the very legitimacy of the regime as keeper of the peace and upholder of legality was predicated on its commitment to fair adjudication. Yet since the Muromachi regime's founding in the fourteenth century, the often unstable hold on power of the shogun and his military governors meant that before they could exercise authority in their courts they had to secure the loyalty of their followers on the battlefield. Even during the regime's heyday, in the late fourteenth and early fifteenth centuries, armed conflict was never too far away. The most effective way to keep local followers from turning into opponents was to dole out titles to land or access to its yield, to create ties of patronage and loyalty.[2]

So, inevitably, even in the best of times, the Muromachi regime established its relationship with the elites it sought to govern in terms of two sources of authority, the official and the lordly. One was conceived as impersonal, predicated on appointment to offices and on conformity to legal and institutional precedent; the other was personal, sustained by bonds that could be as mutable as they were deeply felt. Access to one enabled the cultivation of the other, as the official right to commandeer resources and requisition lands made possible the growth of lordly influence and the forging of relations with other families, through marriage (and dowries) and rewards for service (in the form of titles and lands). Members of the officialdom could draw upon these relations in arenas not directly connected with the exercise of the authority granted by their office—for instance, in the course of competition with other elite houses.

Since antiquity authorities both national and local had combined the formal investiture that came with membership in the administrative apparatus of the state with more personalistic chains of command built on bonds of patronage. If in times of relative peace and prosperity the two forms of authority were not invariably at odds with each other, in times

2. Conlan, "Largesse."

of unrest, when central authority faltered, the contradictions between the official and the lordly became harder to ignore. In the fourteenth century, and even more so in the fifteenth, the official and the lordly met and clashed epochally over the issue of landholdings, as members of the regime tried to balance their guarantee of the legal order with their cultivation of reliable followers.[3] By the time the Muromachi shogun assumed power in the mid-fourteenth century, local conflict and the privatization of land (more on this below) had conspired to weaken the state, depriving it of much of its coercive power; local authorities answered to the shogun not only as representatives of a state that preceded the establishment of the shogunal regime, but as men at arms who had risen to prominence by fighting at the shogun's side. The regime's legal specialists, no doubt channeling the leadership's political frustration, acknowledged the dilemma that confronted the authorities in a supplementary law (*tsuikahō*) issued in 1357 (article 79), in which they tried to spell out guidelines for rewards to followers that would not infringe on the rights of high-ranking proprietors.[4]

This chapter is not about the best of times. It is about the decades after 1450, when the shogun's reach in the provinces faltered, and the institutions of local governance were tested by political conflict and outright civil war. The chapter considers land and jurisdiction over land as they emerge in the context of adjudication. In a series of documents chronicling lawsuits and various parties' efforts to document their claims to lawful entitlement a picture emerges, not only of the regime's sometimes contradictory definitions of its role, of its claims to public, official authority and its cultivation and exercise of that authority in ways that were private and familial. Also revealed, despite the patchiness of the age's documentary record, are the emergence and legal sanction of new forms of land tenure, predicated not only—or not primarily—on preexisting title but on actual possession and administration of a holding. This chapter finds, linked in complex ways to ambiguities surrounding the right to adjudicate and the reasons for doing so, tensions over the

3. Bisson, *Crisis of the Twelfth Century*, 573–82. Bisson speaks of "public order" and "customary coercive lordships" (p. 574).

4. For the original, see Satō S. and Ikeuchi, *Chūsei hōsei shiryōshū*, 38; in English, Grossberg, *Laws of the Muromachi Bakufu*, 58–59.

definitions of entitlement themselves, and the conditions for upholding formal rights to land and its revenues. Conversely, asking what made for a strong claim to rightful ownership of land helps bring into focus the question that confronted those who were asked to evaluate such claims (or who arrogated for themselves the right to do so): How was their jurisdiction understood, and how was land part of it? In attending to the practices of rule and the performance of authority during decades of civil strife, to the enduring tension between the official and the lordly, this chapter considers whether the prolonged civil war that embroiled the east and the rest of the country, and rapidly reduced the reach of the Muromachi regime, also undermined the usefulness, or the appeal, of the regime's *official* authority. But the point is not so much to dwell on institutional change. Rather, in the pages that follow, I grapple with the ways in which Kantō elites imagined themselves, their roles, and their rule over both people and the landscape, at the intersection of private property and political jurisdiction.

To do so, I consider the authorities' conduct over the course of a number of incidents, or cases, as recorded in various documents and sets of documents issued by those same authorities. These cases include disputes over landholdings, as well as less contentious (but not less problematic) petitions for confirmation of rights, and lists of behaviors forbidden in specific locations, issued in the form of placards of prohibitions:

Case no. 1 — Dispute between Ōishi Sadashige and Bannaji over holdings in Ashikaga Estate (1454), adjudicated by Ashikaga Shigeuji, Lord of Kamakura

Case no. 2 — Dispute between Bannaji and Sano Moritsuna (and Moritsuna's relative Yatsukunugi) over holdings at Kariyado (1455–56), adjudicated by Ashikaga Shigeuji, Lord of Koga (and mediated by Sano Moritsuna)

Case no. 3 — Dispute between Rokuōin and the Chiba brothers over holdings at Akatsuka (1462), adjudicated by the Uesugi and the Lord of Horigoe, Ashikaga Masatomo

Case no. 4 — Disputes between Nagao Tadakage and Nagao Kageharu; and Nagao Tadakage and the villagers of Kozukue over holdings at Shiba and Kozukue, respectively (1475), negotiated by Nagao Tadakage

Case no. 5	Letter granting three villages to Kō no Morohisa (1469) Letter confirming holdings of thirteen hamlets to Motegi Mochitomo (1471) Hōkokuji land registers (1477)
Case no. 6	Dispute between Hōkokuji and Ōta Dōkan over holdings at Naze (1471), mediated by Nagao Kagenobu
Case no. 7	Dispute between Kaneko and the monks of Zenkōji who claimed holdings at Hiranuma (after 1483?) also claimed by a local warrior, mediated by Ōta Dōkan and others
Case no. 8	Prohibitions (1472, 1498, 1504, 1506, 1512) issued by Nagao, Nagano, Yokoze, Uesugi, Hōjō

A Short History of an Old System

If disputes over land demanded so much of the attention and the resources of the regime in the fifteenth century, what, exactly, was at stake? What did landholdings look like in the late Middle Ages?

By the fifteenth century all land was, practically if not nominally, private. In the Kantō as in the rest of the archipelago, the countryside was made up of countless landholdings, ranging in size from individual villages (*gō*) to sprawling manorial estates (*shōen*) that covered tens of square kilometers and numerous villages. Legally, too, these holdings came in a variety of configurations: theoretically about half of the land belonged to the state, but for centuries it had been entrusted to a variety of parties (such as provincial governors, powerful temples, and shrines) that managed the holdings for their own profit.[5] The other half of the land was part of frankly private manorial estates. Most of these estates were centuries old. In a process that had gained momentum between the tenth and twelfth centuries, estates had been established by removing public land from the tax rolls and granting title to it to powerful aristocratic houses, temples, and shrines.[6] At the same time, these estates had

5. On Tōdaiji and the Ōuchi in Suō Province, see Arnesen, *Medieval Japanese Daimyo,* 93–131; on Uesugi rule of Kōzuke, and how they gained control of the provincial offices of the old imperial administration (*kokuga*) and its perquisites by the turn of the fifteenth century, see Kubota, "Chūsei kōki Kōzuke," 54.

6. Cf. Keirstead, *Geography of Power.*

also been subtracted from the jurisdiction of state officials, making private and public lands into distinct if complementary spheres of authority.[7] In the fourteenth century, the distinction between private and public lands had been erased in law as well as in practice, replaced by a more pragmatic distinction between warrior lands and aristocratic/temple lands.[8] In the fifteenth century, all that remained of the original classification were landholdings' official designations, although even those were commonly confused in actual practice, so that estates would be called villages, for example, and imperial holdings would be called estates.

The growing control exercised collectively by the warrior gentry over holdings private and public was at least in part the product of the culture of absentee proprietorship pervasive among the capital elites, who before the turn of the sixteenth century seldom or never traveled to the provinces to manage, or even to monitor management of, their lands. Since their inception, manorial estates had been founded on the collaboration of on-site managers, who did the actual work of promoting the development of arable lands, and elites in Kyoto, who provided the political prestige and institutional access necessary to secure the status of estate for new lands, and with it the exemptions from state taxation and corvée.[9] Local warriors had entered the scene at the turn of the thirteenth century, when they were called upon to assist with the smooth operation of estates in a time of unrest by the Kamakura shogunate (1185–1333), the first of the military regimes.[10] Charged in particular with forwarding rents to distant proprietors, these warriors had soon created new problems, appropriating for themselves ever-increasing portions of the revenues of estates entrusted to them. In countless lawsuits between

---

7. With a metaphor that applies perfectly to control of public lands in medieval Japan, Geoffrey Koziol ("Political Culture," 56) has compared royal rule in France in the eleventh and twelfth centuries to "Swiss cheese, substantial but perforated with great holes."

8. Ihara, "Muromachi-ki tōgoku honjoryō shōen no seiritsu katei," 24–25, 28–29.

9. Sato, "Early Development of the *Shōen*"; Sato, "Ōyama Estate and Insei Land Policies."

10. Technically, Minamoto no Yoritomo only received the title of shogun in 1192, though his de facto ascendancy was recognized at the end of the Genpei War (1180–85). Yoritomo himself, moreover, did not seem to put much stock in that title, and would probably have been surprised to see his rule was thought to have begun only in 1192.

elite proprietors and provincial warriors, national authorities (both the imperial and shogunal courts) had upheld the rightful claims of the estate proprietors, but had been increasingly forced to recognize the inadequacy of verdicts ordering warriors to desist from encroachment. By the end of the thirteenth century, the courts had acknowledged the need for a compromise solution: contested estates would be split down the middle in a process known as "halving the land" (*shitaji chūbun*). Property of one half would be transferred outright to the warrior manager, on condition that in the other half he relinquish oversight and cease all interference.[11]

The next assault on the prerogatives of the courtly proprietor class occurred in the middle of the fourteenth century, as the recently established Muromachi shogunate struggled to pacify the country in the face of widespread resistance. In provinces throughout Japan, the new regime appointed its most dependable followers as military governors. The office, which dated back to the turn of the thirteenth century, had previously been far more limited in jurisdiction—more of a constable than a governor. The military governors of the Muromachi regime were allowed gradually to take control of the headquarters of provincial administration (*kokuga*), and of the public lands they oversaw. At the same time, in an effort to support the war effort, the shogunate issued decrees authorizing military governors involved in campaigns to commandeer half of the annual dues owed by estates in the provinces in which they were fighting. These decrees, the so-called half-payment decrees (*hanzeirei*), were first issued in 1352 for a select number of explicitly designated provinces, but were then expanded to all the provinces at war in 1355.[12]

---

11. Mass, "*Jitō* Land Possession in the Thirteenth Century"; Nagahara, "Decline of the *Shōen* System," 267–68.

12. Suppl. arts. 57 and 78. Satō S. and Ikeuchi, *Chūsei hōsei shiryōshū*, 29–30, 82–83; Grossberg, *Laws of the Muromachi Bakufu*, 49, 58. The provinces specified in art. 57 were all in central Japan: Ōmi, Mino, Ise, Shima, Owari, Iga, Izumi, Kawachi. See Ihara, "Muromachi-ki tōgoku honjoryō shōen no seiritsu katei," 18–19, 31–34. Akira Imatani ("Muromachi Local Government," 237–40) characterizes the new policy as a curb on the lawlessness of military governors. In English, see Wintersteen, "Muromachi *Shugo* and *Hanzei*"; Hall, *Government and Local Power*, 205–6; Conlan, *State of War*, 85, 98, 224–25. In English-language scholarship the general trend has been to treat the decrees as concessions to the autonomy of military governors. The notable exception

Only two years later, in 1357, yet another supplementary article acknowledged a more profound violation of estates' integrity, in addition to an expansion of the geographical scope of the policy, by instructing military governors to requisition not half of the dues produced by estates in their assigned provinces, but rather half of the *land* of those estates.[13] Detailed exemptions for various categories of estates, and clarifications, were issued at the time and in subsequent decrees.[14] Still, the expansion of authority claimed by the regime was momentous, and its impact on absentee proprietors in the capital profound. It left all holdings exposed to the risk of confiscation, and demanded costly litigation to overturn the pronouncements of military governors who often requisitioned lands in their provinces without too much verification of each holding's status and exemptions.

The partitioning of estates throughout the country, along with the principle that the imposition of levies to support the regime's military operations would be carried out on a province-wide basis rather than estate-by-estate, has been adduced as evidence that the shogun and his provincial representatives were intent on doing away with the very framework of estates or that, at the very least, the interests of the warrior elite were antithetical to those of the proprietary class. In this view, the estate system was superseded by the establishment in the provinces of warrior holdings and, soon enough, warrior domains.[15] This interpretation, variously refined and elaborated over the years, has remained influential, particularly in the West.[16] Yet almost simultaneously a

---

is Mikael Adolphson (*Gates of Power*, 215), who mentions the decrees only in passing, but sees them as a protection for proprietors.

13. Satō S. and Ikeuchi, *Chūsei hōsei shiryōshū*, 38; Grossberg, *Laws of the Muromachi Bakufu*, 58 (suppl. art. 79); Satō S., *Nanbokuchō no dōran*, 207–11.

14. For example, suppl. art. 97, in 1468; Satō S. and Ikeuchi, *Chūsei hōsei shiryōshū*, 43–44; Grossberg, *Laws of the Muromachi Bakufu*, 64.

15. Nagahara, *Nihon hōkensei seiritsu katei no kenkyū*; Nagahara, *Nihon chūsei shakai kōzō no kenkyū*; Satō S., "Muromachi bakufu ron"; Minegishi, *Chūsei no tōgoku*, 71–98.

16. This may be due, in part at least, to Nagahara Keiji's remarkable engagement with English-language scholarship. See, for instance, his "Landownership under the Shōen-Kokugaryō System"; as well as his essay in the *Cambridge History of Japan*, cited in Note 11 above, which appears after an essay on local power in the Muromachi period but concerns itself with the adverse effects on the estate system of the rise and lawlessness of stewards (*jitō*) in the thirteenth century.

countervailing interpretation was proposed to the effect that, far from disregarding the rightful entitlements of estate proprietors, the regime did its best to ensure they were upheld in the face of continuous pressure from those very same local warriors it was trying to win over. Those who espouse this perspective have drawn attention to the solicitude with which the shogunate enforced the exemption of certain types of imperial, aristocratic, and temple holdings from the half-payment decrees, and to its efforts to redefine the legal parameters within which estates and public lands were variously classified. According to these scholars, the warrior elite was supportive rather than adversarial toward the estate system; the system was profoundly transformed by the decrees of the fourteenth century but it did not collapse until the Muromachi regime did, after the middle of the fifteenth century.[17]

From the point of view of the present study, the latter interpretation holds a twofold appeal: first of all, it is more accommodating of the possibility that institutional apparatuses could change, even profoundly, without contemporaries losing the sense of experiencing a recognizable and fundamentally coherent system. In terms of estates' function not only as units of production but also as spatial and affective frameworks (a topic that I treat more fully in the next chapter) this seems significant.

---

17. Kurokawa, "Shugo ryōgokusei to shōen taisei"; Kurokawa, "Chūsei kōki no ryōshusei"; Miyagawa, "Shōensei no kaitai"; Tanuma, "Muromachi bakufu, shugo, kokujin." For an overview of the debate, see Itō, "Chūsei kōki shōensei ron no seika to kadai." Much of the debate hinges on the association between *shiki* (literally "jobs" but in most respects more along the lines of "shares" or "stocks") and sociopolitical hierarchies. The system of *shiki* was predicated on the vertical stratification of functionally distinct entitlements to the lands' revenues: there were *shiki* that designated and remunerated those who served as patrons or administrators in the capital; others for those who managed a holding on site, or coordinated the collection and forwarding of dues; others yet spelled out the rights and duties of individual peasants. This structure helped ensure the political preeminence of members of the proprietary class who monopolized higher (patron and absentee administrator) *shiki*, drawing revenues from multiple estates at once while cultivating ties with holders of lower (managerial) level *shiki* holders in each. The progressive partitioning of estates "territorialized" and so flattened the purely revenue-based vertical structure. To scholars who see the *shiki* system as the most salient characteristic of the estate system the transformation of *shiki* brought about the end of estates.

Second (and as a consequence of the first point), the latter interpretation is more capable of accommodating the discrepancy between the regime's intent (to stand as a stalwart of law and order) and actual, long-term consequences (the eventual undoing of the Kyoto aristocracy's control over the better part of the country's agricultural revenue). If anything, in linking the fortunes of estates and the Muromachi regime, the latter interpretation may postulate too quick a demise for the shogunate in the second half of the fifteenth century.

Rather than simply attempting to date the demise of the manorial estate as a tenurial system on the basis of an agreed-upon set of characteristics, I believe we should consider how long the shogun, the military governors, the deputy governors, and the other officials of the Muromachi regime understood their offices to entail a commitment to uphold law pertaining to land. Trying to answer such a question in the context of the Kantō region is especially intriguing, for the region's size, and its geographical and political distance from the center, force us to think anew about the intersection of authority, absenteeism, and local society in the fifteenth and early sixteenth centuries.

Civil war broke out in the east more than a decade before it did in Kyoto, testing the ability of the proprietor class and the warrior elite to retain control of the administration and the flow of revenue from distant estates before the fighting spread to central and western Japan. Unlike the rest of the country, the Kantō was governed not from Kyoto (or not only from Kyoto), but from a special office in Kamakura, which oversaw the activities of the various military governors in the region on behalf of the shogun. The Kamakura Office, as it is known, although clearly subordinate to Kyoto, functioned as a small-scale, provincial replica of the shogunal administration, as a judicial center for disputes concerning estates that in other corners of the country would be taken to Kyoto. The elites in Kyoto had never cared to leave the capital to administer their lands directly, in situ, because of the great distances separating them from their scattered lands throughout the archipelago, and because of a long tradition of distaste for the backwardness of the provinces. Until its collapse in 1455, functionaries in the Kamakura Office (and the great temples in and around the city), despite proximity to most of the territory they oversaw and the lands they held in the region, had imitated their counterparts in the capital and resided in Kamakura, acting as absentee proprietors to their nearby lands.[18] In this sense, the Kantō case provides insights applicable to the rest of Japan, by offering a strong reminder that absentee rule was driven by assumptions about life on the land and the nature of property no less than by logistics: shorter distances did not produce closer oversight.

The story of the region in the decades after 1455 is one of uneasy rethinking of practices that were as widespread as they were old, of contending with the realization that endemic strife meant not only frequent mobilization, but the end of the life made possible by distant oversight.

The Official and the Lordly

Late in 1454, about a month before ordering the assassination of his chief official and plunging the eastern provinces into turmoil, the Lord of Kamakura, Ashikaga Shigeuji (1438–97), sent out two official letters (*migyōsho*) informing litigants of his ruling in a dispute. The letters were written and signed by two functionaries in Shigeuji's chancery, yet they convey Shigeuji's own frustration toward a member of his provincial administration who had taken control of several holdings belonging to a temple, Bannaji, without proper authorization. The first of the two letters is directed at the man Shigeuji wished to censure, a man named Ōishi:

> The estate agent (*zasshō*) of Bannaji tells us you have not complied with instructions twice before, that concerning various parts of this temple's holdings in Ashikaga Estate, Shimotsuke Province, you stop whatever [you are doing], for it is imperative that nothing further be excused. Does this [not] fairly invite punishment? Ultimately, you must swiftly stop encroachment. What His Highness [Shigeuji] has decreed is that you be punished, if you still do not heed His ruling. Hence, the matter conveyed is as stated.[19]

The other letter was sent to the monks of Bannaji, who had evidently petitioned the authorities when Ōishi tried to seize that temple's lands:

18. Yamada, "Muromachi-ki Kantō no shihai kōzō to zaichi shakai," 81–83.
19. *TKS* 1:354, no. 46 (Bannaji monjo). The letters are dated Kyōtoku 3.10.28 (1454).

> Regarding Bannaji's holdings in various parts of Ashikaga Estate, Shimotsuke Province: Because Ōishi Suruga no kami has gone so far as to wantonly enter them [i.e., take possession of them], time and again rulings have been handed down, but he apparently has not complied. Does this utmost fault not fairly invite punishment? What His Lordship has decreed is that ultimately, even if the matter should come to a disturbance, [He] firmly supports this, that the holdings are entirely the property of the temple. Hence, the matter conveyed is as stated.[20]

The two missives introduce several salient aspects of adjudication on the eve of the civil war. They make clear the political orientation of the Lord of Kamakura and his administration: in 1454, the eastern representatives of the Muromachi regime remained intransigent in their refusal to allow even a prominent local warrior such as Ōishi to exploit his position within the Kamakura Office to seize lands for himself and his followers. Various members of the Ōishi family had served as deputy governors in the provinces of Musashi and Kōzuke, and their stature did not diminish during the civil war. In the 1480s the poet Banri wrote, "The twenty or so districts of Musashi all follow [Ōishi Sadashige's] orders."[21] Moreover, as the letters show, bound up with the regime's political stance on landholding was a continuing reliance on centralized procedures of adjudication, as disputes occurring throughout the east were handled in Kamakura and not, locally, by the governors of the various Kantō provinces. Complaints were presented to the authorities in Kamakura and rulings were communicated to litigants according to a well-established protocol. What, then, was that protocol?

---

20. *TKS* 1:354, no. 45 (Bannaji monjo). The two missives, which constitute our only record of the suit, are preserved in the archives of Bannaji (the letter addressed to Ōishi is actually a copy, sent to the temple for its information).

21. Ichiki, *Baika mujinzō chūshaku*, 4:58–62. On Ōishi posts, see *Shinpen Saitama kenshi tsūshi hen* 2:496. According to Sugiyama Hiroshi ("Shugo ryōgokusei no tenkai to Ōishi-shi"), the Ōishi could boast of a three-generation tenure as deputy governors of Musashi, ending around 1440. Actually the Ōishi, despite their involvement in the local machinery of the regime, had far weaker ties with Shigeuji than with the chief official he would soon assassinate, so Shigeuji's anger at their encroachment probably transcended what might be expected from a judicial and institutional conflict. On the political maneuvering of the Ōishi at this time, see Katsumori, *Nagao-shi no kenkyū*, 210.

When on-site managers or deputies or stewards failed to forward all or part of the year's dues from an estate or when, as in this case, a local warrior tried to wrest control of a holding from its rightful proprietor, that proprietor would send an agent (*sata zasshō*) to file a complaint at the court of the Kamakura Office.[22] Documents reveal that before the suit was filed formally, the prospective plaintiff would often approach one of the members of the court asking for intercession (*kuchiire*)—either to effect an out-of-court settlement or to improve the chances of the suit being accepted.[23] What followed was an inquiry carried out by the warrior authorities (*buke gosata*). Once the suit was filed, the court might issue a summons to the encroaching party (Ōishi, in this case) instructing him to produce a statement justifying his actions, after which the plaintiff (the estate agent) could submit a rebuttal. If further investigation was deemed necessary, a round of questioning might follow.[24] Upon reaching a verdict, the court would send it to local authorities (typically, the office of the deputy governor), which would proceed to circulate and enforce it.[25] Shigeuji's letters to Bannaji and Ōishi Suruga no kami refer to this notification in their final remarks ("the matter conveyed is as stated").

The courts of the Kamakura Office ceased to function when war broke out in 1455, pitting the supporters of Ashikaga Shigeuji against those of the Uesugi (and the shogun), and the two warring factions abandoned Kamakura in favor of a variety of different headquarters better suited for campaigning. Or rather, the office's courts *in the city of Kamakura* ceased to function. Both Shigeuji and the Uesugi continued to hear suits in their respective strongholds, maintaining certain procedures and

---

22. Ihara, "Tōgoku shōen nengu no kyōjō shisutemu to kokkateki hoshō taisei"; see also Nakayama, "Shimōsa seibu chiikisei kara mita Kogane-ryō keisei no zentei," 49.

23. See for instance *GKS* 7, no. 1777 (Unchōan monjo); *KKS* 1, no. 197 (Hōkokuji monjo).

24. Yamada, *Kamakura-fu to Kantō*, 125–30.

25. In practice, though, as Uejima Tamotsu has shown, the verdict was handed down to the plaintiff, who delivered it to the governor, who in turn issued an executive order, which the plaintiff then delivered down the chain of command, as local offices issued further orders (quoted in Saitō, "Jungyō, uchiwatashijō no kakutoku to sōden," 75). See also Sakai, "Ōnin no ran to zaichi shakai," 130–31, 143; and Fukushima, "Tōgoku shōen ni okeru tōchigyō to shiki."

adapting others to the new circumstances without renouncing claims to official authority over the whole plain. There is evidence, for instance, that Shigeuji, who moved to a wartime stronghold in Koga (and was henceforth known as the Lord of Koga), tried to reestablish the courts of the Kamakura Office there.[26]

Despite disruption of the office's daily operations, neither faction lessened its emphasis on the official character of its authority. Soon after the outbreak of hostilities, for instance, between the spring of 1456 and the summer of 1457, Shigeuji repeatedly weighed in on a dispute involving (once again) Bannaji and one of Shigeuji's own prominent followers, Sano Moritsuna.[27] At stake was the village of Kariyado, a holding in Ashikaga Estate (Map 2.1). Truth be told, Shigeuji had contributed to the problem. Exercising his lordly prerogatives, he had granted the village to a relative of Moritsuna, as reward for meritorious service on the first day of the war with the Uesugi.[28] Bannaji immediately lodged a complaint, claiming that the village of Kariyado was a "fundamental holding of the temple" (*konpon gojiryō*) and thus inalienable.[29] The case dragged on, despite Shigeuji's ready acknowledgment (reiterated in successive messages sent by Moritsuna to the temple) that the monks had submitted documentation clearly proving Bannaji's rights to the village. Shigeuji and Moritsuna noted that there had been no official ruling on the matter in recent years so, in order to reach a favorable verdict, an inquiry would have to be conducted. In a letter to the temple, Shigeuji assured the monks that this would happen in a matter of days.

Shigeuji's own brief communiqué to Bannaji and Moritsuna's more detailed letters to the temple—which cite Shigeuji's communiqué—emphatically call for respect of Bannaji's rightful claims, but they both

26. Inagaki, "Koga kubō to Shimotsuke," 29–34.

27. *Sano shishi tsūshi hen*, 509–12. The documents detailing the case are, in chronological order, *TKS* 1:557, no. 524; 1:533, no. 445; 1:586, no. 605; 1:534, no. 447; 1:587, no. 608; 1:511, nos. 388, 389 (Bannaji monjo).

28. For the dating of the letters, which record the day and the month of composition, but not the year, see Minegishi, in *Kindai Ashikaga shishi* 1:263–65; and Satō H., *Chūsei tōgoku no shihai kōzō*, 210–30.

29. *TKS* 1:557, no. 524 (Bannaji monjo). We no longer have copies of the letters written by the monks at Bannaji, and must reconstruct the gist of their arguments from references to them in Shigeuji and Moritsuna's replies.

Map 2.1. Distribution of disputed landholdings (shown here are holdings discussed in cases 1–4 and 6–7).

also defend the legitimacy of the grant made to Moritsuna's relative. Indeed, Shigeuji had decreed that Moritsuna's relative should "receive this holding in particular, and firmly have it in his possession,"[30] and that, "When [Moritsuna's relative] obtained Our acknowledgment, there was detailed evidence of his long service to Moritsuna!"[31] In other words, both men's letters emphasize that, however clear the evidence submitted by Bannaji's monks to prove the temple's rights to the village, Shigeuji had not acted lightly in bestowing the land on a loyal follower. This was

30. *TKS* 1:533, no. 445 (Bannaji monjo).
31. *TKS* 1:587, no. 608 (Bannaji monjo).

not an attempt to justify an abrogation of Bannaji's title, or a renunciation of the impartiality of judicial authority in favor of more expedient ties with eastern warriors. The objection to the monks' request simply to void the grant and the announcement of an inquiry both appealed to law and protocol: the investigation was a formal procedure carried out in the context of proprietors' lawsuits against encroaching locals. Further, it was pursuant to laws issued by the Muromachi regime—dictating reassignment in cases of erroneous expropriation and bestowal of lands that were exempted—that a resolution was at least in part delayed while a different parcel of land (*jiyo no chi*) was sought for Moritsuna's relative (halfway through the year and the agricultural cycle).[32] Even in the early, heady days of war, when rewards were especially important to secure the support of local warriors still uncertain on the party to join, we should view Shigeuji's stance as a performance of eminently public authority.

The letters regarding the dispute over the village of Kariyado bring to our attention three more, interrelated phenomena, variously conceivable in terms of "presence on the land," whose interplay I analyze in the rest of this chapter. The first concerns the evolving nature of authority over land in the provinces, as seen in the ambiguous role played in the proceedings by Moritsuna, who was not only a follower of Shigeuji but also one of his leading commanders. In the letters Moritsuna appears to serve as a go-between, relaying Shigeuji's rulings and trying to allay the monks' anxieties. He also acts as his relative's advocate in the dispute, stressing his exemplary service at an especially sensitive juncture (on the day of the assassination of the Kantō deputy, Shigeuji's chief official). But Moritsuna's investment in the outcome ran deeper still. Obscured by his care to avoid making this kinship explicit and thus drawing attention to himself is Moritsuna's direct interest in the disputed village, as a magnate who controlled a nearby estate and already cast a long shadow on the area around Kariyado. In Moritsuna's multiple levels of engagement in the case we glimpse the complex, tangled interests that made

32. Suppl. arts. 79 (1357), 84, 85 (both 1367), and 97 (1368); Satō S. and Ikeuchi, *Chūsei hōsei shiryōshū*, 38, 39–40, 43, respectively; Grossberg, *Laws of the Muromachi Bakufu*, 58, 60, 61, 64, respectively.

recourse to both official and lordly justifications of authority appealing to the different levels of the warrior elite.

The second dimension of "presence on the land" is evoked by the repeated references in the missives to a deputy (*daikan*). This man had been sent to the village by Bannaji during the dispute, presumably to try and collect rents on the temple's behalf, or to forestall Moritsuna's relative from taking possession of the village. He was deemed by Shigeuji and Moritsuna to be trespassing and in violation of the peace, and an impediment to the settlement of the dispute. Absentee proprietors, as we shall see, increasingly relied on such deputies to manage their holdings and stem the loss of revenue caused by the encroachment of local warriors. By virtue of their role, the deputies often found themselves at the intersection of law and private interest—often *their own* private interest—caught between distant proprietors and recalcitrant local communities.

Following from the first two is a third phenomenon related to "presence on the land": at the heart of the dispute between the temple and the warriors was not a disagreement over entitlement (that is, over who had the stronger claim); it was a disagreement on *definitions* of entitlement. Looming over the negotiation was the growing recognition of the significance of actual possession of land. We see it in the tension between Bannaji's claim that the village was a "fundamental holding" and Shigeuji's initial ruling that Moritsuna's relative have the holding in his possession, as his property (*chigyō o itasubeki no mune*). Although expressed in the course of an exchange meant to reach an amicable settlement, the opposition was between two definitions that were not so much incompatible as incommensurable: whereas in demanding restitution of the village the temple stressed entitlement, in making the grant to his follower's relative Shigeuji had emphasized possession and presence on the land. Recourse to documentation of formal rights was meant to appeal to the official character of Shigeuji's authority—to his desire to be seen as an official. Emphasis on actual possession was more consonant with lordly conceptions of patronage. As we shall see, the emergence, during the civil war, of actual possession as a category of legitimate property was intertwined in complex ways with the persistent tension between the lordly and the official. Variously combined in the lawsuits of the time, these three phenomena provide the impulse for much of the adjudication carried out in the Kantō after the middle of the fifteenth century, whether in the western reaches of the region, which were governed by the Uesugi family, or in the eastern, which were under Shigeuji's sway.

As loyal representatives of the shogun, the Uesugi leaders were no less interested in emphasizing their official role. And, as exemplified by another series of letters, produced between the end of 1462 and the early days of 1464, the Uesugi had to confront disputes very much like the one we have just seen. The cast of characters was nearly a replica of the previous case's: a temple with proprietary rights to a holding, a local warrior, to whom that holding had been granted by the authorities in the region, and the representatives of the Muromachi regime, who were now called upon by the proprietor to mediate the crisis produced by their own grant.

The suit shows the representatives of the struggling Muromachi regime torn between their two roles as enforcers of lawful order and leaders of coalition armies. The contested holding was once again a village, Akatsuka, in Musashi Province. Not much is known about the history of this village, although one brief mention in a chronicle is germane to this case: Akatsuka makes an appearance in *Kamakura ōzōshi* (The great book of Kamakura), when the story is told of how an army loyal to Shigeuji defeated two scions of the ancient Chiba house, early in 1456. The two brothers beat a hasty retreat, and one of them took refuge in Akatsuka.[33] The village makes no further appearances in the chronicle, but we know that it was still in Chiba hands in late 1462 when Rokuōin, a cloister in Kyoto, sent an agent to file a suit demanding restitution of its holding. In a ruling delivered to the Chiba leader, the court decreed that "in accordance with Kyoto's [i.e., the shogun's] ruling," the holding "must swiftly be returned to the temple's agent."[34] Similar injunctions were sent to the chancery of the Uesugi, urging compliance.

---

33. *Kamakura ōzōshi*, 53. The chronicle details events in the eastern provinces between 1379 and 1479. Its author is unknown, and its date is uncertain, though it is believed to have been written not too long after the last of the events it details.

34. *SKS* 5, no 931 (Rokuōin monjo); see also *KKS* 1, no. 182 (Rokuōin monjo). It is unclear whether the cloister's agent filed his complaint both in Kyoto and in the Kantō. The first of the documents related to the case states that "Buei [Shibukawa Yoshikane, the chief official to the shogun's brother in the east] received a great many petitions, so first of all he handed down a ruling." The actual reach of the Lord of Horigoe and his administration was notoriously short, so it is possible that the initial order was not heeded and a new petition, in Kyoto, became necessary.

The ruling was issued by the Lord of Horigoe (r. 1457–91), a younger brother of the shogun sent to the east to replace the rebellious Shigeuji as representative of the regime. During his years in the east, the Lord of Horigoe remained an outsider. He had little military power of his own in the region; his political authority only lasted as long as the Uesugi and the shogun remained at odds with the Lords of Koga. Once that conflict ended, he found himself left aside, having outlived his political usefulness.

Formally, the head of the Uesugi family, as Kantō deputy, was ranked below the Lord of Horigoe, but in practice he served as that lord's military protector and as leader of the forces loyal to the Muromachi regime in the east.[35] Along with the post of Kantō deputy, the head of the main Uesugi house also monopolized the military governorships of two provinces (Kōzuke and Musashi). A junior Uesugi house held the governorship of another province (Sagami), giving the extended Uesugi family formal jurisdiction, as well as military control, over the whole western half of the plain. Since the Uesugi governed both as Kantō deputies and as governors of Musashi, the village of Akatsuka was doubly under the family's jurisdiction. And since the Chiba brothers were Uesugi partisans in the war against Shigeuji, it comes as no surprise that members of the Uesugi family's inner circle of advisors would be called upon as both messengers and enforcers.

Nor were the Uesugi entirely innocent here. The very first of the decrees issued on the matter by the Lord of Horigoe's officials opened with a terse recapitulation of the legal and political dimensions of the dispute: "As for the village of Akatsuka, in Musashi, a holding of Rokuōin: because it differs from other temple lands, [His Highness] believes that the fact that it was assigned as commissariat rice land in the first place was unwarranted."[36] As it happens—although the letter is not explicit about this point—the holding differed from other temple lands in that it had been presented to the cloister by no less of a patron than a consort of the

35. Not coincidentally, the deputy governorship of Izu province, where the Lord of Horigoe had his seat, was held by Terao Reishun, a member of the inner circle of the main Yamanouchi house, who acted as a go-between in the exchange regarding Akatsuka. *SKS* 5, nos. 921, 922 (Rokuōin monjo).

36. *SKS* 5, no. 920 (Rokuōin monjo), also in *KKS* 1, no. 176.

shogun, in 1383,[37] and was, the letter intimates, among the holdings excluded from requisition and the half-payment decrees issued by military governors (such as the Uesugi)—decrees which were often used as political tools, to provision troops mustered by loyal local magnates (such as the Chiba).[38]

Like Moritsuna, the Uesugi leadership found itself forced to go back on a promise of reward. Unlike Moritsuna, though, who had interceded on behalf of a relative and a petty local warrior, the Uesugi had been buying the support of one of the region's most storied families. Also unlike Moritsuna, the Uesugi seem to have had little part in adjudicating the proprietor's appeal, suggesting, in this case at least, that their involvement in the reversal of the original grant was more narrowly limited to assistance in obtaining Chiba Sanetane's compliance (one of the letters was sent by the court to the deputy governor of Musashi, an Uesugi appointee, in accordance with established procedure). Nearly a decade of intense turmoil had not brought about a significant breakdown of the mechanisms guaranteeing the rights of absentee proprietors—if anything, it was in the earlier case, right after the beginning of hostilities, that the distinctions between advocacy and adjudication, office and interest, were more blurred. After all, if the Uesugi had overreached by expropriating and reassigning a holding that should have been off limits, they did so within the framework of the authority of military governors in times of war. In the earlier case, instead, Moritsuna, by supporting his relative's acquisition of the village of Kariyado, had been working to expand his own sphere of lordly influence, from Sano Estate to Ashikaga Estate, where the disputed village of Kariyado was located. Indirect testament to Moritsuna's success may be found in the 1509 memoir of a local monk, *Shōin shigo* (The private words of Shōin), and its account of the siege of the small stronghold of Yatsukunugi (the residence of Moritsuna's

37. *SKS* 5, no. 593 (Rokuōin monjo).

38. As a postscript to the events of 1464, it is interesting to find part of the yearly dues from Akatsuka donated by the Chiba to a local temple, Hōjiji, in 1492 (a sign that they retained, or regained, control of the village after the episode discussed above; *KKS* 1, no. 239 [Shōgetsuin monjo]); Akatsuka is mentioned again in a register of lands compiled by the Hōjō of Odawara in 1559, according to which "six villages in Akatsuka" belonged to one "Lord Chiba" (see Sugiyama, ed., *Odawara-shū shoryō yakuchō*, 77).

relative). In a telling slip, the author matter-of-factly—and mistakenly—locates the stronghold in Sano Estate rather than Ashikaga Estate, suggesting that by the turn of the century the Sano family's influence on the surrounding countryside was so pronounced that even locals could be confused as to what was where, and whose.[39]

Ambiguous Distinctions

As war continued and years passed, the pressure on landholdings grew, and even the greatest attention to law and procedure could hardly keep local warriors at bay. Still, even after the Ōnin War in Kyoto (1467–77) diverted the shogun's attention from faraway eastern provinces, proprietors continued to expect their lawsuits to yield results and the authorities to restore their rights. A letter preserved in the archive of Unchōan, a hermitage of Engakuji, an important Zen temple in Kamakura, attests to this persistent expectation. The letter is a request for intercession sent by a monk from another Zen temple in Kamakura, Tōkōji, to a man named Mamiya. We know very little about him, though surviving evidence suggests he was a magistrate at the court of the Lord of Horigoe.[40] The letter is undated, but its statement that, "For thirty years and more, since [the beginning of] the great disturbance, our temple has been completely cut off from control of its holding [in Izu province]" indicates that it must have been written sometime after 1485.[41] According to

---

39. *Shōin shigo*, 821a.

40. This is far from certain: the Mamiya were a family in Izu, where the Lord of Horigoe had his court. Yet at this late a date (1485 or later) the Lord of Horigoe had retired from active political involvement in the affairs of the Kantō, after the peace treaty of 1483 between Shigeuji and the shogun.

41. *GKS* 7, no. 1777 (Unchōan monjo). *Kanagawa-ken no chimei*, 309b–c, proposes 1472–73 as a date, identifying the disturbance mentioned in the letter as the disorders that took place in the Eikyō era (1438–40) instead of those of the Kyōtoku era, which set off the civil war in 1455. This interpretation is doubtful, as the disorders of Eikyō were over fairly quickly, and order in the east was restored, so the notion that Tōkōji would have been unable to regain its lands seems improbable. Further evidence to support the later date is found in the reference to Nagao Kagenobu, chief retainer to the Yamanouchi Uesugi house, who is mentioned by his posthumous name, Sōtoku, and who died in mid-1473 (for Kagenobu's posthumous name, see *Sōrinji denki*, 438a). Finally, reference to Kageharu's rebellion, which broke out in 1476, means this must be later than that.

the letter, Nagao Kagenobu, chief retainer of the Uesugi at the time, had handed down a judgment several years before. In what was evidently a compromise of sorts, he had mandated the forwarding of a fixed sum of 30 *kanmon* a year. Nevertheless, the letter says, "Since the rebellion of [Nagao] Kageharu," which had begun in 1476, "this too has been interrupted." Proprietors in Kamakura were increasingly pressed to secure a steady flow of revenue even from holdings in nearby provinces (Izu, in this case), but continued to turn to the courts of the Uesugi and the Lord of Horigoe as the most credible venues for redressing violations by local warriors. These authorities, too, struggled to maintain order in the eastern provinces, but it is significant that they continued to try to curb lawless behavior, and that they continued to do so as officials of a regime that was losing its ability to actually support its representatives in the provinces.

Reasons for warrior elites' enduring loyalty to proprietors are manifold, and belie the clear-cut distinctions between litigants and arbiters, between officials and lords. Lords like Shigeuji, or the Uesugi, had longstanding ties with important temples in Kamakura and throughout the Kantō, relations of patronage and collaboration in governance that dated back to the days of the Kamakura Office and would continue during decades of civil strife, through peacetime and wartime monetary donations, prayers, and gifts.[42] They also had more personal relations: Shigeuji's brother, for instance, known in contemporary documents as Lord Yukinoshita, was the chief administrator (*bettō*) of the Tsurugaoka Hachimangū, an important shrine in Kamakura. Yukinoshita makes frequent appearances in documents, mediating disputes, and wielding his influence.[43] Monks, at Zen temples in particular, also doubled as financial brokers, often assuming the post of deputies to the holdings of absentee proprietors and warriors, taking charge of forwarding rents and advancing their own funds (their temple's funds) to cover management costs, in the form of loans.[44] Temples, which were themselves absentee

42. See, for instance, *KKS* 1, no. 230 (Hōshōji monjo); *TKS* 1:109, no. 1; 1:199, no. 3 (Henshōji monjo); *TKS* 1:522, no. 413; 1:551, no. 502 (Bannaji monjo); *TKS* 3:375, no. 15 (Jisha kojō).

43. See *TKS* 1:342, no. 10; 1:586, no. 605 (Bannaji monjo); *TKS* 2:130, no. 51 (Nasu monjo); *GKS* 7, nos. 1726, 1758 (Bannaji monjo).

44. Anzai, *Hōkaiki shōenshi no kenkyū*, 163–72.

proprietors, in other words, were also deeply involved and invested in the prosperity of the holdings of warriors, and the imbricated economic interests of the religious and warrior elites provided ample incentives for the latter to exercise their authority as bulwarks against lawlessness.

Even more immediately, though, the eastern representatives of the foundering Muromachi regime stood up for absentee proprietors because they, too, were absentee proprietors. All prominent eastern families had accumulated portfolios of holdings over the decades, scattered throughout the Kantō and beyond. Based in Kamakura, temples and high-ranking members of the administration had come to control a significant portion of the lands in the region. Their holdings tended to concentrate in the southern reaches of the plain, around Kamakura itself, but also near major transportation nodes, like roads and rivers; much of the farmland in central Musashi produced income for the ruling elite.[45] Still, the holdings of individual families could be scattered far apart, so even when war began and warriors moved out of Kamakura, close monitoring of all their holdings—let alone permanent presence there—remained problematic. As a result, the antagonism between men like Sano Moritsuna and Chiba Sanetane and temples like Bannaji and Rokuōin could be real and transformative in some cases, but in others the interests of these parties could be aligned, even difficult to tell apart.

Certainly absence from one's lands in a time of military upheaval was as hazardous for a powerful warrior as it was for any proprietor. At the end of 1475, Nagao Tadakage (?–1501), who had just been named chief retainer of the main house of the extended Uesugi family, was confronted with unrest in several of his holdings in the southern reaches of the plain, and struggled to collect income from them.[46] The Nagao family provided much of the real power behind the authority of the Uesugi, and its wealth was well known at the time. In a measure of the correlation between landed assets and political influence, Sadamasa, head of a junior branch of the Uesugi, famously (and bitterly) remarked: "During forty years and more of upheavals, we have exerted ourselves loyally for the success of the main house, yet the lands we hold are still but half of

45. Yamada, "Muromachi-ki Kantō no shihai kōzō to zaichi shakai," 78–81.

46. We do not know the exact date of Tadakage's appointment. According to *Sōrinji denki*, his predecessor and natural brother, Kagenobu, died on Bunmei 5.6.13 (1473).

those of the Nagao."[47] Extensive though they were, the many lands of the Nagao were dispersed throughout the Kantō region, and like other absentee proprietors, the family did not manage its holdings directly. Oversight and collection were contracted out to a deputy—in this case, a high-ranked monk at Unchōan, in Kamakura (though more often in other cases the post was given to a local warrior).[48] At the end of 1475, then, Nagao Tadakage tackled the problems in his holdings by writing a series of letters to his deputy at Unchōan.[49]

These problems can be ascribed in part to a specific contingency, to the tension mounting in the region, as the signs grew harder to miss that an uprising would soon be launched against the Uesugi and their recently appointed chief retainer, Tadakage, by Tadakage's disgruntled nephew, Nagao Kageharu. The holdings in questions, it appears, were part of a portfolio associated with Tadakage's new post, which Kageharu claimed for himself. But Nagao Tadakage's difficulties in collecting dues from his holdings are also symptomatic of the broader challenges that increasingly confronted eastern elites in the late fifteenth century, as they tried to shore up their revenue bases while distracted by the demands of

---

47. *SKS* 5, no. 1019 (*Koshōmon*). For a variant version, see *KKS* 2, no. 50 (Shimabara Matsudaira bunko).

48. See, for instance, the long letter sent by Nagao Kagenobu to Ōta Dōkan on the matter of the position of deputy in the village of Uetaya, a holding of Chōjuji. Kagenobu opposed the appointment of a follower of Dōkan on the grounds that another family, the Shimane, had already farmed land in Uetaya and served as deputy for generations. *KKS* 1, no. 199 (*Kokan zassan* 6).

49. Yamada ("Kamakura Unchōan to Nagao Tadakage") dates the letters to a year between 1473 and 1476, on the basis of content, the beginning of the tenure at Unchōan of Tadakage's deputy, Junchō, and the evolution of Tadakage's monogram (*kaō*). In particular, Yamada comes to the 1476 limit on the grounds that the letters describe a still peaceful relationship between Tadakage and his nephew Kageharu (who would rebel that year). This *post-quem-non* limit, however, should be moved back to 1475, as Kageharu rose up in arms in the sixth month of 1476, and any letter written at the end of the year could not fail to reflect the new situation. My guess, in fact, would be that the letters were written in 1475, because of Tadakage's reference to "the year before last" in one of the letters. Assuming Tadakage acquired control of several of these lands along with the post of chief retainer, and made arrangements for the payment of dues at that time, in 1473, the reference would recommend a 1475 date. (Cf. Nishigaya, "Bushū Kozukue-jō," 148, where the holding is described as being a perquisite of the post of deputy governor.)

ongoing campaigning. The delays that now vexed Tadakage involved only a small fraction of the family's holdings, but the structural tensions they reveal in the circumstances of the region's elite are significant. In his letters, moreover, along with familiar claims and behaviors, we catch a glimpse of the variety of avenues available for resolution, and of the complex interplay of different dimensions of authority, often embodied in the same person.

Two of the holdings in particular, the villages of Shiba and Kozukue, are of interest in the present discussion. Both were located in the southern reaches of Musashi Province: Shiba was on the bay; Kozukue a half day's walk north from Shiba (about twenty-one kilometers; see Map 2.1).[50] Both holdings were a short trip from Kamakura and Unchōan; both were far (about a hundred kilometers) from Tadakage's residence at the time, near the northern edge of the plain, at the Uesugi headquarters in Ikatsuko. In Shiba the problem was caused by an interloper, a man sent by Nagao Kageharu to collect dues from the village—a way, for Kageharu, to stake his claim to the holding. In response, Tadakage instructed his deputy to station men in the village, but to avoid armed confrontation with the interloper. "It would be an unconscionable mistake, and inappropriate, if [Kageharu]'s underling were killed." In fact, even a forcible eviction might be undesirable, for "if [Kageharu's] agent should bring over reinforcements as well, it will inevitably come to battle. It would very much be against our wishes if matters escalated for just one underling."[51] Rather, the strongmen accompanying Tadakage's deputy should compel payment of the yearly dues, and make clear to the peasantry of Shiba that if they paid the dues to Kageharu's man, they would be required to pay them again to Tadakage. Eventually the interloper returned north to Kageharu's fortress, perhaps intimidated by the deployment of the strongmen. Betraying the tension beneath the surface of the happy ending, Tadakage closed the incident with praise for his deputy's decision to station two warriors in the village: "Vying firmly to hold all of that land is most fitting."[52]

50. Both locations are in present-day Yokohama. Kozukue was on the southern banks of a river, the Tsurumigawa.

51. *GKS* 7, no. 1845 (Unchōan monjo).

52. *GKS* 7, no. 1847 (Unchōan monjo).

The second crisis, in Kozukue, unfolded at the same time, though the outcome is unknown. In Kozukue, a local warrior, one Narita Mikawa nyūdō, refused to forward the dues from the holding on grounds that "this year [the crops] have all been a loss"—an explanation that Tadakage in his letter curtly dismisses as "unacceptable."[53] Upon visiting the holding two years prior (when he received it as part of his chief retainer portfolio?[54]), he had negotiated a flat rate to be paid every year "regardless of losses." It is easy to imagine that Tadakage's hard line did little to endear him to local residents at this time. Indeed, there is some oblique but suggestive evidence that this confrontation precipitated a falling out between Tadakage and Kozukue's village elite. When Nagao Kageharu raised his banners in revolt, the following year, the "Kozukue castle warrior band" (*Kozukue jōshū*), as one source calls it, took up arms by his side.[55] And when Tadakage and the armies loyal to the Uesugi quickly turned the tide against Kageharu, the stronghold in Kozukue became a rallying point and a refuge for rebel forces until it eventually capitulated.[56]

Tadakage's troubles resemble those of the monks at Bannaji, or at Tōkōji, even beyond the obvious aspects I have underscored so far. All of these incidents reveal the importance of deputies hired to collect dues from holdings, and suggest the pressures that shaped their contracts with proprietors. During their respective crises, nearly two decades apart, both Bannaji and Tadakage sent deputies to run interlopers off their land. In the earlier case, the interloper was Sano Moritsuna's relative, and since we learn about the episode in Moritsuna's letters, we encounter a deputy who is accused of trespassing and disturbing the peace; in the later case, in

53. William Wayne Farris (*Japan's Medieval Population*, 175–76) finds that local droughts occurred in 1475 and 1476, but does not specify where; also, rivers flooded in the Kantō plain in 1482, according to the annals (*Nendaiki*) of Akagi, a shrine in current Maebashi; quoted in *Gunma kenshi tsūshi hen* 3:753.

54. Some indirect evidence of this can be found in the history of the village, which had been numbered among the holdings of the Naganuma family of Shimotsuke Province until a powerful Uesugi leader took it over in the early 1400s. That the Nagao obtained this parcel of land only recently, and directly from the Uesugi, further suggests its link to the Uesugi–Nagao relation. See Shinkawa, *Shimotsuke chūseishi shinkenkyū*, 41.

55. *Kamakura ōzōshi*, 61.

56. *Ōta Dōkan jō*, 640a–b, 643b.

which our vantage point is reversed, Tadakage's deputy was sent to *confront* the interloper and restore the peace. Their different perspectives notwithstanding, both accounts present one point without controversy: deputies—and often armed deputies—were necessary to establish a presence on the land, as residents could not be counted on to forward yearly dues or to resist the encroachment of aggressive local magnates.[57]

To be sure, the practice of hiring deputies, bound by contract to collect and deliver a percentage of the yield or a fixed sum, is evidence of proprietors' struggle to control their far-flung interests. Opting for a flat, annual payment—as was the case in Tōkōji's letter, as well as in Tadakage's—points at once to considerable bargaining power on the part of proprietors in an age of strife, and to anxiety about the disruption of shipments. Yet as both Tadakage's assiduous contact with his deputy, and the intimation that Bannaji could rein in its own man, suggest, proprietors were far from relinquishing their claims to holdings, or entrusting themselves to the conscientiousness and lawfulness of locals. What the frequent appearances of deputies in late fifteenth-century documents signal is a recognition, on the part of all concerned, that title had to be supplemented with presence on the land ("Vying to firmly hold all of that land is most fitting").

Crises like the ones faced by Nagao Tadakage were not entirely new to the late fifteenth century, though the ongoing civil strife made them more common and more difficult to resolve. The logistical obstacles that military mobilization placed between proprietors and their scattered landholdings gave a new salience to definitions of entitlement to land predicated on presence. Possession and legitimate control of a parcel of land (*chigyō*) was hardly a novel concept, but new articulations gained currency.[58] Lands that were "not actually possessed" (*fuchigyō*) came to be juxtaposed, more specifically, to lands that were "actually possessed" and

57. Anzai, *Hōkaiki shōenshi no kenkyū*, 198–226; Yamada, *Kamakura-fu to Kantō*, 329–65; Nagahara, "Shōen kaitaiki ni okeru ukeoi daikansei."

58. On the evolution of the meaning of *chigyō*, Miyagawa Mitsuru ("Shōen to Chigyō," 101) has observed that, "In the Kamakura period, the word *chigyō* had designated possession of land under a claim of title, and some legal protection was given to this protection. By the sixteenth century, *chigyō* generally meant possession at the sufferance of higher authority."

administered (*tōchigyō*). Proprietors had begun to make the distinction beginning with the turmoil of the fourteenth century, as their rights to estates in distant provinces were threatened by local warriors;[59] the process continued through the heyday of the Muromachi regime, and into the civil war. A register produced in 1478 by Ninnaji, a wealthy temple in Kyoto, divides landholdings into two sections: "Part one: A summary of documents relating to lands actually possessed and administered" and "Part two: a summary of holdings not possessed and administered."[60]

Around the same time (in 1477), Hōkokuji, a temple in Kamakura, obtained Ashikaga Shigeuji's imprimatur for its own register, for which the same taxonomy was employed:

*Holdings of Hōkokuji, actually administered and possessed (*tōchigyō*):*

Item	Shinkōji, within Shimoyabe Village, in Oyamada Estate, Musashi.
Item	Naze hamlet within Akiba Village, in Yamanouchi Estate, Sagami.

Holdings of Kyūkōan, a pagoda founded [by Hōkokuji], actually administered and possessed:

Item	Tokiwa hamlet in Fukazawa, Sagami
Item	In the same province: in Nanasawa: half of the settlement; in Ono: half of the settlement; in Funako: half the settlement.

*Holdings of Hōkokuji, not administered and possessed (*fuchigyō*) since the current disorders:*

Item	Tama Village, in Yamabe Estate, Kazusa Province

Holdings of Kyūkōan, not administered and possessed since the current disorders:

Item	Ka[y]ama-hongō, in Kisai district, Musashi
Item	Hirunuma, in Ninomiya, Kōzuke Province
Item	Aoya, in Shida Estate, Hitachi Province
Item	Kitadono's portion, in Ichinomiya, Sagami.[61]

---

59. Fukushima, "Tōgoku shōen ni okeru tōchigyō to shiki," 161–64.
60. *GKS* 7, no. 1765 (Ninnaji monjo).
61. *GKS* 7, no. 1756 (Sagami monjo).

Needless to say, these categories were not employed solely in registers compiled by absentee proprietors: in an undated letter (most likely also written in 1477), Shigeuji confirms the rights of a local warrior, Yokoze Kunishige, to actual possession and administration (*tōchigyō*) of two holdings, Ryōmai and Sonoda.[62]

Clearly, "actual administration" (or "actual possession") was becoming more than a description of fact; it was evolving into a category used by proprietors to distinguish—quite apart from the legitimacy of formal titles—between lands irrevocably lost and lands from which some revenue could still be expected.[63] Shigeuji had not been as specific when he had granted possession (*chigyō*) of Kariyado to Moritsuna's relative, and Tadakage had not addressed the legal status of Shiba and Kozukue when he called for presence on the land. Still, it is clear that such presence—on the part of a proprietor or his deputy—was crucial to the continuing recognition of a proprietor's entitlement.[64] While in most documents of this sort the word *chigyō* is employed, with less emphasis, Yokoze Kunishige managed to get Shigeuji to actually sanction his control of the land as *tōchigyō*. But what was the value of such sanction, especially when it registered the powerlessness of authorities in the face of lands recognized and now officially categorized as lost? I shall return, in the next chapter, to what actual administration meant to local warriors who lived on the land; here I would like to try to answer the question from the point of view of the authorities who granted such sanction.

Obviously the act of granting legal sanction to holdings was itself a central concern to lords like Shigeuji. But a political act that ostensibly advertised the limits of a political actor's reach is worth considering

62. *GKS* 7, no. 1823 (Yura monjo). The most plausible date is 1477 because that is when the Iwamatsu (and the Yokoze, their followers) switched their allegiance from the Uesugi to Shigeuji who, in the course of negotiating the Iwamatsu defection, would have been asked to confirm their rights to all lands recently acquired. The lands of the Iwamatsu and the Yokoze are the subject of Chapter 3.

63. I have not examined the record in western Japan, but Fukushima Noriko's essay, cited in Note 59 above, is largely based on holdings in Shinano Province, so the phenomenon was not limited to the Kantō.

64. Mostly the word *tōchigyō* appears in registers of lands. For the occasional exception, see for instance *Ōta Dōkan jō*, 635b; *GKS* 7, no. 1732 (Nakanoin monjo).

further, to expose the broader conditions that made it appealing to those involved. Hōkokuji's register was certainly not the only document whose validity Shigeuji confirmed. In 1469, he had granted a petition (*mōshijō*), submitted by one of his supporters, Kō no Morohisa, to three holdings, the village of Ōkubo in Ashikaga Estate, Shimotsuke, and the villages of Tomori and Oe, both in Musashi.[65] Two years later, in 1471, he had sent a letter of confirmation (*andojō*) to another local warrior, Motegi Mochitomo, for seven hamlets in Yamane, Shimotsuke, and six hamlets in Natsushima, Sagami.[66] Strikingly, the majority of Kō's and Motegi's claims (three out of five) were to lands beyond the limits of Shigeuji's actual authority. Nor was that pattern exceptional; in the case of the holdings claimed by Hōkokuji, the portion that lay in the western half of the Kantō (in Uesugi territory) was even larger: nine out of eleven (Map 2.2). So why were these plaintiffs appealing to Shigeuji, and why was Shigeuji accepting their petitions?

By recognizing that proprietors might have rightful claims to lands they no longer actually possessed within *his* sphere of authority (as seen especially in Hōkokuji's register), Shigeuji confessed to a certain lack of actual power. Most embarrassing was the easy comparison between the situation in the provinces under Shigeuji's control and that in those loyal to his Uesugi rivals: while most of the temple's total holdings were in the western half of the plain (and thus under the jurisdiction of the Uesugi) all of the holdings over which control had been lost were in the eastern half. It was in the eastern half of the plain, where Shigeuji held sway, that Hōkokuji's proprietary rights had been disregarded; it was Shigeuji who had failed to stand up for them. The register is organized primarily in terms of lands controlled and lands lost, and does not advertise this unflattering comparison, but the geographical data is appropriately detailed and specific for this sort of document, in plain view for anyone choosing to see it. Whether or not drawing attention to this situation was the main reason for submitting the register to Shigeuji's judgment rather than the Uesugi's—after all, given the option, a plaintiff might

65. *SKS* 5, no. 959 (Kō monjo).
66. *TKS* 2:53, no. 44 (Motegi monjo).

Map 2.2. Holdings confirmed by Ashikaga Shigeuji, Lord of Koga (case no. 5).

have brought this sort of case to Shigeuji anyway, as former Lord of Kamakura—it is hard to shake the suspicion that the temple's leadership was hoping to move the Lord of Koga to action.

At the same time, Shigeuji was making a rather bold claim. By issuing documents that adjudicated claims *throughout* the Kantō region, that did not distinguish between territories controlled by his allies and his enemies when assessing proprietors' entitlement to lands, Shigeuji made a show of disregarding the bearing of political and military contingency on matters of judicial authority. In actuality he ruled as the Lord of Koga and no more, but in his decrees Shigeuji continued to act as highest representative of the Muromachi regime in the Kantō, and this despite his ongoing conflict with the shogun's representatives, the Uesugi. Symbolizing his denial of the collapse of the Kamakura Office (which, in truth, he had played a major role in bringing about), Shigeuji continued to date the documents he issued according to the era that had been current at the beginning of the conflict, and that had long been replaced, in the rest of Japan, by a succession of eras hopefully conceived to usher in a new peace. Even as an embattled shogunate paid less and less attention to the state of the provinces, in other words, the representatives of the regime, in the east at least, continued to style themselves as defenders of lawful order, as rulers of a jurisdiction spelled out by appointment to office rather than by the outcome of military campaigns.

Thus construed, the registers and letters of confirmation reveal a certain straining for lands lost, far away—for none of the holdings in need of judicial confirmation was near the residences of the plaintiffs. They also reveal a continuing reliance on the part of provincial warriors and temples, as they fought to keep their distant holdings, on institutional venues of adjudication, which still retained the prestige of centuries of precedent, even after decades of civil war had sapped much of their actual power to enforce verdicts. In this sense, what may seem like a certain deafness to the realities of civil war on the part of warrior elites—not only because these bold pronouncements of enduring authority flew in the face of mounting disorder and political fragmentation, but also because they failed to acknowledge the enticements of a more sustainable local rule—was actually supported by the continuing expectations of provincials, who were not so quick to do away with the weakened representatives of a foundering regime.

In the divided Kantō, warriors like Kō no Morohisa and Motegi Mochitomo could choose between two courts. In submitting their cases to Shigeuji, they were certainly motivated by their relations to him as a lord; they did not turn to the Uesugi, with whom they had no ties, simply because the lands in question were in the western half of the Kantō. So lordship mattered at least as much as jurisdiction, and certainly the rhetoric of authority that informs the political acts of Shigeuji (and of the Uesugi, in the western half of the plain) underplayed the lordly side of rule. Yet with regard to land, at least, we would oversimplify if we discounted the claims to jurisdictions created by the Muromachi regime, and the resilience of office.

Lordly and institutional dimensions of authority were neither new nor entirely contradictory and, indeed, picking them apart in contemporary practice can be extremely tricky. As the regime's legal specialists had long recognized in devising new taxonomies of landholdings, the distinction between public and private could be less than useful, for the authority obtained by virtue of appointment to office was commonly exercised in forms that were private, when not outright proprietary. Conversely, positions that would be acquired through relations of service and displays of private loyalty were not qualitatively different from offices in the machinery of the state. For instance, leaders of the Nagao family, who monopolized the "private" post of chief retainer to the main Uesugi house, also—concomitantly and consequently—had a stranglehold on the "public" offices of deputy governor for the provinces of Kōzuke and Musashi. The absence of a sharp differentiation was plainly visible when in 1473 Nagao Kagenobu suddenly passed away, and the inner circle of the Uesugi leadership decided to appoint Kagenobu's younger brother, Tadakage, as his successor to the post of chief retainer. As it became apparent that Kagenobu's son (and Tadakage's nephew), Kageharu, had expected to be chosen for the position and had taken umbrage for what he considered a personal slight, the Uesugi leadership tried to find a compromise solution: with no sense that incommensurable positions were being traded, Tadakage was asked to yield the office of deputy governor of Musashi, which he had held since before his selection as chief retainer, so that his nephew could be appointed.[67] (Tadakage refused, and Kageharu eventually rose in rebellion, as noted above.)

In wartime documents especially, where personal exhortations and injunctions often take the place of more deliberative and procedural communiqués, the difference between official adjudication and private negotiation becomes elusive. We have seen some of the slippage between these two spheres in the suits and negotiations over Kariyado and Aka-

67. *Kamakura ōzōshi*, 60; the idea is attributed to Ōta Dōkan, though in documents he wrote he is less explicit about the plan: *KKS* 1, 208 (*Kokan zassan* 6); *Ōta Dōkan jō*, 637a.

tsuka. But as war progressed, the ambiguity went beyond the dual personas and conflicting interests of individual warriors like Sano Moritsuna. The correspondence concerning Shiba between Nagao Tadakage and his deputy, which we saw above, is a case in point. In the same letter in which he conveys his instructions in decisive, even heated language, Tadakage also admits to consulting with another powerful warrior on the matter: "Ōta Dōshin has returned to [his castle in] Kawagoe, so I am waiting for him to join the camp again. . . . Certainly instructions will be sent out again by Dōshin to his men in the vicinity."[68] In the mid-1470s, when Tadakage wrote his letter, Dōshin (1411–88?) was one of the Kantō region's elder statesmen. As the former chief retainer to the most powerful of the junior lineages of the Uesugi, the Ōgigayatsu house, his status was comparable to Tadakage's. The two were related, as Dōshin's main consort was Tadakage's sister. Still, Tadakage's eagerness to consult with his brother-in-law on the disturbance caused in Shiba by his nephew Kageharu was likely more than a matter of personal appreciation for Dōshin's insights.

The village of Shiba was in southeastern Musashi, so Tadakage held sway over it both privately, as proprietor, and officially, as deputy governor of that province. Requesting Dōshin's mediation, then, would appear to mark a retreat from official prerogatives on Tadakage's part. Upon further scrutiny, though, the opposite might be closer to the truth: had Tadakage not been a party in the dispute, thus complicating matters, a case such as the one in Shiba would normally be ruled upon by the office of the deputy governor. In effect, Tadakage was calling upon Dōshin to avoid the potentially dangerous perception of a conflict of interest. And the care with which Tadakage, as one of the parties involved, instructed his deputy to avoid any show of force that might lead to an escalation of violence evinces his desire for an amicable (or at least a judicial) solution to the crisis, one that emphatically turned away from a more personalistic, and possibly more violent, reaction to aggression.

Dōshin certainly had the stature to intervene in a dispute between two members of the Nagao family; he also had more authority in the southern corner of the Kantō than almost any other contemporary. Before

---

68. *GKS* 7, no. 1845 (Unchōan monjo).

formally retiring and relinquishing all his official titles in 1447 and the family headship in 1455, Dōshin had held the post of deputy governor of neighboring Sagami Province, just a short distance from Shiba, where Kamakura (and Unchōan, home to Tadakage's deputy) stood. At the same time, in another example of the complex interplay of official and lordly exercise of authority, by serving (along with his son) as castellan of the recently erected fortresses of Kawagoe and Edo in central and southern Musashi, Dōshin had also become a dominant political figure in that province. There is little evidence to suggest that Tadakage was invoking one dimension of Dōshin's authority rather than the other when he requested his assistance. Nor were there only two personas from which to choose: Tadakage also turned to Dōshin in another capacity, as one chief retainer seeking the advice of another—a post that embodied the ambiguous space between the officialdom of the Muromachi regime and the lordly leadership of local warrior bands by being both familial in conception and institutional in character.

This ambiguity was compounded by the peculiar situation in the Kantō, where the Uesugi acted as military governors of several individual provinces but also oversaw a wider jurisdiction as Kantō deputies. As was often the case for provincial governors, the Uesugi's most important followers (the Nagao and the Ōta) served at the same time in different capacities (as deputy governors and as chief retainers). Had the Uesugi ruled only one province, their deputies, too, would have governed one province in their capacity as deputy governors and overseen the warriors of that province in their capacity as chief retainers.[69] Because the Uesugi had multiple posts and ruled several provinces, though, the prerogatives and jurisdictions of the posts of chief retainer and deputy governor (which were often held by the same person) were not coterminous. The post of chief retainer, which conferred authority over the whole of the Uesugi warrior band, came to entail a broader jurisdiction and gradually subsumed those of the various deputy governors.[70] In theory, head

69. Yet another possibility, which was also quite common, was for a warrior house to hold the governorships of multiple, noncontiguous provinces. In this case, the head retainer and the deputy governor might not be the same person.

70. Kuroda M., *Chū-kinsei ikōki no daimyō kenryoku to sonraku*, 47–56. Originally, military governors in the Kantō answered directly to the head of the Lord of Kamakura.

retainers such as the Ōta and the Nagao exercised different kinds of authority over different groups of people: they commanded the Uesugi followers in one capacity and provincial residents in another. In practice, as in the case of Ōta Dōshin's intervention in the controversy over Shiba, even the actors themselves might not always have been too certain, or too self-reflective, about which role they were playing.

A good illustration of the overlapping character of these complex networks of authority (and meaning) is offered by a letter sent in 1471 by the chief retainer to the main Uesugi house, Nagao Kagenobu, while at the head of an army that was attempting to topple Ashikaga Shigeuji's stronghold in Koga: "The outrageous behavior of Ōta [Dōkan] in your temple's holding in the hamlet of Naze is unlawful. We said that he may borrow provisions for one foot soldier, solely for the duration of the present campaign, and that is all. That he has gone ahead and [collected] land dues [from the whole hamlet] surely has to be at odds [with what was authorized]! [His lordship] must decree [thus]."[71]

The letter is addressed to Hōkokuji, the same temple that seven years later would request Shigeuji's confirmation of its rights to various holdings, including Naze. What makes this brief message interesting here is the considerable number and variety of parties involved in the dispute. The document we have now is a copy held in the temple's archives. The original, according to a notation on the letter itself, was held by Lord Takuma, that is, Uesugi Noriyoshi, head of a junior house of the Uesugi family. Indeed, the body of the letter appears to be addressed to him, and it is his word that Kagenobu solicits at the end of the message. Why send copies of the letter both to Hōkokuji and Lord Takuma? In 1395, Naze had been donated to the temple by Lord Takuma's grandfather, to support prayers for the repose of the souls of his own father, mother, and grandfather.[72] The longstanding connection between Lord Takuma's

---

The Kantō deputy was the most important official within the Kamakura Office but did not have jurisdiction over the governors. See Minegishi, *Chūsei no tōgoku*, 233–37. After 1455 and the division of the plain, the Kantō deputies seem to have absorbed many of the functions of their erstwhile superiors, including oversight of governors. While this is no more than a supposition, it agrees with Kuroda Motoki's conclusions on the relationship between the Uesugi head retainers and the deputy governors.

71. *KKS* 1, no. 197 (Hōkokuji monjo).

72. Quoted in *Kanagawa-ken no chimei*, 186b.

family and the temple suggests that the monks at Hōkokuji turned to him as a patron, seeking his intercession with the authorities (in this case, Kagenobu, the author of our document). Lord Takuma probably wrote a petition on the monks' behalf, which is why Nagao Kagenobu sent his reply to him.[73]

The holding, the hamlet of Naze, was in Sagami, and thus, officially, within Ōta Dōkan's jurisdiction as deputy governor of that province. Certainly in times of upheaval, a deputy governor, acting on orders from the governor, would have been well within his prerogatives to extract from a holding far more than provisions for one foot soldier. The man charged with adjudicating the matter, Nagao Kagenobu, would have outranked Dōkan as chief retainer of the main house of the Uesugi (at the time, Dōkan was chief retainer of the Ōgigayatsu, a junior house). But formally, at least, in terms of the two men's offices in their respective provincial administrations, Kagenobu's jurisdiction as deputy governor of Musashi and Kōzuke Provinces would not have entitled him to brand as "unlawful" (*kusegoto sōrō*) the conduct of Dōkan, his counterpart in Sagami Province. Yet reference in the letter to the collection of a precisely stipulated levy suggests that as commander in chief of the Uesugi armies Kagenobu had authority over all of the various houses of the extended family. Kagenobu's apparent respect for the rights of a proprietor (Hōkokuji) and the official dimension of governance was undoubtedly heightened by his concern for the displeasure of an important Uesugi lord (Takuma Uesugi Noriyoshi). In an ironic twist, as commander in chief of all Uesugi followers, Kagenobu called into question and reined in Dōkan's authority as deputy governor just as Dōkan exercised a prerogative designed expressly to help deputy governors during military campaigns.

The Problem of Jurisdiction in Wartime

Decades of civil strife and permanent mobilization, while disruptive, and destructive, seem to have occasioned less reconsideration of ideas about land and adjudication than we might expect. To be sure, the mobility of rulers (more on this in Chapter 4) made the procedural formalism

73. Here I follow the interpretation of the compilers of *KKS*.

of the lawsuits once brought before the Kamakura Office difficult to reproduce. The letters issued by the chanceries of the Uesugi and the Lords of Koga suggest not so much the procedures and formal adjudication of tribunals as the rewards and confirmations of warlords. Particularly in the 1490s and after 1500, reports on campaigns, exhortations to join the fray, congratulations and thanks for valor in battle make up the majority of extant letters, with legal disputes over landholdings a seemingly lesser concern. Yet battle (of which there was a lot) and conquest (of which there was surprisingly little) seem to have wrought no cataclysmic change in the ways rulers justified their rulings. When, after three decades of on-again, off-again campaigning, the Uesugi made their peace with the Lords of Koga (Shigeuji and his successor, Masauji) in the early days of 1483, the two parties remained ensconced at opposite ends of the Kantō, each maintaining lordly networks of influence in half of the plain. Yet the persistent geographical halving of the Kantō plain went unremarked upon in favor of an imaginary reestablishment of pre-1455 hierarchies and jurisdictions. As if the region could be brought back together under the aegis of an imaginary Kamakura Office, we find Masauji (r. 1483–1512) issuing instructions to various Uesugi leaders on matters of military strategy and land rights. In one case he even revisited the village of Tomori, one of the three villages for which his father, Shigeuji, had granted rights to Kō no Morohisa in 1469 despite having no real control over the area. After the peace with the Uesugi, Masauji could once again enforce the authority he had never formally renounced.[74]

More startling, perhaps, is a document that seems to suggest not only that the rapprochement allowed once again for suits to be decided and verdicts enforced across the *whole* plain, but also that the thirty-year war might have left the tenurial landscape untouched. The document in question is a letter, sent by Ōta Dōkan to a fellow supporter of the Ōgigayatsu Uesugi house, on the thirteenth of the eighth month of an unspecified year. As with the previous dispute (over Naze), here too the complexity of the situation that is hinted at in our one extant document is illustrative of the large cast of characters typical of these incidents,

74. *GKS* 7, no. 1865 (Hikobe monjo); *TKS* 1:342, no. 10; 1:353, no. 41 (Bannaji monjo).

and of the intricate web of interests that various authorities had to contend with.

In the letter, Dōkan pleads the case of a third party, a local warrior named Kaneko, who had misguidedly joined Nagao Kageharu's rebellion a few years back, but had then reconsidered and submitted to the Uesugi again, sending his son as a hostage to prove his loyalty. Following a pattern typical of the age, another local warrior had apparently taken advantage of Kaneko's momentary lapse of reason and taken possession of the land (in the idiom of the day, Dōkan accuses this opportunistic warrior of "running rampage [*iran*] in the village"). As we have seen with other powerful warriors, here Dōkan intervened not in an official capacity—he was, after all, deputy governor of Sagami, while the events in question were taking place in Shimōsa, far beyond the institutional boundaries of his jurisdiction. Rather, his was the intercession of an influential patron. In his letter, Dōkan draws attention away from Kaneko's recent political lapse, focusing instead on his history as a landholder: Kaneko had successfully managed the holding for a long time before the uprising (as deputy for the proprietor, a Zen temple in Kamakura) and should see his position restored.[75] Dōkan concludes the letter by beseeching its recipient, who resided in the vicinity, to stop the interloper's misconduct.[76]

To a number of familiar themes—an absentee proprietor, a local warrior acting as deputy (or on-site manager), a negotiation between provincial magnates acting as proxies for petty local warriors—the letter adds at least one new angle: how were the elites, whether in their official or in their lordly guises, to manage the problem of actual enforcement across shifting political and military boundaries? Concretely, how were they to treat local warriors (followers or enemies), to assess their conduct, when political aims moved along with boundaries?

---

75. Dōkan also mentions Kaneko and his involvement in Kageharu's rebellion in *Ōta Dōkan jō* (638a), where he describes him as being a resident of Kosawa, in northwestern Sagami Province.

76. *SKS* 5, no. 1004 (Ōbaiin monjo), also *KKS* 1, no. 233. For the role of the letter's recipient in this incident, one Saeda Oi no suke, I follow the interpretation of the compilers of *KKS*.

The holding in dispute, a village named Hiranuma, was in Shimokōbe Estate, an estate long associated with the Lord of Koga, in a province, Shimōsa, which was east of the Tonegawa and had been continuously under the control of Shigeuji and his allies.[77] Hiranuma's location alone has led to the assumption that Dōkan must have written his letter after the peace between Shigeuji and the Uesugi, for no follower of the Kantō deputy would have been able to exercise any influence on lands controlled by the Lord of Koga as long as the two parties were at war with each other.[78] Yet this very same observation raises a host of new questions: If, but for a brief period, Kaneko had a long history of unwavering loyalty to Dōkan (and, by extension, to the Uesugi), why did Shigeuji allow him to retain control of Hiranuma? If, on the other hand, Kaneko had managed to cultivate good relations with the Lord of Koga even while ostensibly serving the Uesugi faithfully, why would Shigeuji have allowed another local warrior to encroach on the village? Considering that Shigeuji had supported Kageharu's rebellion in hopes of weakening the Uesugi, why would Kaneko's participation in the rebellion have been held against him?

Both the war between Shigeuji and the Uesugi and Kageharu's rebellion are known to have cost local families their lands, by forcing them to take sides and leave indefensible holdings at the mercy of other families that sided with the enemy. In the case of Kageharu's rebellion, which concluded with the victory of the Uesugi, families that had risen in arms with the rebels were, in several cases, wiped out entirely (the Toshima family being the most prominent example). *Ōta Dōkan jō* (Ōta Dōkan's letter), our eyewitness account of the rebellion, is nothing less than an extended appeal by Dōkan to the Uesugi leadership, to reward its supporters and reconsider some of the more rash land requisitions it had ordered in the wake of the fighting.[79] But Kageharu's rebellion had been an internal affair of sorts, a conflict within the Nagao family and the

77. Inagaki, "Koga kubō to Shimotsuke," 25, 29.

78. The notes to the document in *KKS* reasonably date the letter between 1483 (the date of the peace) and 1485 (Dōkan was assassinated in 1486, on 7.26, while the letter is dated 10.13).

79. *Ōta Dōkan jō*, 635b–644b.

ranks of the Uesugi family. The thirty-year-long standoff between the Uesugi and Shigeuji had taken on a far stronger territorial dimension, with the west under the Uesugi and the east under Shigeuji. That conflict had tested both sides' ability to continue to claim authority over the whole region.

Shigeuji could ignore this territorial reality with impunity when he confirmed the lands of Motegi Mochitomo, Kō no Morohisa, and Hōkokuji. The case of Kaneko and the village of Hiranuma, though, forces us to reckon with our assumption that in the new state of affairs, with the plain divided, proclamations like Shigeuji's had no real effect aside from political theater. What effect did the political and military confrontation that consumed the resources of the Kantō elites for so long have on the patterns of, and assumptions about, landholding? It may be useful, in this instance, to remember that Dōkan's intercession, while on behalf of Kaneko, was also certainly aimed at protecting the interests of Hiranuma's absentee proprietor, a temple in Kamakura (the letter opens by addressing the temple's concerns, not Kaneko's: "I have communicated with the monks of Zenkōji by letter, and there definitely must be no changes [to their title]!"). Temples in the city fell under Dōkan's purview as deputy governor of Sagami, but here Dōkan's letter seems driven by broader concerns, by the same purpose behind Shigeuji's confirmation of Hōkokuji's register: lawlessness, or the strategic displacement of a petty warrior loyal to the enemy, could not be condoned when it affected the central mandate of the Muromachi regime—the protection of the rightful entitlements of temples (and aristocrats, in other parts of the country). Allowing another local warrior to wrest control away from Kaneko would have been an abdication of the authorities' claims to supervision and adjudication of differences concerning land. In this respect, Dōkan's aims and attitudes and Shigeuji's were aligned.

The controversy over Hiranuma in the 1480s, and the various confirmations issued by Shigeuji over a decade before that, add to the picture of a ruling elite that was ambivalent about its own role. They do not in any way undermine the evidence that the turmoil of war unseated and dispossessed a great number of warrior families throughout the Kantō between the middle of the fifteenth century and the early decades of the sixteenth. Rather, they counterbalance our image of the civil war as an age in which those who could not directly control their lands—backed up by military force, as often as not—were doomed to lose all claims to them and all revenue from them. Certainly holdings were requisitioned and reassigned as political and military opportunities presented themselves, but self-aggrandizement was only encouraged when it was compatible with the goals, and self-perception, of the region's ruling elite. As conspicuous as the disorder of civil war is the Uesugi and the Lords of Koga's firm, even obstinate attachment to the modes of governance on which they had built their ascendancy in the heyday of the Muromachi regime—even after that same regime had lost much of its visibility, and all of its actual reach, in the eastern provinces.

Prohibitions

The constitutive ambiguity of this continuing attachment during the years of civil war, and the ongoing coexistence of lordly and institutional aspects of authority, are vividly captured by a body of documents produced by local lords and representatives of the regime throughout the years of war: prohibitions (*kinzei*). These formulaic documents actually had a long history, for they had been issued by the authorities since the fourteenth century, although their usefulness grew along with unrest. As other documents bearing evidence of functioning courts of law grow sparse in our records at the turn of the sixteenth century, prohibitions come to be perhaps the best encapsulation of the complexity of claims to public authority over individual holdings and places in wartime. These brief pronouncements—letters listing behaviors that would not be tolerated by authorities—were used to produce placards that were posted (usually on temple grounds), enjoining troops billeted nearby from wreaking havoc within the sacred precincts or in the surrounding countryside. The following prohibition, for example, was issued in 1498 by Nagao Akitada:

> Prohibitions
>
> As for the bamboo and trees and mountains and fields and brushwood et cetera in Unchōan's holding in the hamlet of Ōda, Kodama District, Musashi: Regarding the fact that cutting and taking of these by all sorts of people has been [carried out] at will, henceforth, no people from other places must enter this [land]. As for the above, should there

be someone who violates the prohibitions, punishment will be meted out. The matter is as stated.[80]

Prohibition placards were arguably the most direct and unmediated form of communication between authorities and the population at large. They were also the most explicit statement of the application to an individual locale of those authorities' mandate to keep the peace. As such they offered an especially public (as in visible) stage on which the ruling elites could enact their role as keepers of peace and order. Listing exhaustively the range of natural resources that are off-limits and addressing one locale with bureaucratic exactness—by using the framework of districts and provinces, hallmark of the state and its territorial jurisdiction—this prohibition and others like it speak with the authoritative voice of institutions, comprehensively addressing all "people from other places." (The prohibitions' implicit potential to address the population at large, it should be noted incidentally, would be realized more fully during the sixteenth century. While at the turn of the century prohibitions remained mainly confined to the precincts and vicinity of temples and shrines, as regional magnates came to employ these publicly displayed injunctions to regulate commoner behavior in villages and towns the legal pronouncements' scope would grow along with their diffusion.)

But prohibitions were issued *on request*. Their peremptory tone disguised their origins and their aims, equivocating on the nature of the authority they claimed to voice. Monks and abbots, or intermediaries traveling on their behalf, often made their way up to the court of a warrior lord to petition for a letter that would protect their temples. We know from the Jesuit missionary Luís Fróis (writing in 1568) that by the late sixteenth century these transactions could have a significant economic dimension: prohibitions were solicited and paid for; they were not issued as part of a systematic and uniform application of provincial rulers' official prerogatives. Further undercutting the injunctions' institutional links and official character, both the issuing lord and the temple expected the primary audience to be made up of the lord's own

80. *GKS* 7, no. 1830 (Unchōan monjo).

army, not the population at large.[81] Practical considerations—the ability to restrain one's men, in other words—apparently overrode formal considerations about the territorial sphere of an official's jurisdiction. This is evident in the quick succession of prohibitions posted in the same temple by different lords, some of whom were asked to draw on their authority as local magnates, while others were simply paid to keep their troops in check on their way through.[82] In this respect, temple and shrine precincts seem to be less the legal ambit for an official's prohibitions than a stage for the reaffirmation of his authority over his own men.

Did the monks assume that the prohibitions issued by one warrior lord and posted in the temple's precincts would be ignored by everyone but his own troops? The expectation of misconduct and violence probably counted more than their actual occurrence, but it is hard to dispel the sense of parcelization of authority that the frequent reissues of the same prohibitions conjure. In 1472 Yokoze Kunishige, a warrior from Kōzuke and the chief retainer of the Iwamatsu family, issued a series of prohibitions for Bannaji.[83] Neither he nor any member of the Iwamatsu held office in the machinery of provincial administration, but Kunishige could claim to be issuing the prohibitions as the commander for one of the forces involved in Nagao Kagenobu's offensive against Shigeuji, which was taking place at that time. In 1512, by contrast, when another warrior from Kōzuke, Nagano Norinari, issued a set of prohibitions for a temple (Chōnenji), he did so entirely on his own authority. It is significant that Norinari refers to his not as prohibitions but rather as injunctions (literally, "wall writings," *kabegaki*), and that the three items in his letter constitute a series of exemptions for the temple rather than restrictions for his own forces:

81. Minegishi, "Sengoku jidai no seisatsu." See also Shibatsuji, "Sengoku daimyō no seisatsu"; Shibatsuji, "Sengoku daimyō no kinzei to seisatsu"; Ōkubo, "Sengoku daimyō monjo ni miru 'kinzei' no kenkyū"; Kobayashi S., *Hideyoshi kenryoku no keisei*; and Ikegami's discussion of prohibitions in *Sengoku no gunzō*, 69–76.

82. *TKS* 1:352, no. 40; 1:353, no. 41; 1:361, nos. 59–60; 1:362, nos. 61–63; 1:363, nos. 64–65; 1:364, nos. 67 and 69 (Bannaji monjo).

83. *GKS* 7, no. 1737 (Bannaji monjo), also *TKS* 1:362, no. 62.

Injunctions:

Item	[In] this temple, no matter how serious someone's crime, if one enters the precincts, he may not be punished.
Item	Throughout the province, someone who has taken the tonsure for particular [political reasons] may not enter the temple.
Item	The mountainous [areas] within temple [lands] may not be foraged.[84]

The expansive purview claimed by Norinari, who addresses everyone and no one in particular in the province, is reminiscent of the authority presumed in the prohibitions issued a decade and a half before by Nagao Akitada. Unlike Akitada, Norinari could not, in fact, draw on the legitimation offered by the Muromachi regime, although it is worth noting that there is no indication that he was acting *against* the authorities—simply, he seems to have been operating independently of them. (In the sixteenth century rising local magnates like Norinari, and then regional warlords like the Hōjō and others, would increasingly claim for themselves the authority to issue such prohibitions.) We can appreciate the concern with land we see in Norinari's injunctions, and the territorial dimension of his jurisdiction, when we view his text against a counterexample of sorts—two sets of nearly identical prohibitions issued by the heads of the Yamanouchi and Ōgigayatsu Uesugi houses in 1506. The Ōgigayatsu prohibitions read:

Prohibition:

As for any troop in our force behaving wantonly or excessively in [E]hara district, Musashi, anyone who should violate the above [prohibition] shall be meted out punishment. The matter is as stated.[85]

---

84. *GKS* 7, no. 1919 (Chōnenji monjo). The interpretation of the second item as referring specifically to political reasons I borrow from Minegishi Sumio's discussion of the document in *Gunma kenshi tsūshi hen* 3:534.

85. From Satomi family letters of the Eishō (1504–21) through Genki (157–73) eras, *KKS* 1, no. 263. The text actually reads "Mihara"; I follow the emendation proposed by the compilers of *KKS*.

The Yamanouchi prohibitions are identical, save for the omission of the phrase "our force" (*tōte*).

Both Nagano Norinari and the two Uesugi houses issued injunctions meant to cover far more than temple precincts. Although Nagano's injunctions alone concern themselves with defining a temple's status as sanctuary, both his and the Uesugi's, posted for all to see, addressed misconduct that harmed local farming communities: the wanton and excessive behavior prohibited by the two Uesugi lords is a commonly used euphemism for looting and illegal foraging. These (and other) prohibitions, in other words, were issued not only to protect the peace, but to protect property. The encroachments and rampaging that so often appeared in documents referring to disputes were now addressed on site, *urbi et orbi*, with direct pronouncements (which just so happened to be issued upon compensation). And both the Uesugi prohibitions and Norinari's instructions were framed in terms of institutional boundaries (provinces, districts) as much as of holding boundaries.

Yet the Uesugi documents, wider in scope because of their vagueness, are also narrower in conception: the Yamanouchi document (the one lacking the specific reference to "our force") may have had a broader geographical and institutional dimension—truly extending to all mischief within the boundaries of Ehara district. But the otherwise word-for-word identical document issued by the Ōgigayatsu does refer to "our force," that is, Ōgigayatsu troops, making clear that in conception, if not in breadth, the Uesugi prohibitions were the product of private lordship as much as they were of any institutionally sanctioned order. It has been suggested that the Ōgigayatsu, who by the turn of the sixteenth century had come to exercise de facto rule over the southern half of Musashi (the province was still legally governed by the Yamanouchi), deferred to the institutional authority of the main house by limiting their prohibitions to their own warriors. This may certainly have figured in the thinking of whoever drafted the prohibitions for the Ōgigayatsu, though, in view of the transactional process leading to their production, we would do better to look for the explanation in the junior house's respect for *familial* hierarchies within the extended Uesugi family (which at the time of the prohibitions had just recently been reaffirmed after several years of armed competition).[86] Nagano Norinari, it is worth remembering, was not especially constrained by his lack of institutional validation when he addressed people "throughout the province," so we should not rush to the conclusion that the Ōgigayatsu were.

In other words, even if addressing the prohibitions to "our troops" was a deferential gesture by the Ōgigayatsu head—and there is no reason to interpret it otherwise—the lordly and the official may be too intertwined, or confused, to pick apart. Not only is the inference too specific for such a small difference in a laconic pronouncement, it also presumes too clear a separation between two guises which, as we have seen so far, were easily switched or conflated. One more illustration: in 1504, Sōun, the first of the Hōjō lords, briefly campaigned in the Kantō, lending his military support to the ill-starred cause of the Ōgigayatsu. As he traveled with his troops along the coast of Sagami Province, Sōun issued a set of prohibitions in Enoshima, a small island just off the coast near Kamakura. Just as the Ōgigayatsu would, two years later, Sōun addressed his prohibitions to "his own troops" (again, *tōte*). The post of governor of Sagami was in the hands of the head of the Ōgigayatsu, at whose behest Sōun was traveling through the province. So it might seem that deference was, indeed, motivated by office. Still, Sōun was not stationed near Enoshima with Ōgigayatsu troops, so there was no special need for such punctilious precision, not if deference is the only way to explain it. Even institutional authority was always embodied by people, by individuals, so respect for it was connected with respect for the person of the office holder (Sōun's respect for the office of the governor of Sagami had been nowhere in sight nine years before, in 1495, when he had conquered the castle of Odawara, in the western corner of the province, from a loyal supporter of the Ōgigayatsu).

More plausibly, Sōun's prohibitions were addressed to his own troops because such prohibitions were both acts of peacekeeping, and thus

---

86. The idea of institutional deference to the formal ruler of the province was proposed by the compilers of *KKS*, in an attempt to draw a distinction between de facto and de jure rule. The emphasis on institutional consciousness may be too narrowly construed: after all, the head of the Yamanouchi held the office of Kantō deputy, which meant that he outranked the Ōgigayatsu leader anywhere in the Kantō anyway, so the debate over who was military governor in Musashi seems irrelevant.

shaped by a certain pretense of selflessness, and acts of patronage building, sustained by the exchange of services and wealth and imbued with the specificity of a personal tie. Sōun provided a local institution seeking *his* assistance with a guarantee of reprieve from looting by *his* troops. By the same token, the small difference in phrasing between the two Uesugi prohibitions reflects the perduring duality in the sources of Muromachi elites' authority: private landholdings were insistently brought under the jurisdiction of officials of the regime; maintaining the peace, an explicitly official endeavor, was actually negotiated in prohibitions as a form of private enterprise.

Implicit here is a link that is worth spelling out: ideas about land and the shape of rule over land went hand in hand. The tensions between the official and the lordly on the one hand, and the acknowledgment as essential of presence on the land (the actual administration of holdings) on the other, emerge as parallel themes in the documents of the period. Official authority, of course, was predicated on the sustainability of a mode of administration and property born of absenteeism, for the courts needed distant petitioners seeking their arbitration as much as those proprietors needed an impartial authority to turn to. Yet lordly authority, too, showed its limits in wartime: certainly it stood to gain from the inevitable blurring of the boundaries of the lawful that accompanied the disorder of war—with warriors taking possession of (and administering directly) the lands once held by enemies or weaker neighbors; with lords granting such lands as rewards in the face of the protests of the rightful proprietors. But if all of this seemingly favored the emergence of a more lordly rule of land and men, the very existence of the distinction between holdings directly administered and holdings no longer actually administered proclaimed the precariousness of a lord's authority. As no higher right was recognized than actual possession, no lord could lay claim to authority that transcended the limits of his military reach.

So although Ashikaga Shigeuji could confirm rights to holdings that lay well beyond the edges of the provinces that answered to him, in the name of his official jurisdiction, lords issuing prohibitions to temples would not even be able to pretend to be addressing anyone but their own troops. The strength of proximity to land and men was also its weakness, for no lord who relied on that proximity could then afford to be away. This trade-off was not lost on warrior elites, from the Uesugi and the Lords of Koga on down to other families that hoped to transcend merely local influence: the Nagao and the Ōta, of course, but also some of the old Kantō families that were less directly tied to the provincial administration of the Muromachi regime. One such family was the Iwamatsu, the subject of the next chapter.

CHAPTER 3

Two Was Better than Eighteen?

In the course of writing a memoir of a life spent in the service of the Iwamatsu family, which he would complete in 1509,[1] the Zen monk Shōin (1438–?) found himself recollecting a series of events that had taken place nearly four decades before, in the early 1470s. The memoir he was composing, *Shōin shigo*, is an extended rumination on the nature of attachment to that most complex and contradictory of medieval corporate identities, the warrior family; it is not a chronological narrative of its author's life, although in the process of detailing his service to the Iwamatsu lords Shōin does provide a vivid eye-witness account of life and conflict in the Kantō in the second half of the fifteenth century.[2]

The memoir also offers us an invaluable perspective on the ways in which warrior families' sense of their own history and of their relationship to land were intertwined. This link, between family history and family lands, is the subject of the present chapter. Whereas the previous chapter analyzed disputes over land as a way of revealing the Muromachi authorities' understanding of their role and their reach, the pages that follow consider tension over land—over its confiscation, confirmation, bestowal—from the perspective of local families. If warrior elites defined themselves as authorities through the process of granting or withholding

1. The text is dated intercalary eighth month of the ninth year of Eishō.

2. For more on Shōin and his relationship to the Iwamatsu family, see Spafford, "An Apology of Betrayal."

titles to land, what did local magnates, who participated in the disputes as plaintiffs or defendants, make of those same lands?

Among the episodes Shōin deemed salient and worthy of detailed retelling was a negotiation in which he had taken part in 1472–73 or, as he puts it, somewhat unhelpfully, "years ago" (*sennen*).[3] Two parties were involved: the Iwamatsu, Shōin's own masters, and the Uesugi, rulers of the western half of the plain and leaders of the coalition of eastern warrior families loyal to the shogun. This particular negotiation was only one of many such talks occurring on a regular basis between warrior families; it was as distinctive in its particulars as it was universal in the issues and impulses to which it provided an outlet, centering on the reward the Uesugi owed the Iwamatsu for performing acts of great valor in their service. The heads of the two families did not take part in the negotiation personally, but rather entrusted their chief retainers with the minutiae of the transaction. The chief retainers themselves, as was entirely common practice, relied on the help of messengers and envoys to relay demands and concessions.[4] Shōin, our memoirist, acted as the envoy in this case, carrying word back and forth between the two chief retainers, and his view of the importance of the talks—because they both helped the fortunes of the Iwamatsu and showcased his skills as a go-between and negotiator—inevitably affects our own assessment of their significance.

For Shōin, of course, it was the specifics that mattered; for us, it is the window that his rich account opens on a widespread phenomenon. Unlike other similar transactions, which survive in formulaic letters that convey the details of the demands made and (when we are lucky) the terms of the final agreement, this negotiation is recollected in a lively and personal account of the two sides' discussions and deliberations. The narrator's closeness to the event he recounts allows us to look beyond the material dimension of relations between great regional lords (the Uesugi) and provincial magnates (the Iwamatsu); it allows us to catch a glimpse of the two parties' perspectives on the event and, more broadly, of the multiple, at times conflicting priorities of late fifteenth-century warriors. A keener sense of the dynamics that the negotiation and its retrospective

3. For more on the date of the negotiation, see Notes 28 and 29 below.

4. Yamada Kuniaki (*Sengoku no komyunikēshon*) provides an in-depth discussion of the use of messengers, couriers, and go-betweens.

account expose is crucial to our view of the transformations wrought by a century and more of civil strife. At the same time, because of the nature of our source, the negotiation has become inseparable from its narration; the account is as much about the vindication of the events at the time of writing, in 1509, as it is about the negotiation itself, which, perhaps not coincidentally, is conjured in living color from a hazy, hard-to-locate past.

The transformations taking place in these years in the patterns of rule, seen as spurred by the exigencies of war, have long been framed by scholars in terms of parallel and interconnected drives toward—to generalize—rationalization of governance: on the one hand, greater lordly intrusion in local rule, concentration of judicial authority, and regulation of commerce and production; on the other, in terms of land tenure, consolidation of previously scattered landholdings, and homogenization and clarification of landholders' jurisdictions and prerogatives.[5] These transformations have rightly attracted the lion's share of scholarly attention, though of course there have been and still are debates about the specific timing and nature of individual trends and developments. Typically, nonetheless, there has been a certain eagerness to find change, partly as a way to identify and describe the antecedents of, and context for, the momentous political reforms of the last few decades of the civil war, which ushered in the early modern period.[6]

---

5. The best outline of this development, and by now a long established milestone in Japanese studies, is John Whitney Hall's seminal, if now dated, "Foundations of the Modern Japanese Daimyo," according to which warlords (*daimyō*) evolved through four distinct phases, each characterized by greater control of resources and territory, more invasive management of their warrior band, and greater centralization than the previous one. The four stages are *shugo daimyō* (military governors), *Sengoku daimyō* (Warring States lords), *shokuhō daimyō* (unification-period lords), and *kinsei daimyō* (early modern lords). Hall, of course, does not intend this schema to be more than an outline, nor does he play down regional differences in the chronology and the manner of change. He further fleshes out his views in an empirical study of Bizen province in his *Government and Local Power*. On warlords' arrogation of judicial authority as a tool for consolidating power, see Katsumata, "Sengoku hō"; Katsumata with Collcutt, "Development of Sengoku Law"; on warlords' interference in villages, see Birt, "Samurai in Passage"; Nagahara with Yamamura, "The Sengoku Daimyo and the Kandaka System."

6. There have been those who have sought to rethink the revolutionary character of the late sixteenth-century reforms by casting doubt on the actual impact of those reforms. In particular, see Brown, *Central Authority and Local Autonomy*.

Here I attempt a different approach, emphasizing not so much change (or its opposite, continuity), both of which are typically observed from the vantage point of the early modern settlement and in order to understand that settlement; rather, I try to take advantage of the opportunity offered by a text like *Shōin shigo.* A careful reading of the memoir's account of these talks focuses our attention on contemporary contexts and attitudes, and replaces the emphasis on structural change and rationalization with a greater willingness to take notice of conflict, indecision, and unintended outcomes. Analysis of the fond retrospective account left by one participant in one dispute, furthermore, complements the reading of broad patterns carried out in Chapter 2, and provides a way to think of warriors' possession of land in terms of emotional attachments; it also shifts the point of view, from those exercising authority over a vast regional jurisdiction in the name of the shogun, to those confronting that authority from their small corner of the plain.

By the end of the process outlined in this chapter, the Iwamatsu had traded their claims to eighteen ancestral holdings dispersed throughout the Kantō plain for rights to two expansive estates right at their doorstep. Seen in retrospect, at least, this settlement fits nicely within the parameters set by later historians: two consolidated holdings represented a far more useful resource than eighteen scattered and indefensible ones. Yet what I analyze here are not so much the settlement's stipulations as the process through which a deal was reached; I stress not so much the events themselves as the interpretation the parties involved decided to give them—all of which emerges powerfully from Shōin's narrative. The Iwamatsu, it turns out, were not comfortable with the outcome at first, uncertain about the cost of an exchange that asked them to give up many of the lands on which their long history and their sense of self were founded.

The Big Picture and the Small

The ruins of Kanayama castle still sit atop a green hill, a short but steep climb from downtown Ōta, a manufacturing city of a little over two hundred thousand on the northern edge of the Kantō plain, a few hours

Fig. 3.1. Ruins of Kanayama castle. Photograph by the author.

north of Tokyo (Fig. 3.1). In the 1470s, with fewer trees on the hill and no city below it, the newly erected fortress of the "Golden Mountain" would have been visible from afar in all directions, towering over the plain. Perched atop a long ridge along a small group of hills that rise apart from the mountains further north, and surrounded by flat farmland, the castle overlooked the southeastern corner of Kōzuke Province. The country around Kanayama is long and narrow, hemmed in by two major rivers—the Tonegawa to the south and the Watarasegawa to the northeast—as they flow toward each other to meet, far downstream, southeast of the castle. Beyond the rivers lay the flat expanse of neighboring provinces, home to other warrior families, some friendly, some not. From his fastness, the lord of Kanayama, head of the Iwamatsu family, could take in the surrounding countryside for kilometers, and no east–west traffic between the rivers and the mountains—no movement of troops—would go unnoticed and unchallenged.

The new fortress, inaugurated in 1469, was designed to be the administrative and symbolic center of the family's newly reunified lands.[7] In the late 1460s, the Iwamatsu were in much need of such symbolism, for they had only just overcome years of internecine struggle and united under the banner of a new lord, Iwamatsu Iezumi (1409–94). Iezumi had been raised in exile far from the Kantō, for his father had incurred the displeasure of the authorities by joining an ill-fated rebellion and had brought the fortunes of his line crashing down with him.[8] Because Iezumi was only a child at the time, his life was spared, but as punishment the headship of the Iwamatsu was transferred to another branch of the family. A young Iezumi first returned to the region in 1440, with an army dispatched by the shogun, but despite his service in that campaign, he was not able to reclaim the headship of the Iwamatsu. Fifteen years later, though, in 1455, the crisis of the Kamakura Office cast the region in turmoil and divided warrior families in two factions, presenting Iezumi with an opportunity.

Loyal to the shogunate, Iezumi sided with its partisans, under the leadership of the Uesugi family. While distinguishing himself among the commanders who fought with the Uesugi, Iezumi also waged a personal campaign to regain the headship of the Iwamatsu from the relatives who had controlled it since his father's disgrace. Because Iezumi sided with the shogun and the Uesugi, his Iwamatsu relatives and rivals sided with Shigeuji, the Lord of Koga, and so, as was so often the case, the regional conflict was played out at a familial level as well, as the two Iwamatsu lines fought on opposite sides and used the war to further their own goals.[9] From the shogun, Iezumi received a number of newly confiscated enemy holdings;[10] from Shigeuji, Iezumi's rivals obtained confirmation of their claims to the headship and to the family's ancestral

7. Saitō Shin'ichi (*Chūsei tōgoku no ryōiki to jōkan*, 90–91) makes a similar point, that the building of castles like Kanayama encouraged the process of absorbing collateral lines, turning junior allies into subordinates, and appointing the heads of cadet families as house elders for the main lines.

8. Satō H., *Koga kubō*, 195; Karasawa, in *Ōta shishi tsūshi hen*, 551; Kubota, "Nanbokuchō, Muromachi-ki no Kōzuke," 40; Minegishi, *Chūsei no tōgoku*, 139.

9. Kuroda Motoki (*Sengoku-ki tōgoku no daimyō to kunishū*, 256–57) makes a similar remark concerning specifically the two lines' roles at the earlier battle of Yūki.

10. *Shōin shigo*, 806a.

lands, as well as a number of new holdings from recently requisitioned lands. As the Uesugi's fortunes improved in the war against the Lord of Koga and his partisans, so did Iezumi's chances in his struggle with his Iwamatsu rivals. Negotiations began, and after several years of rapprochements and renewed suspicion between the two parties, Iezumi finally returned to the family holdings as the winner in the late 1460s, and gathered all of the Iwamatsu's relatives and retainers around himself.[11] A great ceremony at Kanayama in the summer of 1469 marked both the inauguration of the castle and the reconciliation of the formerly rival factions of the family.[12] The fortress visibly realized the unification of Iezumi's rule over his family and his holdings, becoming a rallying point for the Iwamatsu and ensuring that the family made its presence felt—and seen—throughout its lands.[13]

The core of these lands was Nitta Estate. The estate had long been dominated by the Nitta, warriors of a family descended from the Minamoto who had settled in the area several centuries earlier. The Iwamatsu themselves were lesser scions of the Nitta family who had risen to prominence in the fourteenth century after the main house had found itself on the losing side of the wars of the 1330s.[14] Staunch partisans of the newly victorious Ashikaga shogun, the Iwamatsu had been rewarded with most of the lands that had once belonged to the senior Nitta line. They had seen their claim to the family's legacy recognized, and with the lands had received the privileges afforded by their new status, for the new military governors dispatched from Kyoto and Kamakura were not allowed to enter Nitta Estate without permission from the Iwamatsu.[15] Their

---

11. Minegishi, "Kyōtoku no ran no futatsu no Nitta Iwamatsu-shi."

12. *Shōin shigo*, 826a. See also Satō H., *Koga kubō*, 204–6; Karasawa, in *Ōta shishi*, 548. Saitō, *Chūsei tōgoku no ryōiki to jōkan*, 89–92.

13. This observation is Kuroda Motoki's (*Sengoku-ki tōgoku no daimyō to kunishū*, 257–58).

14. An excellent family tree of the larger Nitta family, covering not only the main line but all the collateral houses up to the late fourteenth century as well, is printed in Koyama, *Chūsei sonraku to shōen ezu*, 87.

15. On the Iwamatsu acquisition of the right to bar entry to Nitta to military governors (*shugo funyū-ken*), see Matsumoto, *Tōgoku shugo*, 288–94. There is some disagreement about the evolution of the status and privileges of the Iwamatsu, and the nature of their relationship with the Kantō deputies and military governors of Kōzuke, the Uesugi. See also Minegishi, *Chūsei no tōgoku*, 103.

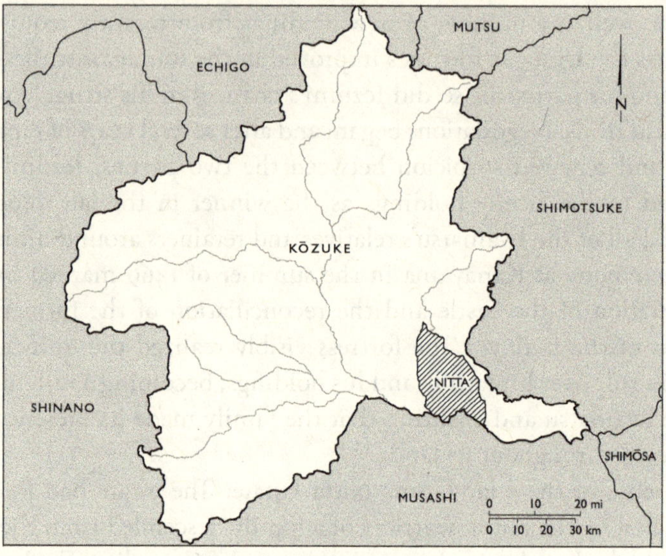

Map 3.1. Nitta Estate in Kōzuke Province.

lineage and the nature of their control of Nitta Estate made the Iwamatsu the most powerful warrior family in southeastern Kōzuke Province (Map 3.1).

Nitta Estate itself was an old and vast estate, established no later than 1157 and covering a surface of approximately one hundred square kilometers in between the mountains, to the north, and the Tonegawa, to the south.[16] Kanayama rose on the estate's eastern edge, and within the

16. The estate extended over the Ōmama alluvial fan, in an area that includes the present-day city of Ōta, as well as parts of the cities of Kiryū, Midori, and Isesaki in Gunma Prefecture, although accurately determining the surface of the estate is difficult, absent precise or certain information on boundaries (its western and eastern borders are thought to have been marked by two streams, the Hayakawa and the Iwasegawa, respectively). A comparison between the map in Minegishi, *Chūsei no tōgoku*, 75, and a modern map suggests a surface of about 100 km²—somewhere between the 87 km² of Manhattan and the 121 km² of San Francisco. (That is, provided we consider the area within the boundaries as we know them and disregard the common statement that the estate covered all of modern Ōta [even before the administrative consolidation of Ōta and Nitta District in 2005, which made Ōta considerably larger].)

boundaries of the estate were at least twenty-five known villages.[17] Different branches of the Nitta family took up residence in these villages, deriving their names from them: Iwamatsu Village was in the southeastern portion of the estate, in the lowlands near the banks of the Tonegawa.[18] As their family rose to prominence in the fourteenth century, the Iwamatsu extended their control over other areas, gradually absorbing the holdings of other families until they came to control the majority of Nitta Estate directly, through collaterals and hereditary followers, or through their tutelary temple.

The competition around the middle of the fifteenth century between the two Iwamatsu lineages was played out in a series of attempts by each side to acquire the holdings of its rivals. As a result of both sides' expansionism, when Iezumi entered Kanayama castle in the eighth month of 1469 he ruled over more of Nitta Estate than any of the Iwamatsu ever had. Iezumi's control over the estate was not complete, though, as not all of it was held by (or of) him, the reunification of 1469 notwithstanding. Consolidation was relative: although the Iwamatsu were supreme in the estate, they held it not as a whole, but as a collection of discrete parcels.[19] Collateral houses still held on to their own lands, and powerful followers like the Yokoze controlled their own significant share of holdings. Further complicating matters, the fragmentation of

---

17. The estimate is conservative: the Nihon shōen Database of the National Museum of Japanese History (Kokuritsu Rekishi Minzoku Hakubutsukan, known as Rekihaku) lists twenty-eight toponyms, twenty-five of which are villages; the remainder are of unclear nature. And it is of course entirely possible that there were other villages that for some reason went unrecorded. Rekihaku Nihon shōen database: http://www.rekihaku.ac.jp/up-cgi/login.pl?p=param/soue/db_param (shōen kōdo 2513001; accessed November 5, 2004).

18. Iwamatsu corresponds to present-day Iwamatsuchō, in southern Ōta.

19. It is worth noting that it is difficult to assess what exactly it meant to control an estate in the late fifteenth and early sixteenth centuries. As a locus of attachment and a source of wealth, Nitta Estate was certainly crucial to the survival of the Iwamatsu. To what degree it continued to exist, institutionally, according to the principles that had guided its establishment, centuries before, is unclear. On this problem, see Ike, "Shōen no shōmetsu to taikō kenchi," 348–51; Yuasa, "Muromachi-ki tōgoku no shōen-kōryōsei," 186–87.

the estate was replicated on the village level.[20] A landholder—be he an Iwamatsu, a Yokoze, a collateral, or another follower—may have held rights to several contiguous villages. The villages were the basic units of administration, but they were not the basic units of landholding, and each of them could comprise individual hamlets, or even individual plots, controlled by a variety of holders. Nevertheless, the main line of the Iwamatsu controlled the vast majority of the lands in the estate, and their paramount position was uncontested.[21]

Nor were the holdings of the Iwamatsu limited to Nitta Estate—or to Kōzuke Province, for that matter. As with other warrior families great and small, the scattering and heterogeneity of landholdings was a product of the piecemeal manner in which the individual items in a portfolio were obtained. The Iwamatsu family retained rights to numerous parcels of land, of varying size, scattered throughout Japan (though mostly concentrated in the Kantō region).[22] A number had come with leadership over the various Nitta lineages; others were acquired by the Iwamatsu themselves, often from the shogun as reward for meritorious service. Land was received from the shogun in Kyoto and (before 1455, at least) from the Lord of Kamakura, as a mark of favor for personal loyalty or as a perquisite of office. Likewise, it could be granted by the Uesugi, as governors of Kōzuke, after being confiscated from a rebellious warrior. Or it might be acquired as a dowry in a matrimonial alliance, or simply purchased with cash from another family: "As for the four villages in Ōkura Estate," notes *Shōin shigo*, marking what it obviously considers a meaningful distinction, "they were ancestral holdings of Lord Kira, in

---

20. Making matters even more complex, villages and other units were by no means stable over time: in his study of medieval Nitta, Koyama Yasunori (*Chūsei sonraku to shōen ezu*, 95–101) includes a table and discussion of the shifting villages within the estate, from the six mentioned in *Wamyōshō* to the nineteen of the twelfth century to the thirty-five of the thirteenth.

21. Minegishi, *Chūsei no tōgoku*, 104–30. See esp. table 11, p. 130, with the breakdown of the land according to families and relations to the Iwamatsu.

22. This situation was not unique to Japan: descriptions of thirteenth-century Rome and post-Conquest England strongly resemble the situation in Nitta Estate. See, for instance, Brentano, *Rome before Avignon*, 17; and Warren, *The Governance of Norman and Angevin England*, 29.

Kyoto. But Yokoze Ryōjun bought them in cash for one thousand *kanmon*. Those were not lands bestowed on him as a reward."[23]

The Deal

The newfound unity of the Iwamatsu family did nothing to resolve the broader conflict that shook the Kantō, and in the early 1470s the plain remained divided, with Uesugi partisans in the western provinces and supporters of the Lord of Koga, Ashikaga Shigeuji, controlling the eastern provinces. The seemingly endless conflict moved along in fits and starts, with periods of limited military activity followed by sudden outbursts of large-scale action.[24] One of these was the offensive launched in 1471, when in the fifth month Nagao Kagenobu (1413–73), the chief retainer of the Uesugi and their most powerful military supporter, "leading a great host, headed against Koga castle," the enemy's main stronghold.[25] By the end of the sixth month the castle was under siege, and Shigeuji had been forced to seek refuge with one of his supporters further south.[26]

Kagenobu's triumph was short-lived, though, and the next spring the great families of the eastern provinces rallied around Shigeuji and launched a counteroffensive. Having turned the tide, they now pressed their advantage, pushing west toward the Uesugi's main camp, which was located just across the Tonegawa, in a place called Ikatsuko. As the

23. *Shōin shigo*, 811a.

24. The war is known to Japanese scholars as the Disturbance of Kyōtoku (*Kyōtoku no ran*), a name coined by Minegishi Sumio in a 1963 article in *Chihōshi kenkyū* ("Tōgoku ni okeru jūgo seiki kōhan no nairan no igi," reprinted as a chapter in his book, *Chūsei no tōgoku*, 233–54). The name stuck even though the disturbance outlasted that era many times over: it began in 1455, during the Kyōtoku era and concluded—if a truce is a conclusion—in 1483, with the so-called "reunification of Town and Country" (*tohi no gattai*).

25. *Kamakura ōzōshi*, 60. A number of letters of congratulation, from both sides, confirm the flurry of military activity: see *GKS* 7, no. 1715 (Kō monjo); *GKS* 7, nos. 1716 and 1717 (Toshima Miyagi monjo, Naikaku bunko); which variously comment on the valor of warriors engaged on both sides at the siege of Tatebayashi, a castle at the eastern tip of Kōzuke, not far from Koga.

26. *Kamakura ōzōshi*, 60. Shigeuji moved to Motosakura, further south in Shimōsa Province (in the town of Shisui, Chiba Prefecture).

chronicle *Kamakura ōzōshi* has it, "there was no break in the fighting, and on the twenty-fourth of the first month of the fifth year of Bunmei [1573], even Uesugi Masazane, the general of the Ōgigayatsu house, perished in battle, aged twenty-four. Wasn't he still a child!"[27] We do not know much about Shigeuji's offensive, how far it got, and where and how exactly Masazane fell.[28] The death of one of the highest lords in the Uesugi ranks, though, underscores the gravity of the crisis their party faced in 1472–73.

Hastily retreating westward from Koga, the commanders of the Uesugi's forces debated the best course of action.[29] Iwamatsu Iezumi, a Uesugi partisan, delegated his longtime chief retainer, Yokoze Kunishige (d. 1495), to participate in the deliberations on his behalf. As the Iwamatsu lord's right-hand man, it was fitting that Kunishige should be charged

---

27. *Kamakura ōzōshi*, 60. Documents show that the fighting continued. *TKS* 3:31, no. 3 (Shirakawa monjo), refers to Shigeuji's flight to the Chiba; *GKS* 7, no. 1745 (Hotchi-shi monjo), suggests the intervention of the Uesugi of Echigo.

28. Satō Hironobu (*Chūsei tōgoku no shihai kōzō*, 103) laments that "for the battles in Musashi there is no evidence in documentary sources." Kuroda Motoki (*Ōgigayatsu*, 29) erroneously attributes to *Shōin shigo* information on Masazane's end. Shichinomiya Keizō (*Kantō kanrei, Uesugi ichizoku*, 184) repeats the idea (presumably deduced from *Kamakura ōzōshi*) that "Masazane died at Ikatsuko in the course of Shigeuji's counteroffensive." If we are to take *Shōin shigo*'s retelling as true, the Ashikaga offensive was stemmed at Kanayama, and Ikatsuko was saved by the Iwamatsu single-handedly. This does not entirely exclude that Masazane was killed in a battle fought somewhere in eastern Kōzuke or northern Musashi at the time.

29. *Shōin shigo* does not clearly situate the negotiation in time, though it is fairly plain that it occurred during the days of Shigeuji's counteroffensive. While most sources do not mention the siege of Kanayama at all, for the most part scholars have agreed upon the overall chronology of this phase of the conflict, leaving the only plausible window for the event between the end of 1472 and the beginning of 1473. The one discordant voice is the entry, "Kanayama-jō," in *NJT* 4:386, which impossibly places the siege in 1471, in the middle of Kagenobu's offensive (and overlapping with Shigeuji's flight south!). The specific source is not given for this reconstruction, though several are listed as having provided material for the entry as a whole. Of these, only two, *Nitta shōden wakumon* and the absurdly jumbled *Nitta shōdenki*, cover the period at hand, but do not discuss the siege, as far as I can tell. So we are left with *Shōin shigo* and its reticence. One more piece of evidence lends some support to my interpretation: a letter from Ōta Dōkan to Terao Wakasa nyūdō characterizes the "difficulties" for the Uesugi party as occurring the year *after* Shigeuji sought refuge with the Chiba. *KKS* 1, no. 208 (*Kokan zassan* 6).

with leading the family's warrior band and negotiating with the high authorities of the Kantō; at the same time, that he was sent to discuss the Iwamatsu family's course of action on his lord Iezumi's behalf was a sign of Kunishige's prestige in Nitta Estate and of Iezumi's prestige vis-à-vis the Uesugi: Iezumi need not personally pay a visit to their chief retainer, Nagao Kagenobu, and receive directions from him.

Across the river, in Musashi Province, the forces under Kagenobu's command were rallying to stave off a siege of the Uesugi main camp. This left the Iwamatsu forces in a quandary: their brand-new castle, Kanayama, stood along the enemy's path. Should the Iwamatsu join the main line of defense at the Uesugi camp, or should they make a stand alone, in Kanayama? "We shall agree to either, without second thoughts," the Iwamatsu representative, Yokoze Kunishige, said to Nagao Kagenobu, in *Shōin shigo*'s retelling.[30] Loath to appear disloyal to the greater cause of the Uesugi, whatever that was, or overly concerned with his lord's own castle and interests, Yokoze Kunishige (and the Iwamatsu) deferred to the commander in chief.

According to *Shōin shigo*, the commander in chief, Nagao Kagenobu, magnanimously, or perhaps just sincerely at a loss for an answer, conceded: "Being, as we are, on the defensive, I'll refrain from deciding this way or that; if deep down in your heart you feel you must protect Kanayama, then you must stay there."[31] But here again our source—by no means *super partes*, it bears remembering—underscores how the commander in chief was aware that either decision would serve to help the Uesugi and their main camp: by staying back and defending Kanayama, Kagenobu said, "You shall certainly be of aid to Ikatsuko's commanders. If Ikatsuko's defenses are strengthened as a result of Kanayama's fighting, you shall have rendered service of great loyalty, unequaled throughout the Kantō. What could surpass this?"[32] This follow-up clarifies that Nagao Kagenobu was faced with a decision of great consequence, and was not sure of his course of action. He was willing to grant the Iwamatsu latitude, as it probably would not harm the camp at Ikatsuko. If on the other hand the Iwamatsu forces' defense should prove successful, Kagenobu's

30. *Shōin shigo*, 823a.
31. *Shōin shigo*, 823a.
32. *Shōin shigo*, 823a.

gratitude—and the Uesugi's gratitude, by extension—would be unparalleled. Crucial here was Kagenobu's abdication of his authority to command the Iwamatsu, his admission of impotence coupled with his willingness to recognize his dependence on others. The way the dialogue is phrased, furthermore, allows Yokoze Kunishige to keep his counsel until *after* Kagenobu has made his concession. According to Shōin's account, the Uesugi's chief retainer read his counterpart's hint correctly—Yokoze Kunishige's desire to hold out in Kanayama—and went on to endorse this course of action before it was proposed.

Responding now to what had become an order from the Uesugi commander in chief, Kunishige set out to make explicit the quid pro quo: "If by chance, protecting our castle by our own strength alone, all of us fighting to our deaths, we should stop the Lord of Koga at the foot of our castle, Ikatsuko's [commanders'] true wishes having come to pass, we shall appeal for an extra amount [of land] as the reward for loyal service."[33] Loyalty—or rather, loyal service—always came with lordly recompense.[34] But quantification of loyalty was not left entirely to the generosity of the grateful. Minute details of the recompense would be negotiated, with the weight of service carefully measured out in holdings. "At that time," Kunishige exhorted Kagenobu, referring to the day when great service would be rendered and the Iwamatsu would put forth their demands for reward, "you must not be remiss in adjudicating the matter."[35] (Here again, it is worth noting in passing, we find in the language of the negotiation the familiar mixture of personalistic, lordly political relations and formal, official procedure.)

The exact quantification of the reward, it seems, was left for later, when the amount of loyalty displayed would be firmly established and plainly visible. As the valor of the loyal was not an individual's virtue (however individually displayed) but the conduct of many ("all of us fighting to our deaths"), rewards should be doled out to satisfy the wishes of all of those who selflessly aided the Uesugi. And because Yokoze Kunishige had not asked to defend Kanayama out of self-interest, it was not self-interest that drove his request for reward, according to our

33. *Shōin shigo*, 823a.
34. See Conlan, "Largesse."
35. *Shōin shigo*, 823a.

source: "I consulted with my companions, who have long been without lands, and each of them, brave to his death, will endeavor to the utmost. On that account, I must say I agreed that they receive the greater part."[36] To this Nagao Kagenobu acceded, hard-pressed for the cooperation of the Iwamatsu and their followers, and the details were postponed until later, with assurances that the demands for recompense would be met swiftly.[37] The whole conversation is recorded by Shōin in his chronicle. Indeed, we learn about it for the first time as Shōin (the character, not the author) quotes it, line by line, to remind Kagenobu of his promise. Holing up in Kanayama castle, the Iwamatsu troops had indeed become a thorn in Shigeuji's side: he could not leave the fortress unreduced and move against Ikatsuko for fear of being trapped between two enemy forces; neither could he, as it turned out, topple the castle, besiege it as he may. Shōin's epic account is vague about dates but richly detailed in its description of what transpired. It would certainly have convinced any Iwamatsu partisan of the inevitability of a rich reward:

> Between the encampment of the Lord [of Koga] and the camp at Ikatsuko lay ten leagues (*ri*). But the Tonegawa separated them, a great river without equal in the Kantō. The river's current was boundlessly wide, and its bottom deep, with white wave crests rising to the sky, flowing swollen. Men and horses could not readily cross back and forth. Yet this foolish old monk found it hard to ponder fate and [sit] quietly, and so day and night I stealthily crossed the waves' difficult spots and went back and forth from Ikatsuko to Kanayama, bringing information to the various commanders. The plans made in the commanders' tent, as a result of the fighting of the bands in the castle, became ever more splendid. Either at daybreak or at nightfall, either by cutting off supply routes or by striking without fear, the warrior bands stopped the many troops and the rabble coming and going from distant provinces to the [besieging enemy] camp, blocking the camp's transit routes. Either lying low in the grass they struck those coming and going to the camp, or with the clouds and rain as their cover they brought back with them the weapons and mounts of those traveling and staying at the camp. In this manner the warrior bands in the castle fought for seventy days and more, and

36. *Shōin shigo*, 823a.
37. *Shōin shigo*, 823b.

even a great army could not achieve military success against them, and so the Lord [of Koga] returned his banners to Ashikaga Estate in Shimotsuke Province, and that was all.[38]

After the dust settled, our memoirist, Shōin, was sent over to remind the commander in chief Nagao Kagenobu of his word. Because of the prowess of the Iwamatsu warriors holed up behind the walls of Kanayama, "the commanders and the warrior leagues at Ikatsuko camp restored the safety of the camp's old splendor without doing a thing," Shōin recalls Yokoze Kunishige boasting, with more than a little hyperbole.[39] "That being the case, I wish to petition on the matter of the reward for our loyalty, which was previously spoken of and decided."[40] When he received Shōin at his headquarters, first thing in the morning, Nagao Kagenobu asked him to draw up a list of the holdings the Iwamatsu wished to receive: "We shall agree to it."[41] Shōin conceded that Kunishige's initial request, before the siege, might have been excessive. "Yet for generations, since the time of the great general,[42] we have had ancestral holdings in eighteen places throughout Musashi and Sagami, and they must be returned to us."[43] In fact, the Iwamatsu held rights to land not only in those two provinces but throughout the Kantō and the whole of Japan. Many of these holdings had slipped away from the family's control, mostly due to distance. Preoccupied with the reunification of Nitta Estate, the two rival factions had had little opportunity to supervise or defend lands scattered far away. Iezumi in particular was forced until 1469 to fight to establish his claim to the headship of the Iwamatsu and could hardly muster the force necessary to stave off the encroachment of other warrior

38. *Shōin shigo*, 820a–b.

39. *Shōin shigo*, 823b. Kunishige's claim sounds particularly inaccurate if we consider the death of Masazane in the defense of Ikatsuko.

40. *Shōin shigo*, 823b.

41. *Shōin shigo*, 823b.

42. The word I translate as "great general" is the one commonly read "*taishōgun*" and translated as "shogun." Here, the first character is actually glossed as "*ō*" rather than "*tai*" by the compilers, so the compound in this case might refer to a "great general" and not to an actual shogun. In my translation of the title I have preferred to err on the safe side, though most probably this is no more than an alternate reading and the compound does in fact refer to Takauji, the shogun.

43. *Shōin shigo*, 823b–824a.

families that controlled the areas where his scattered holdings lay. Much less had he been able to clamor for the restitution of those lands that had long since fallen into others' hands.

The last seventeen years of upheaval, since Ashikaga Shigeuji had rebelled and abandoned Kamakura to relocate to Koga in 1455, had left landholders and their claims in an awkward position. The chain of authority over which Shigeuji had presided had now been replaced by two factions at war: in the western half of the plain, claims and disputes that would once have been addressed by the Kamakura Office now had to be directed to the Uesugi in Ikatsuko. Needless to say, the Uesugi had no actual power over issues arising in the east of the plain. Those would have to be arbitrated by Shigeuji, the Lord of Koga. And since a warrior family had to choose which side to back, lands that fell under the jurisdiction of the enemy had to be written off (as seen in Chapter 2, lords like Shigeuji would forswear their right to requisition and reassign lands only in specific instances, when not doing so would cast doubt on their legitimacy). In the Iwamatsu dispute, Shigeuji, who supported Iezumi's rival, had guarded the family's portfolio of lands as part of the endowment of the junior line, going as far as granting it some of the lands he confiscated from the Uesugi. How the Iwamatsu reunification affected the claims of the family in the eastern provinces is unclear, because of the lack of documentary evidence of any kind, though it is reasonable to imagine Shigeuji reallocating the lands under his jurisdiction to allies more loyal.[44]

Now that they had gained considerable leverage over the Uesugi leadership by virtue of the standoff at Kanayama, the Iwamatsu had their best chance to retrieve their lost lands. But the transaction quickly came to an impasse. Having guaranteed his support for the Iwamatsu petition—indeed, having given the Iwamatsu carte blanche about submitting their requests ("if you draw up a list of the lands you desire we shall agree to it"[45])—Kagenobu now balked. "We are in an awkward position regarding those lands: the Kawagoe as well as various families of Musashi and Sagami have displayed great loyalty since the disorders

44. For example, see *TKS* 2:93, no. 44 (Motegi monjo).

45. *Shōin shigo*, 823b.

of the Ōei and Eikyō eras [1394–1428 and 1429–41, respectively] and we must sanction their rights on the holdings they actually possess and administer."[46]

The "lands they actually possess and administer" were the lands that had once belonged to the Iwamatsu and that the family no longer ruled because of distance and war. Lands "not actually possessed" were holdings for which the rightful holders could do little more than display the tokens of rightful entitlement; others ruled them, others taxed them. These others, as it happens, were followers of the Uesugi or, as in the case of the Kawagoe, powerful collaterals. The Kawagoe were more generally known as the Ōgigayatsu Uesugi, but on occasion they were called by the name of one of the fortresses in Musashi, which they had made their home base. The Ōgigayatsu were trusted allies of the main Uesugi line and had been rewarded for their support, it seems, with the lands of the Iwamatsu—presumably before Iezumi gained the upper hand in his family and the Iwamatsu as a whole sided with the Uesugi. Other (lesser) families from Sagami and Musashi had also benefited from Uesugi largesse. They may have had ties to the Ōgigayatsu, whose power base was in those two provinces, though it is equally likely that Iwamatsu lands outside of Kōzuke—in Sagami and Musashi—were simply divvied up among local families to which the Uesugi owed gratitude.

It is not perfectly clear in *Shōin shigo* whether Kagenobu is saying that he had to sanction the claims of the de facto holders or that he will have to confirm them now, but what *is* apparent is that the Uesugi—or Nagao Kagenobu as their deputy—were compelled to recognize the fait accompli of their supporters' encroachments: the expression Shōin quotes Kagenobu as using, to sanction actual possession and administration of a holding (*tōchigyō mōshisata o itasu*), leaves no doubt that the lands in question were already in the hands of other families. Taking back lands from these local magnates now would be problematic, as these families had rendered loyal service—that is, had lent conspicuous military support—over many years. The dissolution after 1455 of the hierarchy of the Kamakura Office, while freeing the Uesugi from the supervision of

46. *Shōin shigo*, 824a. Both eras witnessed disturbances in the Kantō stemming from tensions between Kyoto and Kamakura.

Ashikaga Shigeuji and elevating them to the highest authority in the region, had also at the same time restricted the geographic scope of their power from eight provinces to three (Kōzuke, Musashi, and Sagami).[47] The pool of lands from which they could select parcels to reward deserving followers had contracted along with their political jurisdiction. The ongoing fighting produced a steady flow of new merit but the relative immobility of the frontline meant that no new lands were available for the Uesugi to confiscate and dole out.

Confronted with Kagenobu's inability to make good on his word, Shōin announced that the Iwamatsu would generously accept a compromise solution: "As for our ancestral holdings, as for the extra lands, in accordance with what was said privately of the portion that is problematic, we have accepted to receive the lesser claim and renounce the greater; is this not at variance with our truest wish?"[48] In other words, although Yokoze Kunishige had been guaranteed whatever he should request—both restitution of ancestral holdings seized by other families and new lands for the Iwamatsu warrior band—he would now settle for a lesser reward. As this clearly went against the Iwamatsu's true desires—and, Shōin implies, Nagao Kagenobu should have been grateful for being let off the hook so easily—surely the Uesugi would condescend to grant at least some compensation for the Iwamatsu's ancestral holdings? "If, in exchange for those lands, we should take possession of just a little of the land in the foothills of our castle, there could be no complaints toward us."[49]

Shōin wastes no time clarifying which land he has in mind: "Fuchina Estate and Sonoda Estate. Our ancestral holdings in Musashi and Sagami should have been returned; therefore, without first debating which is more and which is less, we say here that we would have these two estates entrusted to us."[50] The Iwamatsu would take two estates, Fuchina

---

47. Izu Province, which had at times fallen under the purview of Kantō authorities, had already become, at this time, the residence and jurisdiction of the Lord of Horigoe, Ashikaga Masatomo. Masatomo was aligned with Uesugi, but Izu remained separate from the three western provinces they governed.

48. *Shōin shigo*, 824a.

49. *Shōin shigo*, 824a. The statement (though not the decision) is actually attributed to Shōin, who was acting as Kunishige's messenger.

50. *Shōin shigo*, 824a.

and Sonoda, in exchange for the eighteen holdings that were being withheld from them. Was this a good deal? Were two estates worth more than eighteen holdings of various sizes? Our chronicler wants us to believe that the Iwamatsu leadership was generous in settling for these two estates. Having set up the defense of Kanayama in terms of epic heroism, any reward short of the restitution of rightfully claimed holdings, of the bestowal of new lands for landless retainers, could only be portrayed as stretching the good will of the Iwamatsu.

As it happened, the lands that Yokoze Kunishige so graciously agreed to receive lay just across the border from Nitta Estate. On Shōin's advice, Kunishige wasted no time in moving into and taking possession of (*nyūbu*) Sonoda and Fuchina: before an auspicious day came around, the Uesugi might change their mind and set new conditions. "Presently," Shōin writes, "Nagao Kagenobu circulated an official directive, disposing that there be no difficulties regarding our actually possessed and administered lands."[51] The circulation of a letter notifying local warriors of the deliberations of higher authorities was one of the prerogatives and duties of the deputy governors, an office that in Kōzuke was also controlled by the Nagao. The reward for loyal service to the Uesugi leadership was therefore invested with the officialdom of service rendered to the public authority of the province, the Uesugi governor, who also happened to be the highest representative of Kyoto in the Kantō. The Uesugi had acquired the right to dispose of requisitioned lands as part of the expansion of their gubernatorial authority in the early years of the fifteenth century and, indeed, the very word used for the bestowal of land to the Iwamatsu, *azukeoku* ("to entrust"), suggests that rights over these two estates were transferred by the Uesugi in their official capacity.[52]

Whereas the old (lost) lands were ancestral holdings, the new ones were *entrusted* to the Iwamatsu. Yet such a seemingly fundamental distinction may have been of consequence only right after the transfer, for time had a way of making rights inalienable. Indeed, Shōin's account

51. *Shōin shigo*, 824a. Literally, "no changes" (*sōi nashi*), meaning that the situation on the ground was to be accepted and legitimated—that the lands were "actually possessed and administered" by the Iwamatsu, who had taken control of them and were present there.

52. Kubota, "Chūsei kōki Kōzuke," 54, 56.

does not linger on the point at all, emphasizing instead the ultimately advantageous nature of the deal. "There are no grounds to doubt in our hearts that the various new lands are a precious gain," Shōin admits in *Shōin shigo*, many years after the fact.[53] They were a precious gain, first and foremost, because they were actually possessed and administered, whereas the old, scattered holdings, eighteen though they may have been, were out of the Iwamatsu's actual reach. Would it have been preferable to recover the ancestral holdings in Musashi and Sagami? What had the Iwamatsu gained in the bargain?

Fuchina lay just west of Nitta Estate, and was made up of some thirteen known villages.[54] Though not as extensive as Nitta, Fuchina had a long history. It was established in 1130 as an estate set aside especially to supply the kitchens of a cloister of Ninnaji, a temple back in Kyoto.[55] Several temple holdings were created and existed (nominally, at least) within the boundaries of Fuchina Estate, and over time local administration passed through a number of warrior families, finally to fall into the hands of the Uesugi in the fourteenth century, possibly as a holding attached to the office of governor of Kōzuke.[56] In yielding the estate to the Iwamatsu, then, the Uesugi preferred to give of their own rather than take lands away from their followers and allies. (It is worth noting that in the 1478 register mentioned in Chapter 2, Ninnaji still listed Fuchina as its holding, albeit among those it no longer administered.)[57]

The case of Sonoda Estate was similar in important respects. Sonoda was Nitta's neighbor to the north.[58] Dating back at least to 1172, it was a long and narrow estate that extended northwest–southeast along the

53. *Shōin shigo*, 824a.

54. The Rekihaku Nihon shōen database lists thirteen village names recorded in sources, but two of them appear to be different ways of writing the same name (Moro Village): http://www.rekihaku.ac.jp/up-cgi/login.pl?p=param/soue/db_param (shōen kōdo 2512001; accessed November 10, 2004). There is also a good map of the estate in *Gunma kenshi tsūshi hen* 3:63.

55. Amino, *Tōhoku, Kantō, Tōkai chihō no shōen*, 54–55; and Rekihaku Nihon shōen database.

56. Kubota, "Chūsei kōki Kōzuke," 54.

57. *GKS* 7, no. 1765 (Ninnaji monjo).

58. *Shōin shigo* (824a, 830b, 831a) calls it "Sonoda no shō," but in other documents it appears as "Sonoda no mikuriya."

foothills of the mountains. The estate is known to have been made up of four holdings variously connected to the Great Shrine of Ise, although part of it at one time produced revenue for the Lords of Kamakura as well.[59] This last detail is significant, for it opens up the possibility that the Uesugi had taken control of Sonoda by force after the war had begun with Shigeuji, the former Lord of Kamakura: as part of the portfolio of landholdings of an enemy, the Uesugi may well have felt at liberty to reassign the lands in Sonoda to their own supporters.[60] Indirect corroboration for this hypothesis comes in the form of a missive, written a few years later, from Shigeuji to Yokoze Kunishige, confirming Kunishige's claims to Sonoda (the missive is undated but was almost certainly produced a few years after the negotiation, between 1477 and 1483; at that time the Iwamatsu shifted their allegiance to Shigeuji). The letter suggests that if indeed the Uesugi had handed over to the Iwamatsu a landholding only recently acquired, the Iwamatsu would have been keen on securing confirmation for their new entitlement to Sonoda from Shigeuji (the land's erstwhile holder) as soon as their relations with him improved.[61] We have no way of knowing why, how, or when exactly the estate was handed over from the Iwamatsu to their Yokoze followers; what seems clear enough is that at the time of the negotiation the lands were the Uesugi's to give away.

It is easy enough to see what Iezumi stood to gain from the new round of negotiations, but what he was expected to give up is more difficult to document. The contents of the Iwamatsu family's portfolio of landed interests are not known to us with any precision. To be sure, there are scattered references in the family's collected documents to lands gained and (far more seldom) to lands lost, but we generally have

---

59. See Yamada, *Kamakura-fu to Kantō*, 261–62; and the Rekihaku Nihon shōen database: http://www.rekihaku.ac.jp/up-cgi/login.pl?p=param/soue/ db_param (shōen kōdo 2510002; accessed November 10, 2004).

60. We know that the Iwamatsu may have had designs on Sonoda since 1471, when a letter from Nagao Kagenobu to Yokoze Kunishige makes an elliptical reference to a decision concerning that estate. *TKS* 4:452, no. 2 (Shūko monjo).

61. *GKS* 7, no. 1823 (Yura monjo). Interestingly, in the same letter Shigeuji also confirms Yokoze Kunishige's actual administration and possession (*tōchigyō*) of another holding, Ryōmai (variously referred to as an estate and a village), which at one point Shōin suggests was obtained from the Nagao (*Shōin shigo*, 811a, 830b–831a).

little more than an impressionistic grasp of the changes that occurred over time. (A detailed profile of the eighteen lost holdings—if it were possible—would shed light on the plight of warrior families with landholdings scattered beyond their reach in a time of war. Here I limit my discussion to a few points salient to our understanding of the negotiation and its significance.) Besides individual documents attesting to individual transactions, two existing rolls tally the family's real and nominal possessions beyond the borders of Nitta. These are known as *Iwamatsu Mitsukuni shoryō chūmon* (A register of the holdings of Iwamatsu Mitsukuni), produced in 1395, and *Iwamatsu Mochikuni honryō tokorodokoro chūmon* (A register of the various ancestral holdings of Iwamatsu Mochikuni), which is not dated—though it can be no earlier than 1435.[62] These two texts tell us of Iwamatsu claims to at least thirteen distinct holdings in the provinces of Musashi and Sagami (Map 3.2). Yet we cannot conclude that these thirteen holdings were surely among the ones Shōin has in mind in his memoir. Assuming that our chronicler is not lying outright and there were indeed eighteen *lost* holdings, it follows evidently that the tallies provided in the two rolls are partial, and that we do not know what portion they represent of the lands the family claimed as its own.

One thing the two rolls do help us see is how diverse and scattered Iwamatsu holdings were, and how complex medieval tenurial arrangements could be. Of the thirteen holdings we know about, two were in Sagami and eleven in Musashi. The eleven holdings in Musashi were spread out through ten of the province's twenty-one districts;[63] they comprised portions of private estates as well as (privately held) public lands and included whole villages, hamlets within villages (*mura*), small units of arable with residences attached to them (*zaike*), and even individual

---

62. *GKS* 5:264, nos. 100 and 101 (Masaki monjo). In a recent essay ("Kyōtoku no ran no futatsu no Nitta Iwamatsu-shi," 75), Minegishi Sumio implies that Mochikuni's register was produced around the beginning of the civil war, for Shigeuji confirmed his rights to several scattered holdings in letters dated 1455.

63. That is, the districts of Tachibana, Obusuma, Hiki, Tama, Ōsato, Hanzawa, Adachi, Koma, Ebara, and Saitama (2). Musashi was classified as a "Great Province" (*taikoku*, the largest of four categories into which provinces countrywide were organized) and was made up of twenty-one districts (see the map in Amino, *Tōhoku, Kantō, Tōkai chihō no shōen*, 207).

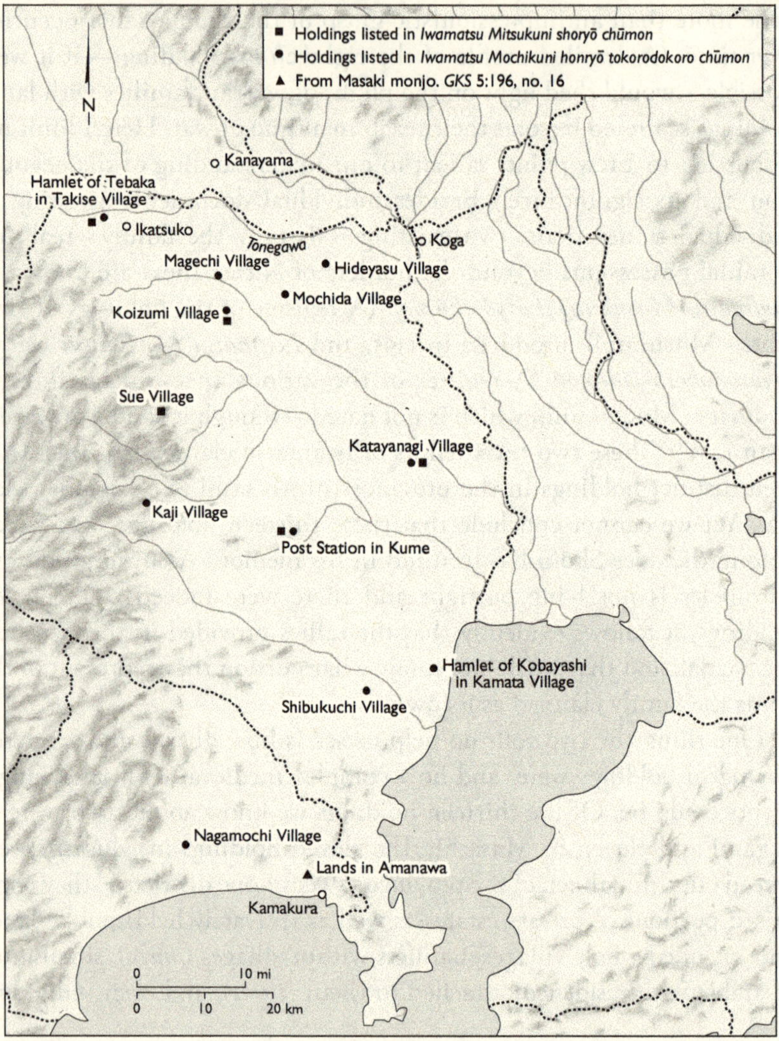

Map 3.2. Tentative identification of some of the eighteen holdings mentioned in *Shōin shigo*.

named plots (*myō*, the basic units for taxation of land). Estimating how much land this added up to is difficult: we often have no idea of the area of these individual named plots, which were the smallest units of farmland taxation but which nonetheless managed to be of variable size, as well as fragmented and scattered throughout a community. The small lands with residences were less fragmented but no less difficult to measure. A whole hamlet, moreover, or a village, might cover a known area, though what percentage of that was actually farmed and assessed—especially in underpopulated and underdeveloped Musashi—is far from clear.

Ultimately, what we *can* know of the Iwamatsu's eighteen holdings comes in the form of impressions—more than guesses but considerably less than certainties. We may not know finally *which* holdings Shōin had in mind, but from the two registers we can nevertheless form a relatively accurate picture of the sort of holdings the Iwamatsu were likely to have: scattered villages—sometimes only small hamlets, or individual plots—surrounded by lands ruled by other magnates. A number of them were along important roads (various branches of the Kamakura Road), or near major rivers (Arakawa, Irumagawa, Tamagawa, and Tonegawa). Taken individually they were not impressive, but their cumulative size—and it bears emphasizing that the Iwamatsu maintained holdings in several other provinces as well—was respectable, especially when we consider that the bulk of the family's lands were in Nitta Estate.

The state of our sources does not allow us to judge the truthfulness of Yokoze Kunishige's tally, or of Shōin's recollection. Kunishige's petition, though, had to be credible; according to *Shōin shigo*, Kunishige's counterpart in the negotiation, Nagao Kagenobu, asked the monk to "draw up a record" of the lands Kunishige and the Iwamatsu desired. However many parcels of land the chief retainer of the Iwamatsu tried to reclaim, Nagao Kagenobu would have been able to examine his request and its merits. Kagenobu's demand for documentation, moreover, further illustrates a pattern we have already encountered, to wit, the existence of a consensual, presumably ubiquitous, reliance on the trappings of a legal and notarial practice through which the elaborate claims and counterclaims of warriors were processed, even in an age of upheaval. Whether or not each item on Yokoze Kunishige's list stood up to scrutiny, it is certain that the Iwamatsu felt they had legitimate claims to those holdings. The indeterminacy of Shōin's expression, of his "eighteen places," is entirely our own problem.[64] The complex histories

64. "Since we followed Shogun Takauji," notes Shōin, referring to the village of Iwamatsu, "for generations it has been the land that gives our family its name," *Shōin shigo*, 805a. The passage reminds us that Shōin had a clear knowledge of Iwamatsu family history, and of its relation to land: he does not place the acquisition of the village of

of individual holdings by no means prevented contemporaries from making circumstantiated and profusely documented claims to specific, clearly located, and minutely known pieces of land. When Shōin refers to the eighteen holdings to which the Iwamatsu claimed an entitlement, he knows precisely which parcels he is referring to. So does Nagao Kagenobu, when he reluctantly confesses to doling them out to other supporters.

Admittedly, neither Shōin the writer nor Shōin the negotiator ever enumerates the lands Kagenobu should return. The lack of precision is no doubt intentional, given our author's otherwise irrepressible penchant for line-by-line, script-like reconstructions of conversations. Perhaps the talks never got far enough for the two sides to sit down and compile a list. Or perhaps writing decades later about the long-lost holdings in the aggregate, Shōin did not find enumeration to be particularly useful, or particularly good storytelling. Be that as it may, the omission of details by both parties—or by the author, retrospectively—suggests a clear understanding of the terms of the negotiation. And so our interpretation of such coyness largely depends on how we view the outcome of the negotiation, in terms of both its concrete stipulations and its symbolic value—on how Shōin (the writer) wants us to view it. Because of the reticence of the documentary record, and its resistance to unequivocal conclusions, all we are left with is the vaguely unsatisfying sense that for the parties involved the terms of the exchange were reasonable, or at least acceptable enough for the negotiation to conclude favorably: eighteen holdings for two estates; distant scattered lands for nearby, contiguous ones. The land areas were roughly comparable, though lacking as we do any quantifiable information on the scattered ancestral holdings this is as close to an estimate as we can get.[65]

Iwamatsu in Takauji's time, but correctly notes that it was since then that the Iwamatsu had become the main house of the extended Nitta family.

65. Sonoda and Fuchina were made up of about sixteen villages between the two of them (twelve villages in Fuchina, four holdings in Sonoda). Given the variable sizes of villages, that is not enough for a hard-and-fast conclusion. Still, it suggests that they were of the same order of magnitude as the lost holdings taken collectively.

Land as Currency, Holdings as Genealogy

Remarks in *Shōin shigo* do provide hints that help identify and date the acquisition of these "eighteen places," or at least narrow down the list of possible matches, but what is more significant is how such remarks shed light on what the Iwamatsu valued in their lost lands. Repeatedly, the chronicle speaks of holdings in "eighteen places, held for generations, since the time of the great general." Shōin does not state so explicitly, but the great general is almost certainly Ashikaga Takauji, the first Muromachi shogun.[66] Although he was not the only shogun to be held in special honor by the Iwamatsu, he is the only one to be consistently remembered with that title.[67] In particular, Takauji is evoked in his official capacity every time a claim to antiquity is put forth. Together, "for generations" and "Shogun Takauji" become a formulaic phrase, a mantra providing the ultimate seal of validation for any claim.[68] A precedent that stood for generations, since the time of the first Muromachi shogun, *must* trump any subsequent development. The association is so firmly established that reference to "generations since the great shogun," even without explicit mention of Takauji, can leave little doubt about who is being called to witness.

Any attempt to piece together more of the picture Shōin suggests with a brief stroke of his brush would distract us from his main concerns as a negotiator and an apologist of the Iwamatsu cause. A quantitative analysis of the negotiation only tells part of the story, and remains blind

---

66. Technically, we cannot speak of a "Muromachi shogun" until Yoshiakira, Takauji's son and successor, completed his palace on Muromachi Avenue in 1381. For the sake of simplicity and clarity, I follow common practice and uniform my usage by considering "Muromachi regime" essentially equivalent to "Ashikaga regime."

67. Yoshinori is revered above all Ashikaga for patronizing the young Iezumi during his exile and enabling the second flourishing of the Nitta family but, perhaps because of his personal relationship with Iezumi, *Shōin shigo* always refers to him as Lord Fukōin.

68. "Our house in the generations since Shogun Takauji," *Shōin shigo*, 788a; "Since we followed Shogun Takauji, for generations it has been the land that gives our family its name," *Shōin shigo*, 805a; "[Ours has been] a house venerated for generations, since the time of Shogun Takauji," *Shōin shigo*, 806a; and, "For generations since Shogun Takauji our inherited title (*kanto*) has been Jibu taifu," *Shōin shigo*, 836b. For references to Yoshinori, see *Shōin shigo*, 788a, 789a, 795b, 805a, 806a, 810a, 833b, and 845a.

to all aspects of the episode that transcended the purely material transaction and that are most important to Shōin. And so our dependence on *Shōin shigo*, while foreclosing certain avenues of research, opens up new ones, closer, perhaps, to the heart of the episode. Shōin's double role as narrator and protagonist of his own narration affords us great intimacy with both his convictions and the mood in the Iwamatsu family. It was *for* (not just *about*) the Iwamatsu that Shōin was writing—with a not-so-subtle wink to posterity.

In exalting his own acumen, bravery, wit, moral uprightness, and learning for the generations to come, our author nevertheless makes repeated professions of boundless admiration for Iezumi, the "second founder" of the family's fortunes, and Kunishige, his brilliant and loyal chief retainer. No doubt, with his memoir Shōin meant to laud his late lords and their heirs (also his lords), and humor their followers. The language of his memoir is largely shaped by this concern, and the text as a whole reverberates with the Iwamatsu's sense of dignity and entitlement. The negotiation of 1472–73 is just one iteration of a motif sounded again and again, but one meant to validate Iwamatsu feelings of (wounded) self-worth through the creation of an episode that encapsulates the family's position and is narrated in a tone consonant with the family's aspirations.[69]

Considered in its economic dimension, the transaction fits squarely within the well-known context of late medieval land tenure and its transformation. The dispersion of a family's resources—the result of hundreds of years of accretion and shedding through inheritance, purchase, bestowal, dowry, donation, relocation, reclamation, encroachment, and litigation—became a liability as several parts of the country spiraled into war. Long-distance travel and movement of goods became arduous,

69. Clearly, this is how later generations of Iwamatsu viewed Shōin's lifework. According to *Nitta Iwamatsu-shi keizu furoku* (*GKS* 5:337), "This memoir was a work written in the Eishō era by a man named Shōinken, [*lacuna*]teenth head of Chōrakuji in Serada. This man was an intimate advisor to [Iezumi], the founder of the second flowering of this house, and from him on to Akizumi, Hisazumi, and Masazumi, over four generations, he recorded the actions of Sōetsu and Sōchū of the Yokoze house of chief retainers."

and oversight of distant assets intermittent. Just like other absentee proprietors, families with particularly fragmented holdings faced serious challenges from interlopers and subordinates, who tested those families' ability to string disparate parcels of lands into a coherent swath of territory and into a defensible whole.

Soon enough, by the middle of the sixteenth century at the latest, it would become apparent that the landscape was being reshaped. The families that had succeeded in molding coherent (and cohesive) domains out of their holdings survived and superseded others that had held sway over loosely knit collections of lands. Crucial to this process of domain building, it seems, was the ability or the failure to consolidate a family's holdings, and to know and manipulate those of followers. Eastern examples of these efforts are the *Odawara-shū shoryō yakuchō* (Service roll of the holdings of Odawara warrior bands, 1559) compiled by the Hōjō family,[70] and the more modest, more precocious, and more dubious *Motegi kashin kyūbun chūmon* (Register of grants to Motegi housemen, 1482).[71]

Rule over a circumscribed area, but with (more) exclusive and far-reaching authority has been posited as a precondition for the gradual creation of new, markedly centralized domains that eventually grew to encompass entire provinces. Compared to the territories loosely strewn together by governors in the fourteenth and early fifteenth centuries—part private property, part lands controlled ex officio and doled out in hopes of securing the loyalty of provincials—the new wartime domains of the late fifteenth and sixteenth centuries were sturdily structured, built from the inside out and invasively managed, in an exercise of authority that reached as deeply as possible into every corner of the lord's jurisdiction

70. Sugiyama, *Odawara-shū shoryō yakuchō.*

71. *TKS* 2:93, no. 45 (Motegi monjo). The original document is no longer extant and available for examination; scholars have pointed to anachronisms in the text (perplexed mostly by such an early date of compilation for a small, and presumably unsophisticated provincial player such as the Motegi family) to cast doubt on its authenticity. See Iinuma Shunsuke, in *Motegi chōshi*, 5:372–81; Shinkawa, *Shimotsuke chūseishi no shinkenkyū*, 285–300; Shinkawa, in *Tochigi kenshi tsūshi hen* 3:614–25; Nagahara, "Motegi-shi kyūninchō kō."

and interfered consistently in his subordinates' affairs.[72] Building on a practice begun in the previous century, sixteenth-century lords came to issue prohibitions and regulations not only to keep the peace, but to regulate market towns and villages.[73] Still far from reaching the level of integration and cohesion of early modern domains, their wartime forerunners of the mid- to late sixteenth century constitute nonetheless a significant move away from the patterns of rule that had been prevalent in the Kantō until the high Muromachi period (1392–1455).

Local magnates with a smaller land base often found themselves at an advantage over their lordly rivals: the narrow horizons of Nitta Estate, for instance, allowed for easier consolidation than the open fields of Musashi and Kōzuke, over which the Uesugi exercised their authority. Although the division of the Kantō into two competing halves ultimately pushed the Uesugi along the path to localization, their eventual attempt to entrench themselves in Kōzuke was belated and half-hearted. Even though they controlled a great many holdings in that province, these were not nearly enough for them to establish a territorial rule comparable to that of local families with lesser pedigrees but deeper roots. The Uesugi had long since relied upon the authority they derived from Kyoto and their ability to add the endorsement of the shogun to the

72. The use of the word *ryōgoku*, commonly translated as "domain," is widespread. A purely historiographical concept, it applies the idea of the proprietary holding (*ryō*) to the provincial framework (*koku*). While the idea works well for Edo period *han*, and to a lesser extent for mid-sixteenth-century warring states, its applicability to the Muromachi order—to the relationship between governors and the provinces they administered in particular—is problematic. Nevertheless, the word is applied as early as the fourteenth century, to provinces that governors came to administer hereditarily. See, for instance, Katsumori, *Nagao-shi no kenkyū*, 238–85, and in the titles of several chapters and sections; Minegishi, *Chūsei no tōgoku*, 243; *Gunma kenshi tsūshi hen* 3:394; and Sugiyama, who uses it even in the title of his article, "Shugo ryōgokusei no tenkai to Ōishi-shi."

73. Kobayashi S., *Hideyoshi kenryoku no keisei*, 201–3. Yamada Kuniaki ("Muromachi-ki Kantō no shihai kōzō to zaichi shakai," 86–87) distinguishes Muromachi authorities and sixteenth-century warlords by noting that the former exercised their authority to shore up the interests of the proprietary class, not concerning themselves with micromanagement of local communities, while the latter showed an active interest in interfering with village society and controlling commercial towns.

favor they bestowed on provincial warriors (hence their dogged continuation of received governing practices even during the years of war). The progressive unhinging of the political order centered in Kyoto left the Uesugi caught up in a network of patronage that no longer had a central underpinning.

The Iwamatsu, by contrast, were in the position to make a timely conversion to a new brand of local rule, predicated on self-contained islands of power: by renouncing their far-flung interests they were able to solidify their hold on southeastern Kōzuke, shoring up their position in the face not only of regional powers like the Uesugi and the Lords of Koga, but also of rival local magnates. The first step in the Iwamatsu's drive toward a tighter control over their followers and lands was Iezumi's unification of the two lines of the family. The ceremony in Kanayama that signaled the renewed unity of the family to friends and rivals also celebrated the reunification of the estate, over all of which the Iwamatsu, now more than ever before, held sway. The concentration of all authority over Nitta Estate, then, was the first step toward the consolidation of all family holdings. In this sense, the Iwamatsu were particularly fortunate in their second step: instead of simply acknowledging the hopelessness of trying to defend their eighteen ancestral holdings, they managed to parley their renunciation into a trade. In exchange for holdings that, in fact, had long ceased to be theirs, the Iwamatsu were able to obtain two estates that tangibly strengthened their position, bordering as they did with Nitta and adding to a growing area of continuous and exclusive Iwamatsu rule.

The new estates bestowed on the Iwamatsu were not controlled by local magnates: expropriating them—indeed, evicting them—would have set off a new round of fighting and further undermined the Uesugi's coalition at a time when it was already shaky. Rather, rights to Sonoda and Fuchina had been held by the Uesugi and by absentee proprietors who had little hope of petitioning for their restitution and no means of recovering them on their own. They lost their lands in Kōzuke very much as the Iwamatsu had lost theirs in Musashi and Sagami. Conversely, when Yokoze Kunishige and Shōin appealed to Nagao Kagenobu for the restitution of the eighteen ancestral holdings in Musashi and Sagami, Kagenobu replied that he was in no position to deny the loyal families of those two provinces confirmation of the holdings they had acquired. In other words, the Iwamatsu holdings had most probably been seized, in some cases at least, by local warriors, Ōgigayatsu/Kawagoe *in primis.* Kagenobu, even as commander in chief of forces loyal to the Uesugi, could do little more than stamp his seal of approval. In previous centuries, income from a village could be earmarked and forwarded to a temple far away; now instead we can imagine an entire holding taken over, more or less by force, by local magnates, as seen in the plight of Tōkōji (in Chapter 2), which stood helpless as all of the income from one of its holdings was siphoned off by interlopers despite Kagenobu's best efforts at mediation.

Seen in this light, the trajectory of the Iwamatsu mirrors that of countless families in eastern Japan during these same years, and their stance in the negotiation, their initial requests, were really a feint aimed at pushing Nagao Kagenobu into a corner, to force him to offer up as compensation their real targets: Sonoda Estate and Fuchina Estate. On paper, the land areas of what was renounced and what was gained were comparable, but in fact the Iwamatsu were trading an entitlement long devoid of any substance for real—revenue-generating—land. (At least one piece of evidence, moreover, indicates that the Iwamatsu had long entertained designs on Sonoda: in a letter written to the chief retainer of the powerful Ōgigayatsu Uesugi sometime before 1471, a provincial magnate named Oyama Mochimasa complained of Yokoze Kunishige's encroachment upon Sonoda, and demanded that the Uesugi put a stop to it.)[74] Not surprisingly, Shōin urged Yokoze Kunishige not to waste any time moving into the two estates and claiming them for the Iwamatsu. His colorful words to Kunishige, who proposed to wait for an auspicious day, are telling: "If we delay for a while, we won't get this done. Did the men of old not say so? 'What is good for heaven and earth is not fitting for the actions of men,' it is said. Today [is the

74. *KKS* 1, no. 198 (Kankōji shozō monjo). The letter is dated (approximately) on the basis of the titles used by Mochimasa to address the letter's recipient (Ōta Dōkan) and refer to Kunishige, both of which changed in 1471. It is not clear whether Dōkan was able to give Mochimasa satisfaction. Mochimasa, who at the time was still backing Shigeuji, shifted sides in 1471.

day]!"[75] Waste any time, and Nagao Kagenobu might go back on his word once again.

But if Shōin's phrasing matters at all here, we would do well to bear in mind the tone he strikes *throughout* the episode—and the memoir. The process of consolidation as I have outlined it certainly captures many of the broad trends that unfolded over a century or so, but it leaves out other voices crucial to our understanding of the period itself—of the mood in 1472–73. It leaves out Shōin's voice, for one, and so in a sense disregards how the Iwamatsu viewed the factors at play in the exchange. It focuses on the broader historical trend—undeniable as it may be—and forgets the moment, and the understanding of contemporaries. It confuses the outcome with the intent.

If we concluded that the "eighteen places" were merely evoked as leverage to obtain something else, we would be left with a number of problems: Why would Shōin go to such lengths to remind his readership—the leadership of the Iwamatsu—of the great cost of the transaction? Assuredly, he wrote after the fact that Iezumi and the Iwamatsu had every reason to be content with the result. Still, in his account he dwells upon the gains far less than he does on the bargaining itself, and his satisfaction is curiously muted for one who never seems to run out of words to praise his own contributions. It undoubtedly made sense, when confronting Nagao Kagenobu, to wax eloquent about Iezumi's attachment to his ancestral holdings: the greater the Iwamatsu's loss was, the greater Kagenobu's obligation to compensate them would be. But would the reevocation of the loss (however distant in the past) not remind the family's leadership of a regrettable concession? These were no run-of-the-mill holdings; these were ancestral holdings, handed down since the days of Shogun Takauji. Further, Shōin was not writing right after the events: the whole of his chronicle was committed to paper more than three decades later. The loss might have been underscored during the negotiation itself, in 1472–73, but there is no reason to assume the author would feel bound to hew to the facts so closely as to risk the displeasure of his own lords after 1509—particularly since there was no need to

75. *Shōin shigo*, 824a.

blandish a long-dead Kagenobu, or his descendants, none of whom would ever read *Shōin shigo* or, probably, hear of its existence.[76]

What if Iezumi had indeed sought the return of the ancestral holdings, and only grudgingly settled for a second-best option? What if the restitution of the holdings was what he truly wanted, and not a feint? Plainly, this is what the text itself wants us to think, if we but heed what it says. This reading would allow us to make sense of some of the peculiarities of the narration, for it explains the emphasis placed on the holdings and the belated mention of satisfaction—real though it certainly was—for the acquisition of two new estates. Also, it satisfies the need to reduce the dishonor for those involved in what seems to have been a bittersweet outcome, by laying the blame on the shoulders not of Shōin and Kunishige but of the Uesugi chief retainer, Nagao Kagenobu. This reading better justifies the space devoted to Kagenobu's rather duplicitous dealing; to his repeated assurances to Kunishige that he would satisfy his requests, which he recognized as legitimate; and then, to his confessing, finally, to signing off on (and condoning) those lands' seizure for the sake of political expediency. Yet as this interpretation irons out one difficulty, it raises another: Why would the Iwamatsu rather recover their old holdings, distant and scattered and, ultimately, difficult to exploit and impossible to defend? I do not wish to suggest that they failed to recognize the bounty that had come their way. By the time Shōin completed his account, nearly forty more years of turmoil would have illuminated the drawbacks of the structure of power on which the Uesugi had founded their primacy. Yet what in retrospect could be seen as a windfall may not have been unquestionably the best course of action at the time.

What I think is important to consider is the way power was perceived, and the variety of ties it was understood to have with land: land

76. We know that *Shōin shigo* was completed in 1509 (*Shōin shigo*, 846b). As for when Shōin began the actual draft, it is reasonable to assume that it was after the death of Iezumi, who is called throughout the text by his posthumous name, Lord Genkeiin, or simply Genkei. Moreover, the text's very structure, more akin to a memoir than a chronicle in its utter disregard for chronology, suggests a retrospective retelling. Still, it is possible that the various scrolls were written at intervals, over an extended period of time, rather than all in 1509.

was viewed and treated as a form of political currency and genealogy. Holdings were currency, most obviously, in that land was the most sought-after reward for loyal service, and thus was, quite literally, bestowed and claimed in accordance with quantifiable expectations. At its most immediate level, the negotiation between Yokoze Kunishige and Nagao Kagenobu was predicated on this shared assumption. The issue of the quantification of the reward for the Iwamatsu—should they succeed in stemming the enemy's advance—was raised even before the plan of action was drawn up for the military campaign. The rest of the negotiation, after the siege of Kanayama, was aimed at sorting out differences in the practical aspects of the recompense, not contesting its theoretical quantification. And never once was it questioned that the currency in which gratitude should be expressed was land, or that gratitude—honor and reward—were, together with loyal service, the glue that held the political order together.

But whereas land served as currency in transactions with other families, in a warrior family's internal dynamics land's genealogical dimension was more central, and was apparent in the way warrior families were, themselves, politically dependent on their lands. They were beholden to them not only economically, for the resources they yielded and the manpower they provided (not least for war); warrior families' ties to their lands were deeper: in them were inscribed a family's identity, its sense of familial continuity, and the evidence of its prestige. Each parcel of land had its history, however obscure and mystifying to us, centuries later; each holding carried in its name associations with the family's past, the memory of the merits through which it was obtained. A holding's name was a sort of heraldic shorthand for a moment in the family's own history—a moment that, by its very nature, reinforced the family's sense of accomplishment and self-worth.[77]

Take the Iwamatsu. Some of their lands came to them from the original Nitta main house, of which the Iwamatsu were once no more than a collateral line: the village of Iwamatsu, for instance, was donated to

77. Scattered holdings (*sanzai shoryō*) were acquired mostly in two ways: as dowries in matrimonial alliances or as rewards for loyal service. See Minegishi, *Chūsei no tōgoku*, 102. For the idea that names of places carried in them social values exemplified by events that occurred in those places, see Basso, *Wisdom Sits in Places*.

Iezumi's forefathers along with other villages beyond the borders of the estate. Having established their residence in the village, the Iwamatsu eventually came to be known by its name. In this sense, not only the village of Iwamatsu but also the other villages that were received at the same time came to be intimately tied to one of the founding moments of the Iwamatsu house, which would eventually go on to succeed to the Nitta main line. The Iwamatsu rose by siding with Ashikaga Takauji in his struggle against Emperor Godaigo and his backers in the 1330s. Among those backers were the members of the main line of the Nitta, so the Iwamatsu's decision to back Takauji represented a dramatic turning point in the family's history.

The momentous decision to side with the Ashikaga boosted Iwamatsu fortunes economically as well as politically, for Takauji, victorious, rewarded them with at least four new holdings in Musashi alone (and backed them in their struggle to emerge as the main house of the Nitta). It is not at all surprising, then, that the later of the family's two extant registers (*Iwamatsu Mochikuni honryō tokorodokoro chūmon*) would reaffirm the Iwamatsu family's rights over three of the four holdings, even though they had been lost forty years before. These lands were not only among the ancestral holdings of the family; their sheer presence on the roll proclaimed unequivocally the magnitude and antiquity of Iwamatsu prestige. Other lands, later, were received from one of the Lords of Kamakura. Like the successive shoguns in Kyoto, the Lords of Kamakura, too, were descended from Ashikaga Takauji; they were the highest authorities in eastern Japan. Yet even the Lords of Kamakura could not confer (and confirm) the sort of prestige the Iwamatsu wished to convey. Shōin's attention is caught by lands held "for generations," since the time of Takauji. For it was those lands that could fittingly reward a family whose loyal service Shōin is fond of deeming "without equal."[78]

78. "Great loyal service, unequaled in the Kantō" (*Shōin shigo*, 823a); "as a reward for loyal service unequaled in the Kantō" (*Shōin shigo*, 810b); even the Lord of Koga would later agree that the Iwamatsu displayed "loyalty without equal among the various houses of the Kantō since the disturbance" (*Shōin shigo*, 787b); and, "His lordship pronounced forthwith that among the various houses ours was of a loyalty unequaled" (*Shōin shigo*, 803a). The word "unequaled" (*musō*) is actually extremely common, and

The Iwamatsu had a complex and at times frustrating relationship with their past and, as a consequence, with the Uesugi. As scions of the Nitta family, the Iwamatsu had historically been in an unusual position vis-à-vis the Ashikaga and their power structure. The Uesugi were part of this power structure, and so were eyed by the Iwamatsu with a mixture of envy and contempt. Shōin likes to trace Iwamatsu relations with the Ashikaga all the way back to the rivalry between Ashikaga Takauji and Nitta Yoshisada, musing about his family's past glory and present decline: "The thinning of our forces is regrettable, I feel. This house's withering is something the Bodhisattva Hachiman's inscrutable will must have decreed. If the lords of Town and Country [that is, of Kyoto and Koga], are not declining, why must our house decline?"[79] Though their paths had since diverged, the Nitta (Iwamatsu) and the Ashikaga had once competed for the same prize: "In antiquity, Ashikaga Takauji and Nitta Yoshisada, following an imperial command, battled like dragons, fought like tigers. . . . Except for Takauji, whom he considered his foe, Yoshisada did not flatter the generals and the fifty thousand riders of other houses, it is said."[80] And never mind that the Iwamatsu began their rise by siding with Takauji, against their own relative and family chieftain Yoshisada.

The principle that bowing to the Ashikaga did not mean bowing to any of their followers is reiterated throughout *Shōin shigo* with a kind of desperate passion. The Iwamatsu had forged with the Ashikaga a special relationship. They had sided with Takauji, implicitly recognizing his suzerainty. Over the years they were rewarded for this stance, and afforded a direct link of subordination to the ruling shogunal family. To it alone did the Iwamatsu—who were, after all, heirs to the Nitta—bow: whenever he can, Shōin reminds his readers that Iezumi had enjoyed the personal favor of the late shogun, Yoshinori (r. 1429–41); he

---

achieving greatness "unequaled in the Kantō" was not as hard as we may imagine. For more professions of uniqueness, see *SKS* 5, no. 1019 (*Koshōmon*); *Shōin shigo*, 831a; *TKS* 2:129, nos. 49, 50 (Nasu monjo); 2:107, no. 71 (Motegi monjo); 3:119, no. 4 (Jōka shoshi monjo); and *TKS* 4:317, no. 21 (Gonaishofuan). Within the narrower confines of Nitta Estate, Kunishige and his son displayed "a loyalty unequaled in this house's ten thousand generations" (*Shōin shigo*, 803b).

79. *Shōin shigo*, 819b.

80. *Shōin shigo*, 803b.

was appointed as one of the three commanders sent to chastise the Lord of Kamakura during the Disturbance of Eikyō, in 1440.[81] As someone who had risen in the world through a personal, direct tie to the shogun, Iezumi bristled at the notion that the Uesugi—mere deputies of the shogun's own official—should demand his allegiance and treat him as a subordinate. Institutionally, the Uesugi were invested with two layers of authority over the Iwamatsu: first, as deputies of the Lords of Kamakura (however estranged they were from Shigeuji at the time of the negotiation) they had ruled over all of the warrior families of the Kantō; now they derived their office—the same office, though with a different set of prerogatives—directly from Kyoto, as they stood behind the "Town" in its conflict with the "Country." Second, the jurisdiction of the Uesugi as governors of Kōzuke Province included Nitta Estate, though the Uesugi were not oblivious to the Iwamatsu family's special ties to Kyoto.[82]

The decline of which Shōin speaks can be seen in terms of the multiple paths to social and political eminence available under the Muromachi regime, and the Iwamatsu's success or failure in traveling them: like many of the old magnates of the northern part of the plain (such as the Oyama, Utsunomiya, Sano, and Yūki families, for instance), the Iwamatsu had not played a central role in the administration of the Kamakura Office. This was part of the reason for the institutional imbalance of power in Kōzuke, and unsurprisingly in *Shōin shigo* the Iwamatsu never frame their relationship with the Uesugi in institutional terms. What matters in the memoir are name, genealogy, status. Here too, though, the Iwamatsu's name shone less than it once had, for the travails of Iezumi's line, and the familial strife that kept its leadership busy for much of the fifteenth century, dimmed the family's luster. For many years it was Iezumi's rivals, the former junior line, who were

81. *Shōin shigo*, 805b.

82. In outlining the relations between the two families, Matsumoto Kazuo (*Tōgoku shugo*, 289–92) describes them not as those between lords and vassals, but as those between governors and traditional local magnates—a jurisdictional relationship, in other words, not one of personal fealty. The statement says more about the looseness of the Uesugi network of attachment than it does about the Iwamatsu's special status.

addressed in documents by the family's ancestral name of Nitta. Iezumi was not honored with the surname Nitta until after the family was reunified, in the 1460s.[83] And that purposeful distinction, made by the Uesugi in addressing Iezumi, was a reminder of yet another distinction of status—of the Iwamatsu family's humble origin as a junior line of the Nitta.

In the end, the concern evinced in the memoir with the Iwamatsu family's dignity should be viewed more as a product of the author's preoccupations in 1509 than as a reflection of significant setbacks experienced in Iezumi's day. Indeed, compared with the vicissitudes experienced by Iezumi's successors (including a confrontation with the Yokoze that required the mediation of the Uesugi to solve), Iezumi's tenure was one of unblemished prosperity. The present from which Shōin so fervently invokes the family's past glory is the author's present, 1509, not the narrative present of the early 1470s. In that earlier, happier time, Iezumi, ennobled by his ties to the shogunal family, only bowed to the authority of the "Town" (the shogun) and the "Country" (the Lords of Koga). The Uesugi themselves had once been deputies of the Lords of Kamakura, and were now siding with the shogun. Perhaps recognizing the predicament of the elite of the Muromachi shogunate—though at the same time failing to understand its full extent—the Iwamatsu denied the Uesugi any institutional credentials. For them the world was divided in two categories: Town and Country on the one hand, and "other houses" on the other. This attitude is best exemplified by another episode, which occurred just a few years after the events discussed here, in 1477. In one of the climactic events in *Shōin shigo*, Iezumi extracts an oath of fealty from family and retainers, trying to ram the Iwamatsu through a difficult transition with a show of force.[84] The first two articles of the oath read:

> Item Other than with the authorities of Town and Country, our warrior bands must not be deployed joining forces with *other houses*.

83. Minegishi, "Kyōtoku no ran no futatsu no Nitta Iwamatsu-shi," 77–79.
84. For the events surrounding the oath of 1477, see *Shōin shigo*, 826b–830b.

Item Should anyone turn his back on this order and join forces with *other houses*, even our son, we shall banish him forever, and deem him unfilial.[85] [emphasis added]

"Other houses" is a not-so-veiled reference to the Uesugi, at a time when the Iwamatsu family was split between continuing to side with them in the war or switching over to the Lord of Koga, Shigeuji. At the same time, "other houses" are all of the local magnates of the plain, with whom Iezumi was loath to interact as a peer. Iwamatsu pride was constructed on the family's uniqueness, a uniqueness consolidated by "generations" of privileged status. Whether in battle or in the political arena, the family's sense of self-worth imposed the exclusion of other families—no help was to be requested from other families, no support that might require gratitude. After all, it was "without borrowing other houses' strength, using our own strength" that the Iwamatsu boasted of stopping Shigeuji's attack.[86] The long way the Iwamatsu had come by 1472–73—from close allies of the Lords of Kamakura, through rebellion, dispossession, exile, division, and then renewed patronage from Kyoto, reunification, and reappropriation of Nitta—this long way and the Iwamatsu refusal to acknowledge its implications provide the backdrop for the negotiation between Yokoze Kunishige and Nagao Kagenobu. The fierce refusal to recognize the family's new role—its decline, unfair even though decreed by the god Hachiman—colors the whole recollection of the talks.

Remarkably, in his retelling of the exchanges between Yokoze Kunishige and Nagao Kagenobu, our apologist never once uses honorific language. The two chief retainers communicate politely, in conciliating tones, surely, but with not a hint of deference on either side. This happens not only in descriptive passages: Kunishige, who would normally be expected to address his counterpart as his social better, uses instead the plainest language, even when seemingly direct quotes are recorded through the use of special suffixes (*sōrō*). For all of Shōin's display of a

85. *Shōin shigo*, 799a–b. See also Satō H., *Koga kubō*, 207; and Minegishi, *Chūsei no tōgoku*, 136–39.

86. *Shōin shigo*, 823b. Note how this is contrasted with Kagenobu's willingness to rely on others—on the Iwamatsu, specifically—to save the day for him.

consumed storyteller's mimetic technique, his manipulation of the tenor of the conversations is the surest sign that his memoir was aimed at a friendly and very partisan readership. By structuring Kagenobu and Kunishige's conversation as a dialogue between peers, Shōin is conveying—none too subtly—the assumption that their parity derives from their respective masters' equal status. Yet, paradoxically, it is the foil itself that reveals the implausibility of the underlying claim: one can fathom the possibility that Iezumi, his mind clouded by the awareness of his own genealogy, may delude himself into conceiving of this relationship with the Uesugi leadership as of one between social equals (or that social parity would translate into political parity), but it is difficult to concede that Yokoze Kunishige, for all of his power within the Iwamatsu circle, could stand beside Nagao Kagenobu, perhaps the most powerful man in the Kantō region.

The asymmetry of the exchange brings home forcefully—and unintentionally—the inconsistency of Shōin's assertion. Kunishige repeatedly travels to Kagenobu's headquarters to present his case; never does the Uesugi general come to Kanayama, or to the Yokoze's headquarters. In the actual negotiation, no doubt, Kunishige himself would have thought it wildly inappropriate to address Kagenobu without the reverence he was due. But in Shōin's oration *pro domo sua*, the disregard for proper etiquette is used to powerful effect to challenge the Uesugi's claim to authority. Or, at least, to affirm the Iwamatsu's freedom from Uesugi jurisdiction.[87]

Shōin shigo's rhetoric spells out the Iwamatsu's position vis-à-vis the Uesugi, and sheds light on the stance their negotiators took in the talks. It articulates the family's reluctance to part from its history, as enunciated through its holdings. Renouncing all claims to lands that had been

87. Truth be told, the Uesugi did accord a particular treatment to the Iwamatsu. Starting in 1364, they stopped circulating notices of their ordinances (*jungyō*) to Nitta Estate, perhaps in recognition of the estate's special exemptions. See Matsumoto, *Tōgoku shugo*, 290–91. Whether this was still the case in the fifteenth century is unclear, as the motor behind the growth of the Iwamatsu's status was provided by the desire of the Lords of Kamakura to create counterweights for the Uesugi. Also unclear is whether the special privilege was attached to the Iwamatsu as a family or to the estate itself.

defining components of their self-image, the Iwamatsu consented to shed some of their status. The fact that some of those eighteen holdings were, most probably, effectively lost to the Iwamatsu long before only confirms this conclusion. In 1472–73, Iezumi was asked to renounce claims to lands he had been unwilling to cede for years, perhaps decades. Although his and his predecessors' dogged insistence on their entitlement had ultimately earned the family two new estates, these two estates came at the cost of accepting the reality of the Iwamatsu family's new position.[88] Valorous though they may be, the Iwamatsu were no longer peers of the Uesugi. In fact, they also had to take a backseat to the Ōgigayatsu (Kawagoe) house, which had been wielding more and more power in the last two generations. The sense of Kagenobu's reply to the Iwamatsu was unmistakable: the Uesugi leadership could not afford to alienate allies in Sagami and Musashi, not to mention their own collaterals, who held sway over much of those two provinces. Indeed, it is in the shape of disorientation caused by the distance between the Uesugi's expectations and the Iwamatsu's that the glaring discrepancy between memory and reality occasionally surfaces in *Shōin shigo*.

So the Iwamatsu, at the end of the day, found their expectations scaled down by events. In effect, they were forced to accept the Uesugi's view of the negotiation: a routine give-and-take with one of the numerous families that supported them in the war—if not with the closest, most subservient, or least powerful of these supporters. As far as the Uesugi were concerned, the Iwamatsu were local magnates, albeit with an illustrious pedigree. To their chagrin, along with Sonoda and Fuchina the Iwamatsu accepted their confinement to Nitta and its immediate surroundings, hemmed in between the Tonegawa and the mountains, on the edge of the plain. The loss of much of their portfolio of scattered landholdings (one which, after all, long predated the negotiation) was emblematic of their loss of status: no longer could the Iwamatsu boast of an outlook that encompassed the whole of the realm. Along with their lands and

---

88. The intensity of the Iwamatsu family's commitment to shaping its historical self-image in terms of its holdings should also be understood as a function of its struggle to recreate unity between long-estranged lineages. See Stein, "Making History English," 106.

economic interests, the Iwamatsu's political ambitions were now confined to a corner of the Kantō plain—albeit a strategically important corner.

Their new territorial, local rule forced them to put less emphasis on, or at least less stock in, their claims to genealogy and prestige. It was not because the specifics were weak or false, but because that sort of claim served to ground a political role the Iwamatsu had long ceased to play—a role that, in truth, offered rapidly diminishing returns to all who clung to it. This the Iwamatsu could not readily bring themselves to acknowledge. Apologetic assertions of ongoing independence from the Uesugi and personal ties to the shogun in the distant capital were mixed with longing for a time when the family was involved in deciding the fate of the realm. Unfortunately for them, by the late fifteenth century the Iwamatsu were no longer in a position to participate in the politics of the "realm as a whole."[89] And so, seeking continuity in a vanishing model of supraregional authority and status, they at once lamented their decline and exalted their flourishing.

For all of their inability to accede to Iezumi's initial demands, Nagao Kagenobu and the Uesugi were nevertheless eager to ingratiate themselves with him. Peers of the Ashikaga they may no longer have been, but the Iwamatsu still stood in a special position among the local magnates within the jurisdiction of the Uesugi. They stood on Kanayama. Within four years, the resilience of this new, formidable fortress would stand in stark contrast to the manifest weakness of the Uesugi's own headquarters at Ikatsuko—symbolizing, perhaps, the passing of an age. Moreover, with a stranglehold over Nitta Estate and newly acquired lands all around it, the Iwamatsu might have been less than they fancied themselves, but were nonetheless a presence the Uesugi had to reckon with in Kōzuke. Even as no more than local magnates, the Iwamatsu held sway over a remarkably large swath of land. This made them stand out in Kōzuke Province, whose warrior class was typically made up of

89. Warren's description of the dispersal of baronial holdings in post-Conquest England—and its effects on barons' mentality—captures the posture of the Iwamatsu with eerie precision: "In consequence [of the dispersal of their holdings] the great barons did not acquire a provincial outlook: they were more inclined to think in terms of the realm as a whole" (*The Governance of Norman and Angevin England*, 57).

petty provincial families that banded together in temporary warrior leagues supporting the Uesugi. To the east, by contrast, in the provinces of Shimotsuke, Shimōsa, and Hitachi, the plain was characterized by a number of long-lived warrior families of distinction and regional power, such as the Oyama, Utsunomiya, Yūki, Nasu, Chiba, Satake, and Satomi. The Iwamatsu, settled at the crossroads of these two worlds, partook of some of the traits of both.

The family tree of the Iwamatsu could stand up to those of most of their eastern neighbors, though the vagaries of their fortunes meant that unlike those eastern neighbors they were forced to suffer the indignity of an outsider (the Uesugi) gaining a stranglehold on Kōzuke Province's governorship and summoning them to participate in military campaigns along with lesser families.[90] Though the Uesugi paid lip service to the Iwamatsu's distinction by keeping their authority out of Nitta Estate, the Iwamatsu could hardly pretend not to be taking orders from a family they considered to be at best their equal—especially as the traditional families of the eastern half of the plain were able to curtail the authority of the sitting governors and interact directly with the Ashikaga, Lords of Koga. The ambiguity of the Iwamatsu's status, neatly exemplified by the family's geographic location, proved to be both a boon and a source of vexation.[91] The family's position, eccentric in the coalition

---

90. Minegishi Sumio (*Chūsei no tōgoku*, 103) suggests that the internal divisions within the Nitta family in the fourteenth century—even before the rivalry that plagued the Iwamatsu in the fifteenth—stunted its growth and prevented it from acquiring the power and status it would have otherwise enjoyed. For instance, the Nitta failed to prevent the Uesugi from gaining a stranglehold on the post of governor of Kōzuke even though the Uesugi were outsiders.

91. Using terms found in contemporary sources, scholars have produced a three-tiered classification of local warriors: *gōzoku* (traditional local magnates), *kokujin* (provincials), and finally *ikki* (alliances of petty land holders). Upon careful scrutiny, this clear taxonomy is difficult to sustain, as it tends to be blurred by differences in usage across time and space. The problem is noted by Kubota Jun'ichi, who analyzes the terminology as it is used in contemporary texts, such as a 1428 entry in *Manzai jugō nikki* (in *ZGR*, suppl. vol. 2, 533–34; also *GKS* 7, no. 1441); in a 1450 letter by Shigeuji quoted in *Kamakura ōzōshi*, 40–41 (also *GKS* 7, no. 1562); and in a 1456 letter, also by Shigeuji, preserved in the Edo-period *Buke jiki* (and cited in *GKS* 7, no. 1628). Kubota ("Nanbokuchō, Muromachi-ki no Kōzuke," 39–40) shows that the distinctions were

supporting the Uesugi but absolutely pivotal along the tense front with the Ashikaga, replicated its unsettled social standing, in between the eastern Kantō of traditional magnates and the western Kantō of petty warrior leagues.[92]

In retrospect, the outcome of the negotiation was extremely advantageous for the Iwamatsu and was symptomatic of broader changes taking place throughout Japan. By exchanging scattered parcels of lands for control of two estates in their very backyard, the Iwamatsu were taking a step in the right direction, toward reinventing themselves as warlords in the following century. Had Iezumi and his deputies lived long enough to see the results, they might have had an easier time resigning themselves to the loss of the family's sense of self, to the shrinking of its horizons. They would have seen the family's interests grow narrower, more intensely local; but they would also have seen its roots grow deeper, as the great houses of the land like the Uesugi were swept away. In 1472–73, though, the Iwamatsu—just as so many others—could not see how, hidden among their day-to-day tactical decisions, were choices that in retrospect would appear to be watersheds. Eager to turn circumstances to their advantage, they were nonetheless unprepared to give up the old for the new; if they made their way into a novel

---

perceived by contemporaries, and that in fact the difference was growing at this time (and was enhanced by Ashikaga Shigeuji). He is especially interested in the one between provincials (*kokujin*) and petty local holders (members of *ikki*), and uses the Iwamatsu as an example of the former to show the substantial differences between them and lower-level warriors. Instead, Matsumoto (*Tōgoku shugo*, 285–88) characterizes the Iwamatsu as traditional magnates among provincials, to emphasize the anomaly of their position in Kōzuke. With three categories used for what were substantially two groups, scholars tend to concentrate on one or the other end of the spectrum. In an attempt to avoid the drawbacks of using the lexicon of the day too literally, Yamada Kuniaki (*Kamakura-fu to Kantō*) refers to the great warrior families as "daimyo class" (*daimyō kurasu*), a phrase that, in its extraneousness to the original context, provides greater flexibility; the terminological fuzziness may better reflect the ever-shifting, situational quality of the vocabulary used at the time.

92. Still, the Iwamatsu also saw themselves as warriors of the highest pedigree within the world of the plain. They viewed themselves as direct supporters of the Ashikaga—which, ironically, was a relationship with the shogun often enjoyed by lowly members of warrior leagues.

localism, they did so grudgingly, all the while turning to look back and lament the loss of what had been. A great many of the more prominent families, with resounding titles and far-flung interests, shared this situation and, no doubt, this attitude. In the case of the Iwamatsu in particular the burden of past splendor, real or imagined with retrospective fondness, acted as a constant diversion from any process of consolidation which, we now feel, was increasingly understood as the key to survival.

CHAPTER 4

No Longer the Age for Camping

When the Iwamatsu embarked on construction of their hilltop fortress of Kanayama early in 1469, Shōin was charged with overseeing the project. He recorded the progress, taking note of the ceremony for the purification of the site and the groundbreaking, which was dedicated to the gods of heaven and earth. He fortified the keep with the Nine-Word Invocation (*kuji*) and the protection of the four heavenly kings. As work neared completion in the eighth month, the Iwamatsu family head, Iezumi, "at an auspicious hour of a propitious day, sent his best wishes and congratulations from Ikatsuko," some twenty kilometers to the southwest, where he was residing.[1] The new castle was inaugurated soon after, with great pomp and circumstance, in a celebration that brought together the recently reconciled lineages of the Iwamatsu (as seen in Chapter 3). On the day of the ceremony, Iezumi rode over to the castle from his residence in Ikatsuko and was welcomed by relatives and housemen, who had traveled out to the edge of the family's lands to greet him. The event was a carefully staged effort to associate the renewed unity and prosperity of the family with its new administrative and military headquarters, the castle of Kanayama. Yet after the festivities were over, Iezumi left Kanayama and returned to Ikatsuko. Our source, *Shōin shigo*, makes little of Iezumi's residence in distant Ikatsuko before the inauguration of Kanayama, and does not say a word about his departure from

1. *Shōin shigo*, 826a.

the new castle afterward. The omission may be no more than a reflection of the anticlimactic character of the return trip; it may also be the embarrassed silence of our otherwise voluble memoirist before a glaring contradiction.

Our author would have been troubled by the association between Ikatsuko and the Uesugi family. As seen in the previous chapter, the conflicted view the Iwamatsu leadership had of its relationship with the Uesugi was central to its efforts at self-definition. The tension between the Iwamatsu family's claims to autonomous prestige and Iezumi's closeness to the Uesugi drives the narrative in *Shōin shigo*: for Iezumi to reside at Ikatsuko before construction of Kanayama was perfectly justifiable; for him to elect to return to the Uesugi encampment at Ikatsuko after establishing a towering fortress at the center of his own lands was puzzling, perhaps a little demeaning, even.

But the episode lays bare another contradiction as well, one that certainly was not a source of great anxiety for our memoirist—one that, in fact, he may well not have recognized at all. This chapter is about this less obvious contradiction: Why, it asks, did the great lordly families in the region prefer to reside in, and rule from, a succession of military encampments (*jin*) even though they commissioned the construction of new castles across the plain, and encouraged local magnates to build castles following their example? In the answer to this question we may find the reasons for Iezumi's return to Ikatsuko; more broadly, making sense of this contradiction means uncovering the ways local and regional elites viewed not only castles, but the particular form of territorial control castles both shaped and revealed.

Some background: the building of Kanayama was not an isolated event. Rather, archaeological evidence has revealed that in the second half of the fifteenth century provincial elites throughout the archipelago engaged in a castle-building arms race. On the grassy expanse of the Kantō plain, in eastern Japan, where central authority faltered and war began early, fortresses sprang up in rapid succession, starting in the 1450s. Soon, travelers in the region found it hard to journey a few miles without seeing or stopping at a castle built by a great lord or a local magnate. What took place in those years was nothing short of a castellan revolution, to borrow a phrase from the study of medieval Europe (what Pierre Toubert has called *incastellamento*). Castles, and groups of castles, became central nodes for control of the countryside, as farmland and villages were now transformed into hinterlands of newly erected strongholds.[2] By 1500, a militarized rural landscape made visible even to a distracted observer new ways of exercising authority and conducting warfare. Castles like Kanayama became central hubs of political and economic power for local warrior magnates trying to exercise unfettered control over the surrounding countryside; they underscored the distinction between their builders and the many petty warriors who lived on the land, in nearby villages. For scholars, this castellan revolution has recently come to provide the driving narrative in the story of local society during the transition between the medieval and the early modern period, between about 1450 and 1600.

Yet Ikatsuko, where Iezumi returned and continued to reside until 1477, even during the siege of Kanayama discussed in the previous chapter, was neither a castle nor a city. It was a military encampment established by the Uesugi family. Seemingly at odds with the age's novel attention to local roots of authority, and apparently aloof from the advantages supposedly afforded by the castellan revolution, the heads of the various houses of the extended Uesugi family, surrounded by powerful local magnates like Iezumi, spent much of the second half of the fifteenth century not in castles but in encampments. If Iezumi's behavior was contradictory, the contradiction was not his alone.

This chapter explores this curious predilection for encampments in the context of the changes ushered in by the militarization of the countryside, by considering what the castellan revolution entailed and what words like castle and encampment meant to contemporaries. If the castellan revolution represents, as it seems, a pivotal moment in the transition between the medieval and early modern social and political orders, what then is the significance of encampments? Were they simply provisional

---

2. Toubert, *Les Structures du Latium médiéval.* Though later scholars have sought to complicate the original picture, Toubert's theory is now widely accepted, and *incastellamento* is believed to have been typical not only of central Italy, where Toubert first found it. See Wickham, *The Mountains and the City*, xxiii–xxv, 36–39, 115–18, 302–6; Debord, "Castellan Revolution"; Koziol, "Political Culture," 52–54, 59–60; Bisson, *Crisis of the Twelfth Century*, throughout, but in particular, 53–55. For an account of the evolution of Kantō castles that mirrors Toubert's *incastellamento*, see Fujiki, "Sengoku Hiki no shiro to mura."

solutions, intermediate stages in a long-term evolutionary trajectory? Or should we make something of their timing, which *coincided* with the diffusion of castles? Examining the political experiment carried out in camps like Ikatsuko enables us to consider the geographic dimensions of political necessity; to tease out regional elites' cultural perceptions and assumptions about their authority and the space in which it operated.

To sketch this chapter's main argument: although castles held the promise of greater control over surrounding lands (and resources), they forced upon local and regional magnates alike a new sort of association between power and place, a new commitment to a single locale. More to the point, in the eyes of the great regional lords whose authority rested on ties to office, castles lacked essential institutional prestige. The name "castle" applied to any stronghold, from a temporary fastness to an imposing structure like Kanayama; and anyone with sufficient resources could build one. Encampments, instead, as we shall see, could be built on an idea of political landscape more congenial to families of the caliber of the Uesugi.

The Castellan Revolution

For generations after 1455, the Uesugi and most of the warrior elite in the Kantō operated in a context of more or less permanent mobilization. It comes as no surprise, in this climate, that warrior families great and small busied themselves in the construction of fortresses in their few moments of respite from campaigning. To name but a few, in 1457, on direct orders from the shogun, the Ōgigayatsu built (or rather, had their followers build for them) the castles of Edo and Kawagoe on their lands and aligned to protect the western half of the plain from the incursions of warriors loyal to Shigeuji.[3] In response, not too far away, the Narita built a castle at Iwatsuki at the behest of Shigeuji, who in turn settled

3. A few different versions of the events exist: according to *Kamakura ōzōshi*, 55, on orders from the shogun the Ōgigayatsu built Kawagoe, their Ōta followers built Edo; according to *Shōin shigo*, 843a, both castles were built by the Ōta with the assistance of several other families, the Ueda, Mito, Haginoya. For Kawagoe Estate as a holding of the Ōgigayatsu, see Ochiai, "Musashi no kuni Kawagoe no shō"; Yuyama, "Ōgigayatsushi no ryōiki," 101–8.

Fig. 4.1. What is left of Hachigata castle, overlooking the Arakawa. The Chichibu hills are visible in the distance. Photograph by the author.

down in Koga and erected a fortress for himself there.[4] As he mulled rebellion, between 1473 and 1476, an aggrieved Nagao Kageharu began work on a stronghold at Hachigata, on the southern bank of the Arakawa, where the river flows out from the Chichibu hills and into the plain (Fig. 4.1). Soon, local warriors began to flock to the castle, or send pledges of support.[5] Among these were the Toshima brothers, who had long controlled the country west of the new castle of Edo. Unhappy to find themselves in the shadow cast by the new Ōgigayatsu stronghold, the Toshima joined forces with Kageharu, putting their network of fortresses—Hiratsuka, Shakujii, Nerima, among others—at his disposal.[6] Most of these castles were tested in battle, variously holding out or quickly falling to sieges. Chronicles, and letters sent by lords to their followers commending them for valiant fighting and casualties sustained, tirelessly record clashes before the walls of castles: of Usui, Kozukue, Kunugida, Yatsukunugi, Tatebayashi, Sano, Sanada, Shiroi, Hirai, Ichikawa, Mizorogi, Koiso, and many more. Fighting was incessant, and most of it, most decisively, took the form of a siege.

Indeed, the number of castles dotting both the countryside and our sources' narratives almost seems to vouch for the castles' indispensability. Pitched battles too were many and bloody, to be sure, but time and

4. On Koga's location, see Inagaki, "Koga kubō to Shimotsuke."
5. *Kamakura ōzōshi*, 60.
6. Kuroda M., "Toshima-shi no metsubō," 216–22.

again defeated armies retreated to their strongholds to weather a storm. By sheer repetition, if nothing else, sources suggest that it was at castles that differences were finally settled. For instance, in 1477, the Uesugi army led by the chief retainer of the Ōgigayatsu, Ōta Dōkan, clashed on the fields of Egota and Numabukuro with the forces of the Toshima. Dōkan was victorious, and the younger of the Toshima brothers died on the battlefield along with many others. The very next day, Dōkan laid siege to the surviving brother, in the family's main castle at Shakujii. In Dōkan's own account, "We negotiated a peace whereby he would return to his previous loyalty [to the Uesugi], whereupon, on the eighteenth, he came out and we met face to face. Further, he told me he would dismantle the stronghold, but in the end it became clear he was tempting me with falsehoods, so on the twenty-eighth I stormed the castle's outer enclosure, and that night he fled."[7]

The fall of Shakujii marked the end of the Toshima family. In a similar vein, the Yamanouchi Uesugi lost battle after battle during the quarrel with their Ōgigayatsu relatives, on the fields of Sugaya, Sanemaki, and Takami in 1488, and then again, disastrously, at Tachikawa, in 1504.[8] Undaunted, they awaited reinforcements holed up in their castles, and then launched a counteroffensive, toppling Ōgigayatsu fortresses in rapid succession—Shiroi, Kunugida, Sanada, and, finally, the enemy's main castle at Kawagoe. The Ōgigayatsu immediately sued for peace. Why did the Ōgigayatsu not capitalize on their battlefield successes by laying siege to the Yamanouchi castles when they had a chance?

The proliferation of new castles certainly transformed the conduct of war, offering greater protection and creating new opportunities for warrior families engaged in military confrontations (that is, most of them, at one time or other). Besieging a castle created new difficulties—besides the self-evident one of storming a keep. Armies now needed enough personnel to blockade access roads, often for an extended time, requiring a long-term commitment of troops and a steady flow of supplies to pro-

7. *Ōta Dōkan jō*, 638b.

8. We know little about the first three battles (see the brief accounts in *SKS* 5, no. 1019 [*Koshōmon*]). Our best source for Tachikawa is the account by Sōchō, quoted in Chapter 1. *Shōin shigo* only briefly mentions the clash at Tachikawa, in which the Iwamatsu participated on the Yamanouchi side (*Shōin shigo*, 845a).

vision them. Sieges that dragged on severely tested the resolution of finicky allies, who were known to pack their things and return home before victory if they felt the costs were outweighing the benefits.[9] Perhaps the Ōgigayatsu lacked the manpower to mount a prolonged siege.[10] In a letter dated 1488, a follower prophetically dissected their chances of defeating the Yamanouchi, noting that the Yamanouchi had long "been the pillars of the Uesugi, and so the various houses protect their banner. Respect for them is unparalleled, and their forces number two hundred thousand riders, they say. The Ōgigayatsu riders number barely one hundred or so."[11]

But the castellan revolution was not merely a matter of resources. The new castles made their military importance felt by forcing invading armies to reckon with the fortresses along their path. Thus, as we have seen in Chapter 3, in 1472 the vast army of allies mustered by Shigeuji for a frontal assault on the Uesugi was held up for more than seventy days trying to topple the castle of Kanayama, which stood near the road Shigeuji's forces were traveling.[12] Unable to overcome the resistance of the far smaller Iwamatsu army holed up behind the ramparts, Shigeuji eventually turned on his heels and made his way back to Koga. Similarly, Ōta Dōkan was compelled to ride out and besiege the Toshima fortress at Hiratsuka, which had been situated in such a way as to obstruct transit to and from Dōkan's own castle.[13] Indeed, the presence of the new fortresses was not only felt by armies on the march. I have spoken of the restructuring of space brought about by the new castles in terms of a militarization of the landscape, but the process reached far beyond the immediate contingencies of mobilization and defense. Soon, castles also changed the path of roads themselves. The "upper road" (*kamitsumichi*) was the main branch of the highway system that ran north–south through the Kantō region and converged on the city of Kamakura, in the south,

9. For a good example of long sieges and departing allies, see *Ōta Dōkan jō* (641b) and *Kamakura ōzōshi* (64) on the siege of Usui.

10. It seems that the Hōjō, who helped the Ōgigayatsu win at Tachikawa, were eager to return home; they did not come back, a year later, to help the Ōgigayatsu break the siege of Kawagoe.

11. *GKS* 7, no. 1803 (Kokin shōsoku monjo).

12. *Shōin shigo*, 819b–820b.

13. *Ōta Dōkan jō*, 640a.

from which the plain had been governed for two and a half centuries until the falling out between Shigeuji and the shogun. Now, the upper road itself splintered into a number of new roads that ran between castles and connected the new towns clustering around, and sometimes within, the walls. Towns that had once thrived as post stations along the road were passed by; some, like Nigabayashi, near the castle of Hachigata, were quickly abandoned when new roads were opened that served nearby castles more directly.[14]

Villages once scattered around the countryside moved, and concentrated in the vicinity of the new fortresses. Recent archaeological surveys and excavations have revealed a series of dramatic shifts occurring in the second half of the fifteenth century, such as a peak in the number of hamlets and dispersed rural settlements that were abandoned, coupled with the appearance of an unprecedented number of new, strongly nucleated settlements located in the immediate vicinity of strongholds. Most (of the few) pre-fifteenth-century settlements excavated to date in the region have revealed patterns of separation between lowlands near riverbeds (where hamlets developed) and plateaus (where ritual functions were situated, with temples and burial grounds), but sites that were first settled in the late fifteenth century show the population moving to higher ground, when it was available, and settling on plateaus.[15]

---

14. Saitō, "Chūsei tōgoku no kaidō to sono hensen"; Asano, "Sengoku-ki jōkan no nendaikan," 86–91; Iimura, "Michi to 'shuku,'" 24–27. It is worth noting, though, that Nigabayashi in particular was also the site of a major battle in 1477 between Nagao Kageharu's forces and Ōta Dōkan's (*Ōta Dōkan jō*, 638b; *Kamakura ōzōshi*, 61). We know that local populations often fled to the hills on such occasions to escape death and kidnapping for ransom at the hands of marauding troops ("The monks were afraid of the troops and as a result they had scattered and run away," *Shōin shigo*, 821a), and it is entirely possible that the site was abandoned as a direct consequence of the battle. On roads, see Saitō, "Chūsei tōgoku ni okeru kasen suiryō to toka"; Saitō, "Kamakura kaidō Kamitsumichi to kita Kantō"; Saitō, "Minami Kantō," 151–80; Kobayashi T., "Suitei Kamakura kaidō Kamitsumichi"; Gotō and Shinkai, "Tama kyūryō no Kamakura kaidō Kamitsumichi"; and Ushiyama, "Shakujiigawa o watari Iwabuchi e."

15. Maekawa, "Chūsei shūraku no dōkō to ryūtsū kikō no saihen"; Taniguchi, "Hakkutsu sareta Toshima-gun"; Yanase, "Bōsō no chūsei shūraku"; Shibata, "Kōkogaku kara mita chūsei Bōsō." See also Harada, "Tonegawa chūryūiki ni okeru shōen no sonraku keikan."

During those same years, moving out of lowlands along with hamlets, warriors built new strongholds on hills or on promontories at the edges of plateaus.[16] Absent those, as was often the case in the Kantō plain, they made do with bluffs overlooking rivers: Shakujii was built on the banks of the river of the same name; Hachigata was perched a little higher, above a bend on the far mightier Arakawa. As local elites moved into these new structures in great numbers, the longstanding residences/mansions in which they had resided (*tate*, or *tachi* in the east), and which had been scattered throughout the countryside like the dwellings of the peasantry, ceased to be used in similarly dramatic numbers.[17] Surveys and excavations have not been equally systematic in every corner of the Kantō region (present-day Ibaraki and Kanagawa Prefectures have not received the same level of scrutiny as Saitama or Chiba Prefectures), but where archaeologists have had a chance to work, their findings have been striking. In Musashi the appearance of new mansions peaked in the fifteenth century (nineteen in the first half, twenty-one in the second), and the disappearance of previously occupied ones gathered momentum after 1450 (three sites abandoned before that, twenty-four in the second half of the fifteenth century, twenty in the first half of the sixteenth). Likewise, the building of new castles and the abandonment of previously used ones both increased dramatically in the first fifty years after the beginning of the civil war (three appearances and zero disappearances before mid-century; eighteen appearances and one disappearance after 1450; two appearances and ten disappearances after 1500).[18]

Countrywide data are still unavailable, but in recent years the publication of reports on excavations prompted by Japan's public works and real estate boom of the 1970s and 1980s has had a dramatic impact on the established view of the evolution of castles. These were once thought to have begun as small mountain strongholds that over time, slowly,

16. Saitō, *Chūsei tōgoku no ryōiki to jōkan*, 53.

17. Shibata, "Chūsei no kakki"; Fujiki, "Naisen no naka no mura to machi to shiro"; Fujiki, "Sengoku Hiki no shiro to mura"; Saitō, "Gaisetsu"; Saitō, *Chūsei tōgoku no ryōiki to jōkan*, 22–30; Kojima, "Ema-shi kan to Ema-shi." On the importance of these *tate*/*tachi*, see for example Gomi, "Tachi no shakai to sono hensen."

18. Inoue Tetsuo, "Minami Kantō ni okeru jōkanseki shutsudo tōjiki," 189–91, especially tables 7 and 8 on p. 190.

migrated downward, eventually giving birth to the sprawling lowland fortresses built by the great warlords of the late fifteen hundreds. The old trajectory had been traced on the basis of the accounts found in war tales (*gunki*) and the still visible remains of early modern castles. A memorable example of the former is the long scene of the siege of Kasagi castle in the fourteenth-century epic *Taiheiki* (Chronicle of the Great Peace), with the outnumbered, heroic troops loyal to the emperor holding off wave after wave of attackers from the shogunal army:

> The more than seventy-five thousand attackers from the four directions climbed over chasms and cliffs, clung to *kuzu* vines, and scaled rocks, until they came before the Hall of the Two Monarchs, close upon the outer gate of the castle. There they rested awhile, looking up into the castle. And indeed they beheld the sovereign's brocade banner floating in the air, its sun and moon of gold and silver shining and sparkling in the bright sunlight. All the space beneath the banner was filled by more than three thousand armored warriors, standing like clouds or mist with joined sleeves and gleaming helmet-stars.[19]

Yet the castle at Kasagi was little more than a collection of ramshackle fortifications thrown up to enhance the protection afforded by the impassable terrain on which the original structure—a temple, for most of its existence, not a fortress—was built. And while scholars have taken aim at the obviously inflated numbers fighting on both sides, the image of the castle itself—here and elsewhere—has lingered on. Nor is it easy to avoid the temptation to trace a line back from majestic monuments like Himeji castle, built at the turn of the seventeenth century and still visited by hundreds of thousands every year.[20] The continuity of the word castle in our sources long suggested continuity in the reality it denoted; changes in location and size were treated as variables modulating

---

19. McCullough, trans., *Taiheiki*, 72. This does not mean that the earlier residences were always discarded; in some cases, as Saitō Shin'ichi (*Chūsei tōgoku no ryōiki to jōkan*, 91–92) notes, they continued to be used alongside the new castles through much of the sixteenth century.

20. The number fluctuates from year to year; in 2009, a near-record 1.5 million people visited the castle, according to an announcement posted on April 16, 2010, on the website of the city of Himeji. See http://www.city.himeji.lg.jp/koho/press/_20781/_21696/_22185.html (accessed September 23, 2010).

an otherwise recognizable identity. Until recently, moreover, analysis of the physical remains of castles was confined to surface surveys of their layout (*nawabari*), which yielded important insights but limited scholarly attention to the newest layers in the development of each structure. Castles typically acquired their final form in the tumultuous closing years of the civil war, at the end of the sixteenth century, so research tended to focus on those years and presume that it was then that castles came to play significant roles.

Only recently has a different picture begun to take shape. No archaeological remains of permanent castle-like structures have been positively dated to the Nanbokuchō period (1336–92), casting doubt on the existence of permanent structures expressly designed for defense before the fifteenth century.[21] Archaeologists now propose that before the building rush of the fifteenth century castles were erected only as temporary redoubts, typically built on high ground to survive an emergency or escape a short-term threat. These quickly assembled and quickly dismantled structures were not expected to sustain an extended siege or hold off a vast invading army. Rather, they were meant to provide refuge during brief, local conflicts. Even less were they built for permanent occupancy. Residential functions were carried out by lightly fortified mansions, built in the vicinity of the paddies and fields tilled by the peasants from whom local warrior notables extracted their livelihood. These mansions were often surrounded by earthworks or a palisade, and sometimes a ditch, which served as much as a sluice for irrigation as it did as a serious moat. The mansions were the space of everyday life; from these a warrior family would administer its lands and exercise whatever public authority it might have. The pre-fifteenth-century fastnesses, on the other hand, were temporary places of refuge, the space of the non-quotidian, as some Japanese scholars have called it.[22] (I shall return to this.)

By comparison the new complexes were imposing. Kanayama, whose construction Shōin oversaw in 1469, was especially impressive: the castle's surface was not so very great, but its remains extend north–south along

---

21. Saitō, "Nanbokuchō, Muromachi-ki no jōkaku"; Saitō, *Chūsei tōgoku no ryōiki to jōkan*, 98. See also Yanase, "Chiba-shi no honkyo no fukugen," 306–8.

22. Nakazawa, *Chūsei no buryoku to jōkaku*, 163–91; Ochiai, "Chūsei tōgoku no jin to geinō"; Saitō, *Chūsei tōgoku no ryōiki to jōkan*, 28, 45.

narrow hilltop ridges for 2.5 kilometers, and east–west for 1.5 kilometers.[23] Perhaps also because of its hilltop visibility, Kanayama became one of the more famous castles in the Kantō (and so in lavishly praising the fortress's defensive capabilities Shōin may have been voicing a commonly held view).[24] Castles erected on more level and open terrain might be more compact: Hachigata, built by Nagao Kageharu in the mid-1470s, covered an area of about 400 by 650 meters;[25] Shakujii, the castle in which the Toshima family holed up to make its last stand against Ōta Dōkan in 1477, extended over a roughly square area about 350 meters to the side (that is, 12.25 hectares).[26] And although excavations have not yielded much evidence of masonry, these castles were protected by significant defenses. Often exploiting impassable terrains (steep bluffs over rivers, hills), fortresses were also surrounded by moats and earthworks. At Shakujii, for instance, archaeologists have excavated dry moats between 2.8 and 3.5 meters deep, with widths between 7 and 9 meters at the top, and 0.7 and 1 meter at the bottom. Along one of the moats traces of an earthen rampart have been unearthed, 7.1 meters wide at its base.

The castles built after about 1450, which I have been calling new castles, consolidated behind stronger, permanent ramparts the functions once divided between mansions and mountaintop fastnesses. These new castles were not simply further downhill than their earlier namesakes, they were fundamentally different, for by providing long-term defensive capabilities to residential and administrative complexes, they now became places of daily life and administration as well as refuge, embodying warriors' claims to both military and political power.[27] Certainly, the transformation that in retrospect seems abrupt was in fact gradual to

---

23. *NJT* 4:386–91.

24. Fukushima Masayoshi (in *Shinpen Saitama kenshi tsūshi hen* 2:943) notes that in the sixteenth century Kanayama was numbered among seven famous castles in the Kantō (the others being Karasawa, Ōta, Oshi, Kawagoe, Umayabashi, and Utsunomiya), though he omits Utsunomiya from his discussion and gives no reason for the fame of these seven castles in particular.

25. *NJT* 5:166–69; Ishizuka, "Hachigata jōseki."

26. *NJT* 5:266–68.

27. In an essay ("Nanbokuchō no shiro kara Sengoku no shiro e") originally published in 1986, historian Owada Tetsuo refers to the transformation from fourteenth- to

those who experienced it: the hesitations of archaeologists in classifying individual structures as mansions or castles attest to the practice of strengthening compounds' defenses piecemeal—retrofitting them by digging deeper and wider moats, building thicker and higher walls.[28] Contemporaries, moreover, less anxious than modern scholars to label and classify, let ambiguous, shifting, ill-fitting terminology reveal some of the change underway around them. In 1488 the poet Banri, traveling by Hachigata, praised the fortress in grandiloquent Sino-Japanese verse: "The ramparts of Hachigata castle—not even a bird could peep past them."[29] Twenty-one years later the linked-verse master Sōchō, less impressed perhaps, or simply more accustomed to this sort of sight, simply referred to Hachigata as "the mansion [*tate*] of Nagao Akikata."[30]

All the same, as the process gained momentum across the region, local warrior notables, who had often been little more than village elites, found themselves at once more clearly separated from surrounding settlements (by moats and walls) and more obviously central to them (by functioning as focal points of previously more scattered villages).[31] Castles soon became the central cores of markets and towns, though there is considerable debate as to whether castles and castellans "attracted" towns, developed them as part of their foundation, or were built on sites of preexistent

---

sixteenth-century castles as one from purely military to political headquarters. The essay was reprinted in Owada, *Chūsei jōkakushi no kenkyū*, 35–48.

28. Hashiguchi, "Tōgoku no bushi kyokan."

29. Ichiki, *Baika mujinzō chūshaku*, 2:2–3.

30. *Azumaji no tsuto*, 488.

31. The separation of the warriors in castles from the nearby community could have drawbacks: Minegishi Sumio (*Chūsei no tōgoku*, 244) argues that in choosing Hachigata as his base of operations, in the center of the plain, Kageharu failed to realize that his ancestral home of Shiroi in Kōzuke was too far away, and to establish ties with the Hachigata area. Karasawa Sadaichi (in *Ōta shishi*, 557) suggests that Kageharu moved to Hachigata precisely because he was aware of Shiroi's peripheral location, but that he did not have time to build ties with local warriors. As for why Kageharu chose Hachigata, one story has it that it was the site of a fort built in the tenth century by the notorious rebel Taira no Masakado (*NJT* 5:166–67). Sekiguchi Kazuya ("Hachigata-jō") dismisses this as "hard to believe." Yamada Kuniaki's systematic survey and map of holdings in the fourteenth and early fifteenth century (*Kamakura-fu to Kantō*, 275) does not show the Uesugi or their followers holding any land in this corner of Musashi. Hachigata, though, was a gateway to the Chichibu hills where the Nagao held land, according to Katsumori Sumi (*Nagao-shi no kenkyū*, 111).

markets and towns.[32] These processes appear to have played out at different levels and on different scales (surely, the building of Hachigata had a greater impact on its hinterland and urbanization than, say, that of a small stronghold at Yatsukunugi did), but everywhere the reorganization of settlement affected the character of warrior presence and dominion on the land. Recent scholarship has underscored the link between the castles built by warriors and the farming communities in the surrounding countryside: Saitō Shin'ichi, for instance, has shown that castles were sited not so much to maximize military/strategic advantages, as to control surrounding territory (a conclusion that parallels the one reached by scholars working on the Holy Land, where crusader kingdoms gave considerable impulse to the western medieval tradition of castle building).[33]

Camps Were Capitals

I suggested above that we should not be surprised that warriors throughout the Kantō region (and the whole archipelago, really) responded to the state of military unrest by building stronger, and then permanent, defenses. Yet although it is not difficult to view this consolidation of functions as a natural, almost inevitable product of permanent mobilization, the case of the Uesugi and their encampments invites us to look more closely at the assumptions about power and space that informed the behavior of warriors of different status, as the prospect of continuous, endless war became ever more real. If building permanent castles in place of mansions was indeed the natural solution to a clearly understood (and agreed upon) problem, then why did the Uesugi—the Yamanouchi in particular, but the Ōgigayatsu, too, if less obviously—build castles yet rule from camps? And what were these camps anyway, that could be used as abodes for years on end?

32. Yanase, "Chiba-shi no honkyo no fukugen," 314–15; Sano, "Mizubori no keifu to jōkamachi no kigen"; Kojima, "Sengoku-ki jōkamachi no kōzō"; Ichimura, *Sengoku-ki tōgoku no toshi to kenryoku*, 395–429.

33. For strikingly similar conclusions reached by scholars of castle building in the Holy Land, see Ellenblum, *Frankish Rural Settlement*, 3–38; see also Molin, *Unknown Crusader Castles*, 50–51.

The most vivid description we have of a mid-fifteenth-century encampment is the one offered, with more than a little gusto, in *Shōin shigo.* The camp in question was used by Shigeuji as he prepared to mount the siege described in Chapter 3:

> As for the forces that accompanied [Shigeuji] from Hitachi, Kazusa, Shimōsa, Awa, and Shimotsuke Provinces, the Yūki, Oyama, Nasu, Utsunomiya, Sano, Sanuki—in total more than eight thousand riders—rode up to him, with the main force and the rearguard somehow arranging themselves in the vicinity. The main force was stationed at Ōtategawara Village and Hachimangawara in this estate [i.e., Nitta Estate, home of the Iwamatsu]. The rearguard was stationed in Okayama plain in Sanuki Estate. The main and rearguard forces were about twenty-five *ri* apart. Looking around in all directions, one's eye could not take in the whole encampment. Wild beasts, fleeing, lost their way; flocks of birds flying away grew exhausted in the clouds; the dust and the smoke from the fires that were started spread wildly and the noon was darkened; the flames from the beacons rose and the night shone brightly.[34]

Of the Uesugi camp at Ikatsuko, instead, the memoir says, "[T]his now was the main camp, as the Uesugi Deputy had petitioned for the Imperial Banner. . . . [I]n total more than seven thousand riders set their camps in the vicinity of Ikatsuko, in [the villages of] Hanzawa, Kowaze, Awase, Mokusai, Hotta, Takise, and Tebakagawara."[35] He also notes, "All day Uesugi [Fusasada] and his Ōgigayatsu relatives made their camp on the plain of Okabe, and in the evening they rode into the main camp at Ikatsuko."[36]

Shōin shigo's author's recollection is factual, if not especially descriptive (hyperbole aside). It says precious little about either camp's defenses and nothing at all about the structures that made up the camps (tents? wooden buildings?). Shōin had lived at Ikatsuko for years, had seen Shigeuji's camp from the walls of Kanayama, and had also, later in life, spent time at the other major camp used by the Uesugi, at Uwado. So he

34. *Shōin shigo*, 820a.

35. *Shōin shigo*, 820b.

36. *Shōin shigo*, 791b. This remark is in the "table of contents" of book 3, the text of which is now lost.

probably did not feel compelled to leave his readers a description of the structures that made up the complexes (often wooden buildings, protected by earthworks), with the likes of which, after all, everyone would have been familiar. What these passages do bother to tell us, though, is no less revealing. It is clear that major camps were sprawling affairs, frequently built along major roads, stretching over the countryside for kilometers on end, and occupying villages all around their chosen site.[37] In the case of Shigeuji's camp Shōin tells us of the vast distance between its vanguard and its rearguard (8 kilometers).[38] In the case of Ikatsuko he provides not distances but rather a list of the villages swallowed up by the encampment (seven of them). We do not have cadastral surveys of those villages for the period in question, nor does our source specify how much of each village was taken up by the various camps, so it is hard to tell exactly how much land Ikatsuko covered. Judging from the approximate location of the villages, though, we can estimate that an area of almost ten square kilometers was disrupted, if not occupied in its entirety (Map 4.1).[39]

Yet *Shōin shigo* does give us some hints as to the layout of the complex as a whole: Ikatsuko, like Shigeuji's and other camps, was an agglomeration of smaller individual camps rather than a single, compact and centrally planned, structure. Both passages mention a "main camp" (*honjin*), where the head of the Yamanouchi—the (Kantō) deputy—had his headquarters. Other warrior houses had their own separate camps, in some cases some way away, so that various lords had to "ride into the main camp." The colorful passage depicting Shigeuji's camp suggests a similar pattern, by referring to a central "main force" (*ōte*). Frequent, if oblique, references in contemporary sources hint at a widespread practice. At the time of the camp in Uwado, the Iwamatsu had their own

37. Matsuoka Susumu ("Sengoku shoki tōgoku ni okeru jin to jōkaku," 2) has also made a similar observation, noting that the word "*zengo*" (around; literally, "before and after") was generally used to situate a camp in relation to known toponyms.

38. Actually, Shōin claims that the distance was 25 *ri* (about 97 km, at 3.9 km/*ri*), exaggerating an already impressive distance tenfold, as Minegishi Sumio notes (in "Kyōtoku no ran ni okeru jōkaku to jinsho"). Interestingly, all the distances provided for this incident appear to be off by the same margin, as if the author were really using a different unit of measure.

39. *Saitama-ken no chimei*, 101b, 746b, 747a, 748b–c, 754a, 826a–b.

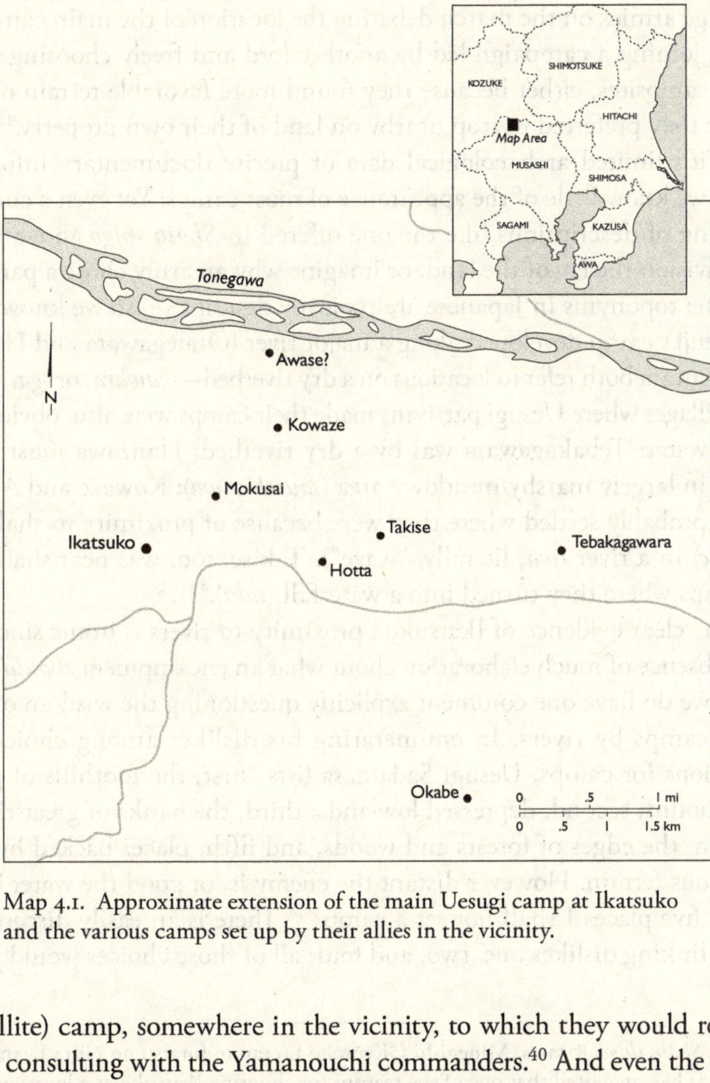

Map 4.1. Approximate extension of the main Uesugi camp at Ikatsuko and the various camps set up by their allies in the vicinity.

(satellite) camp, somewhere in the vicinity, to which they would return after consulting with the Yamanouchi commanders.[40] And even the commanders themselves could be encamped at some distance from one another: in the letter that bears his name, Dōkan refers to Nagao Tadakage's camp as being "a little distant."[41] *Shōin shigo* tells of commanders

40. *Shōin shigo*, 845a.
41. *Ōta Dōkan jō*, 639b.

of large armies on the march debating the location of the main camp; of allies joining a campaign led by another lord and freely choosing their own campsites, either because they found more favorable terrain or because they preferred to stop nearby on land of their own property.[42]

With limited archaeological data or precise documentary information, we know little of the appearance of most camps. Yet even a cursory reading of descriptions like the one offered in *Shōin shigo* above helps us envision the lay of the land, or imagine why an army chose a particular site: toponyms in Japanese are typically descriptive, so we know that Shigeuji's camp developed along a major river (Ōtategawara and Hachimangawara both refer to locations on a dry riverbed—*kawara*, or *-gawara*); the villages where Uesugi partisans made their camps were also, obviously, near water: Tebakagawara was by a dry riverbed; Hanzawa must have been in largely marshy/meadowy area (*sawa*/*-zawa*); Kowaze and Awaze were probably settled where they were because of proximity to shallows (*se*/*-ze*) in a river (*wa*, literally, "wave"). Takise, too, was near shallows, perhaps where they turned into a waterfall (*taki*).[43]

The clear evidence of Ikatsuko's proximity to rivers is ironic since, in the absence of much elaboration about what an encampment *should* look like, we do have one comment explicitly questioning the wisdom of setting camps by rivers. In enumerating his dislikes among choices of locations for camps, Uesugi Sadamasa lists "first, the foothills of great mountains; second, depressed lowlands; third, the banks of great rivers; fourth, the edges of forests and woods, and fifth, places backed by impervious terrain. However distant the enemy is, or good the water is, in these five places I shall not set a camp."[44] There is an easily discernible logic linking dislikes one, two, and four: all of those choices would yield

---

42. *Shōin shigo*, 821a–b. Minegishi ("Kyōtoku no ran to futatsu no Nitta Iwamatsushi," 76) has suggested that one of the reasons for choosing Ikatsuko as a location for a camp was its proximity to the lands of the Iwamatsu, who were deeply involved with the encampment from its inception.

43. The exact details of the fifteenth-century terrain have been erased by the systematic riparian engineering that took place after World War II, and such features as shallows and rapids can only be imagined in place of the cement that lines most rivers.

44. *SKS* 5, no. 1019 (*Koshōmon*). Elsewhere, Sadamasa also refers to ideal (idealized?) camp layouts; Shōin, too, cites the "eight camps" established in Chinese military thought, with names like "bird," "cloud," "heaven," and so forth (*Shōin shigo*, 820a).

the higher ground, or the advantage of being less visible, to an attacking force. The aversion for camps near riverbanks may be connected to that for places backed by impervious terrain, perhaps out of concern for foreclosing one's own avenues for escape; most of the rivers in question, moreover, were actually fairly shallow, gravelly, and seasonal, so that in the dry months of the year they would have hindered easy transit without providing too much actual protection against attackers. Be that as it may, it is clear that not everyone in the Uesugi leadership agreed with Sadamasa (both Ikatsuko and Uwado were established right by rivers), but the existence of views so contradictory helps us understand why different warrior families chose to maintain their own separate camps, each located to their leaders' liking.

In recent years various sites at both Ikatsuko and Uwado have been excavated.[45] Three excavated sites thought to be associated with the Ikatsuko camp suggest that the camp proper (excluding the more distant satellite compounds used by allies) extended for about two or three kilometers from east to west at the northeastern tip of the Honjō plateau, in northern Musashi Province (now Saitama Prefecture).[46] North of the site lies the alluvial plain of the Tonegawa, the greatest of the rivers that produced the Kantō plain. The Tonegawa's alluvial plain is separated from the plateau itself by a small river, the Onnaborigawa, which flows eastward and has eroded the northern edge of the plateau, producing bluffs some four to twelve meters high. Southeast of the site are two more rivers, the Koyamagawa and the Shidogawa, which flow together some eight hundred meters away, so that the site is surrounded on three sides in what one of the reports has deemed "a natural fastness" (*shizen no yōgaichi*).[47]

---

45. Higashiikakko Iseki Chōsakai, *Higashiikakko, Kawaramachi*; Honjō-shi Iseki Chōsakai, *Higashiikakko Shiroato iseki*; and Honjō-shi Iseki Chōsakai, *Higashiikakko Akasaka Iseki.* Reports from Uwado have yet to be published; for some information on the dig there, see Ogino, "Kawagoe kanseki." See also *NJT* 5:138 (although for certain sites *NJT* has been quickly growing obsolete, as data from excavations conducted in the last decade or two finally become available).

46. Minegishi ("Kyōtoku no ran to futatsu no Nitta Iwamatsu-shi," 76), presumably referring to the whole complex, including satellite camps, estimates an east–west extension of six kilometers.

47. Honjō-shi Iseki Chōsakai, *Higashiikakko Shiroato iseki*, 2.

Similarly, the camp called Uwado in our sources stood on the western bank of a river (the Irumagawa), in central Musashi (in the modern city of Kawagoe).[48] The core of the site coincided with the grounds of the mansion of the Kawagoe family, which by the second half of the fifteenth century no longer existed, and the precincts of a temple called Jōrakuji.[49] Preexisting structures were often reused (requisitioned) for military encampments, and it would seem that the central portion of Uwado was laid out on what had been a burial ground used by that temple.[50] The camp was established by the Yamanouchi at the turn of the sixteenth century, at the height of hostilities during the war of the "Two Uesugi," and was meant to provide a staging ground for attacks on the nearby fortress of Kawagoe, where the Ōgigayatsu were ensconced at the time. Uwado's natural defenses were more formidable than those at Ikatsuko had been. The fast current of the Irumagawa separated the two camps, though it is clear that Uwado did not rely solely on the river to stave off enemy sallies. Excavations have uncovered traces of two rings of moats on the northern and western edges of the central portion of the camp (the outer moat three to seven meters wide), along the outer side of an earthen rampart. Other moats have been found within the earthworks, perhaps serving to further subdivide the inner compound (although these moats do not seem to be associated with earthworks, so perhaps they were not intended to create distinct enclosures, as was common practice with castles).[51]

A fair amount of fortifying was carried out at both encampments, raising a host of questions about their temporary nature, and about the

48. Until recently there was very little archaeological information on Uwado: *NJT* 5:66–68 does not have an entry on the Yamanouchi camp itself, though it does mention the locale in connection with the residence of the Kamakura-period Kawagoe family. Sekiguchi Kazuya ("Kawagoe-shi yakata") explicitly mentions the link between the two structures and suggests that the site should be known not as the Kawagoe family residence (*Kawagoe-shi yakata*) but as the Uwado castle (*Uwado-jō*). More recently, the connection has been made in Ochiai, "Musashi no kuni Kawagoe-kan," esp. 47–51; Tanaka S., "'Yamanouchi Uesugi-shi no kawarake' to wa."

49. *Kaikoku zakki*, 501a.

50. Nor was this exceptional: during the dispute that rocked the Iwamatsu family in 1495, troops were stationed in the burial grounds where the grave of the recently deceased patriarch, Iezumi, was. *Shōin shigo*, 837b.

51. Ogino, "Kawagoe kanseki," 163.

traits setting apart camps, mansions, and castles (of both the temporary and permanent varieties). In some ways, encampments may evoke the old temporary redoubts: emergency, ad hoc spaces of refuge apart from routine administration and the everyday. Much has been made of the difference between permanent castles as spaces of everyday life and their temporary forerunners, conversely conceptualized as spaces apart. Archaeological evidence has reinforced this characterization by highlighting the functional separation of highlands (plateaus, hills, mounds, slopes) as spaces reserved for ceremonial functions, for temple and shrine precincts and burial grounds.[52] Military encampments, too, had a long history of proximity to sacred spaces like temple and shrine precincts, and liminal spaces like mounds and slopes.[53] In this sense, the Yamanouchi's use of the grounds (and burial grounds) of Jōrakuji at Uwado was hardly innovative. The provincial temples established by the old imperial state (*kokubunji*), for instance, had a long tradition of offering asylum to transient populations and functioning as hospitals for the needy. In the Middle Ages, because of that tradition and the auspicious presence of a deity, provincial and other temples came to be used as defensive structures during peasant insurrections. Soon, warriors too were stationing their armies in or near the precincts (and as a paradoxical, if perhaps inevitable consequence, battles were often waged nearby, visiting destruction upon temples and shrines even as they functioned as havens).[54] Nor were other temples, or shrines, exempted. Indeed, the prohibitions discussed in Chapter 2, posted in temple and shrine precincts to stop soldiers garrisoned nearby from marauding and assorted outrages, attest to the frequency with which religious complexes were *compelled* to offer hospitality to campaigning armies.

The liminality of the sorts of places often selected for camps—hills, slopes, mounds (which were often overgrown artificial burial mounds

---

52. Writing about the early modern period, Barbara Ambros (*Emplacing a Pilgrimage*, 22) has drawn on the Foucauldian notion of heterotopias to stress mountains' character as places apart. See also, on Kumano, Moerman, *Localizing Paradise*.

53. Marra, *Representations of Power*, 62–65; Nakazawa, *Chūsei no buryōku to jōkaku*, 163–64.

54. Oishio, *Kokubunji no chūseiteki tenkai*, 222–23; *Ōta Dōkan jō*, 639b; *Shōin shigo*, 821a–b.

dating from a thousand years before), and even dry riverbeds—has made the emergence of the new castles in the fifteenth century seem like a complete break. As for the camps used by the Uesugi, the temporary and non-quotidian character they shared with the old fastnesses may lead to the assumption that they were fundamentally different from the new permanent fortresses, which were making the conduct of war a matter of everyday business.[55] Yet it is easy to overstate the differences between the new, permanent castles and camps, or the similarities between camps and temporary castles. The notion of a temporary space, to be applied indifferently to mountaintop redoubts and to camps, should be rethought in the context of the endemic warfare of the fifteenth century, as should the juxtaposition between quotidian (*nichijō*) and non-quotidian (*hinichijō*) spaces, which can be misleading in its seeming clarity.

To be sure, truly temporary camps were still used, camps meant to last but the length of a brief foray against a neighbor. Ōta Dōkan's retelling of his experience chasing down Nagao Kageharu's rebellious supporters all around the plain between 1477 and 1481 mentions thirty-four camps by name (most of these used for no more than a few days).[56] But the camps built by the Yamanouchi Uesugi at Ikatsuko and Uwado were something different. To begin with, the word "temporary" seems singularly inapposite for Uwado, which stood from 1497 to 1505, or Ikatsuko, which operated even longer, from 1457 to 1477.[57] One may argue that in the long run twenty years and eight years were not terribly long stretches, although contemporaries did not take them to be short-lived (even the most permanent of Japanese structures tended to be built of wood, after all, so long-term durability remained an elusive proposition).

The different circumstances of the two camps' ends adds to the uncertainty: Ikatsuko's life was cut short by its sudden and embarrassing collapse at the hand of Kageharu, who blockaded the roads around the

55. Ochiai, "Chūsei tōgoku no jin to geinō," 37–38. Ochiai describes camps as temporary structures, and quintessential medieval spaces of authority, without really elaborating on what made them typical of the Middle Ages as against the later period of civil war.

56. *Ōta Dōkan jō*, 636b–44a passim.

57. Morita, "Monjo, kiroku kara mita Ikatsuko-jin"; Ochiai, "Musashi no kuni Kawagoe-kan," 51–53; Tanaka S., "'Yamanouchi Uesugi-shi no kawarake' to wa," 67–68.

camp, forcing the Uesugi to leave before supplies ran out. Ikatsuko was destroyed by an enemy (always a possible end for a defensive structure), not dismantled voluntarily by the Uesugi.[58] Nor was its end immediately apparent to all: Ōta Dōkan attempted a brief revival of the camp a few months later before concluding that continuing unrest in the area made the idea inadvisable. Uwado's fate, on the other hand, may seem to suggest that the camp was never meant to last, for it was discarded soon after the Ōgigayatsu capitulated and vacated the castle of Kawagoe for the victorious Yamanouchi. Given Uwado's proximity to Kawagoe, though, it is not surprising that when hostilities with the Ōgigayatsu were over and the enemy was made to surrender the fortress, the Yamanouchi should choose to make that their residence, rendering the camp redundant.[59]

And we may question whether the two camps' eventual demise set them apart from castles as *programmatically* short-lived—whether, in other words, camps were intended to fill the need for temporary military structures created by the diffusion of permanent castles. After all, there is no indication that temporary castles ceased to be built after permanent ones appeared on the scene; and temporary castles, too, could be built for the narrow purpose of pressuring, or besieging, an enemy. A rich vocabulary referring to such "siege castles" appears frequently in contemporary documents.[60] In recording that a siege castle was established on a particular occasion, these sources would seem to suggest that such structures were thrown together on short notice—distinct from the permanent, residential strongholds produced by the castellan revolution. Yet what was a siege castle for one source was just a castle for another (the Toshima brothers' Hiratsuka, for instance), confusing our taxonomies and intimating that in the late fifteenth and early sixteenth centuries mansions and castles of various sorts were perceived along a spectrum

---

58. *Kamakura ōzōshi*, 61; *Shōin shigo*, 839a.

59. It is worth noting that it was not because of Uwado's superior capabilities that the Yamanouchi triumphed over the Ōgigayatsu. Rather, we may say that it was because of the castles at Kawagoe and Edo that the far less powerful Ōgigayatsu managed to withstand the Yamanouchi until 1505.

60. For instance: words like *taijō* and *mukaijiro* (opposing, facing castle), *tsukejiro* (a castle "against").

defined by function, and thus amenable to change as need dictated new uses for existing structures.[61] And this is more indication that, no matter how much they endeavored to build castles that would withstand the passing of time along with the onslaught of enemies, to contemporaries the effects of the castellan revolution may have been visible only cumulatively. In being discarded after use, Uwado met a fate that was neither especially remarkable nor defining of the difference between castle and camp. Camps did not stand apart by virtue of their temporary character (however variously measured).

By and large, contemporary sources do seem to distinguish between camps and other military structures more consistently than they do between, say, (new) castles and residences.[62] On his way through the Kantō in 1502, the poet Sōchō noted in his travel diary, matter-of-factly, "A place called Uwado is presently the site of the encampment of the Yamanouchi."[63] Yet this does not mean that structural difference outweighed functional similarity: years later, Sōchō, revisiting the military standoff between

---

61. Saitō (*Chūsei tōgoku no ryōiki to jōkan*, 62–66) distinguishes terminologically between the terms *taijō*, *mukaijiro*, and *tsukejiro*, which he then concedes were functionally analogous; Nakazawa Katsuaki (*Chūsei no buryoku to jōkaku*, 243–54) analyzes the terminology of castle building (though focusing on early medieval sources). He notes that fortresses would be referred to either as *yōgai* or *jōkaku*, and concludes that the designation depended not on their size or structure but on their affiliation: rogue, "adulterine" castles were consistently called *jōkaku*, whereas strongholds erected with the consent or at the behest of public authorities such as the shogunate or the local governor were invariably *yōgai*. Alas, the actual pattern outlined by Nakazawa does not fit the evidence in the late fifteenth century: in *Ōta Dōkan jō*, 638a, a castle built by the Toshima is called a *yōgai* even though it is unambiguously a rebel outpost.

62. Matsuoka Susumu ("Sengoku shoki tōgoku ni okeru jin to jōkaku," 2–3) suggests that camps were not mistaken for castles because castles and camps were structurally hard to confuse, though he makes a specious distinction by drawing attention to two instances in which, conversely, castles are referred to as camps (both are from one source, *Ōta Dōkan jō*). A more convincing explanation, one compatible with Matsuoka's broader point, is that contemporaries often used the word camp metaphorically to refer to a seat of authority. In another letter, not quoted by Matsuoka, Dōkan refers to Ashikaga Shigeuji's residence in Koga—a castle—as his "main camp." (*KKS* 1, no. 208 [*Kokan zassan* 6]). Still, other texts exist in which camps and castles seem to be conflated: *Kamakura ōzōshi*, 64, once refers to the building of a "temporary camp-castle" (*kari no jinjō o kamaekeru*), while a letter from 1496 speaks, all-encompassingly, of a "camp-castle siege-camp" (*jinjō taijin*) (*GKS* 7, no. 1820 [Utsue monjo]).

63. *Sōgi shūenki*, 673.

the two Uesugi in another diary, would observe, "The Ōgigayatsu were allied with [Hōjō] Sōun and held Kawagoe and Edo. The Yamanouchi held Uwado and Hachigata."[64] Militarily, at least, Sōchō's failure to draw a distinction between Uwado, on the one hand, and Kawagoe, Edo, and Hachigata, on the other, suggests that permanence and impermanence did little to set apart the castles from the encampment.

So why camps? What was it about camps that was appealing? What *can* we say about them?

Sprawling, probably messy complexes though they were, Ikatsuko and Uwado undoubtedly served as more than temporary military facilities. During their years in operation, Ikatsuko and Uwado were the main centers of consumption in the plain, the capitals of the embattled Yamanouchi Uesugi polity.[65] In the only moment of reflection he committed to paper on the subject, Ōta Dōkan remarked: "As for the camp at Ikatsuko, for thirty years the Imperial Banner had stood here, but as a result of an unforeseen event [i.e., Kageharu's attack], [his lordship] was forced to retreat from the camp."[66] All manner of mishaps and blunders are presented as "unforeseen events" (*ryogai daimoku*) in fifteenth-century sources. Still, even while overstating the camp's long years of service by a considerable margin, Dōkan's statement confirms that, had it not been for Kageharu's rebellion, the Uesugi would have been more than happy to maintain their court at Ikatsuko for years to come. And the passage also makes clear that Ikatsuko functioned *as a court*, not simply a staging ground for campaigns: the imperial banner—representing the mandate to pacify the eastern provinces in Kyoto's name—unambiguously defined Ikatsuko as a seat of public authority. *Shōin shigo* echoes this view, implying as a matter of course that a camp could be a site worthy of a court: "As for the camp in Ikatsuko, this was now the main camp, as the Uesugi Deputy had petitioned for the Imperial Banner."[67] When the Yamanouchi leadership wrested Hachigata castle from Kageharu a few

64. Horton, *Journal of Sōchō*, 9; Uzawa, *Sōchō Suruga nikki*, 5–6.

65. They were also the cultural capitals of the region, as linked-verse production and political centers were closely connected; see Yata, *Chūsei Sengoku-ki kenryoku kōzō*, 115–31; Morita, "Yamanouchi Uesugi-shi no kyoten ni tsuite."

66. *Ōta Dōkan jō*, 637b.

67. *Shōin shigo*, 820b.

months after hastily abandoning the camp at Ikatsuko, Dōkan noted, "the Banner was moved to this castle,"[68] as if to underscore that what had mattered about the move was not only the family head who moved, but the office and mandate he represented. The chronicle *Kamakura ōzōshi* is even more explicit: "As for Akisada [the Kantō deputy and head of the Yamanouchi Uesugi], he unfurled the Imperial Banner in the castle at Hachigata, and this became his home castle (*ijō*)."[69]

Running through all of these casual comments is the shared understanding that the presence of the imperial banner conferred on a residence—whether a main camp or a residential castle—the status of a public office. Successive heads of the Yamanouchi Uesugi resided at Ikatsuko, surrounded by collaterals and more distant relatives, house elders, chief retainers, and allied lords. Iwamatsu Iezumi's return to Ikatsuko after the inauguration of Kanayama, which opened this chapter, must not have seemed noteworthy to the many other lords who were residing at the camp. Nagao Kageharu, too, lived at Ikatsuko, only departing in anger when he was passed over for appointment as chief retainer to the Yamanouchi.[70] And the various deputy governors of the provinces under Uesugi rule moved their chanceries to the camp and ran day-to-day administrative business from there: as we saw in Chapter 2, Kageharu's rival for the post of chief retainer, his uncle Nagao Tadakage, managed the payment of dues in faraway estates without leaving Ikatsuko.[71] In other words, Ikatsuko (and later Uwado) soon became the nuclei of urban developments. The blockade that ultimately brought the camp to an end was effective chiefly because Ikatsuko had developed beyond a purely military, defensive facility, attracting merchants and trade: "[The enemy] blocked merchants' transit to and from the Ikatsuko camp. Whether

---

68. *Ōta Dōkan jō*, 641a.

69. *Kamakura ōzōshi*, 63. See also Kinoshita, "Yamanouchi Uesugi-shi ni okeru kanto to Kantō kanreishiki," 23–25.

70. *Kamakura ōzōshi*, 60; *Shōin shigo*, 838b–839a.

71. And of course, house elders like Terao Reishun maintained contacts between Ikatsuko and Uesugi commanders when they were away: see *SKS* 5, no. 922 (Rokuōin monjo); *KKS* 1, no. 208 (*Kokan zassan* 6). See also Ochiai, "Musashi no kuni Kawagoe-kan," 51–52.

battling along the roads or clashing in villages, the attacks on families and homes were beyond count," notes Shōin.[72]

Nor were the powerful warriors who resided at the camp roughing it: ceramics excavated at the Ikatsuko and Uwado sites tend to be of very high quality, befitting the palatial seats of the loftiest lords of the Kantō. Confirming a pattern verified in sites associated with warrior families' residential headquarters across the region, a significant number of commercially obtained wares have been found among the locally produced specimens.[73] Excavation at one of the Ikatsuko sites has yielded significant amounts of imported white porcelain (*hakuji*) and celadon (*seiji*), along with domestic ceramics like Seto wares and a Tenmoku bowl.[74]

---

72. *Shōin shigo*, 838b. For Ikatsuko as a market town, see Asano, "Hōjō ryōgoku no jōkan to tōjiki," 233–34.

73. Asano, "Tōgoku ni okeru zaichi doki no seisan to ryūtsū," 400–401; Inoue Tetsuo, "Minami Kantō ni okeru jōkanseki shutsudo tōjiki," 174–75. For a discussion of Chinese ceramics found at the residences of local magnates, see Taniguchi, "Hakkutsu sareta Toshima-gun," 74–78.

74. Asano, "Sengoku-ki jōkan no nendaikan," 47. Asano actually feels the numbers are too small (porcelain 31, celadon 22, glazed Seto 8, *tenmoku* 1) for the Kawaramachi site to be the central part of the camp, as scholars believe. In an essay on the excavation of ceramics at Uwado, Koizumi Isao ("Kawagoe-kanshi no hakkutsu") mentions several similar finds, which he dates from the twelfth and thirteenth centuries (and possibly, for some items, the fourteenth), particularly a Southern Song (1127–1279) variety of celadon now known in Japan as *Kinuta seiji*, which has very seldom been found beyond the city limits of Kamakura, and another variety of celadon from southern China known in Japan as *Shukō seiji*. What is puzzling about the article is that, despite its recent date of publication, Koizumi discusses the site solely in terms of the 1970s excavation of the old residence of the long-extinct Kawagoe family. Koizumi notes the remarkable extension of the site, but nowhere mentions that the remains of the Kawagoe family residence were subsequently overlaid with the Uwado encampment (the very size of the complex is striking for a middling family like the Kawagoe, less so for an encampment of the Yamanouchi Uesugi). It is entirely possible that some of the potsherds recovered at the site were given an earlier date because of the site's putative association with the Kawagoe; a later date would also explain why ceramics seldom found beyond the "capital city" of Kamakura would be recovered in the middle of Musashi. This seems even more likely in consideration of Hashiguchi Sadashi's revision of the chronology of so-called square mansions to the end of the Middle Ages. See Hashiguchi, "Chūsei hōkei kyokan o meguru shomondai"; Hashiguchi, "Chūsei tōgoku no kyokan to sono shūhen."

But among the potsherds archaeologists have recovered at Ikatsuko, Uwado, and other sites associated with the Yamanouchi Uesugi, the ones that have generated the most interest and debate are a type of low-fired, unglazed ceramics known as *kawarake* (Fig. 4.2). These earthenwares, dishes and cups in particular, are typical of the Middle Ages, when they were produced in bulk as disposable ritual vessels.[75] Their ritual significance far exceeded their material value; their recovery at Uwado and Ikatsuko, in vast numbers and in specific locations within the camps, offers us hints, I believe, not only about encampments' ritual dimensions, but also, more broadly, about the functioning of authority in late medieval Japan. *Kawarake* allow us to make sense, politically, of the tricky juxtaposition of the quotidian and the liminal, and to figure out the appeal of camps in an age of castles.

In the fifteenth century, with the formalization of the ceremonies of state performed by the shogunate (*buke girei*), the production of *kawarake* earthenware was standardized in its sizes and shapes for use during the official ritual calendar, in banquets such as the "Ceremony of Three Libations" (*shikisankon*). In this ceremony, which was typically performed in ancient-style halls (*shindenzukuri*) reserved for functions of state,[76] the shogun and his highest-ranking followers would take turns drinking sake from a cup that was passed around while propitiatory toasts and offers of food were made to the gods.[77] The combination of the stateliness of the venue and the intimacy and sharing of the actual ceremony was designed to reinforce personal and political bonds among members of the highest elites.[78]

75. Cort, "Disposable but Indispensable"; Hattori, "Kawarake."

76. Kumakura (*Nihon ryōri no rekishi*, 75) notes the choice of venue, but characterizes the choice merely in terms of a preference for the solemnity of tradition. For an in-depth analysis of the Ashikaga rulers' self-conscious use of different architectural conventions to bolster their regime, see Stavros, "Building Warrior Legitimacy in Medieval Kyoto."

77. See the discussion of *shikisankon* in Rath, *Food and Fantasy*, 67–71. My thanks to Professor Rath for showing me a copy of his manuscript before publication. Kumakura has provided description of the ceremony in two recent works, *Nihon ryōri bunkashi*, 142; and *Nihon ryōri no rekishi*, 75–78. See also *Shōin shigo*, 834b, which most probably refers to the same ceremony, albeit without naming it explicitly.

78. For an important new study of the centrality of ritual in late medieval Japan, see Conlan, *From Sovereign to Symbol.*

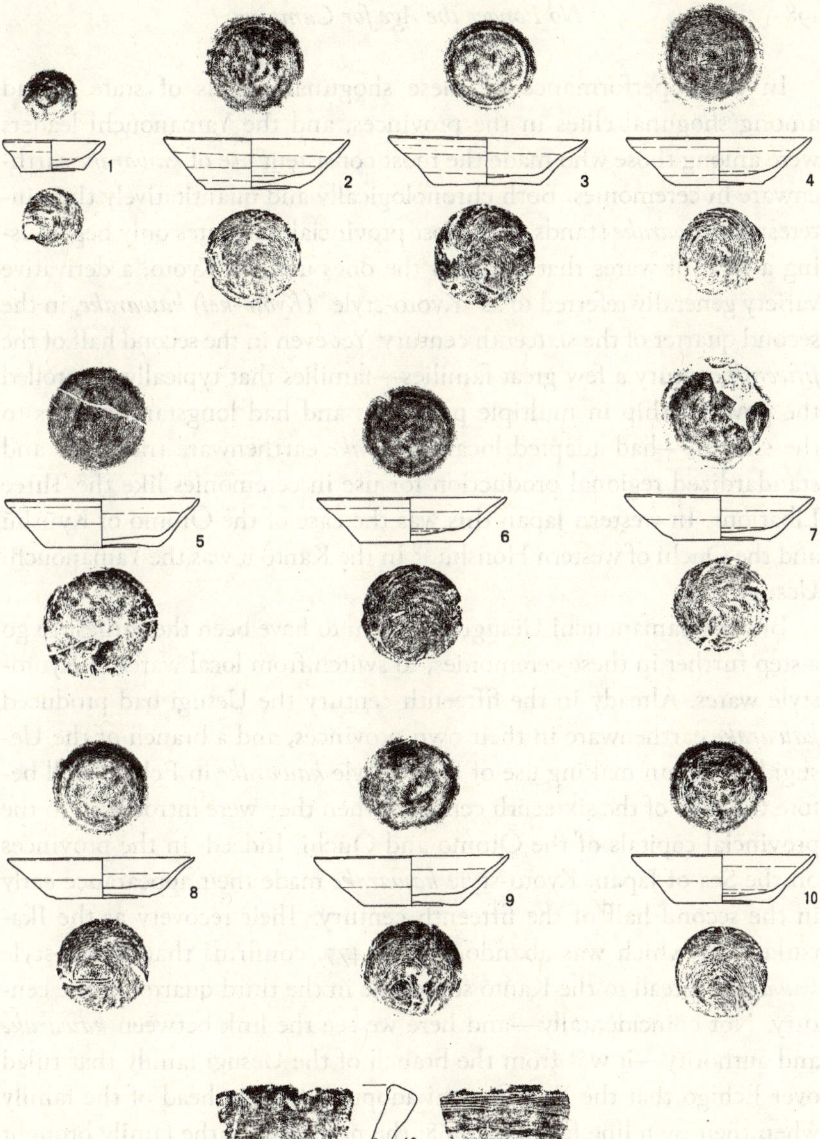

Fig. 4.2. *Kawarake* unearthed at the site of the camp of Ikatsuko. From Honjō-shi Iseki Chōsakai, *Higashiikakko Akasaka Iseki*, 10; used by permission.

In time, performance of these shogunal rituals of state spread among shogunal elites in the provinces, and the Yamanouchi leaders were among those who made the most consistent use of *kawarake* earthenware in ceremonies. Both chronologically and quantitatively their interest in *kawarake* stands out. Most provincial magnates only began using a style of wares that imitated the ones used in Kyoto, a derivative variety generally referred to as "Kyoto-style" (*Kyōto-kei*) *kawarake*, in the second quarter of the sixteenth century. Yet even in the second half of the *fifteenth* century a few great families—families that typically controlled the governorship in multiple provinces and had longstanding ties to the shogun—had adapted local *kawarake* earthenware traditions and standardized regional production for use in ceremonies like the Three Libations. In western Japan this was the case of the Ōtomo of Kyūshū and the Ōuchi of western Honshū.[79] In the Kantō it was the Yamanouchi Uesugi.

But the Yamanouchi Uesugi also seem to have been the earliest to go a step further in these ceremonies, to switch from local wares to Kyoto-style wares. Already in the fifteenth century the Uesugi had produced *kawarake* earthenware in their own provinces, and a branch of the Uesugi had begun making use of Kyoto-style *kawarake* in Echigo well before the turn of the sixteenth century, when they were introduced to the provincial capitals of the Ōtomo and Ōuchi. Indeed, in the provinces on the Sea of Japan, Kyoto-style *kawarake* made their appearance early in the second half of the fifteenth century. Their recovery at the Ikatsuko site, which was abandoned in 1477, confirms that Kyoto-style *kawarake* spread to the Kantō sometime in the third quarter of the century. Not coincidentally—and here we see the link between *kawarake* and authority—it was from the branch of the Uesugi family that ruled over Echigo that the Yamanouchi adopted the new head of the family when their own line failed in 1468; the new head of the family brought the (Kyoto-style) wares from Echigo with him when he moved to Ikatsuko. Archaeologist Tanaka Shin has called this subgroup of Kyoto-style wares "Yamanouchi-style" (*Yamanouchi-kei*) *kawarake*. Leaving a trail as they spread southward throughout the regions controlled by the Yama-

79. Tanaka S., "'Yamanouchi Uesugi-shi no kawarake' to wa," 74; Hattori, "Kawarake," 437.

nouchi, these Yamanouchi-style *kawarake* have been recovered from sites at Hirai, in southwestern Kōzuke, and Hachigata, in northwestern Musashi (which the Yamanouchi took over after defeating Nagao Kageharu), as well as Ikatsuko and Uwado (Map 4.2).[80]

The form and style of the wares, homogeneous and recognizable throughout the various residences of the Yamanouchi, served to strengthen the cohesion of armies made up of warriors of disparate lineages and families. That the new heir would bring *kawarake* with him from Echigo was no anomaly: Yamanouchi-style *kawarake* have been found at all the sites associated with the family (Map 4.3). Indeed, the vessels' homogeneity and distribution suggest that the Yamanouchi produced the *kawarake* earthenware at kilns they controlled and transported them to their various residences throughout the eastern provinces. Supporting this interpretation, and confirming the vessels' exclusively ritual uses, *kawarake* tend to be more plentiful at the center of Yamanouchi sites and fewer on the margins, where they are outnumbered by locally produced wares.[81]

Implicit in these observations is the possibility of using the diffusion of different styles of *kawarake* to trace the bonds that were established between families through adoptions—the patterns of genealogical, marital, strategic affiliation that underpinned the avowedly institutional authority of families like the Uesugi. Locally, the ascendancy of one style of *kawarake* over another mirrored the ascendancy of one family or one lineage over others, and the distribution of Yamanouchi-style *kawarake* has revealed a story of Yamanouchi influence over areas not previously associated with the family's power. An example is the castle of Iwatsuki, once believed to have been built by the Ōgigayatsu in the 1450s. Recent scholarship has shown that it was in fact the fruit of the labor of the Narita family, which supported Shigeuji in his decades-long war against the Uesugi. Later, after a peace was negotiated in 1483, the Yamanouchi managed to have one of the sons of their chief retainer adopted as heir by the Narita—a poorly documented event that is confirmed nonetheless

80. Tanaka S., "'Yamanouchi Uesugi-shi no kawarake' to wa," 68–69.

81. Akimoto, "Sengoku-ki kita Kantō no kawarake," 264. Asano Haruki ("Tōgoku ni okeru zaichi doki no seisan to ryūtsū," 400–401) has noted the difference between the wares recovered in Ikatsuko and in contemporary sites nearby. For a diagram of *kawarake* diffusion, see Ono, "Jōkan shutsudo no tōjiki," 130–34.

Map 4.2. Diffusion of Kyoto-style *kawarake.*

by the appearance at Iwatsuki, shortly before the turn of the sixteenth century, of Yamanouchi Uesugi style *kawarake* earthenware.[82]

82. Aoki, "Iwatsuki jōseki"; Kuroda M., *Sengoku-ki tōgoku no daimyō to kunishū*, 60–64.

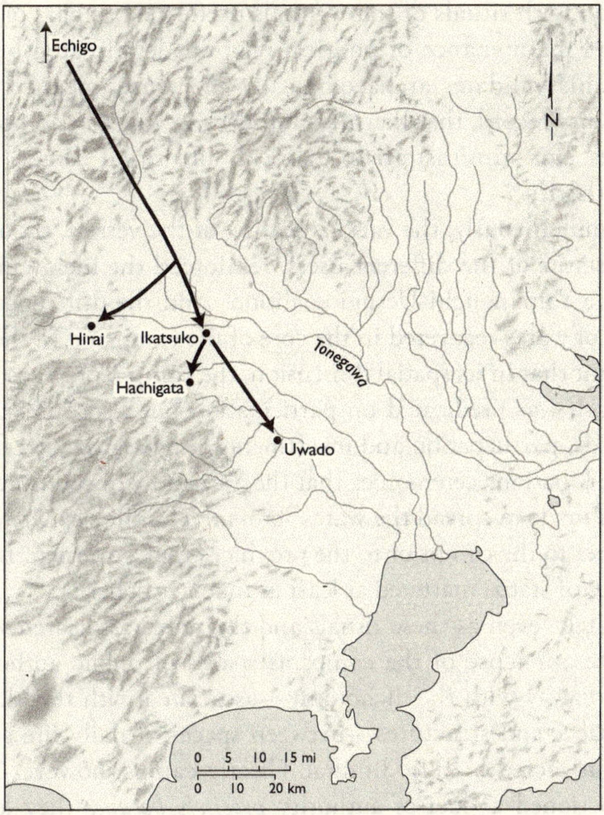

Map 4.3. Distribution of Yamanouchi-style *kawarake* in the Kantō.

By using a type of ceramics made in self-conscious imitation of the ones used in the capital region, the Yamanouchi emphatically traced their affiliation and affinity with the shogunal house in the capital. The copious presence of these wares at Uwado, where the Yamanouchi held court and waged war on their Ōgigayatsu relatives, coupled with their absence at nearby Kawagoe, where the leadership of the Ōgigayatsu had its headquarters, underscores these vessels' exclusive association with what we would call rituals of state carried out by the Yamanouchi heads—who monopolized the highest, region-wide offices in the shogunal administration. Much of the space of the encampments was thus conceived in connection with rituals of state, rituals performed as part of the cultivation and maintenance of political relations legitimated by the shogunate. This validates archaeologically the sense, gleaned from the documentary record, that Ikatsuko and Uwado were not ad hoc military complexes, but administrative, political, and ritual centers—seats of public authority.[83]

Yet, simultaneously, the various scaling of the vessels, thought to reflect the status of the different users, reinforced the hierarchical structure of the Yamanouchi Uesugi coalition. And the difference between the types of wares recovered in the core of the camp and in the outlying areas meant that in its spatial dimension, the camp represented a regime whose reach was predicated on participation but also on exclusion. In other words, participation and investment in the regime was felt during the Three Libations ceremonies that the Yamanouchi sponsored; but no effort was made to spread the wares across the family's sphere of authority, whether to the camps or to the provinces they governed. In the end, differences of status mattered at least as much as cohesion.[84]

Ultimately, even as these rituals and the wares associated with them complicate our sense of the camps as spaces of public authority, they help us do away with the dichotomy—associated with the idea of temporary spaces and structures—between spaces of daily life and spaces set apart as sacred because liminal. Clearly camps, however impermanent, functioned as loci of authority *precisely because* they lent themselves to the performance of functions both ritual and routinely administrative, for good management of the affairs of state, even at its most secular, was closely associated with and dependent on sacred spaces. For instance, provincial temples and provincial shrines (the temples' Shintō counterparts) were commonly established in the vicinity of the provincial

---

83. In discussing an encampment established in the fourteenth century, Ochiai Yoshiaki ("Chūsei tōgoku no jin to geinō," 44–49) has pointed out the importance of the propitiatory performance, by one of Shigeuji's forefathers, of ritual dances long associated with the imperial court as a way of enhancing his authority.

84. Hattori Mitsuyoshi ("Kawarake kara mita Hōjō-shi," 13–15) has shown how the Hōjō of Odawara, too, later in the sixteenth century, made use of different types of *kawarake* to spell out status differences throughout the plain.

capitals of the old imperial state, which by the fifteenth century had developed into full-fledged urban centers. (The walled precincts of these capitals, too, no less than temples and shrines, were often repurposed as camps.)[85] It is no coincidence that the Ōtomo and Ōuchi, who distinguished themselves among provincial governors by the care with which they adopted the formal rites elaborated in Kyoto, performed the Ceremony of Three Libations in their provincial capitals, much as the Uesugi did in their encampments.[86]

The Language of Place and Authority

Yet it is worth returning to the point that the Yamanouchi chose to rule the western Kantō from a seat of power that for all of its functional and ceremonial affinities with contemporary fortresses (not to mention cities), was persistently, and exclusively, referred to by sources at the time as an encampment. Something about Ikatsuko's and Uwado's character as encampments mattered.

The word these sources use for encampment, *jin*, is a tricky one, for it makes no distinction between the physical space of the encampment and the activity for which such an encampment was used—that is, the military campaign. To distinguish the two, historians occasionally describe the physical place using cognates with more specific connotations (*jinsho*, a campsite; *jinrui*, a camp's earthworks). Invariably given to colorful descriptions, Shōin recalls how he "went around and beheld the layouts of the two camps, which faced each other separated by difficult terrain, [and realized] they were fortifications without equal in this country."[87] But by and large fifteenth- and sixteenth-century writers keep

---

85. Ogawa, *Chūsei toshi "Fuchū" no tenkai*, 31–35, 503–33; Fukasawa, "Chūsei no Musashi Fuchū"; Saitō, "Minami Kantō," 157–58.

86. Hattori, "Kawarake," 437; Tanaka S., "'Yamanouchi Uesugi-shi no kawarake' to wa," 73–74. A slightly different twist on the practice is the one offered by the Shimazu of southern Kyūshū, who seem not to have used *kawarake* in great quantities during the sixteenth century even as they did perform a version of the Ceremony of Three Libations (in other words, utilizing different kinds of ceramics for banquets other than the ceremony). See Kusunose, "Sengoku-ki Shimazu-shi ni okeru shushoku kyōō girei."

87. *Shōin shigo*, 801b.

on the vague side with the generic *jin* (and it is useful to add, parenthetically, that there is no terminological distinction between a camp lasting ten weeks and one lasting ten years).

Commonly used phrases and compound words denoting the creation of an encampment, like *jin o toru* and *chōjin su* (or *jin o haru*) refer, clearly enough, to the establishment of a facility. Uesugi Fusaaki "set a camp in a place called Ikatsuko in Musashi,"[88] while Dōkan less momentously, a few years later, "set a camp nearby, in a place called Murayama, in this province,"[89] or "arrived and set a camp at the monastery in Kanaya."[90] One Akabori Kōzuke no kami received a letter of congratulations for his valor: "You led the troops from Tottori against the place where Nagao [Kageharu] had made his camp, whereupon, without it coming to a battle, [his troops] withdrew and scattered."[91] Marking its concreteness, the camp is typically associated with a landmark, a place name. These phrases (*chōjin su*, in particular) evoke the image of a complex spreading out across the countryside. At the opposite end of a camp's life, phrases like *jin o harau* similarly imply the existence and the dismantling of a camp *structure*: "Seeing the camp dismantled [the defenders] sallied forth from the castle."[92]

Other compounds, like *shutsujin*, are less concerned with the physical space of the encampment. *Shutsujin* means not so much to exit a camp as to set off on a campaign. For example, in 1471, during the course of a major offensive launched by the Uesugi against Shigeuji, the distant shogun wrote an urgent letter to one of his supporters, enjoining him to rendezvous with the advancing army: "Time and again we have spoken about this. In each and every matter, if you serve loyally, *deploying your troops* without further ado, the pacification [of the realm] will not be turned back" (emphasis added).[93] In this case the exiting of the camp is purely metaphorical, as the recipient of the missive, Uesugi Fusasada, governor of Echigo Province, was being ordered to set off with an army

---

88. *Kamakura ōzōshi*, 55.
89. *Ōta Dōkan jō*, 640b.
90. *Ōta Dōkan jō*, 642a.
91. *GKS* 7, no. 1792 (Akabori monjo).
92. *Kamakura ōzōshi*, 64.
93. *TKS* 4:319, no. 29 (Gonaishofuan).

from Funai, the capital of that province (a town, not a camp), and cross the mountains to join the offensive. Even more confusing is another phrase, *kijin su*, which literally means "to return to the encampment,"[94] but also means "returning from the campaign" (as long as Ikatsuko and Uwado stood, the two meanings could be one and the same, of course).[95] The bigger picture here is that *jin* were no less an *activity* than they were a place—and an activity entailing a great degree of mobility, no less.[96]

The association between power and place is pervasive in medieval Japanese—and well known—and typically took one of three forms. Among local warriors, social status was marked by the use of ceremonial titles received from the court—often appointments to the old imperial governorships, which by the late Middle Ages were dispensed liberally as empty honors with no actual duties attached to them (nor any jurisdiction over the province of nominal appointment). In fact, over time they had come to be hereditary, and were used by members of a lineage to signal their claims to legitimate succession: the head of the Sōja house of the Nagao family commonly signed his letters as "Governor of Owari" (*Owari no kami*); the head of the Yokoze, chief retainer of the Nitta Iwamatsu, was commonly called "Governor of Shinano" (*Shinano no kami*); a warrior from a family of lesser status, like the Motegi, might be known as "Lieutenant Governor of Kazusa" (*Kazusa no suke*).[97] Such titles represent a view of place wholly divorced from geography—a place constituted in purely institutional and ceremonial terms.

---

94. *Kamakura ōzōshi*, 62; *Shōin shigo*, 845a.

95. *Kamakura ōzōshi*, 62; *KKS* 1, no. 199 (*Kokan zassan* 6).

96. Examples of the word *jin*, alone, referring to an activity: *KKS* 1, no. 197 (Hōkokuji monjo); comments in *Kamakura ōzōshi*, 64, about a campaign being long (*chōjin*); *TKS* 1:490, no. 338 (Bannaji monjo); *GKS* 7, no. 1866 (Hotchi-shi monjo); *Shōin shigo*, 832b.

97. Even the word sinecure here seems to imply too much of an actual office: with only sixty-seven provinces to draw from, and hundreds of warrior families in need of a title, appointments were redundant, with several families sharing the same governorship (just in the Kantō "Shinano no kami" was used by the Yokoze, Ōmori, Nikaidō, Unakami, and a branch of the Ōishi. In Echigo, it referred to members of a branch of the Nagao). For studies based on the hereditary and nominal character of these and other titles, see Sawaki, "Sengoku bushō no kanto juryōmei to jitsumyō"; Nagatsuka, "Sengoku bushō no kanto, juryōmei"; Tsunoda, "Ashikaga Takauji to Imagawa Yoshimoto no kanto, juryō"; Kinoshita, "Buke kanto toshite no sama no kami"; Kinoshita, "Buke to shishiki taifu"; Kinoshita, "Chūsei kōki ni okeru buke to kantō juryōmei."

A second kind of link to place was apparent in surnames: most warriors boasted of real or fictive descent from ancient warrior clans (*uji*), themselves often descended from the imperial family. On especially important occasions, warriors would be known to sign documents with such prestigious names—Fujiwara, Taira, Minamoto, Tachibana, and so forth. Soon, though, warrior families adopted more prosaic names, which designated narrower segments of an extended kinship group—typically a single lineage or house. Uesugi began as one such surname, as did Ashikaga, or Nagao (most of these surnames derived from toponyms, such as the name of an ancestral manorial estate). By the fifteenth century, though, these groups had developed multiple lineages of their own and grown unwieldy. As junior lines moved away from the family residence, they often changed their surnames to signal the establishment of separate houses. These new surnames, too, were drawn from the names of the locales chosen for the new branch house's residence (Iwamatsu is an example, taken from the name of a village in Nitta Estate; Yamanouchi and Ōgigayatsu, likewise, were names derived from the two families' "neighborhoods" of residence within the city of Kamakura, before the civil war).

A third, closely related form of association between power and place was in the choice of informal titles of address for important personages and office holders. The shogun himself was seldom referred to by his formal title (*Seii taishōgun*, Great General for the Pacification of Eastern Barbarians). More commonly, he was called the Lord of Muromachi, from the street in Kyoto on which he built his palace.[98] Seen from the Kantō region, where individual street names and neighborhoods in the distant capital may have been less immediately evocative of the power of place, he was called Lord of Kyoto or, simply and impressively, Kyoto.[99] In the Kantō, Shigeuji was the last in a line of Ashikaga chieftains known

98. Stavros, "Locational Pedigree"; see also Mass, "The Mixing of Past and Present," 61–64.

99. It is worth noting, at the risk of stating the obvious, that conventional periodization in Japanese history also evinces a bias toward place (over people): whereas dynastic regimes in Europe are normally referred to by the name of the reigning family (Carolingians, Capetians, Ottonians, Angevins, Bourbons), their premodern Japanese counterparts are distinguished by the name of the place they elected to use as their seat of authority: Nara, Heian, Kamakura, Muromachi, Edo.

as the Lords of Kamakura, so called because they presided over the Kamakura Office in the town of the same name. When Shigeuji relocated from Kamakura to Koga at the beginning of the Kyōtoku Disturbance (1455–83), he came to be known (along with his successors) as the Lord of Koga. These titles—sobriquets, really—were the only ones Shigeuji had, titles that conveyed no information about his position in the hierarchy of the Muromachi regime.[100]

In this regard—in terms of the traditional representation of power as place—the Yamanouchi Uesugi may seem to have been something of an anomaly, for they associated their governance less with a seat of authority than with the announcement of a mandate, symbolized and given visibility by the imperial banner: they ruled from a camp because their role as high representatives of the shogun was initially validated and expressed by campaigning against Shigeuji. Even as other notables came to be called lords of here or lords of there, the Yamanouchi chieftains seem to have remained steadfastly placeless. Unlike Shigeuji, defined exclusively by his abode, the head of the Yamanouchi Uesugi had an actual post—that of Kantō deputy—but that title seldom appears in chronicles and correspondence to, from, and about him.[101] Most often, the Yamanouchi Uesugi chieftain was called no more than *yakata*.[102] The title *yakata* is curious, as it signifies "residence"—the Yamanouchi residence—without any geographic specificity; as if to say "the residence of the Yamanouchi lord," wherever that may be.

Yakata was not a Yamanouchi exclusive. It could be used by anyone who was referring to an important warrior leader he recognized as his

---

100. The one exception I have come across is in reference to Ashikaga Takamoto (1485–1535), third of the lords of Koga, who is referred to as the "Kantō general" (*Kantō jōshō*) in a 1517 document (*KKS* 1, no. 278) in which Ashikaga Yoshitane, the shogun, is referred to by his formal title, *seii taishōgun*. The word "general" (*jōshō*) refers to a military commander of the highest rank, though in this case it seems to be used as a mark of honor rather than a specific military or institutional designation.

101. It appears occasionally in travelogues (*Baika mujinzō* and *Sōchō shuki*) and in chronicles and memoirs (*Shōin shigo, Kamakura ōzōshi, Sōrinji denki*); as often as not, it appears simply as "deputy" (*kanrei*), shorn of both geographic and institutional specificity (in *Shōin shigo, Kamakura ōzōshi, Sōrinji denki*, and *Ōta Dōkan jō*).

102. *TKS* 4:452, no. 2 (Shūko monjo); *SKS* 5, no. 1019 (*Koshōmon*)—here it seems to refer to Akisada but it might be used as a general statement; *GKS* 7, no. 1753.

own lord. In the case of the head of the Yamanouchi Uesugi, for instance, the title was used by the house elders, but also by Ōta Dōkan—who served as chief retainer to the Ōgigayatsu but recognized the Yamanouchi head as the pinnacle of the extended Uesugi family and therefore often spoke of him as *yakata*.[103] On the other hand, in *Shōin shigo*—whose author was a steadfast proponent of the autonomous stature of the Iwamatsu—the title was used not for the head of the Uesugi but for the various heads of the Iwamatsu.[104] The title, in other words, was highly relational, as its use was predicated on a level of affiliation with the lord to whom one referred. If it was a reference to a place, it certainly was not a useful one in finding the locus of power it denoted. So it is intriguing that in a letter to one of the Yamanouchi elders, Dōkan once used another title, Lord of the Outer Fortifications (*sōgamae-sama*), probably in reference to the Uesugi head.[105] Like *yakata*, *sōgamae-sama* points to a locus of authority without naming it, without situating it beyond its function; compellingly, even more than *yakata* it evokes without naming it the encampment where the Yamanouchi lived during those years (Ikatsuko).

Needless to say, the pervasive links between power, office, and place were not articulated in terms of toponyms alone. Or, rather, links to toponyms were part of a broader conceptual framework, one that overwhelmingly structured medieval Japanese conceptions of space and place as a hierarchy. As seen in Chapter 1, even poetic geography was articulated in such a fashion. The sociopolitical hierarchy of premodern Japan was linguistically mapped onto the territory—its dynamics embedded in the vocabulary of place and movement. Just as geography gave shape to provincial warriors' status relations, the landscape itself was made of people, so to speak, and partook of the language and the structure of social hierarchy: a locale was "up" or "down" from another,

---

103. *Ōta Dōkan jō*, 636b, 637a, 637b. In a tally of expenses produced by a temple in Musashi in 1502 (*KKS* 1, no. 253 [Shōmyōji monjo]) it is the head of the Ōgigayatsu who is referred to as *yakata*, though in a similar document compiled by the same temple in 1506 (*KKS* 1, no. 260 [Shōmyōji monjo]) both the heads of the Ōgigayatsu and the Yamanouchi receive that title (the head of the Yamanouchi is referred to as "*yakata* of Sugaya," from the location of his encampment at the time, in 1505).

104. *Shōin shigo*, 824b, 825a, 826a, 826b, 830b, 832a, 833b, 843a.

105. *KKS* 1, no. 208 (*Kokan zassan* 6). The compilers suggest, plausibly, that this refers to the Uesugi head, Akisada.

just as one man might rank above or below another.[106] Kyoto, because of the overwhelming institutional, social, and cultural prestige it derived from centuries spent as the locus of highest authority—first the imperial court, more recently also the shogunal court—was by definition the apex of this political geography, and journeys to and from the capital always involved ascent and descent.[107] (Clearly, no consideration of topography was involved in Kyoto's loftiness, as the city, sitting in a basin surrounded by hills, was nonetheless "up" from any outlying locale.) As a consequence of the capital's preeminence, the provinces were looked down upon and traveled down to—their institutional subordination reflected in their imagined geographic placement below Kyoto. A journey to the Kantō, in the remote east, was always conceived as a descent from the lofty heights of the capital.[108] *Shōin shigo*—written by a man of the east—describes Iwamatsu Iezumi, at the head of a shogunal army, making preparations "at the beginning of his trip down to the Kantō."[109]

What is significant about such hierarchies of space (some of which survive in modern Japanese, if less ubiquitously) is that places were not intrinsically higher or lower. Loftiness and baseness were ways of mapping political, and thus contingent, relations of power and authority. To put it in more concrete terms, one headed down from Kyoto to Kamakura (all the more so if at the head of a shogunal army); one sent a letter down from Kamakura to Musashi, or Kōzuke; one traveled down from wherever a personage of high rank held court or resided.

---

106. Similar analyses of premodern Japan's hierarchical space can be found in Nenzi, *Excursions in Identity*, 21–26; and Wigen, *A Malleable Map*, 34–37.

107. In *Shōin shigo* and in general it seems that Kyoto is used mostly to refer to the shogun, while Raku—a term borrowed from the name of one of China's imperial capitals, Luoyang—is reserved for the physical city, along with Miyako. For contemporary references to Kyoto as Raku(yō), see *Sōrinji denki*, 434b, 438a; *Shōin shigo*, 805b; *SKS* 5, no. 1019 (*Koshōmon*); *TKS* 4:329, no. 69 (Gonaishofuan).

108. In the early modern period, the region around Kyoto came to be known as "Kamigata" (literally, "upwards"). A letter by Nagao Akikage (undated but written sometime in the first quarter of the sixteenth century) is generally cited as an early example of such usage; Uesugi Sadamasa appears to use the word with that meaning in 1489. *SKS* 5, no. 1019 (*Koshōmon*).

109. *Shōin shigo*, 805b. The original sentence implies a whole trip, concluded with Iezumi's arrival. "The beginning of the arrival" would be awkward in English.

A lord's court was his "seat" (*za*, or *goza* in the honorific form), so it is fitting that the verb *gozaru* (made by adding a verbal ending to the noun *goza*) should come to be used to mean "to be present." In other words, the language so strongly associated with the locus of authority was really predicated on the metonymical representation of those who held that authority.[110] As a result, it also comfortably accommodated the mobility of these seats of authority along with the mobility of those who, literally and figuratively, sat on them. The representation of authority in terms of places (that is, the representation of those who held authority in terms of places) also necessarily meant that the physical spaces in which authority was performed—the court that issued verdicts adjudicating land disputes, for instance, or the chancery that issued a deputy governor's call to arms—existed but feebly apart from the men that worked there. Courts were moved (*goza o utsusu*; *dōza su*) in the train of a great lord, and in an age of perpetual strife, when calls to arms were issued more or less daily, "to move a court" would also mean "to launch a campaign."[111]

The Uesugi, of course, had to maintain power over several provinces, and so, practically, the uprootedness and mobility of an encampment suited them perfectly. Wherever they *were* was a court. In this sense, the most distinctive trait of camps was not that they were temporary, but that they were—rhetorically, at least—mobile.

The putative mobility of encampments, their rootlessness, brings us back to the contradiction that opened this chapter. If, as seems more and more likely, the second half of the fifteenth century was defined by a castellan revolution, by the rush to improve one's odds by building better

---

110. A similar conception of authority (sovereignty) and territoriality also informed the empire of the Inca. According to Susan Elizabeth Ramírez (*To Feed and Be Fed*, 13–56), the word Cuzco, long thought to have meant "the navel" and to have been used to refer to the imperial capital (a sort of *umbilicus mundi*), really referred to the person of the reigning sovereign, so that the center of the empire (and of the *ecumene*) was wherever he was.

111. For example, "[The Yamanouchi] requested that his lordship set out from his seat to fight," and, "Although several months went by, his lordship, having set out from his seat, did not have evidence of a fitting military success" (*Shōin shigo*, 844b); or the Uesugi chief retainer discussing the particulars of "his lordship's moving his seat to this castle" (*TKS* 1:570, no. 565 [Bannaji monjo]).

defenses, what were the enticements for local warriors or great regional lords *not* to rely on the permanent walls of fortresses? One explanation is logistic: unlike the petty local magnates who built strongholds to solidify their control on the nearby countryside and defend it from aggression by neighbors, the Uesugi drew income from landholdings that were broadly scattered and thus not conveniently policed with a single fortress, however grand. Hence their lack of enthusiasm for castle building.[112] This interpretation certainly has its merits, though the problems posed by a portfolio of dispersed lands were hardly unique to the Uesugi: as seen in Chapter 3, the Iwamatsu (and many other families) confronted just such a problem. But the Iwamatsu built Kanayama, and other families built other castles. And even within the extended Uesugi family, the Ōgigayatsu, whose lands were located across the region, built castles at Edo and Kawagoe (one could say that they responded to the challenge of dispersed lands by building dispersed castles). So an understanding of the Yamanouchi leaders' seeming reluctance to build residential castles (though they did, at various times, take over Hachigata from Nagao Kageharu and Kawagoe from the Ōgigayatsu) should not be sought in their feelings about castles per se, as structures meant to ensure control of the surrounding hinterland.

The Uesugi's mobility was less a rejection of the advantages offered by castles than a refusal to accept the fragmentation of the plain that grew more and more pronounced with each new disturbance. Fragmentation was exploited, and exacerbated, by the castles great and small that local magnates were constructing to shore up their respective spheres of influence. These new castles crowded the landscape, sometimes simply to assert a family's power over nearby hamlets and villages, sometimes to encroach on neighbors and foes' freedom of movement. Ikatsuko and Uwado, by contrast, existed because the Uesugi's own definition of authority rested on their capacity to attract local magnates to their court, men like Iwamatsu Iezumi. Castles could certainly work as effective headquarters, but encampments like Ikatsuko grew in direct proportion to the ability of the Uesugi to encourage the residence of warriors who had compelling

112. This is the point made in Yamazaki, "Yamanouchi Uesugi-shi no jōrui," 125, 141–42.

reasons to stay put in their own strongholds instead. The authority of the Uesugi needed to transcend the local because it drew on the prestige of the shogunate, whose claims, though little more than claims at this time, remained countrywide. Like the kings of England after the Norman Conquest, whose courts traveled around the country adjudicating controversies and dispensing justice, the Yamanouchi Uesugi needed, or at least benefited from, a court that was in the fullness of its authority wherever they were.[113]

Not coincidentally, the Yamanouchi Uesugi did not lay out Ikatsuko or Uwado in the heart of their own lands, as most warrior families did when building castles, or setting up their satellite encampments. Rather, they chose the locations for their camps on the basis of a Kantō-wide outlook: Ikatsuko was near the main route connecting the north and south of the plain; Uwado was built, as an aggressive statement, only a short way away from Kawagoe castle, in the heart of the estate of the same name (which belonged to the Ōgigayatsu, against whom the Yamanouchi were waging war at that time). Certainly, as archaeologist Tanaka Shin has argued, the rituals revealed by the *kawarake* that have been excavated at the Uwado site were meant to reaffirm the cohesion of the Yamanouchi coalition in the face of Ōgigayatsu resistance, in the heart of Ōgigayatsu lands. Still, the camps themselves, with their location and layout, tell a more complicated story, about the Uesugi, their conception of authority, and its inherent contradictions. On the one hand, we can understand the presence of *kawarake*—and thus, ultimately, of the Yamanouchi court itself—as a proclamation that all land in the western Kantō provinces was open to them and the institutions they represented and embodied, and that they could elevate Kawagoe Estate to a stage for the performance of rituals of state just as readily as any other place. Thus, inasmuch as the castellan revolution is interpreted as the creation of

113. I am not suggesting that the authority or the claims to authority of the Yamanouchi were comparable to those of the kings of England in scope but simply that there were remarkable similarities in the ways in which both enforced and manifested their authority in a highly fragmented political landscape. Analogies with the Mughal rulers in India in the sixteenth and seventeenth centuries are in some ways even more striking, for those rulers too traveled around their domains to keep local gentry in check, electing to reside in camps rather than in palaces or cities. See Schimmel, *Empire of the Great Mughals*, 77–80.

residential headquarters for rising local warriors, the Yamanouchi reliance on mobile courts displayed the family's claim to superiority and its abiding commitment to a model of governance that was provincial and regional (if not national), but most certainly not local.

On the other hand, though, the camps' own hierarchical structures, revealed by the uneven distribution of ceramics, and the scattering of satellite encampments in the surrounding countryside, attest to different facets of a fragmentation the Uesugi were not able to overcome. The physical fragmentation of the camps reminds us of the strongly patrimonial character of authority, even when that authority was exercised in the name of institutions. If the new castles perpetuated the parcelization of the landscape, the solution adopted by the Uesugi—the nominally mobile encampment that enabled their itinerant exercise of authority—could only be partly successful. When an army on the march through lands officially governed by its commanders chose its campsites (and thus its path) on the basis of the distribution of the participating troops' holdings, clearly, then, even authorities who could mobilize vast armies in the name of the shogunate were acknowledging the persistent limits on the territorial dimension of their jurisdiction. In occupying the lands of their Ōgigayatsu rivals the Yamanouchi may have stated otherwise, but the Uesugi polity was, to the end, built in the interstices between lands held by others.

CHAPTER 5

The Pointillist Plain

Weeks before his death in 1502, an ailing Sōgi, accompanied by a number of his students, made his way south through the Kantō. Over the course of the previous thirty-some years, Sōgi had established himself as the most influential and sought-after poet in Japan. In a pattern that had since become common among linked-verse masters, he had taken to traveling through the provinces, leading *renga* sessions and imparting instruction on the finer points of the art to local warriors eager to burnish their credentials as men of culture. Because Sōgi himself had left a famous account of the first of his tours of the provinces after a trip through the Kantō, it is fitting that his last journey would be recorded in a travelogue (*Sōgi shūenki*, The last days of Sōgi) by one of his companions, the poet Sōchō. Sōchō's matter-of-fact prose describes the party's departure from the provincial capital of Echigo by the Sea of Japan, its trip over the mountains, across the Kantō plain, past the town of Kamakura on the Pacific coast, and up into the hills again at Hakone Yumoto, where Sōgi passes away.[1] Throughout the journey, concerns about Sōgi's rapidly deteriorating health shape the party's itinerary and affect its pace. Even periods of repose at warriors' mansions are a mixed blessing, as the hosts' excitement over Sōgi's presence keeps the old master busy composing poetry and refereeing linked-verse sessions.

---

1. The travelogue does not end with Sōgi's death, but continues to include Sōchō's return to Suruga Province.

For our purposes, the most striking incident in the travelogue occurs in between stops, and has little to do with poetry. "A place called Uwado," Sōchō writes, "[at] the crossing of the Irumagawa in Musashi Province, is presently the site of the encampment of the Yamanouchi. We rested there for over twenty days; as there were many men of taste, we composed thousand-verse *renga* and so forth. Moving to the village of Miyoshino and Kawagoe, we stayed there for more than ten days, and at the beginning of the seventh month we reached a residence called Edo."[2]

One would scarcely know from Sōchō's account that the poets traversed a no-man's-land between two embattled fortresses; that the Ōgigayatsu were holding out against their Yamanouchi relatives in the fortresses of Kawagoe and Edo; and that the camp at Uwado had been established just across the river from Kawagoe for the very purpose of harassing the forces in that castle. Although Sōchō's mention of an encampment suggests military mobilization, nowhere does the poet bother to clarify that Sōgi and he and other members of their party were making their way *across an active frontline*, visiting first the headquarters of the besieging army and then the stronghold of the besieged. To be sure, earlier in his account Sōchō does hint at the present state of political unrest as he travels north to meet Sōgi in Echigo: "A conflict broke out between the Yamanouchi and the Ōgigayatsu, and all of the Eight Provinces [of the Kantō] have been divided between the two sides; even for wayfarers it is difficult, I hear. Thanks to the good offices of acquaintances here and there, I even waded through Musashino, made my way past Kōzuke, and reached the provincial capital of Echigo around the first day of the ninth month."[3]

Most of Sōchō's contemporary readers would have known that Kawagoe was the main castle of the Ōgigayatsu and understood perfectly the implications of his laconic statement. Perhaps because it went smoothly—or because, really, the travelogue was meant exclusively as a quiet account of the last days of Sōgi's life—this remarkable crossing is

---

2. *Sōgi shūenki*, 674. Another, slightly different, version of the passage is printed in *Sōgi shūenki* (ann. Tsurusaki and Fukuda), 449.

3. *Sōgi shūenki*, 673. Sōchō actually writes the name as "Ōginoyatsu."

barely noted at all.[4] Which is a pity, because we know little about what it was like to travel across a military frontier or, for that matter, about what the frontier itself was like. Two decades later in another travel diary, *Sōchō shuki*, Sōchō once again left an account of a crossing between warring families. This time, he provided greater detail:

> We were accompanied to the town by many people and palanquins from Moritaka. Anonotsu has been desolate for more than ten years, and nothing but ruins remains of its four or five thousand houses and temples. Stands of reeds and mugwort, no chickens or dogs, rare even to hear the cawing of a crow. The wind and rain at the time were terrifying. Our escorts all returned home and no others arrived to meet us. We lost our way, and after wandering in the wrong direction we hired a local foot soldier on the advice of an acquaintance. The soldier took us two leagues to a place called Kubota. That night the party sent by Kajisai, equipped with palanquins and such, found us.[5]

This incident is often cited by scholars to illustrate the perils of travel in an age of strife, and the hardships facing poets and literati who had to seek out the patronage of local warriors to make a living: Sōchō perfectly conveys the anxiety of the stranded traveler, endangered not so much by the war itself as by nightfall in a desolate, isolated area.[6] The rain may have been less terrifying for a seasoned traveler than our diarist would have us think, but we should not lightly dismiss the palpable relief that greeted the arrival of the tardy welcome party.[7] The passage also

---

4. H. Mack Horton (*Song*, 104) surmises as much, when he writes that *Sōgi shūenki* was "crafted with stylistic finish as a single statement," unlike later works which admitted "a good deal more 'non-poetic' vocabulary." See also Etō, *Sōgi no kenkyū*, 245–57, passim; Kaneko, *Sōgi tabi no ki shichū*, 101–25 (which is actually a heavily annotated presentation of the text itself); Kaneko, *Sōgi no seikatsu to sakuhin*, 19; Tsurusaki, *Sengoku o yuku rengashi Sōchō*, 78–81; and Okuda, *Sōgi*, 226–31; for Sōgi as seen through Sōchō's travelogue, see Kishida, "Sōgi no kage."

5. Horton, *Journal of Sōchō*, 16. The passage is from *Sōchō shuki*, which covers Sōchō's life and travels during the years 1522–27. Uzawa, *Sōchō Suruga nikki*, 14–15.

6. Tsurusaki, *Sengoku no kenryoku to yoriai no bungei*, 30; see also Tsurusaki, *Sengoku o yuku rengashi Sōchō*, 9–10. In the latter work in particular Tsurusaki goes to some lengths to prove that the desolation encountered by Sōchō was the product of war, not some natural calamity.

7. Tsurusaki (*Sengoku no kenryoku to yoriai no bungei*, 30) goes so far as to call the poet's description somewhat of an overdramatization, caused perhaps by his dejection

vividly illustrates the logistics of frontier crossing and offers a glimpse of the nature of the boundaries that separated the territories of different warrior houses. Although the anecdote takes us away from the Kantō plain—the events Sōchō records took place in the mountains of Ise Province, in central Japan—the contours of the situation it outlines were surely typical of the rest of the country as well. It is one of the more explicit references to issues that are implicit or hinted at obliquely in other sources dealing with travel, territory, and boundaries.

It was common practice for visiting artists and other highly regarded guests to be escorted by local guides as they traveled through a warrior house's lands.[8] Sōchō's considerable distress was no doubt heightened by the unexpected failure of the planned rendezvous: everything was definitely *not* as it should be. Indeed, if guides were necessary on a warrior family's own lands (remember Sōchō's tour of Musashino, in the company of Mita Ujimune and his son, in Chapter 1), all the more were they needed to help with the delicate passage through a contested military frontier. Escorts would hand a visitor over to their counterparts from a neighboring (hostile) family, in a sort of relay. Unlike border crossings between modern states, though, there was no barrier or checkpoint separating the two parties and helping negotiate the transition; protocols surely existed, as Sōchō's night in the rain intimates, but we know little about the specifics. In remembering his time among the ruins of Anonotsu, Sōchō darkly paints a picture he had barely suggested in his earlier travelogue: transit from one warrior family's lands to those of a neighbor

---

at being abandoned outdoors in the rain at dusk. Sōchō had found himself in a similar plight in 1509, when, at the end of a day's journey, he had reached his destination (a local warrior's mansion), only to find that the drawbridge had already been raised and he could not gain admittance. The poet's worry at the impasse was clearly matched by the wariness with which locals welcomed travelers after dusk (*Azumaji no tsuto*, 488). For another contemporary reference to the dangers of darkness, see articles 3 and 19 of Hōjō Sōun's house precepts, *Sōunji-dono nijūikkajō*, 353 and 355–56, respectively; in English, see Steenstrup, "Hōjō Sōun's Twenty-One Articles," 289–303.

8. Explicit mention of escorts is not always made by travelers in their accounts, unless there was something remarkable about the situation or the escort (or lack thereof, as in the case of Sōchō's misadventure). For references to escorts, see *Shirakawa kikō* (Kaneko, *Sōgi tabi no ki shichū*, 7–26; S. Carter, "Sōgi in the East Country," 180); *Azumaji no tsuto*, 491–97; *Tsukushi michi no ki* (Kaneko, *Sōgi tabi no ki shichū*, 27–100; Kato, "Pilgrimage to Dazaifu," 347, 349–50); *Shōin shigo*, 793a.

occurred in a gray area where affiliation could be ambiguous and settlement sparse—especially when the two families were at war.

This final chapter is about passages and crossings—over the landscape and across boundaries—and about what they may tell us of the territorial shape taken by authority. It follows recent scholarship that has analyzed the emergence of early modern territorial states (domains, in the case of Japan) by considering processes occurring at the polities' edges rather than their centers, and finding correlations between shifts in the configuration and conceptualization of boundaries, and ideas about rule over land.[9]

To highlight the different dimensions of rule over territory, both in terms of policies and vocabulary, the chapter also confronts another sort of boundary: the larger study's chronological limits. It provides an epilogue to the story told thus far by tracing the history of the region past the end of Uesugi rule and into the domain of the Hōjō. The contrast between the two regimes is instructive. The Hōjō were newcomers to the Kantō and their attention to the opportunities for reorganizing the landscape to suit their political ends has long been recognized. But by straddling the chronological boundary of the medieval political order, I do not wish to highlight only the differences between what came before and what came after. Rather, juxtaposition of the political landscapes under the Uesugi and the Hōjō reveals both the extent of the shift brought about by the change of regime and the continuities that hindered the transition to a radically different conception of territorial governance.

In the absence of a wealth of sources as eloquent as Sōchō's travelogues, I try to tease out contemporary ideas from unreflective references scattered about documents concerned with other matters. I consider in particular the different words used to describe different sorts of boundaries and travel between places, and the ways in which lexical distinctions did or did not overlap with actual ones. Various types of boundaries appear in our sources, their differences spelled out by the kinds of spaces they set apart: there were the borders between administrative and political jurisdictions such as provinces and districts; there were the

9. I am thinking in particular of Sahlins, *Boundaries*; see also Edwards, *Families and Frontiers*.

borders between villages, or estates, which delimited proprietary or usufructuary rights to arable land; there were, finally, frontiers, which could overlap with the other two types of boundaries when political and proprietary rights collided. In English, I note in passing, the work of distinguishing among these three categories is done by two words: "border" and "frontier" ("boundary" and "border" I use more or less interchangeably, opposed to "frontier"). In the discussion that follows, I limit use of "border" and "boundary" to those boundaries created by the organization of formal entitlements (provinces, districts, estates, etc.), whereas I use "frontier" or, more often, "military frontier" to refer to those political boundaries produced by the de facto occupation of land, and as the result of military campaigns and settlements.[10] The distinction provides a useful way of focusing on the differences between inherited spatial frameworks and the eventual production of a new, more markedly territorial conceptualization of authority. Moreover, as we shall see, contemporary usage in letters, memoirs, and chronicles actually confirms the awareness of a differentiation between borders and frontiers.[11]

Lastly, I should clarify that I use the term frontier with a connotation closer to the one that has been employed in scholarship produced in or about Europe, rather than in the sense given to it by Frederick Jackson Turner and those who have followed and critiqued him in studies of North America. I do not, in other words, use frontier to refer to a more or less broad area of contact between cultures, but rather, more narrowly, to a variously fortified and contested boundary. The frontiers that divided warriors in the fifteenth and sixteenth centuries were not, obviously enough, spaces of contact between different cultures, and linear boundaries did not form through a process of settlement and fixing of broad frontier regions. The latter notion is of difficult application in the case of Japan, where the concept of (essentially) linear borders, established along with the imperial state in the seventh and eighth centuries,

10. I follow the practice outlined by Daniel Power ("Introduction. Frontiers," 2) of using frontier as "a political barrier between states or peoples, often militarised."

11. The distinction was not unique to Japan: Peter Sahlins ("Natural Frontiers Revisited," 1425–26) discusses the difference that existed in France and in French between frontiers (where one polity faced another militarily) and boundaries (the linear limits of that polity's suzerainty).

retained currency, at least formally, throughout most of the Middle Ages. Although a trajectory leading from broad frontiers to linear boundaries may not fit conditions in fifteenth- and sixteenth-century Japan, I do not entirely eschew the notion of frontiers as constituted by broad zones of exchange. In its purely spatial dimension, the idea that the margins of different—and frequently hostile—territorially conceived potentates or domains could come in contact in broad zones rather than in sharply traced military fronts is one that fits well with the accounts Sōchō left us.

Boundaries and Frontiers

Consider Sōchō's choice of words: Sōgi and he uneventfully "move" (*utsuru*) from Uwado to Miyoshino and Kawagoe. The verb is unremarkable, its meaning seemingly neutral. It denotes travel, generally to and from a place, and is often associated with changes of residence, whether temporary or more permanent. For instance, Iwamatsu Iezumi "moved to Kanayama" and stayed there for some time after the rout at Ikatsuko.[12] "[Nagao] Kageharu moved to Nagai castle" after the fall of his previous fortress.[13] Uesugi Akisada "crossed the Tonegawa and moved to Kawachi."[14] Yet *utsuru* is not the most commonly used verb in contemporary documents. Far more frequent is *koyu*, "to go over," or, more literally, "to cross over."[15] In document after document the word describes, say, warlords crossing rivers, travelers making their way over mountain passes, and armies heading into neighboring provinces.[16] No less often (surprisingly perhaps) *koyu* simply refers to travel from one location to another: on orders from the Iwamatsu, "the envoy Intō went over to Kanai

12. *Shōin shigo*, 839a.

13. *Ōta Dōkan jō*, 642a.

14. *Ōta Dōkan jō*, 637b.

15. Writing "to go over" in English has the advantage of capturing the flavor of the original without the translation sounding too contrived, or completely disregarding English usage. It is important to note, though, that within the limits of my knowledge of other European languages, verbs for "coming" and "going" do not carry any connotations of "crossing."

16. For instance, in *Ōta Dōkan jō*, 637b, 638b, 641a, 643a; *Sōrinji denki*, 443a; *SKS* 5, no. 1019 (*Koshōmon*); *Shōin shigo*, 792b, 833b, 842a, 844b.

castle";[17] Ōgigayatsu Uesugi Sadamasa told a retainer, in a letter, "As my messenger you are going over to Kawagoe";[18] Ōta Dōkan reminded the Uesugi leadership that "several times Kageharu sent over emissaries" to seek a negotiated settlement;[19] or that—away from the cares of a world in turmoil—his own "aged parent, the lay priest, had gone over to Sōrinji, in Shiroi."[20]

At first glance, the word seems to have lost any strict link to the idea of crossing a boundary or a threshold. If indeed the connotations of "moving" and "crossing" had blurred, it should come as no surprise that even Sōchō—whose prose is incomparably richer than the formulaic writing typical of the missives quoted above—does not bother to make the distinction. The temptation, then, is to suppose that the fuzzy vocabulary mirrored a fuzzy political landscape. But if Sōchō does not feel compelled to name the frontiers he crosses, or even to speak of crossing, we should not assume that he or anyone else involved in such a trip was unaware of the passage from one territory to another. It seems improbable that the special access granted to literati—who are sometimes thought to have been able to transit through otherwise impassable areas by virtue of the popularity of the services they offered—would make them unaware of the logistic problems confronting anyone planning to cross an active military frontier. Sōgi, in *Shirakawa kikō*, and even more so Sōchō, in *Azumaji no tsuto*, are clearly aware of the obstacles that wars placed across their paths. Just because, in *Sōgi shūenki*, Sōchō does not cite the mobilization in the area around Kawagoe, it in no way means he was oblivious to it.[21] The question is what did territory mean to late medieval Japanese as they traveled over the land, and how do the forms taken by borders and military frontiers help us understand the regions they defined? Why was all travel, all movement, a crossing?

---

17. *Shōin shigo*, 837b.

18. *SKS* 5, no. 1019 (*Koshōmon*).

19. *Ōta Dōkan jō*, 636b.

20. *Ōta Dōkan jō*, 640a.

21. For various explanations of Sōgi's convoluted Kantō itinerary in *Shirakawa kikō*—predicated on different degrees of freedom of movement ascribed to poets in times of war—see Kaneko, *Rengashi to kikō*, 126–28; Okuda, *Sōgi*, 38–39; and Ramirez-Christensen, *Heart's Flower*, 135.

It is worth taking a step back to examine the vocabulary that organized space as both property and jurisdiction—to consider the use of the word "border" (*sakai*). Curiously, perhaps, references to borders are as sporadic as those to crossing are ubiquitous. No more than a handful of documents openly mention them or even implicitly hint at them. Even more significant than the small number of such references are the ways and the contexts in which the word "border" is used. The same character is used for both the border around a province and that around an estate, suggesting that political jurisdiction and family property were or could be perceived as homologous. Certainly, as we have seen, the ambiguities in the separation between lordly and official authority meant that the parallel distinction between private holdings and territorial jurisdiction was prone to disappear as well, so it should come as no surprise that the two were not marked apart lexically.[22] (Because this chapter draws mainly on what I have called unreflective pronouncements, though, it would be wise to consider the degree to which the lack of terminological differentiation between provincial and estate borders might also be a product of the relative lack of consideration contemporaries gave to boundaries as concepts.) Of the infrequent mentions of boundaries in late fifteenth- and early sixteenth-century documents, one lone border around an estate represents the exception among relatively more numerous references to borders between provinces. This remarkable imbalance may be explained by the paucity of surviving documents on disputes between villages, which often took the form of conflicts over boundaries (or over particular water rights that were affected by contested boundaries), and which Japanese scholars tend to view as the most characteristic and widespread of disputes during the decades of civil war.[23]

Provinces had mattered for centuries as political and administrative units. In the Muromachi period, governors and deputy governors ruled

---

22. Ike Susumu examines the same process of conflation, but takes the word *kuni* (variously, "province," "country," "state") as his subject. Ike, "Sengoku-ki no 'kuni' ni tsuite."

23. Yamamoto, "Sengoku daimyō ryōgoku 'sakaime' chiiki"; Noritake, *Sengoku daimyō ryōgoku no kenryoku kōzō*, 320–41; and Marushima, "Sakaime no jōdai to 'roji chisō,'"; Sasaki, "Sengoku-ki 'sakaime' ni okeru ryōshusō no dōkō."

and levied taxes on a provincial basis, but when the political order centered on the shogunate faltered, the province ceased to be the main unit of territorial organization. Provinces, of course, survived as places of daily life besides narrower forms of identification like individual villages or estates, or broader ones, like the Kantō as a whole. Petty warriors continued to band together in leagues, in times of emergency; in the late fifteenth and sixteenth centuries, these local leagues retained—even increased—their provincial foundations, and came to be known as the "Musashi league" or the "Kōzuke league" (*Bushū ikki* and *Jōshū ikki*, respectively). But these organizations were not part of the official apparatus of the Muromachi regime, and their provincial identification was the product of the conditions specific to the western half of the plain; no counterparts emerged in the areas under the control of the Lords of Koga, in the eastern half.[24]

If we consider the Kantō as a whole, and warriors of higher pedigree along with the smaller holders who formed leagues, these forms of provincial attachment are less visible; when our sources talk about movement and political space, the significance of provinces and their boundaries remains ambiguous. It is therefore worth examining some of the passages in which borders and frontiers appear. Although borders are not mentioned frequently in contemporary documents, when a provincial boundary does appear, it is generally identified precisely: writing to one of his supporters in the eastern half of the plain, Ashikaga Shigeuji observed that "[Uesugi] Akisada is holding back on the border of Musashi and Kōzuke, and in a matter of days there will surely be another clash."[25] Significantly, the border between the provinces of Musashi and Kōzuke was provided by various rivers—one of them in particular, the Tonegawa, was the largest and most important river in the Kantō plain. Other borders between Kantō provinces are seldom mentioned.

Considering that both of the provinces mentioned in the letter were under the authority of the Yamanouchi Uesugi, one wonders whether the border between them was noteworthy *because* it overlapped with a major river: the river's size, not the boundaries' political significance,

24. Kuroda M., *Sengoku daimyō to tozama kunishū*; Kuroda M., *Sengoku-ki tōgoku no daimyō to kunishū*.

25. *GKS* 7, no. 1757 (Motegi monjo); also in *TKS* 2:112, no. 85.

provided the threshold here. (This is a little of a paradox, for although the overlapping of a provincial boundary with a river may well have increased the boundary's actual significance from a military standpoint, studies have shown that rivers like the Tonegawa tended to function, in peacetime at least, far more as connections, as poles of attraction, than as barriers.)[26] The fading of provincial lines—from political relevance, if not from people's imaginations—was no doubt accentuated by the special situation in the Kantō: here one extended family, the Uesugi, held nominal authority over several contiguous provinces (as far as the authority of the shogunate went, at least), so the borders between them were little more than internal subdivisions. At various times during their tenure the Uesugi had appointed warriors of different families as deputy governors of each province, but by the late fifteenth century even these posts came to be monopolized by the members of one family, the Nagao. Provinces continued to be cited even as the lines dividing them grew less important; as a part of the shared spatial syntax of contemporary Japanese they provided a verbal grid within which to locate places. At least by the second half of the fifteenth century, though, they were seldom coterminous with actual political spheres.[27]

We should not dismiss the lack of attention to provincial boundaries within the Kantō as a necessary product of precedent—of a century in which the region in its entirety had constituted a supraprovincial administrative sphere under the aegis of the Kamakura Office. The eastern branch of the Muromachi regime did not bequeath the Kantō any conspicuous sense that the region was or ought to be one polity, or at least one unit of

---

26. On the ways in which the rivers hindered and shaped circulation in the Kantō, see Saitō, "Chūsei tōgoku ni okeru kasen suiryō to toka"; on the Tonegawa as a pole of attraction, see Hagiwara, "Chūsei Tonegawa bunkaken to shūkyō." Hagiwara's findings are consistent with those of recent research on borders and frontiers in medieval Europe. See Power, "French and Norman Frontiers"; and Edwards, *Families and Frontiers*, 158, 165. On the Tonegawa, see also Ogasawara, "Tōgokushi no butai toshite no Tonegawa, Hitachigawa no suimyaku"; Saitō, "Joron"; Saitō, "Kamakura kaidō Kamitsumichi to kita Kantō"; Arai et al., "Kodai, chūsei no Nakagawa ryūiki o saguru"; Kondō Y., "Tonegawa no henryū." On the relative irrelevance of provincial boundaries from the point of view of local village communities, see Yata, *Nihon chūsei Sengoku-ki no chiiki to minshū*, 299–317.

27. For an illuminating study of the evolution of the syntax of space (of different spatial "templates") in a medieval European context, see Smail, *Imaginary Cartographies*.

administrative jurisdiction without internal demarcation: the most common reference to the region as a whole, the "Eight Kantō Provinces" (*Kantō hasshū*) rather pointedly stressed its composite character. A boundary between distinct jurisdictions was more likely to be acknowledged than one between areas governed by the same family, but the significance of such an acknowledgment remains ambiguous at best. In 1478, Dōkan wrote, "Honma Ōmi no kami, Ebina Saemon no jō, a resident of Kai Province named Katō, and besides them, men from the border with that province [Kai], consulted with each other and, on the fourteenth of the previous month, headed against our allies' camp."[28] Here Kai is mentioned simply to establish where the events took place, and who took part in them; the passage is not about political space, it is about people. These are not "the armies of Kai," but forces cobbled together by warriors living near the border. Mention of the boundary itself is purely descriptive too: these warriors reside near the provincial boundary, Dōkan seems to be telling his superiors, and are therefore understandably prone to involve themselves in the affairs of the Kantō. Moreover, emerging from Dōkan's mention of warriors near the Kai border, and from Shigeuji's mention of Uesugi forces holding back near the Musashi-Kōzuke border, is the idea that provincial boundaries were less lines than zones, important not when they were crossed but when they were inhabited.

Just how tenuous the association was between provinces and political action becomes apparent as we read on: "Setting off before the sky grew light and crossing the Kai provincial border I headed against Katō's stronghold and scattered [his forces]; beginning with a place [along] the Tsurukawa I had [the area] set on fire, and so pacified all of Sagami, east and west."[29] Even as Dōkan launched his raid into a neighboring province, his focus was the residence of the Katō. In his own account, Dōkan did not attack or invade Kai Province itself—he is simply providing a convenient landmark for his story. As the letter plainly states, his concern was not the pacification of Kai, but of Sagami. Quelling the forces from Kai was a way to return peace to Sagami. Another source covering the same incident, *Kamakura ōzōshi*, echoes Dōkan's account:

28. *Ōta Dōkan jō*, 640b.
29. *Ōta Dōkan jō*, 641a.

"Pursuing [the enemy], he crossed the border of Kai and attacked Katō's stronghold."[30] The provincial border itself does not appear to have been defended, or to have represented an obstacle; the Katō warriors sought refuge not in Kai, but in their fortified residence, on their family lands.

Still, both Dōkan and the chronicle mention the boundary crossing, registering the persistent power of the old provincial framework to organize space meaningfully—this, at a time when Japan lacked for neither political structures nor conflicts that could create new spheres of power and authority, new ways of dividing up the landscape. As we shall see, new frontiers did take shape, and even though preexisting administrative borders continued to provide a backdrop of sorts, they determined neither the layout nor the character of the emerging boundaries.

Now, as mentioned, the word "*sakai*," which I have been translating as "border" and "boundary," referred mostly to the demarcations of the old imperial units of territorial administration and of privately held estates; compounds derived from the same character (*kokkyō*, *kunizakai*), which I also render in English as "border" and "boundary," were used more specifically for provinces. What these words did not designate, in the Kantō at least, were the shifting and often contested frontiers of rival potentates' spheres of influence, between, say, the lands of the Ōta and their Ōgigayatsu lords in eastern Musashi. That writers in the fifteenth century should have made such a distinction is sensible. Both provinces and estates were legally defined and clearly identified—though frequently contested—swaths of (mostly) contiguous territory. Neither of these sorts of territories were directly linked to or defined as spheres of political power: provinces had long ceased to represent the privileged framework for authority (which, especially under the Uesugi, was exercised through familial structures even as it was justified in terms of public appointment); estates provided more adequate settings for emerging structures of local rule, but were still as fragmented and contested internally as they were intelligible as wholes. They were more coherent as units of production than as spheres of authority.

Yet if perceived analogies between landholdings and the administrative subdivisions inherited from the old imperial state were clear enough

30. *Kamakura ōzōshi*, 63.

to invite use of the same spatial vocabulary, the possibility of discoursing, eventually, about province- or region-wide *domains* built upon warrior family's own holdings in estates was not far off. There is some indication that certain families at least were beginning to think in those terms, as the main houses asserted their supremacy over collaterals and gained a degree of direct control over the totality of the estates where they resided. The case of the Iwamatsu, colorfully preserved in *Shōin shigo*, exemplifies the choices facing local warriors, as they were compelled to trade in the genealogical validation offered by scattered holdings, accumulated over the course of generations, for the less familiar but more secure profit derived from a wide swath of contiguous landholdings. *Shōin shigo* chronicles the decision itself, and for all of its celebratory rhetoric cannot hide the pain and anxiety that the process cost the Iwamatsu. It also seems to acknowledge, in one of the author's many paeans to his Iwamatsu masters, that at the end of the transformation, lordship had acquired a new dimension. It is, of course, the worth of great warlords that matters: "[Iwamatsu] Masazumi's skill in particular—he is a valiant warrior of unequalled character; we should call him a hero worthy of a thousand men."[31] But the concrete shape this prosperity takes is also important: "Sturdy borders, and a fate of morning dew and evening clouds—What must we ask for?!"[32] *Shōin shigo* probably speaks literally when it asks for sturdy borders, despite the accompanying weather metaphor.

But which borders does Shōin have in mind? Certainly not those of Kōzuke. The Iwamatsu had never claimed to be lords of the whole province, even when they insisted on treating the great houses of the land as their peers. Moreover, provinces had never been something to defend. As Dōkan implies in his letter, provinces were places *in* which (not *over* which) battles were fought. By the time Shōin recorded his memoir, in

31. *Shōin shigo*, 817b.

32. *Shōin shigo*, 817b. To the best of my knowledge, the phrase is Shōin's. The expression "morning dew" (*asatsuyu*) is relatively common both in Chinese and Japanese literature and is a stock metaphor for the ephemerality of life. The exact reference of the "evening clouds" (*boun*), though, is elusive; its locus classicus is a poem by the Tang poet Du Fu (712–70) about the distance separating him and his friend and fellow poet Li Bo (701–62), which does not really seem to fit the passage in *Shōin shigo*.

1509, the Iwamatsu had moved beyond the consolidation of their home base, Nitta Estate, settling into neighboring Fuchina and Sonoda. The borders he evokes may have been not the ones around Nitta but the ones encompassing all of the family's lands, or—a slight but important difference—the borders around each of the family's individual holdings. After all, as seen in Chapter 3, the Iwamatsu were paramount in Nitta, but not alone: their collateral lineages had portfolios of holdings in and around the estate, and even the Yokoze maintained lands of their own.

Nonetheless, even with these provisos the case of the Iwamatsu shows how the association of the house's holdings with one or more whole estates held the promise of a lordship that identified a family's landholding with a sphere of political influence. The identification is what allows Shōin to speak of *sturdy* boundaries—not just clearly delineated, but safe, well-defended. This process of consolidation and expansion was often carried out less peacefully than the Iwamatsu managed to do according to *Shōin shigo*. Whether or not warriors were inclined to imagine their lands as territorial domains, the narrow or broad portions of landscape they controlled were given coherence by contiguity and a uniform recognition of a lord's authority over them. That coherence was often hard won, through drawn-out armed confrontations with neighbors.

So, one wonders, why do we not see, in contemporary sources, more instances of the word "*sakai*" used in reference to the limits of real political and military control, in discussions of frontiers that are contested and fought over? When the whole country was mired in civil war, with new fronts opening up daily between neighboring magnates ever more inclined to seek redress for their grievances on the battlefield rather than in the arbitration of a diminished shogunate, the scarcity of references to fronts is puzzling. If "borders" and "frontiers" fail to crop up more regularly in a corpus of documents devoted primarily to invasions and campaigning, to extolling the loyalty of followers in military crises and memorializing one's own martial prowess in battle, what should we make of the idea of emerging territorial domains?

With the exception of one ambiguously phrased mention by Dōkan ("I set off for eastern Kōzuke and seized several enemy border holdings"), the word "*sakai*" does not appear to have been used to refer to military frontiers.[33] Even assuming that the word I translate here as "enemy border" (*tekkyō/tekisakai*) does indeed refer to a frontier (and not to a provincial boundary that is worth mentioning because enemies happen to hold lands on the other side), still, the word is extremely unusual in medieval texts generally. The earliest usage I know of (which coincidentally is from the Kantō) is in *Yūki-shi shin'hatto* (The new law code of the Yūki family), compiled in 1556, about seventy-five years after Dōkan left us the account of his incursion.[34] The time difference, I argue below, matters. But let us put chronology aside for a moment. What is clear from the passage is that Dōkan was not interested in the frontier (or provincial border) per se, but rather in the individual enemy holdings to be seized there. In this sense, then, and despite his striking use of the word "border" in association with a military front, Dōkan is describing an incursion that was analogous in conception to the one he conducted in Kai against the Katō.[35]

---

33. *Ōta Dōkan jō*, 639a.

34. The compound *tekkyō* (which fails to appear in João Rodrigues's 1603 *Vocabulario da Lingoa de Iapam*, incidentally) has been glossed broadly as "enemy land" in *Yūki-shi shin'hatto* and in other texts as late as the first half of the nineteenth century—a gloss that is both curiously vague and dependent on modern ideas of territoriality. The article in the Yūki code is no. 79 (Ishii et al., *Chūsei seiji shakai shisō, jō*, 267–68). For the later examples of usage, see *Nihon kokugo daijiten*, in the Japan Knowledge database (http://japanknowledge.com [accessed December 19, 2011]). My thanks to Professor David Eason, who unearthed the Yūki reference during the course of an extended discussion of the word *tekkyō*.

35. Another, similarly ambiguous example comes from the Tōkaidō region, to the west. In *Sōchō shuki*, Sōchō writes of his 1527 visit to a castle at Utsuyama, on the "border of three enemy provinces" (*sankakoku no teki no sakai*) to indicate a military frontier. See Uzawa, *Sōchō Suruga nikki*, 188–89; and also Horton's translation, *Journal of Sōchō*, 151. Saitō (*Chūsei tōgoku no ryōiki to jōkan*, 289) cites this passage as an example of a frontier between domains at war although, really, the word *sakai* here arguably refers to the "three provinces." *Which* three provinces he had in mind is another problem entirely: Utsuyama, in the current city of Kosai, Shizuoka Prefecture, was on the border between Tōtōmi and Mikawa Provinces—two provinces, not three. Sōchō appears to be confused about Utsuyama's location, writing of the castle that it was "on the provincial border," and then going on to state that "sentries keep watch day and night for possible attacks from Owari, Mikawa, or Shinano," thus suggesting that these were the three provinces he had in mind and that he had placed the castle on the wrong border.

Telling is that the connotation of the word "*sakai*" is ambiguous where a conflict overlaps with a preexisting provincial boundary, and that a provincial boundary becomes politically significant when it happens to coincide with a military frontier: during the second half of the fifteenth century, the area in question had become perhaps the most contested theater in the ongoing conflict between those loyal to the Lords of Koga and the Uesugi, and had shifted sides repeatedly as one party gained the upper hand or a local family decided to change camps. Therefore, even though a provincial boundary survived nearby, it was the advancing and retreating of armies that gave territorial manifestation to the current state of political allegiances. The standoff between Ashikaga Shigeuji and the Uesugi lasted decades and became the grand conflict that marked the political geography of the era and produced the broad, overarching framework in which other, more circumscribed disputes erupted from time to time in the plain. The frontier to which it gave rise, though, remained the only one to develop on a regional scale until the appearance of the Hōjō at the turn of the next century.

If, indeed, as late as the turn of the sixteenth century boundaries were seldom connoted as frontiers in Kantō documents, a generation later Sōchō would introduce his crossing in central Japan by plainly stating, "The area beyond the Kumozugawa and Anonotsu is on the frontier of this province's fighting, making it difficult to pass."[36] Yet this was no provincial boundary. In the Japanese text, Sōchō calls it a border (*sakai*), but there can be no doubt that he is alluding to a military frontier.[37] The slippage we see in Sōchō's account—from boundary to frontier—may recall the ambiguity of Dōkan's expression, some forty years before. But the realities the two writers were grappling with were different. In the case of Dōkan, the boundary and frontier were conflated by circum-

36. Uzawa, *Sōchō Suruga nikki*, 14. Horton's translation (*Journal of Sōchō*, 15–16) is more elegant, but omits the word "frontier": "There has been fighting in this province beyond Kumozugawa river and Anonotsu, making it difficult to get from place to place."

37. Admittedly, Sōchō refers to the boundary using a less common character (the one used in the name of the port city of Sakai), but since Sōchō's and the more common character share the reading "*sakai*" it seems unwise to make too much of his usage.

stance; the provincial boundary and the lands occupied by the enemy were close enough that in a time of unrest mentioning one could evoke the other. In Sōchō's travelogue, instead, the frontier between two competing houses is equated with a frontier between political entities *in the absence* of any preexisting institutional demarcation. The proximity of a river probably contributed to Sōchō's choice of the word "boundary," even though what he proceeds to describe in his account of a frightening night in the rain is hardly a linear boundary, but rather a broad, depopulated zone of attrition.

At its barest, the different senses of boundaries come down to the distinction between Dōkan's continuing association of the word "boundary" with the provincial apparatus and Sōchō's greater willingness to identify warriors' spheres of influence and occupied lands as territorial units. We may attribute this, partly, to different geographical conditions: the openness of the Kantō's flat, open landscape, with few strong landmarks or demarcations (ridges, ravines) to create recognizable "areas" that could transcend this or that holding or village, contrasts with the narrower horizons that characterize much of the rest of Japan.

Yet more significant, I suspect, is the passage of time. In a country in the throes of ongoing civil war, the twenty years separating Sōgi's last journey and Sōchō's rainy night in the open brought about dramatic if often unacknowledged changes in the political landscape—even in the Kantō. The appearance of the word "boundary" to signify a military frontier would seem to signal the beginning of a transformation (or of contemporaries' awareness of one) in the ways rulers exercised their authority over territory, one consonant with Shōin's reference to *sturdy* borders. Indeed, it was during those twenty years that the Hōjō family of Odawara went from being a new and not entirely welcome southern neighbor to being the ultimate threat to the survival of the Uesugi and the political order of the Muromachi regime in the Kantō.

The parallel evolution of ideas about borders and territorial polities is not unique to Japan. In European history, as mentioned, considerable research has been conducted both on the ways in which the creation of linear boundaries in the early modern period was used to bolster new ideas about the state, and on the ways in which the tenurial fragmentation of the Middle Ages conditioned ideas about boundaries, frontiers, and the territoriality of governance.[38] Writing about the creation of a frontier in medieval Spain, Eduardo Manzano Moreno has drawn attention to the link between the structure of land tenure and governance and the perception of boundaries: "One of the essential features of the medieval European landscape was its lack of cohesion and unity: its discontinuity meant that the whole territory of medieval Europe was, in itself, a frontier. One can find this pervasive frontier in feudal enclaves, which fragmented and divided the territory in such a way that crossing from one to another meant passing through the jurisdictions of different lords."[39] Written about medieval Spain, and Europe in general, this description could not fit Japan better. The Kantō was made up of a constellation of tiny holdings—some no larger than a portion of an estate or a village—loosely bound together by familial ties and alliances.

From afar, an imaginary political map of the region in the second half of the fifteenth century might appear to be divided between two clearly defined camps, separated by the Tonegawa and Watarasegawa as well as by provincial borders: the supporters of Ashikaga Shigeuji, the Lord of Koga, to the east; to the west, the partisans of the Uesugi, former deputies of Shigeuji now taking orders directly (and exclusively) from the shogun back in Kyoto. If one looked harder, though, a little closer, one would see these two large groups lose definition, their territorial cohesion disintegrate in a dizzying jumble of individual local families, each with scattered landholdings interspersed with those of neighbors. Much like a pointillist painting, our imaginary political map of the Kantō would *seem* to consist of a small number of broad territories, homogenously colored to denote the territories controlled by each of the two coalitions. Observed close-up, the multitude of tiny, distinctly colored dots (the holdings of individual houses) that help create the larger spheres of influence of the Lords of Koga and the Uesugi reveal

38. Sahlins, *Boundaries*, 55–59; Sahlins, "Natural Frontiers Revisited"; Manzano Moreno, "Creation of a Medieval Frontier."

39. Manzano Moreno, "Creation of a Medieval Frontier," 36. The same idea is expressed by Sergio Boffa (*Warfare in Medieval Brabant*, 53) in the context of the logistics of medieval European warfare: "Medieval principalities were geographical entities that were difficult to defend. The protection of a territory made up of many domains of which some were enclaves within foreign or enemy lands was not easy to organise."

themselves in all their variety and dispel the impression of unity. Each of these dots could change color autonomously of those that surrounded it, as each local warrior house was liable to switch sides at any time to protect its interests, or to engage in its own feuds with neighbors or collaterals.

In this light, the scarcity of references to borders is consistent with the sense of a ubiquitous frontier seen in the widespread use of a verb meaning "to cross over" in place of the plainer "to go": in a landscape carved up into pockets of authority, every journey was a crossing of sorts—through the lands of followers, allies, collaterals, neutral parties and, occasionally, enemies. The paradox is most apparent when we stand in the shoes of the great regional lords, such as the Uesugi leaders. Between 1455 and 1493 they held sway—nominally, at least—over three provinces: Kōzuke, Musashi, and Sagami (and, to a degree, Izu). Their right to rule rested on a monopoly of two sets of titles, those of governors of the three provinces and of Kantō deputy. Increasingly, the real authority of the Uesugi derived from their ability to lead local warriors in battle against the Lord of Koga (and reward them accordingly) as much as it did from any official appointment from Kyoto. As they moved about the plain shoring up defenses against enemy raids and orchestrating counterattacks across the Tonegawa, the Uesugi and their deputies must have been keenly aware of the fragmentation of their sphere of authority, and of the insignificance of provincial borders.

The tension between warriors' political pretensions and the territorial articulation of those pretensions played out differently at different levels. In the case of the Iwamatsu, the claims to authority that derived from sway over Nitta, Sonoda, and Fuchina remained limited because of the survival in the Kantō of multiple levels of lordship and the coexistence of multiple, concentric spheres of authority, often at odds with each other. The Iwamatsu family's lordship—for all of its expansion beyond the boundaries of Nitta—still corresponded to its property: if the family had on its hands something of a proto-domain, this had not yet transcended the sphere of what Ishimoda Shō calls a patrimonial state.[40]

40. The notion of a "patrimonial state" (*kasansei kokka*)—presented in Ishimoda, "Kaisetsu"—is cited in Satō H., "Sengoku-ki kokkaron," 380. In a similar vein, speaking of Europe, Sahlins ("Natural Frontiers Revisited," 1427) quotes Herbert Rowen's

Whatever the cohesiveness of the Iwamatsu's sphere of authority, beyond the confines of their own, strong borders, they still owed loyalty and service to the Uesugi. Yet if distant history and a sense of self slowed families like the Iwamatsu in their move toward consolidation and, gradually, a kind of lordship that fused landholding and political authority, the Uesugi, from their lofty perch high above all eastern warriors (with the exception of the Lords of Koga), had to contend with far greater hindrances. Compelled by their vast, dispersed wealth and by their long identification with authority over multiple provinces, granted to them by an ever more feeble shogunate, they continued to govern in their curious peripatetic fashion well into the sixteenth century, seemingly blind to the wisdom of settling down as many of their subordinates were doing. And while they enabled the consolidation of the lands of followers, they took no such action for their own, failing perhaps to see the advantages even as they advertised them for others.

After the end of the camp at Uwado, at the turn of the sixteenth century, the Uesugi gradually conformed to the dominant trend of the day and made their headquarters in castles. As we have seen, the growth and spread of fortresses profoundly affected the conduct of warfare, for wars were won or lost as castles stood or fell.[41] Dōkan is said once to have declared, "tranquility and danger in arms rest on the ruler's castle."[42] The expenditure entailed in the construction of vast new strongholds could be met only by warrior houses capable of extracting considerable resources from their holdings, so that infrastructural projects on such a scale both demanded and resulted from success in forging consolidated

---

characterization of early modern states in terms of "proprietary dynasticism." Sahlins adds, "Jurisdictional sovereignty in early modern France meant that the crown accumulated rights to specific domains—fiefs, bailiwicks, bishoprics, seigneuries, boroughs, and even villages. Alongside and overlapping these 'feudal' forms of dominion were administrative circumscriptions created by the crown. As seen from the periphery, the lesson was clear: the kingdom was not a coherent territorial entity consistently 'bounded' in a linear sense."

41. Noritake, *Sengoku daimyō ryōgoku no kenryoku kōzō*, 330–32; Matsuoka, *Sengoku-ki jōkangun no keikan*, 263; for an example of this phenomenon in Europe, see Vann, "Twelfth-Century Castille."

42. Quoted in Sugiyama, *Sengoku daimyō Gohōjō-shi*, 401. The statement could, alternatively, refer to "tranquility or danger in Musashi."

and extensive holdings, or from a continuing ability to defend scattered ones. For instance, as the site for their new castle in the 1450s the Ōgigayatsu chose Kawagoe Estate, which they had recently acquired. They built another fortress at that time, in Edo, though for decades neither of them would become the family's center of operations.

In a sense, the Uesugi failed to see all of the possibilities—and all of the dangers—that these new castles carried with them. For one thing, they did not bother to assert strong control over the fortresses they held. The affiliation of Kawagoe and Edo was ambiguous at best: when Dōkan, who had served as castellan of Edo for the Ōgigayatsu, became too powerful in the eyes of his lords and was eliminated, the Ōgigayatsu again missed the opportunity to make the two castles fully their own. New deputies were sent to Kawagoe and Edo—men of lesser authority and prestige (and autonomy), but deputies nevertheless, who managed the fortresses for the absentee Uesugi. By the 1490s the Ōgigayatsu heir was residing in Kawagoe, but the head of the family was still ensconced in the family's ancestral residence, in Kasuya Estate.[43] The Yamanouchi, too, after experimenting with camps and itinerant courts, came to rely on castles, though they took a less than active approach, refurbishing a castle built by the rebel Nagao Kageharu (Hachigata), or taking over one built by the Ōgigayatsu (Kawagoe, for a while), rather than building one themselves, and making it their permanent seat. And Hachigata, like Edo and Kawagoe, was garrisoned and managed by deputies: Banri describes it as a stronghold of the Kantō deputy (that is, the head of the Yamanouchi), but Sōchō speaks of it as a residence of the Nagao.[44]

This newfound reliance on castles seems to have had a curious effect. Ever more prone to holing up in their many fortresses, the Uesugi became no more entrenched in one locale than they ever had been: the heads of the family toured their castles or sent their deputies to manage them as they continued to live in their residences of many generations. The plain, from their point of view, became even more fragmented, even more a collection of points.

43. For evidence of Ōgigayatsu residence in Kawagoe, see *SKS* 5, no. 1019 (*Koshōmon*). The 1489 letter was written to the castellan of Edo, thus also showing that the Ōgigayatsu were not managing that castle directly.

44. Ichiki, *Baika mujinzō chūshaku*, 2:2–3; *Azumaji no tsuto*, 488.

Without the backing of shogunal authority, the Uesugi family controlled a network of patronage, not a domain. Kageharu's rebellion made painfully clear that the provinces of Kōzuke, Musashi, and Sagami formed a whole under the aegis of the Uesugi, but a whole entirely predicated on consensus. When the young Nagao lord rose up in arms, the whole territory of the plain turned into a frontier—or multiple frontiers: one immediate effect of the political discontinuity of the landscape was the absolute lack of a coherent frontline. No linear front could form because the lands of the various contenders were thoroughly intertwined, and nothing like Hadrian's Wall or the Great Wall of China could be built along the line delimiting a threshold between "us" and "them." In war even more than in peace the significance of the pointillist analogy used to describe the situation in the Kantō becomes apparent: politically speaking, the plain was made up of points rather than areas. As a result of the tenurial fragmentation of the time, any journey was from one point on the map to another rather than from one region to the next. The Uesugi, in their peregrinations, "crossed" from holding to holding, from retainer to retainer. In time, even as they confronted the growing demands of defense and mobilization with their castles, the plain remained a composite of largely autonomous local interests and their jurisdiction no more than islands of rule. To borrow again from the situation in medieval Europe, the Kantō "was composed of many domains set within other territories, friendly, neutral or hostile. It was therefore sometimes necessary to ask permission to pass through a neighbouring territory in order to enter one's own domain or enemy lands."[45] In times of unrest, this posed an obvious challenge.

This fragmented landscape brings us back to the problem of frontiers. The linear boundary, the word "*sakai*," may not have lent itself to describing the areas of attrition produced by a discontinuous, fragmented language. But as armies marched or rode into each other's lands or set up defenses to prevent such incursions, a word *did* exist to describe what we would call military frontiers. This word, though, clearly owed more to a logic of crossing and passing through a parcelized landscape than it did to the recognition of a central authority that organized the

45. Boffa, *Warfare in Medieval Brabant*, 181.

land as coherent expanses of territory, divided by linear or quasi-linear boundaries. In 1471, Utsunomiya Shigetsuna wrote a letter of commendation to one of his warriors, who had acquitted himself well during a recent campaign against the rival Nasu family of northern Shimotsuke Province: "I am most moved and delighted by your strenuous effort in the fighting of the past twenty-fifth and twenty-sixth, at the time of the attack at Shimonasu-guchi."[46] Shimonasu-guchi sounds like a place name. In fact, the toponym here is Shimonasu, an estate, and the word *kuchi* (or the suffix *-guchi*) means "entrance." What Shigetsuna is saying, then, is that his follower fought valiantly during clashes in the vicinity of Shimonasu.

Japanese commentators occasionally gloss the suffix *-guchi* with the vague term "area, direction" (*shūhen*, *hōmen*).[47] But in an undated letter to unnamed allies, Ashikaga Shigeuji observes, "As for our forces fighting at Bushū-guchi—this will happen in a day or two, and so Intō will convey the details to you."[48] Clearly, Shigeuji cannot be speaking of combat "in the Bushū area," that is, in Musashi. The province was expansive, and even granting that Intō was meant to convey further details to the recipient, the indication would have been so vague as to be utterly useless. Why even bother adding the suffix at all? If *kuchi* is meant to indicate an area, it is incongruously narrow for a whole province. Then again, "area" can be far too broad a translation as well.

Rendering *kuchi* more plainly as "entrance" makes more sense sometimes: writing about his exploits in the third person, Dōkan recalled how he "set a camp nearby, in a place called Murayama, in this province; his relatives Zusho no suke and Rokurō approached Okumiho from both entrances."[49] If there can be two ("both") *kuchi*, then the word must indicate a discrete place, not simply a general vicinity. Okumiho, in the mountains of Sagami, was in a long, narrow valley, and Dōkan sent

---

46. *TKS* 4:22, no. 1 (Tomatsuri monjo).

47. That is the explanation provided for Shimonasuguchi in *Motegi chōshi* 2, doc. 83; Kuroda Motoki translates the word as *hōmen*, speaking of an attack on Edo (*Ōgigayatsu*, 108).

48. *GKS* 7, no. 1826 (Shūkomonjo). The name of the addressee is missing from the letter, as is the year of composition. The reference is to the go-between, a warrior called Intō, who is referenced as a messenger in *Shōin shigo* (831b, 837b, 846a).

49. *Ōta Dōkan jō*, 640b.

his relatives to approach it from both ends. The idea that *kuchi* would refer to a point of access is perfectly sensible—almost inevitable, even—in the context of a mountainous landscape. Yet as Shigeuji's letter shows, it is when the word is *not* found in connection with a narrow valley that things get confusing. One last example, drawn from Shōin's memoir—a passage I have already quoted in Chapter 4: "[The enemy] blocked merchants' transit to and from the Ikatsuko camp. Whether battling along the roads or clashing in villages, the attacks on families and homes were beyond count. As a result, the camps of [the troops from] Echigo and this province were in distress, and so we for our part opened up Nitta-guchi."[50] In this case, the "entrance" is to Nitta Estate, and it is being opened by the Iwamatsu to help relieve the blockade imposed on the camp at Ikatsuko by Nagao Kageharu. Here, too, the suffix must refer to a place more specific than a general vicinity, if the Iwamatsu warriors were to open it up, either to send reinforcements or to welcome troops seeking a way out of Kageharu's encirclement.

The word's resistance to a single translation has to do not only with the lack of an equivalent in modern English; it is also a product of our expectations about its possible meanings and of our assumptions about the contexts in which it was used. All of the examples I have cited, and the overwhelming majority of those I have encountered, point to the locations of military campaigns.[51] Sōchō, for instance, never uses the word in his travelogues, though he seldom shies away from naming the places he visits and the sights he sees (needless to say, the word never shows up in Sōgi's more rarefied travelogues, either). Its appearances in letters and chronicles consistently relate to the movement of troops and the sites of battles, identifying a place name as a path into a particular locale, whether an estate, a valley, or a province. As in the case of Shimonasu-guchi,

---

50. *Shōin shigo*, 838b.

51. For other examples of the word used as a suffix after a toponym, see *GKS* 7, no. 1762 (Oyama monjo); *KKS* 1, no. 241 (Takeuchi Bunhei-shi shozō monjo); *Ōta Dōkan jō*, 635b; *Shōin shigo*, 790b, 839a–b; *SKS* 5, no. 1019 (*Koshōmon*); *GKS* 7, no. 1826 (Shūko monjo); for its use alone, see *GKS* 7, nos. 1822, 1872 (Abo monjo and Irobe monjo, respectively); *KKS* 1, no. 243 (Kōmyōji monjo); *TKS* 2:104–65 (Motegi monjo); 2:130–51; 132–58 (Nasu monjo).

Nitta-guchi, or the two *kuchi* leading into Okumiho, these access points did not simply sit in the general vicinity of the toponyms to which they were affixed. They were the way into them.

Not coincidentally, these entranceways were expected to become sites of clashes between armies, and were guarded accordingly: as *Shōin shigo* tells us, the Iwamatsu "opened up Nitta-guchi." When incursions were launched against enemy lands, wherever the defending forces arrayed themselves that place name would be a *kuchi*, if only for the occasion.[52]

The consistent representation as access points of thresholds that we might be tempted to think of more as linear boundaries or frontiers speaks to a different way of conceptualizing the distribution of authority on territory. Portraying frontiers—the unstable and often contested boundaries separating neighboring states or domains—as more or less narrow, more or less hazy buffer zones caught in the process of settling into a linear border does not help us here.[53] Usage of the word *kuchi*, on the other hand, suggests that the fragmentation of holdings that was prevalent in Japan, which hindered the agglomeration of coherent, contiguous domains, also discouraged contemporaries from viewing the spaces between themselves and their neighbors as lines. Rather, the

52. The best illustration of this practice (that I have come across) is in two texts from beyond the Kantō: *Asakura shimatsuki* (33, 36, 38, 43) and Inoue T., Kuwayama, and Fujiki, *Kaetsu tōsōki* (*Asakura shimatsuki, Kaetsu tōsōki, Esshū gunki*, 328, 329, 330, 331, 332, 333, 339, for example), two sixteenth-century war tales immortalizing the struggle between the Asakura of Echizen and the Kaga *ikki*. These texts attach the suffix *-guchi* to a number of already established toponyms, and only when describing military deployment. There are no other attested uses of those place names with the *-guchi* suffix, suggesting that the compound did not become a distinct toponym in its own right. Yata (*Nihon chūsei Sengoku-ki kenryoku kōzō*, 236–38) offers the only discussion of the word I have encountered, and notes that usage associated *kuchi* with locales near frontiers. Moving from the word's most obvious meaning, Yata associates *kuchi* with staging points, such as inns and post stations, but does not really go beyond, to question what use of such a word means about conceptions of territory. Conversely, Matsuoka Susumu ("Iwaki-ryō sakaime no jōkangun to chiiki shakai") uses the word *kuchi* to refer to various fronts/frontier zones surrounding the lands of the Iwaki family of Mutsu in the sixteenth century, but only as shorthand, not in connection with contemporary sources.

53. Power, "Introduction. Frontiers," 3–6.

sometimes empty lands separating rival houses were described in terms of the points that provided access and transit between them. Some compelling if indirect corroboration for this interpretation comes from several other, unrelated languages, across which we find analogous usages: words denoting borders or frontiers often carry, as alternative or original connotations, meanings such as "gate," "way," or "pass."[54] And in the Japanese context, writing about a different sort of passage—between different levels of exclusion and sacredness on an early modern period mountain, Ōyama—Barbara Ambros has noted that the threshold was represented by a *torii* or a stone gate.[55] If we accept that the "frontier" was discussed in terms of a passage, no great leap of imagination is necessary to note how defensive structures would come to be associated with the passage they were set up to monitor, how these defensive structures came to stand for the frontier more generally.

In another of his undated letters of commendation, Shigeuji acknowledges the service of one Abo Ujiyasu, a warrior who had once petitioned for confirmation of his holdings in northern Musashi: "We hear that on the past tenth of the month you set out against Takayama Estate, storming the enemy castle. Though it is not the first time, we feel that [yours] is the height of loyalty. As for that access point, in consultation with our allies, you must continue to block it."[56] Takayama Estate was in southwestern Kōzuke, just across the river from the residence of the Abo, and although the context suggests that Abo crossed over into the neighboring province, the access point in this case must be connected to Takayama specifically, rather than Kōzuke in general. Abo's assault was probably part of an offensive against the Yamanouchi Uesugi, who had one of

---

54. Manzano Moreno ("The Creation of a Medieval Frontier," 46) discusses the etymologies of the words used to indicate the frontier in several languages, including Latin and Arabic. He notes that the Arabic notion of *thagr* (frontier) is also used (although less commonly) to mean "opening," "gate," and "pass" and that this meaning is found in words of the same root in other Semitic languages. In Latin the word *limes* originally denoted a military road or pass, and in the Byzantine Empire the Greek *kleisurai* also had a similar etymology, denoting "passes" or "defiles." And another Arabic word (*darb*) used in Asia Minor has two meanings, of "frontier" and "gate," "way," and "pass."

55. Ambros, *Emplacing a Pilgrimage*, 38.

56. *GKS* 7, no. 1822 (Abo monjo). On the Abo family, see Itō K., *Musashi bushidan no ichiyōtai*, 169–77.

their most important holdings and fortresses in nearby Hirai, and the suggestion here is that by taking the local castle, Abo was blocking not only Takayama, but also transit to and from Hirai. When Shigeuji speaks of "blocking that access point," then, he must be instructing Abo to hold the castle that guarded the passage.[57] He implies that the castle *was* the passage, and lets us catch a glimpse of the relationship between territory—boundaries, in particular—and fortifications.

Domains: An Epilogue

Much changed with the arrival of the Hōjō. They appeared abruptly, interfering in the affairs of the Uesugi as the conflict between the Yamanouchi and the Ōgigayatsu headed toward its climax in 1504–5. In fact, the Hōjō had been advancing from the west—quietly at first, ever more menacingly with each new conquest, since 1491. Hōjō Sōun's (1432–1519) subjugation of Izu Province must have been a blow to the Uesugi, but his advance into Sagami in 1495 after the capture of Odawara (which would become his main castle) seems to have attracted relatively little notice; the Ōgigayatsu even requested Sōun's help to defeat the Yamanouchi. Only after matters settled down between the "Two Uesugi" did it become apparent that their preoccupation with each other had allowed the Hōjō to gain a strong foothold in Sagami. Kamakura fell to Sōun in 1512, and from then on the Hōjō advance became the main threat for the Uesugi. In 1524 Edo fell to the enemy with surprising ease, and despite repeated attempts was never retaken. Then, the staunch resistance put up by some of the great houses of Musashi—the Mita and Ōishi, sometimes the Ōta—stymied the Hōjō for several years. When the last line of defense, Kawagoe, finally fell in 1546, the surviving Uesugi retreated north to their castle at Hirai in Kōzuke. Under attack again, they resisted only until 1552, then they withdrew from the Kantō and sought

57. Again, Manzano Moreno's discussion of frontiers in Semitic and Indo-European languages is providential, showing how the word *thagr* (frontier), sometimes refers to a single castle, as in the case of Zaragoza. Castles, he notes, "were perceived as a series of 'passes' which controlled the access to a given territory. This perception fits well with the character of the frontier described above, as it highlights the discontinuity and irregularity of the frontier landscape" ("The Creation of a Medieval Frontier," 46).

refuge in Echigo, over the hills.[58] The last of the Ōgigayatsu perished in the fall of Kawagoe, and when the fighting was over, several provincial magnates submitted to the Hōjō.[59] The realignment of provincial magnates like the Mita, Ōta, Ōishi, and Fujita, among others, allowed the "southern warrior bands," as the Uesugi called them, to sweep through Musashi and quickly launch an assault on the last bastion of the Yamanouchi.

The submission of local families is significant in two ways. First, it reveals how disconnected from the warrior houses of Musashi and Kōzuke the Uesugi had become over the decades. As the Yamanouchi were evicted unceremoniously, their former followers remained firmly entrenched in their lands, warily negotiating a settlement with the invaders. That the Hōjō could replace the Uesugi at the apex of the plain's political hierarchy without too much disruption was a function of the autonomous prosperity enjoyed by local magnates (the Hōjō brought along their own retainers and rewarded them handsomely, mostly drawing from the holdings of the vanquished Uesugi and their loyalists).[60] Hōjō rule over the Kantō, while facing its fair share of challenges from warlords of nearby provinces, remained remarkably smooth in its day-to-day dealings with local families.

Reconciliation with most of the Kantō elite also entailed another consequence. As conquerors from another region, the Hōjō were largely free from the shackles of precedent that had limited the Uesugi's ability to enact or even imagine deep changes in the way territory was ruled. The Hōjō negotiated settlements and made concessions, but from their lofty position as victors. At the same time, because pacification was achieved by leaving in place local magnates, the Hōjō had to make allowances for the peculiarities of the region's political and tenurial geography, even as they tried to take advantage of their position as outsiders to reshape the conquered lands to their liking.

58. Kuroda M., *Ōgigayatsu*, 79–90; Sugiyama, *Sengoku daimyō Gohōjōshi*, 400–408; *Gunma kenshi tsūshi hen* 3:500–506; Katsumata, "Jūgo-jūroku seiki no Nihon," 21–23.

59. Katō, "Hōjō Ujiteru ni yoru Hachiōji-ryō shihai no kakuritsu," 241–42; *Shinpen Saitama kenshi tsūshi hen* 2:492–94.

60. Ikegami, "Sengoku daimyō ryōgoku," 47–48, 68–71.

Ultimately the reconciliation proved to be short-lived. The survival and dubious allegiance of a number of local magnates in areas recently subjugated became an urgent problem as Hōjō armies advanced from their stronghold in Odawara. Over the next generation, the Hōjō proceeded to neutralize many of the magnates that posed a threat to their hegemony—mostly through marital alliances and the forced adoption of Hōjō heirs, which led to the absorption of local warrior houses into the Hōjō power structure. The recognition of the continuing political relevance of the old Kantō elites—implicit in these dealings—spurred not only the assimilation of recalcitrant families but also the establishment of a strong network of jurisdictions founded on castles.[61]

This phenomenon is especially noticeable in the shape taken by local rule, in the role and organization given to the castles that dotted the landscape. Hōjō-sponsored land surveying has justly been the focus of a great deal of scholarship, in an attempt to clarify how the lords of Odawara interfered with existing tenurial patterns in order to solidify their grip on the region.[62] The novel ways in which they made use of castles, though, were at least as significant, and contributed directly to shape a new form of territorial authority. Certainly the Hōjō did not demolish all existing fortresses in order to clean the slate. Castles like Edo, Kawagoe, Matsuyama, and Hachigata played a crucial function in the machinery of Hōjō governance, and have come to be associated far more closely with their sixteenth-century masters than with their original builders: rain-stained lettering on an explanatory placard, put up for

61. Ikegami, "Sengoku daimyō ryōgoku," 87. A bizarre exception to the pattern was and remained the Kira house of southeastern Musashi, which continued to enjoy almost unfettered autonomy. The Kira seem to have participated in none of the Hōjō's campaigns, nor to have had to suffer the ignominy of a survey of their lands; they survived, it seems, as a peaceful and more or less ignored enclave in the heart of Hōjō territory. See Ogino Minahiko, "Musashi no Kira-shi."

62. Birt, "Samurai in Passage"; Nagahara with Yamamura, "Sengoku Daimyo and the Kandaka System"; Katsumata with Collcutt, "Development of Sengoku Law"; Owada, *Gohōjō-shi kenkyū*; Katō, "Hōjō Ujiteru ni yoru Hachiōji-ryō shihai no kakuritsu"; Ikegami, "Sengoku daimyō ryōgoku"; Fujiki, "Daimyō ryōgoku no keizai kōzō"; Kuroda M., *Sengoku daimyō ryōgoku no shihai kōzō*; Asakura, "Gohōjō-shi no kenryoku kōzō"; Sawaki, *Gohōjō-shi to ryōgoku kei'ei*; and Noritake, *Sengoku daimyō ryōgoku no kenryoku kōzō*.

the lonely visitor on the grounds of what used to be Hachigata castle by town officials in present-day Yorii-machi, Saitama, devotes a line and a half to the eighty years before Hōjō rule and four lines to the forty years between the arrival of Hōjō Ujikuni and the castle's fall to Toyotomi Hideyoshi in 1590.

In Hachigata and elsewhere, the Odawara warlords did endeavor to expand and refurbish the castles they took over.[63] The Hōjō took pride in the their fortifications, which are noted for the advances they display in military technology.[64] Their fondness for castles was not reflected merely in their attention to infrastructure, for militarily and administratively castles would eventually become the backbone of the family's Kantō-wide domain. The functions they performed starting around 1555 have come to define Hōjō rule and exemplify the innovations that set the warlords of the sixteenth century apart from the military governors and local magnates of the fifteenth.[65] The case of the Hōjō is nonetheless remarkable, for attention to the geographical distribution of castles as well as to their administrative uses enabled the development, from the very early years of the family's rise, of a new link between land and authority, one which produced the territorial domains of this period.

Although the Hōjō inherited many of the fortresses that, individually, had played key roles under the Uesugi, in the aggregate these looked very different. And it was in the aggregate, quite clearly, that the Hōjō meant for them to be employed. From their inception, locations for castles had been affected by topography and the proximity of transportation routes.[66] But each family built its own, on its own lands—logically enough, since fifteenth-century castles emerged as a response to local conditions. The Hōjō took a different approach, as they slowly made their way into the plain. Hōjō forces fanned out from Odawara, in the southwestern corner of the Kantō, subjugating or winning over the warriors they encountered on their path. Fragmented though it was—not only subjected to the vicissitudes of war, but shaped by the same tenurial

---

63. *NJT* 5:167; Sekiguchi, "Hachigata-jō," 216–17.

64. Saitō, "Kōzuke no kuni Nakayama-jō."

65. *Kanagawa kenshi tsūshi hen* 1:1027; Ikegami, "Gohōjō-ryō no kuji ni tsuite"; and Asakura, "Gohōjō-shi no ryōgoku shihai."

66. Saitō, *Chūsei tōgoku no ryōiki to jōkan*, 55–57.

idiosyncrasies that characterized the holdings of the local magnates they conquered—the Hōjō advance *did* have a moving frontline, a military frontier of sorts. Because they were outsiders, and their takeover took the form of invasion rather than uprising, the Hōjō had the opportunity to use their castles in a different way. They were integrated into the moving frontier—indeed, more than any other factor, they shaped it.

The castles built by the Hōjō, and the ones they chose to refurbish and expand, were situated favorably not to rule a holding, or an estate; they were meant to protect and ensure the expansion of a domain that was growing to encompass several provinces. A map of the most vital fortresses garrisoned by the Hōjō at the apogee of their power, just before their ill-advised and ill-fated showdown with Toyotomi Hideyoshi, clearly plots a relationship between the parts (the castles and their hinterlands) and the whole (the domain). The situation in 1590 need not concern us here, but the map also provides a chronology of the Hōjō advance—much like the rings in the trunk of a tree—and a geography of their frontier. Irei Masao has posited that the main castles—the most imposing, the ones where troops were mustered—were arranged in concentric rings (Map 5.1). The widest ring, the one farthest from Odawara, stretched across the provinces of Kazusa, Hitachi, and Shimotsuke. Most of those fortresses rose east of the Tonegawa, beyond what had ever been the limits of Uesugi control, and only became part of the Hōjō's defense network in the years after the Uesugi departed. Closer to Odawara were some of the castles that had dominated the Kantō since the time of the war between the Yamanouchi Uesugi and Ashikaga Shigeuji: east to west, in an arc that guarded the hither bank of the Tonegawa, were Edo, Iwatsuki, Kawagoe, Matsuyama, and Hachigata. Closest to Odawara stood the strongholds that monitored access to Sagami Province—and again, *access* was the key feature of a frontier: Hachiōji, Kozukue, Tamanawa, and Misaki.[67]

How do we know that these were concentric frontiers, that together they formed defensive rings? Are we connecting the dots arbitrarily, or were the Hōjō themselves spacing their strongholds systematically? Irei's scheme is admittedly a little contrived, in that it presupposes an

67. Irei, "Odawara-eki," 113–14.

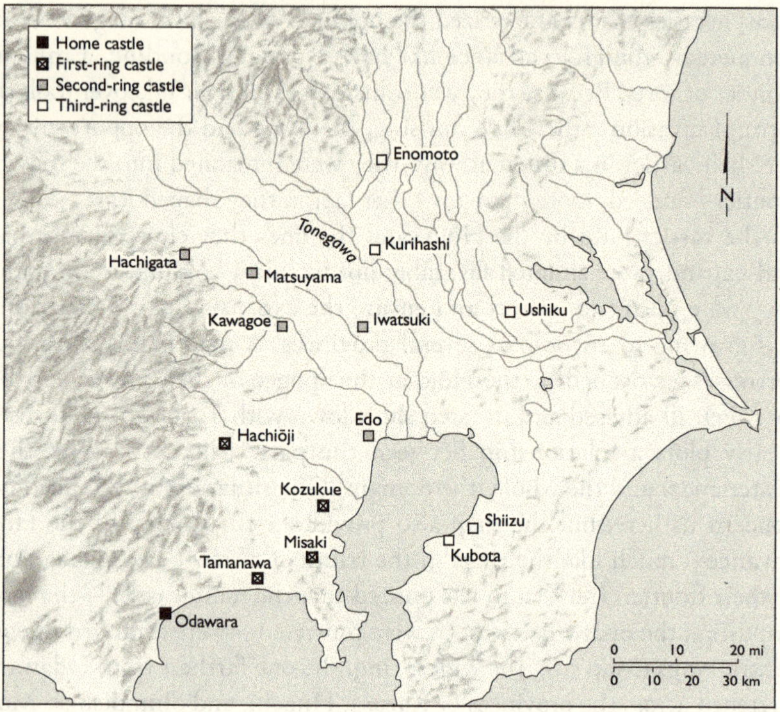

Map 5.1. The concentric rings of the Hōjō family's branch castles.

awareness, from the start, of the overarching northeastward direction to Hōjō expansion. Hachiōji, for instance, was actually established *after* Edo, Kawagoe, and the castles in that ring, rather than before (this is because at that time the family's expansion was aimed at Musashi rather than at the Kantō as a whole).[68] But there is also some evidence that the Hōjō were not simply reacting to the situation they found. Even early on, as they quelled resistance in Izu and slowly ate away at Uesugi territory in Sagami at the turn of the sixteenth century, the Hōjō began to

68. On the chronology of the assimilation of the Tama region around Hachiōji, as revealed by surveying that accompanied its conquest, see Katō, "Hōjō Ujiteru ni yoru Hachiōji-ryō shihai no kakuritsu," 241–49. For a glimpse of how warlords in other parts of Japan tackled the problem of reorganization of newly annexed borderlands, see Yamamoto, "Ryōgoku 'sakaime' chiiki," 70.

reorganize the landscape: they divided the whole territory of Izu, then Sagami, and eventually Musashi, into districts. These were not the ancient districts that were outlined in the early tenth century *Engi shiki* (Procedures of the Engi era) and that had organized local administration of the imperial state ever since. The new lords of Odawara drew up their own from scratch. Some of the new districts were produced by consolidating or breaking up old districts; others instead codified the importance of several castles by drawing jurisdictions around them.[69]

It was not until the development of what historians have called the "branch-castle domainal system" (*shijōryō-sei*) in the second half of the sixteenth century that castles became the basic units for all facets of administration (taxation, adjudication, bestowal and confirmation of land rights, troop mobilization), but from the start they played a pivotal role in reshaping local rule. It was through districts and district heads that taxes were collected and, as I mentioned earlier, several of the new districts were designed around castles and their hinterlands. In this system castellans—district heads who were also in charge of a castle—were also entrusted with mustering troops.[70] Hōjō forces were organized in various "bands" (*shū*), each assigned to a castle, and under the command of a castellan. And although these troops did not necessarily reside or even hold much land in the area under the jurisdiction of the castle, the composition of the warrior bands tended to be more local as one moved away from Odawara and the Hōjō homeland, toward the frontier.[71] This differentiation among the warrior bands, captured in the entries of *Odawara-shū shoryō yakuchō* (Service roll of the holdings of Odawara bands, 1559), was probably not intentional. Rather, it reflects the evolving nature of Hōjō rule: in peripheral regions, where the warlord's authority was not yet solidly established, meddling and reorganization from Odawara are less apparent.[72]

69. Owada, *Gohōjō-shi kenkyū*, 207; Asakura, "Gohōjō-shi no ryōgoku shihai ni tsuite," 344–48.

70. Arimitsu, "Chiiki kokka no shikumi," 144–45. (Arimitsu follows Kuroda M., *Sengoku daimyō Hōjō-shi no ryōgoku shihai*, 177–90.)

71. Minegishi Sumio ("Sengoku jidai no 'ryō' to ryōgoku," 341) makes the statement in his examination of Kōzuke.

72. Ikegami, "Sengoku daimyō ryōgoku," 50; Irei, "Odawara-shū shoryō yakuchō kenkyū," 430–34; Sawaki, *Gohōjō-shi no kiso kenkyū*, 102–9.

Yet it is clear that the Hōjō were sensitive to the special needs of governance in outlying areas. They did not hesitate to change the distribution of their castles as contingencies changed. When the frontier moved away from Matsuyama, in northern Musashi, the Hōjō not only loosened their control on that castle, allowing it a greater degree of autonomy, they actually *demolished* several of the smaller fortresses they had built in the former frontier region, in order to ensure that the castellan of Matsuyama could rule more strongly.[73] When a castle guarded a frontier, the lords of Odawara would involve themselves more actively in its management, assiduously sending out instructions to the castellan, and supervising construction and repairs.[74] In the Hōjō's understanding, castles functioned as parts of networks, not as individual strongholds.[75] Especially on the frontier, the hinterland of major castles was dotted with other smaller fortresses, carefully and regularly spaced out.[76] The networking of castles was paralleled by their functional diversification, as smaller fortresses designed to monitor traffic along access routes were interspersed with larger ones entrusted with defense from an invading army. In one case at least, the Hōjō built a castle in a place called Nakayama, in the mountains of Kōzuke. The place name "Nakayama" ("inner mountains," "mountains between") was commonly used to designate boundaries that ran through mountainous regions, so the Hōjō's choice of location signaled militarily, topographically, and even toponymically their understanding of that castle's function.[77]

---

73. Matsuoka, *Sengoku-ki jōkangun no keikan*, 265; on the ways in which strongholds in frontier areas of other parts of the country, too, were built differently according to the strategic nature of each frontier, see Matsuoka, "Iwaki-ryō sakaime no jōkangun to chiiki shakai," 8–25.

74. Shimoyama, "Gohōjō-shi no jōkaku kanri to shiro fushin"; Nishigaya, "Sengoku jōkaku."

75. Matsuoka, *Sengoku-ki jōkangun no keikan*, 250–300.

76. Owada, *Gohōjō-shi no kenkyū*, 245–53. Owada speculates that the homogenous distribution of castles in northwestern Musashi, for instance, was devised to ensure that the chime of a bell sounding an alarm could be heard from one castle to the next.

77. The interpretation of the usage of the toponym is Kuroda Hideo's (*Kyōkai no chūsei*, 37–63). Kuroda also cites a locale called Nakayama no kuchi ("entranceway to the mountains between"), confirming the link between *kuchi* and boundaries. See also Saitō, "Kyōkai ninshiki no henka"; Saitō, "Kōzuke no kuni Nakayama-jō." Studies of Hōjō and their castle-building practices have contributed significantly to our

An example gives us a sense of how far the Kantō had come since the Uesugi. Writing to his castellan in Edo on the eve of the arrival of the Hōjō, in 1489, Ōgigayatsu Uesugi Sadamasa elaborated at length on his ongoing feud with the Yamanouchi, on the assassination of the scheming Dōkan (which Sadamasa himself had ordered), and on the ineptitude of his adopted son and heir, Tomoyoshi. The aging warrior's concern for the future of the Ōgigayatsu house is expressed conventionally, yet it is hard to escape the uncanny feeling, upon reading the details of his letter, that Sadamasa was somehow prescient. What is remarkable is not so much his prophecy that the fortunes of his house would come to an end with his heir—which in a sense they did, although the Ōgigayatsu struggled on, diminished, for three more brief generations—but his lucid perception that danger would come from neighboring provinces rather than the Yamanouchi. One cannot but think of Hōjō Sōun when Sadamasa warns, "From other provinces unimagined thieves will come openly; no doubt they will do as they please with the Kantō."[78]

Sadamasa's warning against aggression from beyond the borders of the Kantō is hardly unique. Other fifteenth-century texts raise similar alarms, and associate distant regions with looming threats and vague foreboding. Danger may come from this or that neighboring province or, generically, from "another province" (*takoku*), as these texts identify the foe with the place name.[79] This sweeping identification between province and warrior house is less likely as attention moves closer to home, and documents discuss families in the Kantō. Just a few years earlier Dōkan had spoken of the forces mustered by "a man from Kai," not of the armies of Kai. Sadamasa, in his letter to Soga, lays out future plans to be carried out "if we pacify the three provinces of Kōzuke, Musashi, and Sagami."[80]

---

understanding of the impetus behind construction, of the way fortresses came to be utilized, and of the role they had in shaping territorial domains. Taking his lead from Matsuoka and Saitō, Nakanishi Yūki ("Sengoku-ki ni okeru chiiki no jōkan to shugo kōken") has studied the distribution of castles in Settsu Province in an attempt to show how the status of a castle—whether it was built by a holder of public office or by a local warrior—affected and was reflected by its location (lowlands or mountains, home bases and hinterlands).

78. *SKS* 5, no. 1019 (*Koshōmon*).

79. *Kamakura ōzōshi*, 60; *Shōin shigo*, 820b, 844b.

80. *SKS* 5, no. 1019 (*Koshōmon*).

In a letter written in the midst of a war that risked tearing apart the Uesugi family's hegemony, the expression Sadamasa chooses is revealing. Just as Dōkan had a few years before, Sadamasa uses the names of the three provinces—Kōzuke, Musashi, and Sagami—purely to provide a setting for the conflict. They are no more than places, three provinces variously split in their support of the two contending factions. When Sadamasa speaks of pacification, he naturally intends that it should be achieved through subjugation of the Yamanouchi. Yet he does not focus on the provinces controlled by his rivals: in Sadamasa's world—or at least in the world portrayed in his letter—no *one* province is associated with one side or the other, even though the Yamanouchi were most firmly ensconced in Kōzuke and the Ōgigayatsu in Sagami. Sadamasa speaks of the pacification of all three provinces because that was the political stage on which the Uesugi had acted for generations. In fact, although the Uesugi were occasionally addressed by the place names of their residences (the castle at Kawagoe, the camp at Ikatsuko—and only in *Shōin shigo*), never were they associated with the name of the individual province these residences were in. Never were the Uesugi, metonymically, "Sō" or "Bu" or "Jō" from the Chinese-style names of the various Kantō provinces under their jurisdiction (Sōshū, Bushū, and Jōshū, for Sagami, Musashi, and Kōzuke, respectively).

The Hōjō, on the other hand, would be. In the late 1550s, they begin to appear in documents, regularly if not exclusively, as "Sō," from the Sinicized name of Sagami Province, where their main fortress, Odawara, stood. Thus, in a letter from 1558, we read of the "conflict between Sō and Bō [Shimōsa],"[81] in reference to the standoff with the Satomi, a family from that province. At the height of the family's expansion in the late 1560s, a series of exchanges meant to sound out the possibility of a truce with Nagao Kagetora (aka Uesugi Kenshin, 1530–78) of Echigo repeatedly bring up "the matter of peace talks between Sō and Etsu [Echigo],"[82] or "the issue of Etsu and Sō."[83] Writing about the Hōjō, their counterpart broaches "the issue of the peace with Sōshū [that is, Sagami]."[84] The

81. *Sengoku ibun* 2, no. 1087 (from *Kii zokufudoki furoku*, 10).
82. *DNK*, vol. 12, bk. 1, no. 510 (Uesugi-ke monjo).
83. *DNK*, vol. 12, bk. 1, no. 514 (Uesugi-ke monjo).
84. *DNK*, vol. 12, bk. 1, no. 518 (Uesugi-ke monjo).

association between the Hōjō and Sagami Province was not a mere reference to location, but rather part of a process of mutual identification between the warrior house and its lands: the Hōjō continued to be called "Sō" even after they subjugated other, vaster, provinces.[85] By the late 1560s they ruled over Izu, Musashi, parts of Kōzuke, Shimotsuke, and Shimōsa, as well as Sagami, and were lending their backing to the last, beleaguered descendants of a family the Hōjō themselves had once served, the Imagawa of Suruga and Tōtōmi. Yet they were called Sō—a name meant to transcend the pure toponym, and represent the whole of the house's conquests. By employing a moniker drawn from provincial rather than local geography—albeit, a provincial geography loosely and imprecisely outlined—the Hōjō signaled their wish to give themselves a synthetic designation, one that might overcome the fragmentation of the region and the persistent, if reduced, presence of autonomous warrior families.[86]

That an element of oversimplification—the perfect and exclusive correspondence between the warrior house and its lands—was included in the Hōjō rulers' portrayal of the balance of power in the Kantō should not detract from its significance. It is telling that rival warlords refer to the Hōjō in this manner, too. The lack of controversy surrounding the Hōjō's use of the name "Sō" is certainly a reflection of the spread among warlords of the practice of taking as their own the name of their provinces of origin (or, as in the case of the Hōjō, of their headquarters). In the case of the lords of Odawara, though, things are more complicated, firstly because the arena in which they contended had always transcended

85. Citing the similar use, by the Mōri of Aki Province, of the word "Gei" (for Aki) even after they had expanded beyond that province's borders, Ike Susumu ("Sengoku-ki no 'kuni' ni tsuite," 3) argues that the names of provinces had remained associated with the old imperial state and the Muromachi regime, and that emerging provincial magnates made use of them simply to refer to their home province. See also Yata, *Nihon chūsei Sengoku-ki kenryoku kōzō*, 255–61.

86. The survival of pockets of land that escaped Hōjō jurisdiction was arguably made easier by the persistent "patchiness" of the territory. Although all lands within the new frontiers of the Hōjō's conquests were nominally under the scrutiny of the Hōjō and produced revenue for them, we have evidence of vast tracts of fallow, empty lands, which the lords of Odawara tried to entice locals to develop. See Asakura, *Gohōjō ryōgoku no chiikiteki tenkai*, 49–68; Noritake, *Sengoku daimyō ryōgoku no kenryoku kōzō*, 174–92.

the limits (and therefore the ability to identify with) a single province; secondly, because unlike the Takeda of Kai, or the Uesugi of Echigo, who had been entrenched in those provinces for centuries, the Hōjō had become paramount in the Kantō only very recently. Their meteoric rise saw them progress from followers of the Imagawa to lords of two provinces (Izu and Sagami) and invaders of a third (Musashi) in just over twenty years. Chronologically, Izu was as close to a home province as the Hōjō ever had; Sagami (Sō) became their headquarters only a few years later, when they selected Odawara as the site for their main castle.

Use of the Sinicized names of provinces to designate warrior houses became common throughout Japan, probably sooner in areas where politics had functioned on a clearer, one-province basis. In Echizen, the Asakura often referred to themselves and their troops as "Etsu," explicitly evoking the ancient Chinese kingdom of Yue (written with the same character as Etsu) to portray themselves as a cohesive and identifiable political entity rather than simply one of a number of warrior families with holdings in Echizen.[87] But if Sō became the new title for the Hōjō family in accordance with the model established in other single-province contexts, it is the application of this name to the vast and heterogeneous landscape of the Kantō that is significant. In the sixteenth century, a language emerged that allowed description of the plain in terms that did not rely on the old geographical terminology—and it is no coincidence that the more literary "Sō" was consistently preferred over the more mundane and geographical "Sagami." What "Sō" enabled was the portrayal of the Kantō—or the portion of it that followed the Hōjō—as a single, nameable, territorially intelligible political unit (names like Sō, in their brevity, may also owe their popularity to the sixteenth-century penchant for abbreviation of proper nouns, which is apparent in so many documents of the period).

The molding of this new territorial coherence was clearly discernible along the edges (to return to boundaries). Indeed, scholars in Japan have singled out the affirmation by sixteenth-century warlords of the right to mediate border conflicts and establish boundaries as a seminal moment in the creation of territorial domains—calling both the process and the

87. See *Asakura shimatsuki*, 27.

end result (not coincidentally) ***bunkoku*** ("province division").[88] The emergence of a clearly conceived frontier region was symptomatic of the formation of an equally clearly structured territorial organization for the domain as a whole; the creation of a well-laid out network of castles was crucial to the development of the kind of domain the Uesugi had never had.[89] Under the Hōjō, peace treaties with hostile neighbors included provisions spelling out the new limits of the contenders' spheres of authority.

These spheres were meant not to be porous, and to define mutually exclusive territories, but they had not yet developed into linear boundaries. Rather, they remained zones—hinterlands of fortresses: they were policed by networks of castles, and defined in terms of whole districts given and taken. When the Hōjō and the Takeda, battling over the spoils of the former Imagawa domain in two districts in eastern Suruga, called for a truce, it was decided that both parties would pull back and leave one empty district between them, as a buffer. The Hōjō would take Izu Province, and the Takeda would take Suruga. But the boundary established by the treaty did not follow the traditional one between the two provinces. Rather, it ran down between the two districts in eastern Suruga that had been contested, so that the Hōjō acquired one whole district in that province. As a concession to the Takeda, the Hōjō renounced two castles they had built in the frontier region. These, at least, were the minutiae of the agreement.[90]

More broadly, this episode is noteworthy for two reasons. It vividly illustrates the solidification of the association between territory and

---

88. Fujiki, *Toyotomi heiwarei to Sengoku shakai*, 1–12. Yata (*Nihon chūsei Sengoku-ki kenryoku kōzō*, 255–57) shows how the word *kokka* (used by warlords to refer to their own domains, but literally meaning "province and house") was understood by the Hōjō themselves as a composite of the family (*kamon*) and the province (*bunkoku*). For an excellent discussion of the use of the word *kokka* over the course of the centuries, see Toby, "Rescuing the Nation from History," 219–22.

89. Working on the San'yōdō region in western Honshū, Tada Nobuhisa ("Jōkaku kōsei kara mita chiiki to sakaime") has gone as far as to construct a model correlating castle distribution with frontier definition. Tada builds on Saitō Shin'ichi's insights on the functional diversification of castles and on Matsuoka Susumu's conclusions on the formation of border regions, claiming that domains with weak centers tended to have hazy frontiers.

90. The whole incident is reconstructed in Noritake, *Sengoku daimyō ryōgoku no kenryoku kōzō*, 320–41.

warrior family, giving concrete manifestation to the new warlords' propensity to redefine the landscape in terms of their own dominion. The traditional border between two provinces was willfully ignored—redrawn—in order to maintain the nominal unity and coherence of the two families' domains. The Hōjō ruled over Izu, and wherever Hōjō rule extended was—or could become—Izu. Gradually ironing out the kinks along the edges and the pockets of autonomous lordship within the territory of their domain, in a process that closely resembles the movement toward a territorial state that characterized Europe in the early modern period, the Hōjō sought "to rationalize its administration and to rectify its limits."[91] Similar challenges confronted warlords all over Japan, who turned to a variety of solutions. In parts of western Japan, warlords could reorganize newly annexed frontier regions only with great difficulty; instead, they relied on what one scholar has called the "special perception of balance" of local warriors, who determined the contours of a boundary by gauging the relative weight of neighboring potentates.[92] In the case of the settlement between the Hōjō and the Takeda, there is no evidence of reliance on local warriors—withdrawal from the frontier castles was complete. Further, recognizing the special exigencies of defense, the lords of Odawara set out to minimize their dependence on local warriors by recruiting troops from other parts of their domain—from their "homelands" in Izu, Sagami, and Musashi.[93] In doing so, they reinforced the perception of unity they had sought to instill in their subjects, deploying forces to the far reaches of Hōjō territory in the name of a new association forged between the warrior house and its lands and evoked through the naming of this new polity.[94]

The strong borders invoked by Shōin for the Iwamatsu family lands in 1509 finally appear as political boundaries in a letter sent out by the Hōjō chancery at the end of 1569: "Within the year, the enforcement of

91. Sahlins, "Natural Frontiers Revisited," 1435.

92. Yamamoto (quoting Akiyama Nobutaka and Kishida Hiroyuki) in "Sengoku daimyō ryōgoku 'sakaime' chiiki," 68–70.

93. Noritake, *Sengoku daimyō ryōgoku no kenryoku kōzō*, 335–38.

94. On this system, see Saitō, *Chūsei tōgoku no ryōiki to jōkan*, 272–87. This particular short-term mobilization toward the frontier was called *ban* (Saitō describes this as meaning "stationing of troops").

the borders throughout the domain must be strengthened, and we appeal to all the able-bodied workers in the three provinces of Izu, Sagami, and Musashi, even in temple and shrine holdings."[95] The borders in question refer ambiguously either to the whole of the Hōjō domain (although the word I translate as domain, *bunkoku,* can also refer to provinces) or to Izu, Sagami, and Musashi, listed individually but addressed collectively.[96] This makes the passage no less significant. The old provincial framework did not need to matter to the internal administrative organization of the domain to retain its relevance as an organizing principle of daily life for those "able-bodied workers" (*ninsoku*) mobilized in the letter. Yet the boundary (*sakaime*), in this case obviously functioning as an active frontier, provides a cohesion not seen, say, in Sadamasa's reference to the pacification of the Kantō provinces, eighty years before. This boundary now delineated a space, whether of provinces or a domain, *over* which battles would be fought.

The creation of a no-man's-land along borders that needed reinforcing signals that the formation of linear boundaries was still a work in progress. More systematically organized networks of castles enabled the restructuring of territory and helped create a frontier region, even as the Hōjō continued to tolerate the idea of a land incompletely occupied or controlled.[97] Reliance on warriors recruited in more firmly controlled

---

95. The letter is dated Eiroku 12.11.23 (December 30, 1569), and exists in two nearly identical versions, from Sueyama Shizuhiko-shi shozō Enari monjo, and Fuji Asama jinja monjo. Printed in *Sengoku ibun* 2, nos. 1339, 1340, respectively.

96. Yata (*Nihon chūsei Sengoku-ki kenryoku kōzō*, 257–58) believes that the distinction between *bunkoku* and *kokka* means that, here, the Hōjō have in mind the old framework of the imperial state's provinces. Given the enumeration of the individual provinces, his view is hard to dismiss entirely (Yata also cites a similar letter by the Takeda, which more obviously lists an aggregation of provinces rather than a unitary domain), although I think he fails to see the importance of the word "border" in this context.

97. Recently, important research has been carried out on the economic and fiscal dimension of this imperfect control of the edges of domains, starting with the frequent dual allegiances of local populations (Yamamoto, "Sengoku daimyō ryōgoku 'sakaime' chiiki"); Minegishi ("Tōgoku Sengoku-ki no gunjiteki kyōkai ryōiki") found that communities on the frontiers were allowed by contending warlords to pay half of their dues to each side, in what amounted to an admission of imperfect control, but also a

areas of the domain betrays an imperfect assimilation of the margins: Hōjō power was at its strongest in their main fortress in Odawara, and in their branch castles; it faded as it moved away from those hubs of authority—hence the presence of castles throughout the countryside and in contested regions. These castles served not only to launch offensives and fend off incursions, but also to reaffirm Hōjō authority along the still hazy edges of the domain. Ironically, then, for all of the changes wrought on the landscape by the strife of the sixteenth century, a traveler like Sōchō might not have experienced border crossing all that differently, had he lived for another fifty years. Even as a rhetoric emphasizing the unity of the domain took root, a domain united both with the lord's house and as a knowable and nameable territory; even as Hōjō policy reinforced this unity through treaties and recruitment and castle building, the poet might have found himself stranded in the middle of an empty, ravaged landscape somewhere between domains, waiting in the rain for someone to come and pick him up.

Nor did the vocabulary of borders and frontiers shift quickly. In 1547, Hōjō Ujiyasu, master of Izu, Sagami, and Musashi, wrote his supporters thanking them for their "fighting at Sōma-guchi" in Shimōsa, during a recent campaign.[98] We would expect this lag, of course, seeing the "stickiness" and malleability of other labels in medieval Japan, which lived on unchanged to designate subtly shifting realities (the word "estate" comes to mind most readily here). We should also look for its reason in the specific context of Hōjō rule, in the persistent parcelization of the landscape, which was still made up of a great number of local holders. The composite nature of territorial authority in even the most centralized of sixteenth-century domains ensured that frontiers could be internal as often as external. Still, the overarching relation between frontiers and authority was being reconfigured: the geographically centerless Kantō ruled by the Uesugi after the shuttering of the Kamakura Office in 1455 was replaced by a very different plain. Defined by an expanding

---

form of truce negotiation in order to maintain the stability of frontier regions, as noted by Noritake (*Sengoku daimyō ryōgoku no kenryoku kōzō*, 274–91). Saitō (*Chūsei tōgoku no ryōiki to jōkan*, 269) termed this the "negative" side of warlord boundary-control policies (compared to the "positive" side represented by frontier castles).

98. *Sengoku ibun* 1, nos. 286, 287 (Sakurai monjo and *Komonjo* 2, respectively).

frontier and a series of concentric lines of defense was a political hub, Odawara, that was even more eccentric to the plain than Kamakura had been, in the southwestern corner of the region. The new frontier, though, was a single, outward-looking one, which could be traced across the plain, from the fields of Musashi to Tokyo Bay. What this new frontier defined was a coherent political space that did not derive from the framework of the old imperial state, the province. The Hōjō did not have a name for their polity (though in changing their own name from Ise to Hōjō in 1524 they signaled their dynastic aspirations) so they used Sō, speaking of a part to invoke an imagined whole. As the Uesugi and others had before them, they issued prohibitions, though they did so not as individuals in the manner of functionaries of the Muromachi regime, but in the name of the Hōjō family, the real name of this new place they were creating in eastern Japan.

Coda

So much changed in the seventeenth century, after the new Tokugawa regime brought the country under its sway, that it is always jarring to be reminded of its reputation as backward-looking and conservative. The dual image of reaction and innovation remains, implicitly, in recent scholarship, which has turned to movement—of bodies, of goods, of knowledge—to articulate the impulses toward freedom found in what was a far more regimented society than Japan had known in the previous centuries. What was once characterized as tension, within the state, between institutional and economic vigor, on the one hand, and entropy, on the other, has been more recently coded as a tension between warrior and commoner societies.[1] Drawing attention to the mutually reinforcing growth of recreational travel among broad segments of the population, and of a vast, commercially available printed literature that documented the cultural and touristic charms of the archipelago and guided the traveler through them, historians have recently argued for links between writings about place and the development of early forms of national, or proto-national, identity.[2] The literature of woodblock publishing invited travelers of all sorts to experience every corner of the archipelago for

1. Vaporis, *Breaking Barriers*; Hur, *Prayer and Play*.

2. An early study drawing attention to this perspective is Toby, "Rescuing the Nation from History"; more recently, there have been several monographs on the subject: Yonemoto, *Mapping Early Modern Japan*; Berry, *Japan in Print*; and Nenzi, *Excursions in Identity*.

themselves—an archipelago which that very literature was charting ever more profusely. Countless maps, gazetteers, and tour guides told travelers about the amenities available at their destination and along the road.

This literature also organized information minutely, in charts, tables, and narratives tailored to a variety of different needs. They told the would-be traveler what to experience, and how. The freedom of movement—which was relative but considerable—was, nonetheless, freedom to move throughout a landscape that was reduced to a fixed backdrop and a stage. Every wayfarer experienced the places he or she visited in ways that were inevitably personal and particular, but the organization of space, and knowledge about it, functioned in creating a countrywide consciousness precisely by denying that travel was a process, and place itself the product of a dialectic engagement of each traveler with a space that was created anew each time. Place was now a taxonomy.

Famous places now sprouted up everywhere, as medieval poetic commonplaces (*utamakura*) were supplemented with notable destinations of all kinds: not only beautiful landscapes immortalized in poetry, but also famous local foods and famous local brothels. Fame and renown multiplied for commercial consumption, which is not to say that medieval place and space were lost, or trivialized. Distinguishing early modern famous places (*meisho*) from medieval *utamakura* and famous places (*nadokoro*) was mostly their quantity, which increased prodigiously, and their new commodification. Conceptually, the old and the new had more in common than they had dividing them. Both proclaimed, or advocated, personal experience within guidelines that the writer proffered to the reader ready-made; indeed the writer himself had largely received the guidelines from a community of like-minded writers who set clear parameters for contents and organization of material (and experience)—be they elegant diction or commercial viability.

Assuredly, political and military conditions in the fifteenth and sixteenth centuries, and a far more limited number of poetic places, had produced a landscape and an experience of landscape that were markedly different from those of the early modern period. Safety was a far greater concern to medieval travelers, as the rainy misadventure of the poet Sōchō recounted in the previous chapter reminds us. Fewer people traveled to fewer destinations. A landscape that by the turn of the nineteenth century would be crammed full of places of note was largely empty (conceptually if not in actual fact) in the fifteenth and sixteenth centuries, punctuated here and there rather than mapped and taxonomized. And in the Kantō, more than elsewhere, the transition was stark: the region was reinvented when the Tokugawa moved their seat to Edo in 1590, quickly going from backwater beyond the pale to hinterland of the country's political capital. The lists of famous places available to medieval writers, and to the occasional medieval traveler, were no less prescriptive than the guides that organized and labeled every corner of the land in the early modern period. They were, nevertheless, both less exhaustive and less visually overpowering. The spatial imagination of the later period was not only relentlessly classificatory but also cartographic in a way that fifteenth- and early sixteenth-century Japanese would not have recognized or, indeed, according to Mary Elizabeth Berry, comprehended.[3]

However prescriptive they were, medieval spatial hierarchies had none of the mathematical rigor of mapmaking; they were vaguer, and more lax. Within the loose network of *utamakura* that poets like Sōchō, Banri, Sōboku, and others might have felt compelled to experience—Musashino, Mount Tsukuba, Nikkō, the Shirakawa Barrier, for instance—lay vast expanses of land that were unremarkable, and went unremarked upon. For a brief time, in the late fifteenth and early sixteenth centuries, poets filled in those blanks with accounts of their interactions with local warriors, creating, so to speak, the literary landscape as they traveled through it. In this sense, at least, the burden of precedent was far greater in the early modern period, for precedent was so much harder to avoid.

But if precedent retained in early modern tour guides the primacy it had enjoyed in medieval travelogues, it was also different in important ways. Early modern precedent was far more capacious than its medieval counterpart in scope and in appeal. It included all manner of places, goods, and services, and in this sense encoded space not only more minutely but more diversely than *utamakura* ever had. Where poetic commonplaces colored the landscape with emotion, early modern famous

3. Berry, *Japan in Print*, 54–103. See also Yonemoto, *Mapping Early Modern Japan*, 8–43.

places filled it with food, drink, shows, *as well as* temples and locales of literary note. The variety of the information now subject to recommendation and validation attests to the different engine driving the organization of place and travel, that is, a competitive publishing market in which success was measured out in comprehensiveness. At the same time, the greater purview of the catalog of famous places was a response to the broader readership enticed to purchase guides and goods. More than ever before, knowledge about the "proper" significance of a place was available to anyone who was interested. The treatises presented by itinerant poets and literati to their patrons are a testimony to the paths to acculturation that opened up throughout the country in the wake of the Ōnin War. Despite the frequent lamentations about the crudeness of provincials' efforts at participation in high culture, those provincials were able to participate. In the early modern period, though, knowledge of the land, which was no longer confined to the literary, no longer required a handmade copy, or acquaintance with a member of the cultural elite; it was available for purchase and even for rental in books printed and reprinted in large runs.[4]

Finally, and consequently, the ordering power of precedent changed between the medieval and early modern periods in one more significant way. What expanded, as if out of awareness that Japan was in a new age, was the very past that was invoked as normative. Chronologically, the early years of the Tokugawa dynasty provided a new age of founding fathers that could be set beside older, though not necessarily more hallowed, ages. If in 1509 a memoir like *Shōin shigo* invoked the name of this or that Muromachi shogun to validate the Iwamatsu family's claims to land and pedigree, early modern writers could also draw on precedents from the early seventeenth century. And not only lofty precedents: tour guides openly stood on the foundations of their own previous editions, and advertised inns that were decades old as readily as they did temples that were centuries old. In early modern texts, time was collapsed along with space, and the medieval, once so persistent, was not so much superseded as drowned out.

---

4. For a perspective on print culture, and its relation with various manuscript traditions, see Pitelka, *Handmade Culture*, 69–72, 111–31.

APPENDIX A

Springs and Autumns in the Kantō

The upheaval that marks the history of the Kantō region in the late fifteenth and early sixteenth centuries does not make for riveting storytelling, as it mostly lacks a clear plot with an obvious climax and charismatic protagonists. Historians typically organize what political and military narrative can be discerned in terms of a succession of discrete conflicts: the Kyōtoku Disturbance, the Rebellion of Nagao Kageharu, the Chōkyō Disturbance, and the Eishō Disturbances. These are described in brief below.

The Kyōtoku Disturbance

The Kyōtoku Disturbance (*Kyōtoku no ran*) takes its name from the era in which it began, and lasted from 1455 to 1483. Like the ones that followed it, it was characterized by long stretches of calm and desultory fighting, which alternated with briefer periods of intense campaigning.

Acting on long-nursed grievances, Ashikaga Shigeuji, Lord of Kamakura, rebelled against his relative, the shogun in Kyoto, head of the main line of the Ashikaga family. In doing so, Shigeuji came into conflict with the Uesugi, who were stalwart supporters of the shogun in the east. Over the decades, when the shogun and the Lord of Kamakura had been at odds, the Uesugi had sided with Kyoto, stirring Shigeuji's resentment. In 1455, the Lord of Kamakura had the young head of the Uesugi assassinated.

The hostility between the Uesugi family and Shigeuji polarized allegiances throughout the plain, deepening a rift between families of differing status that had been a source of tension within the Kamakura Office. For years before the outbreak of hostilities the Uesugi family had monopolized the administration of the office, excluding most of the old Kantō families from governance. Begrudging Uesugi ascendancy, these families now widely backed the Lord of Kamakura. Most of them had their lands in the eastern part of the plain, which now turned into territory friendly to Shigeuji. The west of the plain was settled by small holders, who as a group had long sided with the Uesugi in order to counterbalance the prestige of the older families. The structural competition between these two levels of warrior society was one of the conflict's deeper causes, and gave it its distinctive geographical dimension, with the course of two rivers, the Tonegawa and Watarasegawa, marking the frontier zone between the two blocks (see Map 0.2).[1]

To take advantage of the support of the old eastern families (Yūki, Utsunomiya, Oyama, Sano, Nasu, Satomi, and others) Shigeuji relocated to his lands east of the Tonegawa, and built a stronghold for himself at Koga, in Shimōsa. He never returned to Kamakura, and he and his descendants soon came to be known as the Lords of Koga (*Koga kubō*).

Across the river, to the west, Uesugi partisans coalesced around two of the family's lineages, the Yamanouchi and the Ōgigayatsu houses. The Yamanouchi house was the main lineage of the extended Uesugi family, and its successive heads controlled the post of Kantō deputy (*Kantō kanrei*), the highest in the Kamakura Office. They were closely related

1. The division of the plain was not complete: when the shogun sent his younger brother Masatomo to take Shigeuji's place in Kamakura, local warriors *from the western part of the plain* put up a stiff resistance, preventing Masatomo from entering the city. The only (near) contemporary text to detail the events of the early years of the disturbance is *Kamakura ōzōshi*, which describes many but not all of the incidents and battles from a bird's-eye view. For a brief account of the situation in the Kantō before the Kyōtoku Disturbance, see Imatani, "Muromachi Local Government," 232–33; for the details of the disturbance itself, see Shinkawa, *Shimotsuke chūseishi no shinkenkyū*, 74–97; Sennohara, *Kantō Sengokushi*, 16–50; Inagaki, "Koga kubō to Shimotsuke," 23–25; Minegishi, *Chūsei no tōgoku*, 233–42; Kuroda M., *Ōgigayatsu*, 16–18, 20–22; *Kindai Ashikaga shishi*, 1:273–80; Satō H., *Koga kubō*, 54–86; Satō H., *Chūsei tōgoku no shihai kōzō*, 99–105; Kubota, in *Gunma kenshi tsūshi hen*, 3:454–67.

and allied with a third Uesugi house, which ruled Echigo, just north of the Kantō. The Yamanouchi also controlled the governorships of Musashi and Kōzuke, and were supported by families that had served as deputy governors there, in particular the Ōishi family and the three Nagao houses. The Ōgigayatsu house, instead, was a junior line of the Uesugi that had risen to prominence recently thanks to the patronage of the shogun. The Ōgigayatsu came to hold sway over Sagami and southern Musashi, and their main deputies and military supporters were the Ōta. Since before the conflict, the Uesugi had derived much of their power from the backing of the shogun, who used successive Kantō deputies to check the sometimes unruly Lords of Kamakura. The war between the Uesugi and Shigeuji, therefore, was also a proxy war between the shogun and Shigeuji. When the Lord of Koga decided to seek a truce and then a peace, he negotiated with the Uesugi in order to reach a settlement with the shogun.

The Rebellion of Nagao Kageharu

The Rebellion of Nagao Kageharu (*Kageharu no ran*) takes its name from a powerful lord who led an uprising against the Yamanouchi house of the Uesugi between 1476 and 1480 (chronologically, this new crisis overlapped with the final years of the previous one). Once again, personal resentments sparked a conflict that grew into a regional conflagration fueled by widespread intrafamilial tensions. The occasion for the uprising was provided by a slight: when Kagenobu, head of the Nagao family and chief retainer (*kasai*) to the Yamanouchi Uesugi, passed away in 1473, his son Kageharu, a young man at the time, fully expected to succeed him. Instead the Uesugi elders selected for the post Nagao Tadakage, younger brother of Kagenobu and uncle of Kageharu. Incensed, Kageharu withdrew with his supporters from the Uesugi court, and plotted revenge.

At the root of the problem, aside from rumors at the time that Kageharu was unfit to follow in his father's footsteps, was the composite, multilineal structure of many warrior families. By the fifteenth century, families like the Uesugi had divided into multiple lineages (houses) bearing the same surname but living apart geographically and economically, and drawing revenues from distinct portfolios of landholdings. This was true not only of the Uesugi, where the Yamanouchi, Echigo, Ōgigayatsu, and other lineages coexisted, but also of the Nasu, Chiba, Ōishi, Ōta, Yūki, and Nagao. In the case of the Uesugi, appointment to office had helped establish a clear hierarchy between the main and the junior houses, and the various lineages managed to coexist for generations in relative harmony. Other families split apart under the strain of competition for leadership and resources. The Nagao adopted their own path: they divided early on into three lines—eventually known as the Nagao houses of Shiroi, Sōja, and Kamakura (later, Ashikaga and Tatebayashi). Unlike their overlords the Uesugi, though, the Nagao never established which of the three houses was the main one and which were collaterals. Instead, the three rotated among them the several posts held by the family (not only that of chief retainer of the Yamanouchi, but also the deputy governorships of Kōzuke and Musashi Provinces).

By the time Kageharu was passed over in favor of Tadakage, the Shiroi Nagao had led the Nagao family for two generations. As the new head of the Shiroi, Kageharu (and his followers) had good reason to expect this to continue. Yet his uncle, Tadakage, who had been born into the Shiroi but had been adopted by the Sōja as a youth, was selected in Kageharu's place, by virtue of greater seniority, experience, and (apparently) competence. As a familial squabble, the crisis pitted against each other, on the one hand, the institutional flexibility of the posts of head of the Nagao and chief retainer of the Yamanouchi Uesugi; on the other, the more rigid practices of patronage, which tended to take on a hereditary, multigenerational character. Kageharu's grievance was not purely personal: when he failed to secure the prestigious post that had been his father's and his grandfather's before him, personal embarrassment was not the greatest concern (though in a status-conscious society it certainly carried its weight); Kageharu had to confront relatives, housemen, followers, and allies, all of whom were bound to him by his house's prestige and power, and dependent on the continuing bounties that flowed from the house's stranglehold on that particular post. Kageharu's setback not only threatened his personal political career, it undermined the basis of his and many other houses' prosperity. Similar pressures compelled warriors throughout the western Kantō, especially the heads of junior houses and families that had been less favored by Uesugi patronage, to throw in their lots with Kageharu against their own relatives.

As noted above, the new disturbance overlapped with the final years of the Kyōtoku Disturbance. Indeed, the Uesugi found themselves attacked on two fronts, for Kageharu, realizing he could not win on his own, forged an alliance with Ashikaga Shigeuji. The Uesugi survived the showdown that ensued; without a decisive victory, Shigeuji and Kageharu found they were unable to maintain the full mobilization of their supporters, and sued for peace with the shogun.

For Shigeuji, involvement in the disturbance had the unforeseen result of bringing about peace with the shogun after nearly thirty years (and retirement from the political scene), but for Kageharu and his partisans, the rebellion concluded in abject failure. Kageharu himself survived, and spent the rest of his life in his residence of Shiroi, in central Kōzuke, but many of the families that fought with him were wiped out. The Nagao family, which had long provided the military muscle behind Yamanouchi Uesugi rule, found itself divided against itself and largely incapacitated, as did another important Yamanouchi partisan, the Ōishi family. As a result, it was Ōta Dōkan, chief retainer of the Ōgigayatsu Uesugi, who took the lead in quelling the rebellion, chasing Kageharu's armies around the plain, defeating them over and over until a truce was negotiated. Dōkan emerged as the leading commander of the Uesugi forces at this time, and his prowess on the battlefield enhanced the political stature not only of the Ōta, but also of their Ōgigayatsu lords.[2]

The Chōkyō Disturbance

A few brief years of calm intervened before the Chōkyō Disturbance (*Chōkyō no ran*), which takes its name from the era in which it erupted, consumed the Kantō between 1488 and 1505. This third disturbance

2. Ōta Dōkan, the chief retainer of the Ōgigayatsu Uesugi, and the commander who led the effort against Kageharu, left behind a long letter detailing his deeds, which is our best source for the events of those years (*Ōta Dōkan jō*). For scholarly reconstructions of the crisis, see Maejima, *Ōta-shi no kenkyū*, 64–79; Maejima, "Ōishi-shi no Ninomiya-jō," 69–73; Katsumori, *Nagao-shi no kenkyū*, 108–18; Sennohara, *Kantō Sengokushi*, 50–58; Yamada, "Nagao Kageharu to Nagao Tadakage"; Kuroda M., *Ōgigayatsu*, 34–43; Satō H., in *Shinpen Saitama kenshi tsūshi hen*, 2:418–22; Minegishi, *Chūsei no tōgoku*, 242–52; Karasawa Sadaichi, in *Ōta shishi*, 557; Shichinomiya, *Kantō kanrei, Uesugi ichizoku*, 185–208; Kubota, in *Gunma kenshi tsūshi hen*, 3:467–80.

pitted against each other the "Two Uesugi," as the Yamanouchi and Ōgigayatsu houses were often called at the time. The conflict was an outgrowth of Kageharu's uprising and the leading role played in quelling it by the Ōgigayatsu and their chief retainer, Ōta Dōkan. After crippling the Nagao, internecine strife now reached the highest level of the Kantō elite, consuming the regime's residual energy in the plain and inviting the interference of neighboring powers. The Hōjō of Izu, in particular, participated in the conflict, called upon by the Ōgigayatsu to lend their troops. Although unable to avert their allies' ultimate defeat, the Hōjō prolonged the conflict, learning more about the Kantō, and the divisions and weakness of the Uesugi. In a matter of years, the Hōjō would return to the plain, with designs of their own.

The war between the "Two Uesugi" was yet another instance of the conflict between senior and junior lineages that had brought about Kageharu's rebellion a decade before. The rise of the Ōgigayatsu had been meteoric, favored by the shogun as a way to check the power of the Yamanouchi. Still, it was a recent affair, and the wealth of the Yamanouchi remained far greater. The tension produced by this structural imbalance took on a decidedly acrimonious cast after the victory against Kageharu and the peace with the Lord of Koga. Ōta Dōkan's success in pacifying the region had generated strong expectations of reward and political recognition, both on the part of Dōkan and of the Ōgigayatsu leaders, which the Yamanouchi quickly disappointed. The Ōgigayatsu, who had opposed reconciliation with Shigeuji, were offended that their position was ignored by the main house after the role they had played in defeating Kageharu. Dōkan undoubtedly made matters worse by writing a long letter to the Yamanouchi leadership, detailing the military service rendered by warriors throughout the plain and accusing the Yamanouchi of thanklessness.

Fearing that Dōkan's displeasure might lead him to rebel as Kageharu had—or simply wishing to undermine their Ōgigayatsu relatives—the Yamanouchi conspired to convince the Ōgigayatsu that Dōkan posed a grave threat to them. Dōkan's eventual assassination, in 1486, and the outcry it produced throughout the Kantō, brought the Uesugi even closer to war, which broke out soon after. Despite losing the support of the Ōta, the Ōgigayatsu managed to defeat the Yamanouchi repeatedly in pitched battles, but were unable to deliver the decisive blow.

Several years of stalemate followed the unexpected death of the head of the Ōgigayatsu, Uesugi Sadamasa, who was killed in 1494 when he fell from horseback while fording the Arakawa. The Yamanouchi eventually broke the stalemate with help from the Uesugi of Echigo and managed, after seventeen years of on-again, off-again fighting, to overcome the Ōgigayatsu.[3]

The Eishō Disturbances

During the Eishō Disturbances (*Eishō no ran*), which followed soon enough, conflicts escalated and multiplied as rebellions broke out, neighboring lords invaded the Kantō, and clashes between houses (the various Nagao, the "Two Uesugi") were replaced by clashes *within* houses. First, in 1507 the head of the Uesugi of Echigo and governor of that province was deposed and killed by his deputy governor, who installed a puppet governor in his place. The head of the Echigo Uesugi had been the natural brother of Akisada, who was head of the Yamanouchi and Kantō deputy. Akisada immediately began preparations for a military expedition to chastise the rebel. After initial success in 1509, the following year the Yamanouchi army was resoundingly defeated, and then crushed during a hasty retreat across the mountains. Akisada perished in battle.

The death of the head of the Yamanouchi prompted a succession crisis, for Akisada had no sons of his own. Vying for the leadership of the Uesugi family and the post of Kantō deputy were his two adoptive sons: Akizane and Norifusa. Akizane was the brother of Ashikaga Masauji, the current Lord of Koga, and had recently been adopted as part of an alliance between the Yamanouchi and the Ashikaga. This dispute soon overlapped with another, for Ashikaga Masauji himself was challenged and eventually unseated by his own son, Takamoto. The Lord of Koga (Masauji) allied himself with his brother Akizane in the fight for the headship of the Yamanouchi Uesugi, and so naturally Masauji's son Takamoto

---

3. Sawaki, *Gohōjō-shi to ryōgoku kei'ei*, 1–20; Kuroda M., *Ōgigayatsu*, 46–53, 60–63; Satō H., in *Shinpen Saitama kenshi tsūshi hen*, 2:438–48; Takagi, in *Tochigi kenshi tsūshi hen*, 3:721–24; Shichinomiya, *Kantō kanrei, Uesugi-shi*, 209–19; Sennohara, *Kantō Sengokushi*, 58–68; Maejima, *Ōta-shi no kenkyū*, 80–91; Shinkawa, *Shimotsuke chūseishi no shinkenkyū*, 130–34.

and the other son of the late Yamanouchi head (Norifusa) banded together against them. Takamoto and Norifusa eventually prevailed in both disputes. In 1512 the Yamanouchi dispute came to an end; Takamoto chased his father out of Koga—although fighting on that front continued until 1518.

But while the Kantō elites were busy fighting each other without quarter, the Hōjō advanced through the southern reaches of the plain, completing their conquest of Sagami Province by 1516.[4] With their new staging grounds in the Kantō plain, the Hōjō soon made inroads in Musashi. The Lord of Koga, Takamoto, was quick to assess the newcomers' power, and in 1521 he arranged a marriage alliance between his son (and successor) and the daughter of the head of the Hōjō family, Ujitsuna. In 1524, Ujitsuna took Edo castle, the main stronghold of the Ōgigayatsu. That same year, he discarded his original family name, Ise, and took the name Hōjō. This new name evoked, as a political manifesto, the memory of the family of the same name that had dominated the Kantō and the country in the thirteenth and early fourteenth centuries. True to that manifesto, Ujitsuna and his successor, Ujiyasu, proceeded to expel the Uesugi and subdue the Ashikaga over the next quarter of a century, until the Kantō was synonymous with Hōjō rule once again.

4. Minegishi, in *Gunma kenshi tsūshi hen*, 3:497–505; Kuroda M., *Ōgigayatsu*, 68–75; Sennohara, *Kantō Sengokushi*, 69–72; Shinkawa, *Shimotsuke chūseishi no shinkenkyū*, 135–38; Ike Susumu, in *Niigata kenshi tsūshi hen*, 2:537–42; Satō H., *Koga kubō*, 101–12; Satō H., *Zoku chūsei tōgoku*, 50–76.

APPENDIX B

Dramatis Personae

ASHIKAGA—The Muromachi regime's ruling family consisted of two lineages, the junior of which was based in the Kantō. The fourteenth-century founder of the shogunate, Ashikaga Takauji (1305–58), chose one of his sons as his successor; to another he entrusted governance of the Kantō region. These two lineages of the Ashikaga coexisted for over two centuries, mostly but not always peacefully, because the Kantō Ashikaga, who ruled from Kamakura and were known as the Lords of Kamakura, bristled at their junior status.

Shigeuji (1438–95; r. 1449–83): last of the Lords of Kamakura, he relocated to the stronghold of Koga, in Shimōsa Province in 1455, after a violent falling-out with his chief official, the head of the Uesugi family, whom he assassinated. Shigeuji and his descendants came to be known as Lords of Koga. The shogun sided with the Uesugi and against Shigeuji, who was branded a rebel.

Masauji (1466–1531; r. 1483–1512): he succeeded his father Shigeuji as Lord of Koga when a peace was negotiated with the Uesugi family (and the shogun) in 1483, after nearly three decades of war. In the war of the "Two Uesugi" (the Chōkyō Disturbance), he sided first with the Ōgigayatsu and then with the Yamanouchi. To seal the new alliance Masauji had his brother, Akizane, adopted into the Yamanouchi house.

Takamoto (?–1535; r. 1512–35): son of Masauji. He overthrew his father and took the title of Lord of Koga for himself.

Masatomo (1435–91): Lord of Horigoe.[1] Masatomo was a younger brother of the eighth Muromachi shogun, Yoshimasa (r. 1449–73), who chose him to replace Shigeuji after Shigeuji left Kamakura. Kantō warriors loyal to Shigeuji prevented Masatomo from entering the town, so he was forced to settle in Izu Province and make his seat in Horigoe. Nominally he was the representative of the shogun in the east, but in fact he was marginalized, especially after the peace between Shigeuji and the Uesugi in 1483.

UESUGI—Originally the heads of the family served the Lords of Kamakura with the title of Kantō deputy but then the two became competitors: after 1455 the Uesugi became the leaders of the coalition opposing Ashikaga Shigeuji in the name of the shogun. The extended Uesugi family was made up of a number of separate houses (lineages).

Yamanouchi—The main house of the Uesugi. Only its heads could be appointed to the post of Kantō deputy and the military governorships of the provinces of Kōzuke and Musashi. A branch of the Yamanouchi held the governorship of Echigo, north of the Kantō, and on several occasions provided heirs to the main house. The Yamanouchi took their name from their original residence in Kamakura, but in the late fifteenth century they largely ruled from various encampments—most notably Ikatsuko, in northern Musashi.

Noritada (1433–55): his assassination, ordered by Ashikaga Shigeuji, sparked the Kyōtoku Disturbance.

Akisada (1454–1510): adopted from the Uesugi of Echigo in 1468, he defeated the Ōgigayatsu in 1505 and led the family as Kantō deputy until his death in 1510.

Norifusa (1467–1525): adoptive son of Akisada. After his father's death in battle, Norifusa allied himself with Ashikaga Takamoto in the Eishō Disturbances and in 1512 won the headship of the Yamanouchi Uesugi and the title of Kantō deputy.

1. Masatomo's title refers to the name of the place where he set his court. He has more commonly been referred to as the Lord of Horikoshi, but since the toponym is pronounced Horigoe, I have used that pronunciation throughout.

Nagao—three lineages; the family long served the Uesugi, with successive heads holding the post of chief retainer (*kasai*) of the Yamanouchi house. Because the Yamanouchi served as military governors of Kōzuke and Musashi, members of the Nagao were deputy governors of those same provinces at various times. The extended Nagao family split into three lineages which did not have a clear hierarchy and alternated in holding the positions of chief retainer and deputy governor. Heirs were frequently adopted from one house into the other. The three houses were each known by the name of its main residence: Shiroi, Sōja, and Kamakura (later, Ashikaga and Tatebayashi).

Shiroi:

For much of the fifteenth century members of this lineage, which had its residence in central Kōzuke, held the post of chief retainer.

Kagenaka (1388–1463) was the chief retainer of the Yamanouchi at the time of Noritada's assassination and led the troops loyal to the Uesugi in the aftermath of that incident, until a new head could be selected for that family. Two of his sons, Kagenobu and Tadakage, had important careers. Tadakage was adopted into the Sōja house.

Kagenobu (1413–73) led the Uesugi forces as chief retainer during some of the years of greater military activity. His sudden death in 1473 created a crisis in the leadership of the Nagao and Uesugi.

Kageharu (1443–1514), Kagenobu's son, was expected to inherit not only the headship of the Shiroi house but also the post of chief retainer of the Yamanouchi. When he was passed over, he withdrew to the castle of Hachigata and launched a rebellion (1476–80).

Sōja:

This house had its main residence in southern Kōzuke.

Tadakage (dates unknown) was Kagenaka's natural son and Kagenobu's younger brother, but was adopted by the Sōja, which had no male heir. He was also deputy governor of Musashi. When his brother Kagenobu died, he was selected by the Uesugi leadership as the new chief retainer of the Yamanouchi.

Kamakura (later, Ashikaga and Tatebayashi):

Members of this house figure less prominently in the events of the late fifteenth and early sixteenth centuries, but came to lead the Nagao during the wars between the Uesugi and the Hōjō.

Ōishi—Powerful warriors of western Musashi, they were strong backers of the Yamanouchi and are known to have served as deputy governors of Musashi. The family was divided during the Rebellion of Kageharu and thus weakened. Around the middle of the sixteenth century, the Ōishi adopted as their heir a son of the head of the Hōjō, Ujiyasu, becoming a de facto junior branch of the Hōjō family.

Ōgigayatsu—Most powerful among the junior houses of the Uesugi. The Ōgigayatsu rose to prominence in the second half of the fifteenth century thanks to the patronage of the shogun, who wished to counterbalance the power of the main house. The Ōgigayatsu came to hold the post of governor of Sagami hereditarily.

Mochitomo (1418–67): ordered the construction of castles at Edo and Kawagoe in the 1450s.

Sadamasa (1443–94): ordered the assassination of his chief retainer and principal military backer, Ōta Dōkan, in 1486. He led the house against the Yamanouchi in the early phases of the Chōkyō Disturbance, but died in 1494 before the conflict was over, in an accident while fording a river.

Ōta—A powerful family in the southern Kantō. The Ōta served the Ōgigayatsu as chief retainers over several generations. On orders from Uesugi Mochitomo, they built the castles of Edo and Kawagoe.

Dōshin (1411–88?): chief retainer of the Ōgigayatsu at the beginning of the war with Ashikaga Shigeuji, he soon yielded the headship of the family to his son Dōkan. He became something of a senior statesman and a patron of the arts.

Dōkan (1432–86): provided the Ōgigayatsu house, and the Uesugi as a whole, with military backing while the Nagao were divided and weakened by Kageharu's rebellion. He was assassinated on Uesugi Sadamasa's orders in the Ōgigayatsu residence of Kasuya.

IWAMATSU—A powerful local family that ruled over Nitta Estate in Kōzuke and traced its descent from the famous fourteenth-century hero Nitta Yoshisada. The Iwamatsu controlled the main road linking Ikatsuko and Koga from their mountaintop castle of Kanayama.

Iezumi (1409–94): led the family back to prominence in the 1460s, after four decades of exile, bringing Nitta Estate under his sway. After siding with the Uesugi (and the shogun) in their fight against the Lords of Koga, Iezumi switched sides in 1477. Iezumi claimed to have helped negotiate the end of the conflict in 1483.

Hisazumi (1461–1511?): Iezumi's grandson. Exiled from Nitta Estate for disagreeing with his grandfather in 1477, he was eventually brought back to inherit the headship of the Iwamatsu, only to be forced into retirement by his own chief retainer, Yokoze Narishige. In his later years, Iezumi was well known as a poet, calling himself Shōjun.

Yokoze—A family of petty warriors with lands in Nitta Estate who rose to prominence under Iezumi and exercised real leadership among Iwamatsu housemen.

Kunishige (d. 1495): Iezumi's chief retainer, he played a central role in the military campaigning of the 1470s and in the negotiations that allowed the Iwamatsu to expand their landholdings to the estates surrounding Nitta.

Narishige (d. 1501?): Kunishige's son. He served as Hisazumi's chief retainer until the two grew estranged. Hisazumi tried to eliminate Narishige and his family, but his coup failed, and Narishige became the warden of the next Iwamatsu leader, Hisazumi's infant son Masazumi.

HŌJŌ of Odawara—Originally housemen of the most powerful family in the Tōkaidō region (the Imagawa), they became warlords in their own right around the turn of the sixteenth century. Taking advantage of the Chōkyō and Eishō disturbances, the Hōjō conquered the provinces of Izu and Sagami. They took the castle of Odawara as their fortress and came to be known as the Hōjō of Odawara (to distinguish them from the thirteenth-century shogunal regents, the Hōjō of Kamakura; also to distinguish the two Hōjō, Japanese scholars often refer to the Odawara lords as Gohōjō, or "latter Hōjō"). The eastward expansion of the Hōjō eventually led them to clash with the Uesugi for domain over the Kantō region.

Ujitsuna (1487–1541): second of the Odawara lords, in 1524 he conquered the castle of Edo and changed the family's name from Ise to Hōjō, signaling his intent to rule the whole region as the original Hōjō had.

Ujiyasu (1515–71): third of the Odawara lords, he defeated the Uesugi in the battle of Kawagoe (1546) and chased the last Kantō deputy from the region.

Bibliography

Note: Primary sources that are published as books with a translator or annotator (e.g., Horton, *Journal of Sōchō*) I have listed by translator. If a text is included in a larger volume, with or without reference to the name of a compiler or annotator, or if the name of the author is not known, I have listed the text by title.

Adolphson, Mikael S. *The Gates of Power: Monks, Courtiers, and Warriors in Premodern Japan*. Honolulu: University of Hawai'i Press, 2000.

Aizawa Masahiko and Hashimoto Shinji, eds. *Kantō suibokuga: Kata to imēji no keifu*. Tokyo: Kokusho Kankōkai, 2007.

Akimoto Tarō. "Sengoku-ki kita Kantō no kawarake: Sengoku daimyō shihai to no kanren." In *Chūsei tōgoku no sekai*, vol. 3, *Sengoku daimyō Gohōjō-shi*, edited by Asano Haruki and Saitō Shin'ichi, 251–86. Tokyo: Koshi Shoin, 2008.

Ambros, Barbara. *Emplacing a Pilgrimage: The Ōyama Cult and Regional Religion in Early Modern Japan*. Cambridge, MA: Harvard University Asia Center, 2008.

Amino Yoshihiko, et al., ed. *Shōen no kaitai*. Vol. 4 of *Kōza Nihon shōenshi*. Tokyo: Yoshikawa Kōbunkan, 1999.

Amino Yoshihiko, et al., ed. *Tōhoku, Kantō, Tōkai chihō no shōen*. Vol. 5 of *Kōza Nihon shōenshi*. Tokyo: Yoshikawa Kōbunkan, 1990.

Anzai Kinji. *Hōkaiki shōenshi no kenkyū: Jikimu undō to daikan ukeoi*. Tokyo: Iwata Shoin, 1994.

Aoki Fumihiko. "Iwatsuki jōseki." In *Sengoku no shiro*, edited by Fujiki Hisashi and Saitama Kenritsu Rekishi Shiryōkan, 177–82. Tokyo: Koshi Shoin, 2005.

Arai Jurō, et al. "Kōdan-kai 'Kodai, chūsei no Nakagawa ryūiki o saguru: Tonegawa, Kosumidagawa no ryūro o chūshin to shite.'" *Saitama kenshi kenkyū* 29 (March 1994): 1–20.

Arimitsu Yūgaku. "Chiiki kokka no shikumi." In *Sengoku no chiiki kokka*, edited by Arimitsu Yūgaku, 128–56. Tokyo: Yoshikawa Kōbunkan, 2003.

Arnesen, Peter Judd. *The Medieval Japanese Daimyo: The Ōuchi Family's Rule of Suō and Nagato*. New Haven, CT: Yale University Press, 1979.

Asakura Naomi. *Gohōjō ryōgoku no chiikiteki tenkai*. Tokyo: Iwata Shoin, 1997.

Asakura Naomi. "Gohōjō-shi no kenryoku kōzō: Hachigata-ryō o chūshin to shite." In *Chūsei tōgokushi no kenkyū*, edited by *Chūsei Tōgokushi Kenkyūkai*, 235–57. Tokyo: Tōkyō Daigaku Shuppankai, 1988.

Asakura Naomi. "Gohōjō-shi no ryōgoku shihai ni tsuite: Gundai to shijōshu o megutte." In *Sengoku-ki tōgoku shakai ron*, edited by Sengokushi Kenkyūkai, 341–56. Tokyo: Yoshikawa Kōbunkan, 1990.

Asakura Shimatsuki. In *Kaitei shiseki shūran*, edited by Kondō Heijō, vol. 6, sect. 28. Tokyo: Kondō Kappanjo, 1900.

Asakura shimatsuki, Kaetsu tōsōki, Esshū gunki. Annotated by Inoue Toshio, Kuwayama Kōnen, and Fujiki Hisashi. In *Rennyo, Ikkō ikki*, edited by Kasahara Kazuo and Inoue Toshio, 326–426. Tokyo: Iwanami Shoten, 1972.

Asakura Sōteki waki. In *Zoku zoku gunsho ruijū*, edited by Kokusho Kankōkai, 10:1–12. Tokyo: Kokusho Kankōkai, 1906.

Asano Haruki. "Hōjō ryōgoku no jōkan to tōjiki: Kita Musashi o chūshin ni." In *Chūsei tōgoku no sekai*, vol. 3, *Sengoku daimyō Gohōjō-shi*, edited by Asano Haruki and Saitō Shin'ichi, 221–50. Tokyo: Koshi Shoin, 2008.

Asano Haruki. "Sengoku-ki jōkan no nendaikan: Kita Musashi ni okeru doki, tōjiki no sosei bunseki o chūshin ni." In *Sengoku no shiro*, edited by Fujiki Hisashi and Saitama Kenritsu Rekishi Shiryōkan, 45–66. Tokyo: Koshi Shoin, 2005.

Asano Haruki. "Tōgoku ni okeru zaichi doki no seisan to ryūtsū." In *Sengoku jidai no kōkogaku*, edited by Ono Masatoshi and Hagihara Mitsuo, 399–408. Tokyo: Koshi Shoin, 2003.

Asano Haruki, and Saitō Shin'ichi, eds. *Chūsei tōgoku no sekai*. 3 vols. Tokyo: Koshi Shoin, 2003–8.

Asao Naohiro, et al., eds. *Iwanami kōza Nihon rekishi*. 26 vols. Tokyo: Iwanami Shoten, 1975–77.

Asao Naohiro, et al., eds. *Iwanami kōza Nihon tsūshi*. 25 vols. Tokyo: Iwanami Shoten, 1993–96.

Ashikaga Shishi Hensan Iinkai, ed. *Kindai Ashikaga shishi*. 6 vols. Ashikaga-shi, Tochigi-ken: Ashikaga-shi, 1975–79.

Aston, W. G., trans. *Nihongi: Chronicles of Japan from the Earliest Times to A.D. 697*. Rutland, VT: Charles E. Tuttle Company, 1972.

Azuma kagami. Annotated by Kuroita Katsumi. In *Shintei zōho kokushi taikei*, edited by Kuroita Katsumi and Kokushi Taikei Henshūkai. Vols. 32–33. Tokyo: Yoshikawa Kōbunkan, 1965.

Azumaji no tsuto. Annotated by Itō Kei. In *Chūsei nikki kikōshū: Kaidōki, Tōkan kikō, Ben no naishi nikki, Izayoi nikki hoka*, edited by Nagasaki Ken, 466–512. Tokyo: Shōgakukan, 1994.

Basso, Keith H. *Wisdom Sits in Places: Landscape and Language among the Western Apache*. Albuquerque: University of New Mexico Press, 1996.

Batten, Bruce L. *To the Ends of Japan: Premodern Frontiers, Boundaries, and Interactions*. Honolulu: University of Hawai'i Press, 2003.

Berry, Mary Elizabeth. *The Culture of Civil War in Kyoto*. Berkeley: University of California Press, 1994.

Berry, Mary Elizabeth. *Japan in Print: Information and Nation in the Early Modern Period*. Berkeley: University of California Press, 2006.

Birt, Michael P. "Samurai in Passage: The Transformation of the Sixteenth-Century Kantō." *Journal of Japanese Studies* 11, no. 2 (summer 1985): 369–99.

Bisson, Thomas N. *The Crisis of the Twelfth Century: Power, Lordship, and the Origins of European Government*. Princeton, NJ: Princeton University Press, 2009.

Boffa, Sergio. *Warfare in Medieval Brabant, 1356–1406*. Woodbridge, Suffolk: The Boydell Press, 2004.

Brazell, Karen, trans. *The Confessions of Lady Nijō*. Stanford, CA: Stanford University Press, 1973.

Brentano, Robert. *Rome before Avignon: A Social History of Thirteenth-Century Rome*. New York: Basic Books, 1974.

Brown, Philip C. *Central Authority and Local Autonomy in the Formation of Early Modern Japan: The Case of Kaga Domain*. Stanford, CA: Stanford University Press, 1993.

"Bushū Edo utaawase." In *Shinkō gunsho ruijū*, edited by Hanawa Hokinoichi, 9:668–71. Tokyo: Meicho Fukyūkai, 1977.

Carter, Paul. *The Road to Botany Bay: An Exploration of Landscape and History*. New York: Knopf, 1988.

Carter, Steven D., ed. *Literary Patronage in Late Medieval Japan*. Ann Arbor: Center for Japanese Studies, University of Michigan, 1993.

Carter, Steven D. *The Road to Komatsubara: A Classical Reading of the Renga Hyakuin*. Cambridge, MA: Council on East Asian Studies, Harvard University, 1987.

Carter, Steven D. "Sōgi in the East Country: *Shirakawa kikō*." *Monumenta Nipponica* 42, no. 2 (summer 1987): 167–209.

Carter, Steven D. "Three Poets at Yuyama: Sōgi and *Yuyama Sangin Hyakuin*." *Monumenta Nipponica* 33, nos. 2–3 (summer and autumn 1978): 119–49, 241–83.

Certeau, Michel de. *The Practice of Everyday Life*. Translated by Steven Rendall. Berkeley: University of California Press, 1988.

Chiba Jōkaku Kenkyūkai, ed. *Jōkaku to chūsei no tōgoku*. Tokyo: Koshi Shoin, 2005.

Conlan, Thomas D. *From Sovereign to Symbol: An Age of Ritual Determinism in Fourteenth Century Japan*. Oxford: Oxford University Press, 2011.

Conlan, Thomas D. "Largesse and the Limits of Loyalty in the Fourteenth Century." In *The Origins of Japan's Medieval World: Courtiers, Clerics, Warriors, and Peasants in the Fourteenth Century*, edited by Jeffrey P. Mass, 39–64. Stanford, CA: Stanford University Press, 1997.

Conlan, Thomas D. *State of War: The Violent Order of Fourteenth-Century Japan*. Ann Arbor: Center for Japanese Studies, University of Michigan, 2003.

Cook, Lewis Edwin. "The Discipline of Poetry: Authority and Invention in the Kokindenju." PhD diss., Cornell University, 2000.

Cort, Louise Allison. "Disposable but Indispensable: The Earthenware Vessel as Vehicle of Meaning in Japan." In *What's the Use of Art? Asian Visual and Material Culture in Context*, edited by Jan Mrázek and Morgan Pitelka, 46–76. Honolulu: University of Hawai'i Press, 2008.

Dai Nihon komonjo, iewake. Tokyo: Tōkyō Teikoku Daigaku, 1904–.

Debord, André. "The Castellan Revolution and the Peace of God in Aquitaine." In *The Peace of God: Social Violence and Religious Response in France around the Year 1000*, edited by Thomas Head and Richard Landes, 135–64. Ithaca, NY: Cornell University Press, 1992.

Edwards, Kathryn A. *Families and Frontiers: Re-creating Communities and Boundaries in the Early Modern Burgundies*. Boston: Brill Academic Publishers, 2002.

Ellenblum, Ronnie. *Frankish Rural Settlement in the Latin Kingdom of Jerusalem*. Cambridge: Cambridge University Press, 1998.

Endō Hiroshi. "Kodai: *Man'yōshū* o chūshin to shite." In *Bungaku no Musashino*, edited by Seikei Daigaku Bungakubu Gakkai, 1–40. Tokyo: Kazama Shobō, 2003.

Etō Yasusada. *Sōgi no kenkyū*. Tokyo: Kazama Shobō, 1967.

Farris, William Wayne. *Japan's Medieval Population: Famine, Fertility, and Warfare in a Transformative Age*. Honolulu: University of Hawai'i Press, 2006.

Fujiki Hisashi. "Daimyō ryōgoku no keizai kōzō." In *Nihon keizaishi taikei*, vol. 2, *Chūsei*, edited by Nagahara Keiji, 237–76. Tokyo: Tōkyō Daigaku Shuppankai, 1965.

Fujiki Hisashi. "Naisen no naka no mura to machi to shiro." In *Jōkaku to chūsei no tōgoku*, edited by Chiba Jōkaku Kenkyūkai, 115–38. Tokyo: Koshi Shoin, 2005.

Fujiki Hisashi. "Sengoku Hiki no shiro to mura." In *Sengoku no shiro*, edited by Fujiki Hisashi and Saitama Kenritsu Rekishi Shiryōkan, 5–26. Tokyo: Koshi Shoin, 2005.

Fujiki Hisashi. *Sengoku shakaishiron: Nihon chūsei kokka no kaitai*. Tokyo: Tōkyō Daigaku Shuppankai, 1975.

Fujiki Hisashi. *Toyotomi heiwarei to Sengoku shakai*. Tokyo: Tōkyō Daigaku Shuppankai, 1985.

Fujiki Hisashi, and Saitama Kenshi Rekishi Shiryōkan, eds. *Sengoku no shiro*. Tokyo: Koshi Shoin, 2005.

Fujiwara Yoshiaki, ed. *Chūsei no michi o saguru*. Tokyo: Koshi Shoin, 2004.

Fukasawa Yasuyuki. "Chūsei no Musashi Fuchū: Sono kūkanteki kōzō to seiritsu o megutte." In *Chūsei tōgoku no sekai*, vol. 2, *Minami Kantō*, edited by Asano Haruki and Saitō Shin'ichi, 57–78. Tokyo: Koshi Shoin, 2004.

Fukushima Noriko. "Tōgoku shōen ni okeru tōchigyō to shiki." *Kokuritsu Rekishi Minzoku Hakubutsukan kenkyū hōkuku* 104 (March 2003): 151–68.

Gomi Fumihiko. "Tachi no shakai to sono hensen." In *Shiro to tachi o horu, yomu: kodai kara chūsei e*, edited by Satō Makoto and Gomi Fumihiko, 225–42. Tokyo: Yamakawa Shuppansha, 1994.

Gotō Takayuki, and Shinkai Hideki. "Tama kyūryō no Kamakura kaidō Kamitsumichi: Machida-shi Notsuta Uenohara iseki o chūshin ni." In *Chūsei no michi o saguru*, edited by Fujiwara Yoshiaki, 59–76. Tokyo: Koshi Shoin, 2004.

Grossberg, Kenneth A., ed. *The Laws of the Muromachi Bakufu: Kenmu Shikimoku (1336) & Muromachi Bakufu Tsuikahō*. Translated by Kenneth A. Grossberg and Kanamoto Nobuhisa. Tokyo: Monumenta Nipponica, Sophia University, 1981.

Gunma Kenshi Hensan Iinkai, ed. *Gunma kenshi shiryō hen*. 27 vols. Maebashi-shi: Gunma-ken, 1977–92.

Gunma Kenshi Hensan Iinkai, ed. *Gunma kenshi tsūshi hen*. 10 vols. Maebashi-shi: Gunma-ken, 1989–92.

Hagiwara Tatsuo. "Chūsei Tonegawa bunkaken to shūkyō." In *Tōgoku daimyō no kenkyū*, edited by Satō Hironobu, 406–16. Tokyo: Yoshikawa Kōbunkan, 1983.

Hall, John Whitney. "Foundations of the Modern Japanese Daimyo." *Journal of Asian Studies* 20, no. 3 (May 1961): 317–29.

Hall, John Whitney. *Government and Local Power in Japan, 500 to 1700: A Study Based on Bizen Province*. Princeton, NJ: Princeton University Press, 1966.

Hall, John Whitney. "Muromachi Japan: A Note on Periodization." In *Japan in the Muromachi Age*, edited by John Whitney Hall and Toyoda Takeshi, 11–14. Berkeley: University of California Press, 1977.

Hall, John Whitney, and Jeffrey P. Mass, eds. *Medieval Japan: Essays in Institutional History*. Stanford, CA: Stanford University Press, 1974.

Hall, John Whitney, Nagahara Keiji, and Kozo Yamamura, eds. *Japan before Tokugawa: Political Consolidation and Economic Growth, 1500 to 1650*. Princeton, NJ: Princeton University Press, 1983.

Hall, John Whitney, and Toyoda Takeshi, eds. *Japan in the Muromachi Age*. Berkeley: University of California Press, 1977.

Hanawa, Hokinoichi, ed. *Shinkō gunsho ruijū*. 25 vols. Tokyo: Naigai Shoseki, 1931–37. Revised edition compiled by Kawamata Keiichi. Tokyo: Meicho Fukyūkai, 1977.

Hanawa Hokinoichi, ed. *Zoku gunsho ruijū*. 37 vols. Tokyo: Zoku Gunsho Ruijū Kanseikai, 1923–33.

Harada Nobuo. "Tonegawa chūryūiki ni okeru shōen no sonraku keikan: Ōta no shō, Shimokōbe no shō o chūshin ni." In *Chūsei tōgoku-shi no kenkyū*, edited by Chūsei Tōgōkushi Kenkyūkai, 379–410. Tokyo: Tōkyō Daigaku Shuppankai, 1988.

Hashiguchi Sadashi. "Chūsei hōkei kyokan o meguru shomondai." *Rekishi hyōron* 454 (1988): 46–57.

Hashiguchi Sadashi. "Chūsei tōgoku no kyokan to sono shūhen." *Nihonshi kenkyū* 330 (1990): 70–97.

Hashiguchi Sadashi. "Tōgoku no bushi kyokan." In *Sengoku no shiro*, edited by Fujiki Hisashi and Saitama Kenritsu Rekishi Shiryōkan, 27–44. Tokyo: Koshi Shoin, 2005.

Hattori Mitsuyoshi. "Kawarake." In *Sengoku jidai no kōkogaku*, edited by Ono Masatoshi and Hagihara Mitsuo, 427–38. Tokyo: Koshi Shoin, 2003.

Hattori Mitsuyoshi. "Kawarake kara mita Hōjō-shi no kenryoku kōzō." In *Chūsei tōgoku no sekai*, vol. 3, *Sengoku daimyō Gohōjō-shi*, edited by Asano Haruki and Saitō Shin'ichi, 13–41. Tokyo: Koshi Shoin, 2008.

Higashiikakko Iseki Chōsakai. *Higashiikakko, Kawaramachi: Kodama Gunshi Kōiki Shichōsonken Kumiai Oyamagawa Kurīn Sentā yukakko kensetsu kōji kankei hakkutsu chōsa hōkoku*, 2 vols. Honjō-shi: Higashiikakko Iseki Chōsakai, 2002.

Hirai Kiyoshi, et al., eds. *Nihon jōkaku taikei*. 20 vols. Tokyo: Shin Jinbutsu Ōraisha, 1979–81.

Hirsch, Eric. "Introduction." In *The Anthropology of Landscape: Perspectives on Place and Space*, edited by Eric Hirsch and Michael O'Hanlon, 1–30. Oxford: Clarendon Press, 1995.

Honjō-shi Iseki Chōsakai. *Higashiikakko Akasaka Iseki: Yamato Un'yu kabushiki kaisha kamotsu shūhai shisetsu kensetsu ni tomonau maizō bunkazai hakkutsu chōsa hōkokusho*. Honjō-shi: Honjō-shi Iseki Chōsakai, 2004.

Honjō-shi Iseki Chōsakai. *Higashiikakko Shiroato iseki: Kabushiki kaisha NTT Docomo idō tsūshin'yō tettō kensetsu ni tomonau maizō bunkazai hakkutsu chōsa hōkokusho*. Honjō-shi: Honjō-shi Iseki Chōsakai, 2004.

Horton, H. Mack. "Renga Unbound: Performative Aspects of Japanese Linked Verse." *Harvard Journal of Asiatic Studies* 53, no. 2 (December 1993): 443–512.

Horton, H. Mack. "Saiokuken Sōchō and Imagawa Daimyo Patronage." In *Literary Patronage in Late Medieval Japan*, edited by Steven D. Carter, 105–61. Ann Arbor: Center for Japanese Studies, The University of Michigan, 1993.

Horton, H. Mack. *Song in an Age of Discord: "The Journal of Sōchō" and Poetic Life in Late Medieval Japan*. Stanford, CA: Stanford University Press, 2002.

Horton, H. Mack, trans. and ann. *The Journal of Sōchō*. Stanford, CA: Stanford University Press, 2002.

Hur, Nam-lin. *Prayer and Play in Late Tokugawa Japan: Asakusa Sensōji and Edo Society*. Cambrdge, MA: Harvard University Asia Center, 2000.

Ibi Takashi. "Edo bunjin no Musashino: Gen'ya kara kōgai e." In *Bungaku no Musashino*, edited by Seikei Daigaku Bungakubu Gakkai, 99–128. Tokyo: Kazama Shobō, 2003.

Ichiki Takeo. *Baika mujinzō chūshaku*. 6 vols. Tokyo: Zoku Gunsho Ruijū Kanseikai, 1993–95.

Ichimura Takao. *Sengoku-ki tōgoku no toshi to kenryoku*. Kyoto: Shibunkaku, 1994.

Ienaga Saburō, et al., eds. *Iwanami kōza Nihon rekishi*. 23 vols. Tokyo: Iwanami Shoten, 1962–64.

Ihara Kesao. "Muromachi-ki tōgoku honjoryō shōen no seiritsu katei: Muromachi-ki saihan shōenseiron no teiki." *Kokuritsu Rekishi Minzoku Hakubutsukan kenkyū hōkoku* 104 (March 2003): 17–41.

Ihara Kesao. "Tōgoku shōen nengu no kyōjō shisutemu to kokkateki hoshō taisei: Muromachi-ki saihan shōenseiron." *Kokuritsu Rekishi Minzoku Hakubutsukan kenkyū hōkoku* 108 (October 2003): 93–120.

Iimura Hitoshi. "Michi to 'shuku'." In *Sengoku jidai no kōkogaku*, edited by Ono Masatoshi and Hagihara Mitsuo, 21–32. Tokyo: Kokin Shoin, 2003.

Ijichi Tetsuo. "Sōchō no *Azumaji no tsuto* shohon kō." In *Nagasawa Sensei koki kinen toshogaku ronshū*, edited by Nagasawa Sensei Koki Kinen Toshogaku Ronshu Kankōkai, 255–74. Tokyo: Sanseidō, 1973. Reprinted in Ijichi Tetsuo, *Ijichi Tetsuo chosaku shū*, 2:616–34. Tokyo: Kyūko Shoin, 1996.

Ike Susumu. "Sengoku-ki no 'kuni' ni tsuite." *Sengokushi kenkyū* (February 2005): 1–12.

Ike Susumu. "Shōen no shōmetsu to taikō kenchi." In *Shōen no kaitai*, edited by Amino Yoshihiko et al., 346–83. Tokyo: Yoshikawa Kōbunkan, 1999.

Ikegami Hiroko. "Gohōjō-ryō no kuji ni tsuite." *Rekishigaku kenkyū* 523 (1983): 1–17.

Ikegami Hiroko. "Sengoku daimyō ryōgoku ni okeru shoryō oyobi kashindan hensei no tenkai: Gōhōjō ryōgoku no baai." In *Sengoku daimyō no kenryoku to shakai*, edited by Nagahara Keiji, 35–103. Tokyo: Tōkyō Daigaku Shuppankai, 1976.

Ikegami Hiroko. *Sengoku no gunzō*. Tokyo: Shūeisha, 1992.

Imatani Akira. "Muromachi Local Government: *Shugo* and *Kokujin*." In *The Cambridge History of Japan*, vol. 3, *Medieval Japan*, edited by Kozo Yamamura, 231–59. Cambridge: Cambridge University Press, 1990.

Inagaki Yasuhiko. "Koga kubō to Shimotsuke." *Tochigi kenshi kenkyū* 7 (1974): 22–34.

Inoue Muneo. *Chūsei kadanshi no kenkyū: Muromachi zenki*. Tokyo: Kazama Shobō, 1961.

Inoue Tetsuo. "Minami Kantō ni okeru jōkanseki shutsudo tōjiki." In *Jōkaku to chūsei no tōgoku*, edited by Chiba Jōkaku Kenkyūkai, 167–92. Tokyo: Koshi Shoin, 2005.

Irei Masao. "Odawara-eki ni okeru Gohōjō-shi no jōkaku taisei." In *Sengoku no heishi to nōmin*, edited by Sugiyama Hiroshi Sensei Kanreki Kinenkai, 113–37. Tokyo: Kadokawa Shoten, 1978.

Irei Masao. " 'Odawara-shū shoryō yakuchō' kenkyū e no teigen: Jōkaku to no kakawari o chūshin ni." In *Gohōjō-shi no kenkyū*, edited by Sawaki Eichi, 426–39. Tokyo: Yoshikawa Kōbunkan, 1983.

Ise monogatari. Annotated by Fukui Teisuke. In *Taketori monogatari, Ise monogatari, Yamato monogatari, Heichū monogatari*, edited by Katagiri Yōichi et al., 109–246. Tokyo: Shōgakukan, 1994.

Ishii Susumu, and Hagihara Mitsuo, eds. *Chūsei no shiro to kōkogaku*. Tokyo: Shin Jinbutsu Ōraisha, 1991.

Ishii Susumu, et al., eds. *Chūsei seiji shakai shisō, jō*. Tokyo: Iwanami Shoten, 1972.

Ishimoda Shō. "Kaisetsu." In *Chūsei seiji shakai shisō, jō*, edited by Ishii Susumu et al., 565–646. Tokyo: Iwanami Shoten, 1972.

Ishizuka Mitsuo. "Hachigata jōseki." In *Sengoku no shiro*, edited by Fujiki Hisashi and Saitama Kenshi Rekishi Shiryōkan, 149–58. Tokyo: Koshi Shoin, 2005.

Itō Kazumi. *Musashi bushidan no ichiyōtai: Abo-shi no kenkyū*. Tokyo: Bunken Shuppan, 1981.

Itō Toshikazu. "Chūsei kōki shōensei ron no seika to kadai." *Kokuritsu Rekishi Minzoku Hakubutsukan kenkyū hōkoku* 104 (March 2003): 5–15.

Kaikoku zakki. In *Shinkō gunsho ruijū*, edited by Hanawa Hokinoichi, 15:184–209. Tokyo: Meicho Fukyūkai, 1977.

Kajihara Masaaki. *Muromachi, Sengoku gunki no tenbō*. Osaka: Izumi Shoin, 2000.

Kamakura ōzōshi. In *Kaitei shiseki shūran*, edited by Kondō Heijō, vol. 5, sect. 23. Tokyo: Kondō Kappanjo, 1900.

Kamens, Edward. *Utamakura, Allusion, and Intertextuality in Traditional Japanese Poetry*. New Haven, CT: Yale University Press, 1997.

Kanagawa-ken Kenminbu Kenshi Henshūshitsu, ed. *Kanagawa kenshi tsūshi hen*. 7 vols. *Genshi, kodai, chūsei*. Yokohama: Kanagawa-ken, 1980–83.

Kanagawa-ken no chimei. Vol. 14 of *Nihon rekishi chimei taikei*. Tokyo: Heibonsha, 1984.

Kaneko Kinjirō. *Rengashi Sōgi no jitsuzō*. Tokyo: Kadokawa Shoten, 1999.

Kaneko Kinjirō. *Rengashi to kikō*. Tokyo: Ōfūsha, 1990.

Kaneko Kinjirō. *Shinkei no seikatsu to sakuhin*. Tokyo: Ōfūsha, 1982.

Kaneko Kinjirō. *Shinsen tsukubashū no kenkyū*. Tokyo: Kazama Shobō, 1969.

Kaneko Kinjirō. *Sōgi no seikatsu to sakuhin*. Tokyo: Ōfūsha, 1983.

Kaneko Kinjirō. *Sōgi tabi no ki shichū*. Tokyo: Ōfūsha, 1976.

Katagiri Yōichi. *Utamakura utakotoba jiten*, revised edition. Tokyo: Kasama Shoin, 1999.

Katō Akira. "Hōjō Ujiteru ni yoru Hachiōji-ryō shihai no kakuritsu." In *Gohōjō-shi no kenkyū*, edited by Sawaki Eichi, 239–65. Tokyo: Yoshikawa Kōbunkan, 1983.

Kato, Eileen. "Pilgrimage to Dazaifu: Sōgi's *Tsukushi Michi no Ki*." *Monumenta Nipponica* 34, no. 3 (autumn 1979): 333–67.

Katsumata Shizuo, with Martin Collcutt. "The Development of Sengoku Law," In *Japan before Tokugawa: Political Consolidation and Economic Growth, 1500 to 1650*, edited by John Whitney Hall, Nagahara Keiji, and Kozo Yamamura, 101–24. Princeton, NJ: Princeton University Press, 1983.

Katsumata Shizuo. "Jūgo-jūroku seiki no Nihon: Sensō no sōran." In *Iwanami kōza Nihon tsūshi*, edited by Asao Naohiro et al., 10:1–57. Tokyo: Iwanami Shoten, 1994.

Katsumata Shizuo. "Sengoku hō." In *Iwanami kōza Nihon rekishi*, edited by Asao Naohiro et al., 8:175–210. Tokyo: Iwanami Shoten, 1975.

Katsumori Sumi. *Nagao-shi no kenkyū*. Tokyo: Meicho Shuppan, 1978.

"Kawagoe senku." In *Zoku zoku gunsho ruijū*, edited by Kokusho Kankōkai, vol. 17, pt. 1, 432–58. Tokyo: Kokusho Kankōkai, 1906.

Keirstead, Thomas. "Gardens and Estates: Medievality and Space." *Positions* 1, no. 2 (fall 1993): 302–6.

Keirstead, Thomas. *The Geography of Power in Medieval Japan*. Princeton, NJ: Princeton University Press, 1992.

Keirstead, Thomas. "The Romance of the Middle Ages." In *The Early Modern "Medieval": Reconstructing Japanese Pasts*, edited by Hitomi Tonomura. In preparation.

Kinoshita Satoru. "Buke kanto toshite no sama no kami." *Rekishi hyōron* 674 (June 2006): 79–93.

Kinoshita Satoru. "Buke to shishiki taifu." *Nihonshi kenkyū* 549 (April 2008): 44–64.

Kinoshita Satoru. "Chūsei kōki ni okeru buke to kanto juryōmei: Zaichi kōkasetsu o megutte." *Nihon rekishi* 730 (March 2009): 17–37.

Kinoshita Satoru. "Yamanouchi Uesugi-shi ni okeru kanto to Kantō kanreishiki no mondai." *Nihon rekishi* 685 (June 2005): 18–31.

Kishida Yoriko. "Sōgi no kage: Sōchō no futatsu no *Shūenki* o megutte." *Bungaku* 3, no. 5 (September–October 2002): 42–54.

Kita Kushi Hensan Chōsakai, ed. *Kita kushi shiryō hen*. 10 vols. Tokyo: Tōkyō-to Kita-ku, 1992–96.

Kobayashi Seiji. *Hideyoshi kenryoku no keisei: Shosatsurei, kinzei, jōkaku seisaku*. Tokyo: Tōkyō Daigaku Shuppankai, 1994.

Kobayashi Takashi. "Suitei Kamakura kaidō Kamitsumichi: Akahama Tenjinzawa iseki no hakkutsu chōsa kara saguru Ofusuma-gun Tsukada-shuku." In *Chūsei no michi o saguru*, edited by Fujiwara Yoshiaki, 37–58. Tokyo: Koshi Shoin, 2004.

Koizumi Isao. "Kawagoe-kanshi no hakkutsu: Saitama-ken Kawagoe-shi." In *Kawagoe-shi no kenkyū*, edited by Okada Seiichi, 347–48. Tokyo: Meicho Shuppan, 2003.

Kojima Michihiro. "Ema-shi kan to Ema-shi: Muromachi-ki no kokujin ryōshu to tate." *Kokuritsu Rekishi Minzoku Hakubutsukan kenkyū hōkoku* 104 (March 2003): 169–83.

Kojima Michihiro. "Sengoku-ki jōkamachi no kōzō." *Nihonshi kenkyū* 257 (January 1984): 30–59.

Kokusho Kankōkai, ed. *Zoku zoku gunsho ruijū*. Tokyo: Kokusho Kankōkai, 1906.

Komuro Eiichi, ed. *Musashino no jōkanshi*. Tokyo: Meicho Shuppan, 1984.

Kondō Heijō, ed. *Kaitei shiseki shūran*. 33 vols. Tokyo: Kondō Kappanjo, 1900.

Kondō Yoshio. "Tonegawa no henryū." *Gunma kenshi shiori* (January 1990): 1–4.

Koyama Yasunori. *Chūsei sonraku to shōen ezu*. Tokyo: Tōkyō Daigaku Shuppankai, 1978.

Koyama Yasunori. "East and West in the Late Classical Age." Introduced and interpreted by Bruce L. Batten. In *Capital and Countryside in Japan, 300–1180:*

Japanese Historians Interpreted in English, edited by Joan R. Piggott, 362–401. Ithaca, NY: East Asia Program, Cornell University, 2005.

Koyama Yasunori. "Kodai makki no tōgoku to saigoku." In *Iwanami kōza Nihon rekishi*, edited by Asao Naohiro et al., 4:231–70. Tokyo: Iwanami Shoten, 1976.

Koziol, Geoffrey. "Political Culture." In *France in the Central Middle Ages, 900–1200*, edited by Marcus Bull, 43–76. Oxford: Oxford University Press, 2002.

Kubota Jun'ichi. "Chūsei kōki Kōzuke ni okeru shugo-ryō no tenkai ni tsuite." *Gunma kenshi kenkyū* 32 (September 1990): 44–61. Reprinted in Kubota Jun'ichi. *Muromachi, Sengoku-ki Kōzuke no chiiki shakai*, 96–126. Tokyo: Iwata Shoin, 2006.

Kubota Jun'ichi. "Nanbokuchō, Muromachi-ki no Kōzuke ni okeru zaichi ryōshu no ikki ni tsuite." *Gunma kenshi kenkyū* 28 (December 1988): 27–44. Reprinted in Kubota Jun'ichi. *Muromachi, Sengoku-ki Kōzuke no chiiki shakai*, 21–46. Tokyo: Iwata Shoin, 2006.

Kumakura Isao. *Nihon ryōri bunkashi: Kaiseki o chūshin ni*. Kyoto: Jinbun Shoin, 2002.

Kumakura Isao. *Nihon ryōri no rekishi*. Tokyo: Yoshikawa Kōbunkan, 2007.

Kumakura Isao. "Sanjōnishi Sanetaka, Takeno Jōō, and the Early Form of Iemoto Seido." In *Literary Patronage in Late Medieval Japan*, edited by Steven D. Carter, 95–103. Ann Arbor: Center for Japanese Studies, The University of Michigan, 1993.

Kuroda Hideo. *Kyōkai no chūsei, shōchō no chūsei*. Tokyo: Tōkyō Daigaku Shuppankai, 1986.

Kuroda Motoki. "Toshima-shi no metsubō." In *Toshima-shi to sono jidai: Tōkyō no chūsei o kangaeru*, edited by Minegishi Sumio, Kobayashi Kazutake, and Kuroda Motoki, 204–24. Tokyo: Shin Jinbutsu Ōraisha, 1998.

Kuroda Motoki. *Chū-kinsei ikōki no daimyō kenryoku to sonraku*. Tokyo: Azekura Shobō, 2003.

Kuroda Motoki. *Ōgigayatsu Uesugi-shi to Ōta Dōkan*. Tokyo: Iwata Shoin, 2004.

Kuroda Motoki. *Sengoku daimyō Hōjō-shi no ryōgoku shihai*. Tokyo: Iwata Shoin, 1995.

Kuroda Motoki. *Sengoku daimyō ryōgoku no shihai kōzō*. Tokyo: Iwata Shoin, 1997.

Kuroda Motoki. *Sengoku daimyō to tozama kunishū*. Tokyo: Bunken Shuppan, 1997.

Kuroda Motoki. *Sengoku-ki tōgoku no daimyō to kunishū*. Tokyo: Iwata Shoin, 2001.

Kurokawa Mamichi, ed. *Kokushi sōsho*. Series 1. 36 vols. Tokyo: Kokushi Kenkyūkai, 1914–17.

Kurokawa Tadanori. "Chūsei kōki no ryōshusei ni tsuite." *Nihonshi kenkyū* 68 (September 1963): 53–63.

Kurokawa Tadanori. "Shugo ryōgokusei to shōen taisei: Kokujin ryōshusei no kakuritsu katei." *Nihonshi kenkyū* 57 (October 1961): 1–19.

Kusunose Keita. "Sengoku-ki Shimazu-shi ni okeru shushoku kyōō girei: 'Shikisankon' to 'kawarake.'" *Hikaku shakai bunka kenkyū* 22 (2007): 22–33.

Lu, David J. *Japan: A Documentary History*. Armonk, NY: M. E. Sharpe, 1997.

Maejima Yasuhiko. "Ōishi-shi no Ninomiya-jō wa Kodama-gun ka." In *Ōishi-shi no kenkyū*, edited by Sugiyama Hiroshi and Kurihara Chūdō, 67–84. Tokyo: Meicho Shuppan, 1975.

Maejima Yasuhiko. *Ōta-shi no kenkyū*. Tokyo: Meicho Shuppan, 1975.

Maekawa Kaname. "Chūsei shūraku no dōkō to ryūtsū kikō no saihen: Etchū ni okeru chūshin shūrakumō ni kanshite." In *Chūsei no shiro to kōkogaku*, edited by Ishii Susumu and Hagihara Mitsuo, 195–214. Tokyo: Shin Jinbutsu Ōraisha, 1991.

Manzai jugō nikki. In *Zoku gunsho ruijū, hōi*, edited by Hanawa Hokinoichi, vols. 1–2. Tokyo: Zoku Gunsho Ruijū Kanseikai, 1931–32.

Manzano Moreno, Eduardo. "The Creation of a Medieval Frontier: Islam and Christianity in the Iberian Peninsula, Eighth to Eleventh Centuries." In *Frontiers in Question: Eurasian Borderlands, 700–1700*, edited by Daniel Power and Naomi Standen, 32–54. New York: St. Martin's Press, 1999.

Marra, Michele. *Representations of Power: The Literary Politics of Medieval Japan*. Honolulu: University of Hawai'i Press, 1993.

Marushima Kazuhiro. "Sakaime no jōdai to 'roji chisō.'" *Sengokushi kenkyū* 43 (February 2002): 24–25.

Mass, Jeffrey P. "*Jitō* Land Possession in the Thirteenth Century: The Case of *Shitaji Chūbun*." In *Medieval Japan: Essays in Institutional History*, edited by John Whitney Hall and Jeffrey P. Mass, 157–83. Stanford, CA: Stanford University Press, 1974.

Mass, Jeffrey P. "The Mixing of Past and Present: Anachronism in Japanese History." In Jeffrey P. Mass, *Antiquity and Anachronism in Japanese History*, 61–64. Stanford, CA: Stanford University Press, 1992.

Matsumoto Kazuo. *Tōgoku shugo no rekishiteki tokushitsu*. Tokyo: Iwata Shoin, 2001.

Matsuoka Susumu. "Iwaki-ryō sakaime no jōkangun to chiiki shakai." *Chūsei jōkaku kenkyū* 16 (2002): 6–29.

Matsuoka Susumu. "Sengoku shoki tōgoku ni okeru jin to jōkaku." *Sengokushi kenkyū* 50 (August 2005): 1–6.

Matsuoka Susumu. *Sengoku-ki jōkangun no keikan*. Tokyo: Azekura Shobō, 2002.

McCormick, Melissa. *Tosa Mitsunobu and the Small Scroll in Medieval Japan*. Seattle: University of Washington Press, 2009.

McCullough, Helen C., trans. *The Taiheiki: A Chronicle of Medieval Japan*. North Clarendon, VT: Tuttle Publishing, 2003. First edition, New York: Columbia University Press, 1956.

McCullough, Helen C., trans. *Tales of Ise: Lyrical Episodes from Tenth-Century Japan*. Stanford, CA: Stanford University Press, 1968.

Minegishi Sumio. *Chūsei no tōgoku: Chiiki to kenryoku*. Tokyo: Tōkyō Daigaku Shuppankai, 1989.

Minegishi Sumio. "Kyōtoku no ran ni okeru jōkaku to jinsho." In *Jōkaku to chūsei no tōgoku*, edited by Chiba Jōkaku Kenkyūkai, 3–16. Tokyo: Koshi Shoin, 2005.

Minegishi Sumio. "Kyōtoku no ran no futatsu no Nitta Iwamatsu-shi." In *Chūsei no nairan to shakai*, edited by Satō Kazuhiko, 63–83. Tokyo: Tōkyōdō Shuppan, 2007.

Minegishi Sumio. "Sengoku jidai no 'ryō' to ryōgoku: Kōzuke no kuni Nitta ryō to Gohōjō-shi." In *Tōgoku daimyō no kenkyū*, edited by Satō Hironobu, 339–79. Tokyo: Yoshikawa Kōbunkan, 1983.

Minegishi Sumio. "Sengoku jidai no seisatsu." In *Sengoku, Shokuhō*, vol. 5 of *Komonjo no kataru Nihonshi*, edited by Minegishi Sumio, 497–511. Tokyo: Chikuma Shobō, 1989.

Minegishi Sumio. "Tōgoku Sengoku-ki no gunjiteki kyōkai ryōiki ni okeru 'hante' ni tsuite." *Chūō shigaku* 18 (1995): 104–17.

Minegishi Sumio, Kobayashi Kazutake, and Kuroda Motoki, eds. *Toshima-shi to sono jidai: Tōkyō no chūsei o kangaeru*. Tokyo: Shin Jinbutsu Ōraisha, 1998.

Minemura Fumito, ann. *Shinkokin wakashū*. Tokyo: Shōgakukan, 1995.

Misumi Yōichi. "Chūsei bungaku ni okeru Musashino to tōgoku." In *Bungaku no Musashino*, edited by Seikei Daigaku Bungakubu Gakkai, 65–98. Tokyo: Kazama Shobō, 2003.

Misumi Yōichi, ed. *Towazugatari, Tamakiwaru*. Tokyo: Iwanami Shoten, 1994.

Mitamura Masako. "Gofukakusa Nijō: Yume o ikiru." *Kokubungaku kaishaku to kanshō* 64, no. 5 (May 1999): 102–9.

Miyagawa Mitsuru. "Shōensei no kaitai." In *Iwanami kōza Nihon rekishi*, edited by Ienaga Saburō, 7:119–61. Tokyo: Iwanami Shoten, 1963.

Miyagawa Mitsuru, with Cornelius J. Kiley. "From Shōen to Chigyō: Proprietary Lordship and the Structure of Local Power." In *Japan in the Muromachi Age*, edited by John Whitney Hall and Toyoda Takeshi, 89–105. Berkeley: University of California Press, 1977.

Mizuhara Hajime. "Towazugatari no kyokōsei o megutte." In *Towazugatari: Chūsei joryū nikki bungaku no sekai*, edited by Imai Takuji et al., 67–86. Tokyo: Benseisha, 1990.

Moerman, D. Max. *Localizing Paradise: Kumano Pilgrimage and the Religious Landscape of Premodern Japan*. Cambridge, MA: Harvard University Asia Center, 2005.

Molin, Kristian. *Unknown Crusader Castles*. New York: Hambledon and London, 2001.

Morita Shin'ichi. "Monjo, kiroku kara mita Ikatsuko-jin." *Chūsei kōkogaku bunken kenkyūkai kaihō* 6 (February 2006): 8–10.

Morita Shin'ichi. "Yamanouchi Uesugi-shi no kyoten ni tsuite: Kōzuke no kuni Itahana o chūshin to shite." *Gunma Kenritsu Rekishi Hakubutsukan kiyō* 29 (March 2008): 103–21.

Motegi Chōshi Hensan Iinkai, ed. *Motegi chōshi*. 6 vols. Motegi-machi, Tochigi-ken: Motegi-machi, 1995–2001.

Murata Shūzō. *Zusetsu chūsei jōkaku jiten*. 3 vols. Tokyo: Shin Jinbutsu Ōraisha, 1987.

Murata Shūzō, ed. *Shinshiten chūsei jōkaku kenkyū ronshū*. Tokyo: Shin Jinbutsū Ōraisha, 2002.

Musashino no kikō. In *Shinkō gunsho ruijū*, edited by Hanawa Hokinoichi, 15:240–41. Tokyo: Meicho Fukyūkai, 1977.

Nagahara Keiji. "The Decline of the *Shōen* System." In *The Cambridge History of Japan*, vol. 3, *Medieval Japan*, edited by Kozo Yamamura, 260–300. Cambridge: Cambridge University Press, 1990.

Nagahara Keiji. "Landownership under the Shōen-Kokugaryō System." *Journal of Japanese Studies* 1, no. 2 (spring 1975): 269–96.

Nagahara Keiji. "Motegi-shi kyūninchō kō." In *Shōensei to buke shakai*, edited by Takeuchi Rizō Hakase Kanreiki Kinenkai, 551–80. Tokyo: Yoshikawa Kōbunkan, 1969.

Nagahara Keiji. *Nihon chūsei shakai kōzō no kenkyū*. Tokyo: Iwanami Shoten, 1973.

Nagahara Keiji. *Nihon hōkensei seiritsu katei no kenkyū*. Tokyo: Iwanami Shoten, 1961.

Nagahara Keiji. *Sengoku no dōran*. Tokyo: Shōgakukan, 1975.

Nagahara Keiji. "Shōen kaitaiki ni okeru ukeoi daikansei." In *Shōen no kaitai*, edited by Amino Yoshihiko et al., 65–104. Tokyo: Yoshikawa Kōbunkan, 1999.

Nagahara Keiji, John Whitney Hall, and Kozo Yamamura, eds. *Sengoku jidai: 1550 nen kara 1650 nen no shakai tenkan*. Tokyo: Yoshikawa Kōbunkan, 1978.

Nagahara Keiji, with Kozo Yamamura. "The Sengoku Daimyo and the Kandaka System." In *Japan before Tokugawa: Political Consolidation and Economic*

Growth, 1500 to 1650, edited by John Whitney Hall, Nagahara Keiji, and Kozo Yamamura, 27–63. Princeton, NJ: Princeton University Press, 1983.

Nagatsuka Takashi. "Sengoku bushō no kanto, juryōmei: Koga kubō Ashikaga-shi to Gohōjō-shi o jirei ni shite." *Komazawa shigaku*, nos. 39–40 (September 1988): 48–58.

Nakanishi Yūki. "Sengoku-ki ni okeru chiiki no jōkan to shugo kōken: Settsu no kuni no jirei kara." In *Shinshiten chūsei jōkaku kenkyū ronshū*, edited by Murata Shūzō, 235–65. Tokyo: Shin Jinbutsu Ōraisha, 2002.

Nakayama Fumito. "Shimōsa seibu chiikisei kara mita Kogane-ryō keisei no zentei." In *Jōkaku to chūsei no tōgoku*, edited by Chiba Jōkaku Kenkyūkai, 43–66. Tokyo: Koshi Shoin, 2005.

Nakazawa Katsuaki. *Chūsei no buryoku to jōkaku*. Tokyo: Yoshikawa Kōbunkan, 1999.

Nenzi, Laura. *Excursions in Identity: Travel and the Intersection of Place, Gender, and Status in Edo Japan*. Honolulu: University of Hawai'i Press, 2008.

Nihon rekishi chimei taikei. 50 vols. Tokyo: Heibonsha, 1979–2005.

Niigata-ken, ed. *Niigata kenshi tsūshi hen*. 9 vols. Niigata-shi: Niigata-ken, 1986–88.

Nishigaya Yasuhiro. "Bushū Kozukue-jō no kenkyū." In *Musashino no jōkanshi*, edited by Komuro Eiichi, 143–211. Tokyo: Meicho Shuppan, 1984.

Nishigaya Yasuhiro. "Sengoku jōkaku ni okeru 'shiro okite' no ichi kōsatsu." In *Sengoku no heishi to nōmin*, edited by Sugiyama Hiroshi Sensei Kanreki Kinenkai, 165–94. Tokyo: Kadokawa Shoten, 1978.

Nitta Iwamatsu-shi keizu furoku. In *Gunma kenshi shiryō hen*, edited by Gunma Kenshi Hensan Iinkai, 5:332–38. Maebashi-shi: Gunma-ken, 1978.

Nitta shōden wakumon. In *Kokushi sōsho*, series 1, edited by Kurokawa Mamichi, 22:431–81. Tokyo: Kokushi Kenkyūkai, 1915.

Nitta shōdenki. In *Kokushi sōsho*, series 1, edited by Kurokawa Mamichi, 22:397–429. Tokyo: Kokushi Kenkyūkai, 1915.

Noritake Yūichi. *Sengoku daimyō ryōgoku no kenryoku kōzō*. Tokyo: Yoshikawa Kōbunkan, 2005.

Ochiai Yoshiaki. "Chūsei tōgoku no jin to geinō." *Nihon rekishi* 617 (October 1999): 37–55.

Ochiai Yoshiaki. *Chūsei tōgoku no "toshitekina ba" to bushi*. Tokyo: Yamakawa Shuppansha, 2005.

Ochiai Yoshiaki. "Musashi no kuni Kawagoe no shō ni tsuite: Nanbokuchō-ki ikō no denryō kankei o chūshin to shite." In *Kawagoe-shi no kenkyū*, edited by Okada Seiichi, 293–338. Tokyo: Meicho Shuppan, 2003. Reprinted in Ochiai Yoshiaki, *Chūsei tōgoku no "toshitekina ba" to bushi*, 51–77. Tokyo: Yamakawa Shuppansha, 2005.

Ochiai Yoshiaki. "Musashi no kuni Kawagoe-kan ni tsuite." *Chihōshi kenkyū* 265 (February 1997): 38–64. Reprinted in Ochiai Yoshiaki, *Chūsei tōgoku no "toshitekina ba" to bushi*, 78–102. Tokyo: Yamakawa Shuppansha, 2005.

Ogasawara Nagakazu. "Tōgokushi no butai toshite no Tonegawa, Hitachigawa no suimyaku." In *Kantō chūshin Sengokushi ronshū*, edited by Tōgoku Sengokushi Kenkyūkai, 118–29. Tokyo: Meicho Shuppan, 1980.

Ogawa Makoto. *Chūsei toshi "Fuchū" no tenkai*. Kyoto: Shibunkaku, 2001.

Ogino Masamori. "Kawagoe kanseki: Yamanouchi Uesugi-shi jinshoki o chūshin to shite." In *Sengoku no shiro*, edited by Fujiki Hisashi and Saitama Kenritsu Rekishi Shiryōkan, 159–64. Tokyo: Koshi Shoin, 2005.

Ogino Minahiko. "Musashi no Kira-shi ni tsuite no kenkyū: Gohōjō-shi no kōbō ni kanren shite." In *Kira-shi no kenkyū*, edited by Ogino Minahiko, 11–114. Tokyo: Meicho Shuppan, 1975.

Oi no kurigoto. Annotated by Shimazu Tadao. In *Kodai chūsei geijutsu ron*, edited by Hayashiya Tatsusaburō, 409–22. Tokyo: Iwanami Shoten, 1973.

Oishio Chihiro. *Kokubunji no chūseiteki tenkai*. Tokyo: Yoshikawa Kōbunkan, 1996.

Okada Seiichi, ed. *Kawagoe-shi no kenkyū*. Tokyo: Meicho Shuppan, 2003.

Ōkubo Toshiaki. "Sengoku daimyō monjo ni miru 'kinzei' no kenkyū: Imagawa-shi o jirei toshite, sono ni." In *Sengoku-ki tōgoku shakai ron*, edited by Sengokushi Kenkyūkai, 71–89. Tokyo: Yoshikawa Kōbunkan, 1990.

Okuda Isao. *Sōgi*. Tokyo: Yoshikawa Kōbunkan, 1998.

Ono Kazuyuki. "Musashino o aruku." In *Tama to Kōshū dōchū*, edited by Arai Katsuhiro and Matsumoto Mikio, 13–37. Tokyo: Yoshikawa Kōbunkan, 2003.

Ono Masatoshi. "Jōkan shutsudo no tōjiki ga hyōgen suru mono." In *Chūsei no shiro to kōkogaku*, edited by Ishii Susumu and Hagihara Mitsuo, 108–40. Tokyo: Shin Jinbutsu Ōraishia, 1991.

Ooms, Herman. *Tokugawa Ideology: Early Constructs, 1570–1680*. Princeton, NJ: Princeton University Press, 1985.

Ōta Dōkan jō. In *Shinpen Saitama kenshi, shiryō hen*, edited by Saitama-ken, 5:635–44. Urawa-shi: Saitama-ken, 1982.

Ōta-shi, ed. *Ōta shishi tsūshi hen: Chūsei*. Ōta-shi, Gunma-ken: Ōta-shi, 1997.

Owada Tetsuo. *Chūsei jōkakushi no kenkyū*. Osaka: Seibundō Shuppan, 2002.

Owada Tetsuo. *Gohōjō-shi kenkyū*. Tokyo: Meicho Shuppan, 1983.

Owada Tetsuo. "Nanbokuchō no shiro kara Sengoku no shiro e: Sono hattatsushiteki kōsatsu." In *Sengoku jōkamachi no kenkyū*, edited by Owada Tetsuo. 35–48. Osaka: Seibundō Shuppan, 2002.

Philippi, Donald. L., trans. *Kojiki*. Tokyo: University of Tokyo Press, 1968.

Pitelka, Morgan. "The Empire of Things: Tokugawa Ieyasu's Material Legacy and Cultural Profile." *Japanese Studies* 29, no. 1 (May 2009): 19–32.

Pitelka, Morgan. *Handmade Culture: Raku Potters, Patrons, and Tea Practitioners in Japan*. Honolulu: University of Hawai'i Press, 2005.

Power, Daniel. "French and Norman Frontiers in the Central Middle Ages." In *Frontiers in Question: Eurasian Borderlands, 700–1700*, edited by Daniel Power and Naomi Standen, 105–27. New York: St. Martin's Press, 1999.

Power, Daniel. "Introduction. Frontiers: Terms, Concepts, and the Historians of Medieval and Early Modern Europe." In *Frontiers in Question: Eurasian Borderlands, 700–1700*, edited by Daniel Power and Naomi Standen, 1–12. New York: St. Martin's Press, 1999.

Power, Daniel, and Naomi Standen, eds. *Frontiers in Question: Eurasian Borderlands, 700–1700*. New York: St. Martin's Press, 1999.

Ramírez, Susan Elizabeth. *To Feed and Be Fed: The Cosmological Bases of Authority and Identity in the Andes*. Stanford, CA: Stanford University Press, 2005.

Ramirez-Christensen, Esperanza. *Heart's Flower: The Life and Poetry of Shinkei*. Stanford, CA: Stanford University Press, 1994.

Ramirez-Christensen, Esperanza. *Murmured Conversations: A Treatise on Poetry and Buddhism by the Poet-Monk Shinkei*. Stanford, CA: Stanford University Press, 2008.

Rath, Eric. *Food and Fantasy in Early Modern Japan*. Berkeley: University of California Press, 2010.

Rekihaku Nihon Shōen Dētabēsu (accessed September 13, 2010). http://www.rekihaku.ac.jp/ up-cgi/login.pl?p=param/soue/db_param.

Sahlins, Peter. *Boundaries: The Making of France and Spain in the Pyrenees*. Berkeley: University of California Press, 1989.

Sahlins, Peter. "Natural Frontiers Revisited: France's Boundaries since the Seventeenth Century." *The American Historical Review* 95, no. 5 (December 1990): 1425–51.

Saitama-ken, ed. *Shinpen Saitama kenshi shiryō hen*. 26 vols. Urawa-shi: Saitama-ken, 1979–91.

Saitama-ken, ed. *Shinpen Saitama kenshi tsūshi hen*. 7 vols. Urawa-shi: Saitama-ken, 1987–91.

Saitama-ken no chimei. Vol. 11 of *Nihon rekishi chimei taikei*. Tokyo: Heibonsha, 1993.

Saitō Shin'ichi. "Chūsei tōgoku ni okeru kasen suiryō to toka." *Tōkyō-to Edo Tōkyō Hakubutsukan kenkyū hōkoku* 4 (1999): 113–33.

Saitō Shin'ichi. "Chūsei tōgoku no kaidō to sono hensen." In *Sengoku no shiro*, edited by Fujiki Hisashi and Saitama Kenshi Rekishi Shiryōkan, 77–100. Tokyo: Koshi Shoin, 2005.

Saitō Shin'ichi. *Chūsei tōgoku no ryōiki to jōkan*. Tokyo: Yoshikawa Kōbunkan, 2002.

Saitō Shin'ichi. "Gaisetsu." In *Zukai Nihon no chūsei iseki*, edited by Ono Masatoshi, 68–69. Tokyo: Tōkyō Daigaku Shuppankai, 2001.

Saitō Shin'ichi. "Joron." In *Chūsei tōgoku no sekai*, vol. 1, *Kita Kantō*, edited by Asano Haruki and Saitō, 3–8. Tokyo: Koshi Shoin, 2003.

Saitō Shin'ichi. "Jungyō, uchiwatashijō no kakutoku to sōden." In *Konnichi no komonjogaku*, edited by Takahashi Masahiko, 3:72–88. Tokyo: Yūzankaku, 2000.

Saitō Shin'ichi. "Kamakura kaidō Kamitsumichi to kita Kantō." In *Chūsei tōgoku no sekai*, vol. 1, *Kita Kantō*, edited by Asano Haruki and Saitō Shin'ichi, 145–68. Tokyo: Koshi Shoin, 2003.

Saitō Shin'ichi. "Kōzuke no kuni Nakayama-jō no kōsatsu." *Chūsei jōkaku kenkyū* 1 (July 1987): 23–24.

Saitō Shin'ichi. "Kyōkai ninshiki no henka: Sengoku-ki kokkyō no iji to kanri." *Shinano* 46, no. 11 (November 1994): 1–23.

Saitō Shin'ichi. "Minami Kantō no toshi to kaidō." In *Chūsei tōgoku no sekai*, vol. 2, *Minami Kantō*, edited by Asano Haruki and Saitō Shin'ichi, 151–80. Tokyo: Koshi Shoin, 2004.

Saitō Shin'ichi. "Nanbokuchō, Muromachi-ki no jōkaku." In *Zukai Nihon no chūsei iseki*, edited by Ono Masatoshi, 74–77. Tokyo: Tōkyō Daigaku Shuppankai, 2001.

Sakai Kimi. "Ōnin no ran to zaichi shakai." In *Shōen no kaitai*, edited by Amino Yoshihiko et al., 105–50. Tokyo: Yoshikawa Kōbunkan, 1999.

Sano Shishi Hensan Iinkai, ed. *Sano shishi tsūshi hen*. 2 vols. Sano-shi: Sano-shi, 1978–79.

Sano Shizuyo. "Mizubori no keifu to jōkamachi no kigen." In *Chizu to rekishi kūkan: Ashikaga Kensuke sensei tsuitō ronbunshū*, edited by Ashikaga Kensuke Sensei Tsuitō Ronbunshū Hensan Iinkai, 207–18. Tokyo: Daimeidō, 2000.

Sasaki Michirō. "Sengoku-ki 'sakaime' ni okeru ryōshusō no dōkō." *Sengokushi kenkyū* 50 (August 2005): 13–18.

Sato, Elizabeth. "Ōyama Estate and Insei Land Policies." *Monumenta Nipponica* 34, no. 1 (Spring 1979): 73–99.

Sato, Elizabeth. "The Early Development of the *Shōen*." In *Medieval Japan: Essays in Institutional History*, edited by John W. Hall and Jeffrey P. Mass, 91–108. Stanford, CA: Stanford University Press, 1974.

Satō Hironobu. *Chūsei tōgoku no shihai kōzō*. Kyoto: Shibunkaku, 1989.

Satō Hironobu. *Koga kubō Ashikaga-shi no kenkyū*. Tokyo: Azekura Shobō, 1989.

Satō Hironobu. "Sengoku-ki ni okeru tōgoku kokkaron no isshiten: Koga kubō Ashikaga-shi to Gohōjō-shi o chūshin to shite." In *Tōgoku daimyō no kenkyū*, edited by Satō Hironobu, 380–403. Tokyo: Yoshikawa Kōbunkan, 1983.

Satō Hironobu. *Zoku chūsei tōgoku no shihai kōzō*. Kyoto: Shibunkaku, 1996.

Satō Hironobu, ed. *Tōgoku daimyō no kenkyū*. Tokyo: Yoshikawa Kōbunkan, 1983.

Satō Shin'ichi. "Muromachi bakufu ron." In *Iwanami kōza Nihon rekishi*, edited by Ienaga Saburō et al., 7:1–48. Tokyo: Iwanami Shoten, 1962.

Satō Shin'ichi. *Nanbokuchō no dōran*. Vol. 9 of *Nihon no rekishi*. Tokyo: Chūō Kōronsha, 1965.

Satō Shin'ichi, and Ikeuchi Yoshisuke, eds. *Chūsei hōsei shiryōshū*. Vol. 2, *Muromachi bakufu hō*. Tokyo: Iwanami Shoin, 1957.

Sawaki Eichi. *Gohōjō-shi no kiso kenkyū*. Tokyo: Yoshikawa Kōbunkan, 1976.

Sawaki Eichi. *Gohōjō-shi to ryōgoku kei'ei*. Tokyo: Yoshikawa Kōbunkan, 1997.

Sawaki Eichi. "Sengoku bushō no kanto juryōmei to jitsumyō." *Sengokushi kenkyū* 9 (February 1985): 22–23.

Schimmel, Annemarie. *Empire of the Great Mughals: History, Art and Culture*. London: Reaktion Books, 2004.

Seikei Daigaku Bungakubu Gakkai, ed. *Bungaku no Musashino*. Tokyo: Kazama Shobō, 2003.

Sekiguchi Kazuya. "Hachigata-jō." In *Zusetsu chūsei jōkaku jiten*, edited by Murata Shūzō, 1:216–17. Tokyo: Shin Jinbutsu Ōraisha, 1987.

Sekiguchi Kazuya. "Kawagoe-shi yakata." In *Zusetsu chūsei jōkaku jiten*, edited by Murata Shūzō, 1:248–49. Tokyo: Shin Jinbutsu Ōraisha, 1987.

Sengoku ibun: Gohōjō-shi hen, edited by Sugiyama Hiroshi and Shimoyama Haruhisa. 8 vols. Tokyo: Tōkyōdō Shuppan, 1989–2000.

Sengokushi Kenkyūkai, ed. *Sengoku-ki tōgoku shakai ron*. Tokyo: Yoshikawa Kōbunkan, 1990.

Sennohara Yasukata. *Kantō Sengokushi (zen)*. Nagareyama-shi, Chiba-ken: Ron Shobō, 2006.

"Setsuboku ryōgin Sumiyoshi hyakuin." Annotated by Kaneko Kinjirō. In *Renga haikai shū*, edited by Kaneko Kinjirō, Teruoka Yasutaka, and Nakamura Shunjō, 245–77. Tokyo: Shōgakukan, 1974.

Shibata Ryūji. "Chūsei no kakki: Tachi to shiro kara jōkan e." In *Chūsei no shiro to kōkogaku*, edited by Ishii Susumu and Hagihara Mitsuo, 170–94. Tokyo: Shin Jinbutsu Ōraishia, 1991.

Shibata Ryūji. "Kōkogaku kara mita chūsei Bōsō no jōkan to mura, machi." In *Jōkaku to chūsei no tōgoku*, edited by Chiba Jōkaku Kenkyūkai, 139–66. Tokyo: Koshi Shoin, 2005.

Shibatsuji Shunroku. "Sengoku daimyō no kinzei to seisatsu." *Sengokushi kenkyū* 10 (August 1985): 28–30.

Shibatsuji Shunroku. "Sengoku daimyō no seisatsu." *Sengokushi kenkyū* 5 (February 1983): 13–14.

Shichinomiya Keizō. *Kantō kanrei, Uesugi ichizoku*. Tokyo: Shin Jinbutsu Ōraisha, 2002.

Shimazu Tadao. *Rengashi Sōgi*. Tokyo: Iwanami Shoten, 1991.

Shimoyama Haruhisa. "Gohōjō-shi no jōkaku kanri to shiro fushin." In *Sengoku no heishi to nōmin*, edited by Sugiyama Hiroshi Sensei Kanreki Kinenkai, 139–63. Tokyo: Kadokawa Shoten, 1978.

Shinkawa Takenori. *Shimotsuke chūseishi no shinkenkyū*. Tokyo: Gyōsei, 1994.

"Shinkei sōzu hyakushu." In *Zoku gunsho ruijū*, edited by Hanawa Hokinoichi, vol. 14, pt. 2, 913–16. Tokyo: Zoku Gunsho Ruijū Kanseikai Kankōkai, 1910.

Shinpen Kokka Taikan Henshū Iinkai, ed. *Shinpen kokka taikan*. 10 vols. Tokyo: Kadokawa Shoten, 1983–92.

Shirane, Haruo. *Japan and the Culture of the Four Seasons: Nature, Literature, and the Arts*. New York: Columbia University Press, 2012.

Shōin shigo. In *Gunma kenshi shiryō hen*, edited by Gunma Kenshi Hensan Iinkai, 5:786–852. Maebashi-shi: Gunma-ken, 1978.

Smail, Daniel Lord. *Imaginary Cartographies: Possession and Identity in Late Medieval Marseille*. Ithaca, NY: Cornell University Press, 2000.

Sōgi shūenki. Annotated by Tsurusaki Hiroo and Fukuda Hideichi. In *Chūsei nikki kikōshū*, edited by Fukuda Hideichi, 449–61. Tokyo: Iwanami Shoten, 1990.

Sōgi shūenki. In *Shinkō gunsho ruijū*, edited by Hanawa Hokinoichi, 22:673–77. Tokyo: Meicho Fukyūkai, 1977.

Sōrinji denki. In *Gunma kenshi shiryō hen*, edited by Gunma Kenshi Hensan Iinkai, 7:432–43. Maebashi-shi: Gunma-ken, 1986.

Sōunji-dono nijūikkajō. In *Chūsei seiji shakai shisō, jō*, edited by Ishii Susumu et al., 353–56. Tokyo: Iwanami Shoten, 1972.

Spafford, David. "An Apology of Betrayal: Political and Narrative Strategies in a Late Medieval Memoir." *Journal of Japanese Studies* 35, no. 2 (summer 2009): 321–52.

Stavros, Matthew. "Building Warrior Legitimacy in Medieval Kyoto." *East Asian History* 31 (2006): 1–28.

Stavros, Matthew. "Locational Pedigree and Warrior Status in Medieval Kyoto: The Residence of Ashikaga Yoshimitsu." *Japanese Studies* 29, no. 1 (May 2009): 3–18.

Steenstrup, Carl. "Hōjō Sōun's Twenty-One Articles: The Code of Conduct of the Odawara Hōjō." *Monumenta Nipponica* 29, no. 3 (autumn 1974): 283–303.

Steenstrup, Carl. "The Imagawa Letter: A Muromachi Warrior's Code of Conduct Which Became a Tokugawa Schoolbook." *Monumenta Nipponica* 28, no. 3 (autumn 1973): 295–316.

Stein, Robert M. "Making History English: Cultural Identity and Historical Explanation in William of Malmesbury and Laȝamon's *Brut*." In *Text and Territory: Geographical Imagination in the European Middle Ages*, edited by Sylvia Tomasch and Sealy Gilles, 97–115. Philadelphia: University of Pennsylvania Press, 1998.

Sugiyama Hiroshi. *Sengoku daimyō Gohōjō-shi no kenkyū*. Tokyo: Meicho Shuppan, 1982.

Sugiyama Hiroshi. "Shugo ryōgokusei no tenkai to Ōishi-shi." In *Ōishi-shi no kenkyū*, edited by Sugiyama and Kurihara Chūdō, 105–14. Tokyo: Meicho Shuppan, 1975.

Sugiyama Hiroshi, ed. *Odawara-shū shoryō yakuchō*. Tokyo: Kondō Shuppansha, 1969.

Sugiyama Hiroshi Sensei Kanreki Kinenkai, ed. *Sengoku no heishi to nōmin*. Tokyo: Kadokawa Shoten, 1978.

Sugiyama Hiroshi, and Kurihara Chūdō, eds. *Ōishi-shi no kenkyū*. Tokyo: Meicho Shuppan, 1975.

Tada Nobuhisa. "Jōkaku kōsei kara mita chiiki to sakaime: Nishi Harima chiiki no chūsei jōkaku o chūshin ni." In *Shinshiten chūsei jōkaku kenkyū ronshū*, edited by Murata Shūzō, 267–94. Tokyo: Shin Jinbutsu Ōraishia, 2002.

Tanaka Shin. " 'Yamanouchi Uesugi-shi no kawarake' to wa." In *Sengoku no shiro*, edited by Fujiki Hisashi and Saitama Kenritsu Rekishi Shiryōkan, 67–76. Tokyo: Koshi Shoin, 2005.

Tanaka Yoshinari. "Hōjō Ujiyasu no Musashino kikō no shingi ni tsuite." *Rekishi chiri* 2 (January 1900).

Taniguchi Sakae. "Hakkutsu sareta Toshima-gun." In *Toshima-shi to sono jidai: Tōkyō no chūsei o kangaeru*, edited by Minegishi Sumio, Kobayashi Kazutake, and Kuroda Motoki, 67–103. Tokyo: Shin Jinbutsu Ōraishia, 1998.

Tanuma Mutsumi. "Muromachi bakufu, shugo, kokujin." In *Iwanami kōza Nihon rekishi*, edited by Asao Naohiro et al., 7:1–50. Tokyo: Iwanami Shoten, 1976.

Toby, Ronald P. "Review Article: Rescuing the Nation from History: The State of the State in Early Modern Japan." *Monumenta Nipponica* 56, no. 2 (summer 2001): 197–237.

Tochigi Kenshi Hensan Iinkai, ed. *Tochigi kenshi shiryō hen*. 25 vols. Utsunomiya-shi: Tochigi-ken, 1973–80.

Tochigi Kenshi Hensan Iinkai, ed. *Tochigi kenshi tsūshi hen*. 8 vols. Utsunomiya-shi: Tochigi-ken, 1980–84.

Tōgoku kikō. In *Shinkō gunsho ruijū*, edited by Hanawa Hokinoichi, 15:268–93. Tokyo: Meicho Fukyūkai, 1977.

Tonomura, Hitomi. *Community and Commerce in Late Medieval Japan: The Corporate Villages of Tokuchin-Ho*. Stanford, CA: Stanford University Press, 1992.

Toubert, Pierre. *Les Structures du Latium médiéval: Le Latium méridional et la Sabine du IXe siècle à la fin du XIIe siècle*. Paris: École française de Rome, 1973.

Tsunoda Tomohiko. "Ashikaga Takauji to Imagawa Yoshimoto no kanto, juryō." *Sengokushi kenkyū*, no. 49 (August 2004): 33–34.

Tsurusaki Hiroo. "Rengashi: Seijitekina, amari ni mo seijitekina hitotachi." *Bungaku* 3, no. 5 (September–October 2002): 55–67.

Tsurusaki Hiroo. "The Poet Shōkō and the Salons of Sakai." In *Literary Patronage in Late Medieval Japan*, edited by Steven D. Carter, 45–62. Ann Arbor: Center for Japanese Studies, The University of Michigan, 1993.

Tsurusaki Hiroo. *Sengoku no kenryoku to yoriai no bungei*. Osaka: Izumi Shoin, 1988.

Tsurusaki Hiroo. *Sengoku o yuku rengashi Sōchō*. Tokyo: Kadokawa Shoten, 2000.

Tyler, Royall. "A Glimpse of Mt. Fuji in Legend and Cult." *Journal of the Association of Teachers of Japanese* 16, no. 2 (November 1981): 140–65.

Ushiyama Hideaki. "Shakujiigawa o watari Iwabuchi e: Tōkyō-to Kita-ku Jūjō Kubo iseki kenshutsu no dōroshi." In *Chūsei no michi o saguru*, edited by Fujiwara Yoshiaki, 77–94. Tokyo: Kokin Shoin, 2004.

Uzawa Satoru, ann. *Sōchō Suruga nikki: Hayashi-ke bon*. Tokyo: Koten Bunko, 1975.

Vann, Theresa M. "Twelfth-Century Castille and Its Frontier Strategies." In *The Circle of War in the Middle Ages: Essays on Medieval Military and Naval History*, edited by Donald J. Kagay and L. J. Andrew Villalon, 21–31. Woodbridge, Suffolk: The Boydell Press, 1999.

Vaporis, Constantine Nomikos. *Breaking Barriers: Travel and the State in Early Modern Japan*. Cambridge, MA: Council on East Asian Studies, Harvard University, 1994.

Walker, Brett L. *The Conquest of Ainu Lands: Ecology and Culture in Japanese Expansion, 1590–1800*. Berkeley: University of California Press, 2001.

Warren, W. L. *The Governance of Norman and Angevin England, 1086–1272*. Stanford, CA: Stanford University Press, 1987.

Wickham, Chris. *The Mountains and the City: The Tuscan Appennines in the Early Middle Ages*. Oxford: Clarendon Press, 1988.

Wigen, Kären. *A Malleable Map: Geographies of Restoration in Central Japan, 1600–1912*. Berkeley: University of California Press, 2010.

Wintersteen, Prescott B., Jr. "Muromachi *Shugo* and *Hanzei*." In *Medieval Japan: Essays in Institutional History*, edited by John Whitney Hall and Jeffrey P. Mass, 210–20. Stanford, CA: Stanford University Press, 1974.

Yamada Kuniaki. "Kamakura Unchōan to Nagao Tadakage." In *Sengoku-ki tōgoku shakai ron*, edited by Sengokushi Kenkyūkai, 131–54. Tokyo: Yoshikawa Kōbunkan, 1990.

Yamada Kuniaki. *Kamakura-fu to Kantō: Chūsei no seiji chitsujo to zaichi shakai*. Tokyo: Azekura Shobō, 1995.

Yamada Kuniaki. "Muromachi-ki Kantō no shihai kōzō to zaichi shakai." *Rekishigaku kenkyū* 626 (November 1991): 78–87.

Yamada Kuniaki. "Nagao Kageharu to Nagao Tadakage," *Nihon rekishi* 600 (May 1998): 117–20.

Yamada Kuniaki. *Sengoku no komyunikēshon: Jōhō to tsūshin*. Tokyo: Yoshikawa Kōbunkan, 2002.

Yamamoto Hiroki. "Sengoku daimyō ryōgoku 'sakaime' chiiki ni okeru kassen to minshū." *Nenpō chūseishi kenkyū* 19 (1994): 67–93.

Yamamura, Kozo, ed. *The Cambridge History of Japan*, vol. 3, *Medieval Japan*. Cambridge: Cambridge University Press, 1990.

Yamamuro Kyōko. "Sengoku no chiikisei." In *Iwanami kōza Nihon tsūshi*, edited by Asao Naohiro et al., 10:161–92. Tokyo: Iwanami Shoten, 1994.

Yamazaki Hajime. "Yamanouchi Uesugi-shi no jōrui ikō no kōsatsu." In *Musashino no jōkanshi*, edited by Komuro Eiichi, 123–42. Tokyo: Meicho Shuppan, 1984.

Yanase Yūichi. "Bōsō no chūsei shūraku: Daichijō shūraku o chūshin ni." In *Chūsei tōgoku no sekai*, vol. 2, *Minami Kantō*, edited by Asano Haruki and Saitō Shin'ichi, 105–28. Tokyo: Koshi Shoin, 2004.

Yanase Yūichi. "Chiba-shi no honkyo no fukugen: Chiba horinouchi, shuku, ichi." In *Sengoku jidai no kōkogaku*, edited by Ono Masatoshi and Hagihara Mitsuo, 305–16. Tokyo: Koshi Shoin, 2003.

Yasuda Noriko. "*Towazugatari* no kyokō: Monogatari sesshu o chūshin to shite." *Nagoya Daigaku kenkyū bungakubu ronshū*, no. 97 (1987): 147–60.

Yasutomi ki. In *Zōho shiryō taisei*, edited by Zohō Shiryō Taisei Kankōkai, vols. 37–40. Tokyo: Rinsen Shoten, 1965.

Yata Toshifumi. *Nihon chūsei Sengoku-ki kenryoku kōzō no kenkyū*. Tokyo: Hanawa Shobō, 1998.

Yata Toshifumi. *Nihon chūsei Sengoku-ki no chiiki to minshū*. Osaka: Seibundō Shuppan, 2002.

Yiengpruksawan, Mimi Hall. *Ḥiraizumi: Buddhist Art and Regional Politics in Twelfth-Century Japan*. Cambridge, MA: Harvard University Asia Center, 1998.

Yogo Toshio. *Sōseki to chihō renga: Shiryō to kenkyū*. Tokyo: Kasama Shoin, 1993.

Yokoyama Shigeru, ed. *Shinkei sakuhinshū*. Tokyo: Kadokawa Shoten, 1972.

Yonemoto, Marcia. *Mapping Early Modern Japan: Space, Place, and Culture in the Tokugawa Period*. Berkeley: University of California Press, 2003.

Yuasa Haruhisa. "Muromachi-ki tōgoku no shōen-kōryōsei to 'gōson' shakai." *Kokuritsu Rekishi Minzoku Hakubutsukan kenkyū hōkoku* 104 (March 2003): 185–221. Reprinted in Yuasa Haruhisa, *Chūsei tōgoku no chiiki shakaishi*, 127–99. Tokyo: Iwata Shoin, 2005.

Yuyama Manabu. "Ōgigayatsu-shi no ryōiki shihai to jōkaku: Muromachi makki no minami Musashi." In *Musashino no jōkanshi*, edited by Komuro Eiichi, 101–22. Tokyo: Meicho Shuppan, 1984.

Zoku Gunsho Ruijū Kanseikai, ed. *Gunsho kaidai*. 10 vols. Tokyo: Zoku Gunsho Ruijū Kanseikai, 1976–77.

Index

Harvard East Asian Monographs

(*out-of-print)

*1. Liang Fang-chung, *The Single-Whip Method of Taxation in China*
*2. Harold C. Hinton, *The Grain Tribute System of China, 1845–1911*
3. Ellsworth C. Carlson, *The Kaiping Mines, 1877–1912*
*4. Chao Kuo-chün, *Agrarian Policies of Mainland China: A Documentary Study, 1949–1956*
*5. Edgar Snow, *Random Notes on Red China, 1936–1945*
*6. Edwin George Beal, Jr., *The Origin of Likin, 1835–1864*
7. Chao Kuo-chün, *Economic Planning and Organization in Mainland China: A Documentary Study, 1949–1957*
*8. John K. Fairbank, *Ching Documents: An Introductory Syllabus*
*9. Helen Yin and Yi-chang Yin, *Economic Statistics of Mainland China, 1949–1957*
10. Wolfgang Franke, *The Reform and Abolition of the Traditional Chinese Examination System*
11. Albert Feuerwerker and S. Cheng, *Chinese Communist Studies of Modern Chinese History*
12. C. John Stanley, *Late Ching Finance: Hu Kuang-yung as an Innovator*
13. S. M. Meng, *The Tsungli Yamen: Its Organization and Functions*
*14. Ssu-yü Teng, *Historiography of the Taiping Rebellion*
15. Chun-Jo Liu, *Controversies in Modern Chinese Intellectual History: An Analytic Bibliography of Periodical Articles, Mainly of the May Fourth and Post-May Fourth Era*
*16. Edward J. M. Rhoads, *The Chinese Red Army, 1927–1963: An Annotated Bibliography*
*17. Andrew J. Nathan, *A History of the China International Famine Relief Commission*
*18. Frank H. H. King (ed.) and Prescott Clarke, *A Research Guide to China-Coast Newspapers, 1822–1911*
*19. Ellis Joffe, *Party and Army: Professionalism and Political Control in the Chinese Officer Corps, 1949–1964*
*20. Toshio G. Tsukahira, *Feudal Control in Tokugawa Japan: The Sankin Kōtai System*
*21. Kwang-Ching Liu, ed., *American Missionaries in China: Papers from Harvard Seminars*
*22. George Moseley, *A Sino-Soviet Cultural Frontier: The Ili Kazakh Autonomous Chou*

23. Carl F. Nathan, *Plague Prevention and Politics in Manchuria, 1910–1931*
*24. Adrian Arthur Bennett, *John Fryer: The Introduction of Western Science and Technology into Nineteenth-Century China*
*25. Donald J. Friedman, *The Road from Isolation: The Campaign of the American Committee for Non-Participation in Japanese Aggression, 1938–1941*
*26. Edward LeFevour, *Western Enterprise in Late Ching China: A Selective Survey of Jardine, Matheson and Company's Operations, 1842–1895*
27. Charles Neuhauser, *Third World Politics: China and the Afro-Asian People's Solidarity Organization, 1957–1967*
*28. Kungtu C. Sun, assisted by Ralph W. Huenemann, *The Economic Development of Manchuria in the First Half of the Twentieth Century*
*29. Shahid Javed Burki, *A Study of Chinese Communes, 1965*
30. John Carter Vincent, *The Extraterritorial System in China: Final Phase*
31. Madeleine Chi, *China Diplomacy, 1914–1918*
*32. Clifton Jackson Phillips, *Protestant America and the Pagan World: The First Half Century of the American Board of Commissioners for Foreign Missions, 1810–1860*
*33. James Pusey, *Wu Han: Attacking the Present Through the Past*
*34. Ying-wan Cheng, *Postal Communication in China and Its Modernization, 1860–1896*
35. Tuvia Blumenthal, *Saving in Postwar Japan*
36. Peter Frost, *The Bakumatsu Currency Crisis*
37. Stephen C. Lockwood, *Augustine Heard and Company, 1858–1862*
38. Robert R. Campbell, *James Duncan Campbell: A Memoir by His Son*
39. Jerome Alan Cohen, ed., *The Dynamics of China's Foreign Relations*
40. V. V. Vishnyakova-Akimova, *Two Years in Revolutionary China, 1925–1927,* trans. Steven L. Levine
41. Meron Medzini, *French Policy in Japan During the Closing Years of the Tokugawa Regime*
42. Ezra Vogel, Margie Sargent, Vivienne B. Shue, Thomas Jay Mathews, and Deborah S. Davis, *The Cultural Revolution in the Provinces*
43. Sidney A. Forsythe, *An American Missionary Community in China, 1895–1905*
*44. Benjamin I. Schwartz, ed., *Reflections on the May Fourth Movement.: A Symposium*
*45. Ching Young Choe, *The Rule of the Taewŏngun, 1864–1873: Restoration in Yi Korea*
46. W. P. J. Hall, *A Bibliographical Guide to Japanese Research on the Chinese Economy, 1958–1970*
47. Jack J. Gerson, *Horatio Nelson Lay and Sino-British Relations, 1854–1864*
48. Paul Richard Bohr, *Famine and the Missionary: Timothy Richard as Relief Administrator and Advocate of National Reform*
49. Endymion Wilkinson, *The History of Imperial China: A Research Guide*
50. Britten Dean, *China and Great Britain: The Diplomacy of Commercial Relations, 1860–1864*
51. Ellsworth C. Carlson, *The Foochow Missionaries, 1847–1880*
52. Yeh-chien Wang, *An Estimate of the Land-Tax Collection in China, 1753 and 1908*
53. Richard M. Pfeffer, *Understanding Business Contracts in China, 1949–1963*

- *54. Han-sheng Chuan and Richard Kraus, *Mid-Ching Rice Markets and Trade: An Essay in Price History*
- 55. Ranbir Vohra, *Lao She and the Chinese Revolution*
- 56. Liang-lin Hsiao, *China's Foreign Trade Statistics, 1864–1949*
- *57. Lee-hsia Hsu Ting, *Government Control of the Press in Modern China, 1900–1949*
- *58. Edward W. Wagner, *The Literati Purges: Political Conflict in Early Yi Korea*
- *59. Joungwon A. Kim, *Divided Korea: The Politics of Development, 1945–1972*
- 60. Noriko Kamachi, John K. Fairbank, and Chūzō Ichiko, *Japanese Studies of Modern China Since 1953: A Bibliographical Guide to Historical and Social-Science Research on the Nineteenth and Twentieth Centuries, Supplementary Volume for 1953–1969*
- 61. Donald A. Gibbs and Yun-chen Li, *A Bibliography of Studies and Translations of Modern Chinese Literature, 1918–1942*
- 62. Robert H. Silin, *Leadership and Values: The Organization of Large-Scale Taiwanese Enterprises*
- 63. David Pong, *A Critical Guide to the Kwangtung Provincial Archives Deposited at the Public Record Office of London*
- *64. Fred W. Drake, *China Charts the World: Hsu Chi-yü and His Geography of 1848*
- *65. William A. Brown and Urgrunge Onon, translators and annotators, *History of the Mongolian People's Republic*
- 66. Edward L. Farmer, *Early Ming Government: The Evolution of Dual Capitals*
- *67. Ralph C. Croizier, *Koxinga and Chinese Nationalism: History, Myth, and the Hero*
- *68. William J. Tyler, tr., *The Psychological World of Natsume Sōseki*, by Doi Takeo
- 69. Eric Widmer, *The Russian Ecclesiastical Mission in Peking During the Eighteenth Century*
- *70. Charlton M. Lewis, *Prologue to the Chinese Revolution: The Transformation of Ideas and Institutions in Hunan Province, 1891–1907*
- 71. Preston Torbert, *The Ching Imperial Household Department: A Study of Its Organization and Principal Functions, 1662–1796*
- 72. Paul A. Cohen and John E. Schrecker, eds., *Reform in Nineteenth-Century China*
- 73. Jon Sigurdson, *Rural Industrialism in China*
- 74. Kang Chao, *The Development of Cotton Textile Production in China*
- 75. Valentin Rabe, *The Home Base of American China Missions, 1880–1920*
- *76. Sarasin Viraphol, *Tribute and Profit: Sino-Siamese Trade, 1652–1853*
- 77. Ch'i-ch'ing Hsiao, *The Military Establishment of the Yuan Dynasty*
- 78. Meishi Tsai, *Contemporary Chinese Novels and Short Stories, 1949–1974: An Annotated Bibliography*
- *79. Wellington K. K. Chan, *Merchants, Mandarins and Modern Enterprise in Late Ching China*
- 80. Endymion Wilkinson, *Landlord and Labor in Late Imperial China: Case Studies from Shandong by Jing Su and Luo Lun*
- *81. Barry Keenan, *The Dewey Experiment in China: Educational Reform and Political Power in the Early Republic*
- *82. George A. Hayden, *Crime and Punishment in Medieval Chinese Drama: Three Judge Pao Plays*

*83. Sang-Chul Suh, *Growth and Structural Changes in the Korean Economy, 1910–1940*
84. J. W. Dower, *Empire and Aftermath: Yoshida Shigeru and the Japanese Experience, 1878–1954*
85. Martin Collcutt, *Five Mountains: The Rinzai Zen Monastic Institution in Medieval Japan*
86. Kwang Suk Kim and Michael Roemer, *Growth and Structural Transformation*
87. Anne O. Krueger, *The Developmental Role of the Foreign Sector and Aid*
*88. Edwin S. Mills and Byung-Nak Song, *Urbanization and Urban Problems*
89. Sung Hwan Ban, Pal Yong Moon, and Dwight H. Perkins, *Rural Development*
*90. Noel F. McGinn, Donald R. Snodgrass, Yung Bong Kim, Shin-Bok Kim, and Quee-Young Kim, *Education and Development in Korea*
*91. Leroy P. Jones and Il SaKong, *Government, Business, and Entrepreneurship in Economic Development: The Korean Case*
92. Edward S. Mason, Dwight H. Perkins, Kwang Suk Kim, David C. Cole, Mahn Je Kim et al., *The Economic and Social Modernization of the Republic of Korea*
93. Robert Repetto, Tai Hwan Kwon, Son-Ung Kim, Dae Young Kim, John E. Sloboda, and Peter J. Donaldson, *Economic Development, Population Policy, and Demographic Transition in the Republic of Korea*
94. Parks M. Coble, Jr., *The Shanghai Capitalists and the Nationalist Government, 1927–1937*
95. Noriko Kamachi, *Reform in China: Huang Tsun-hsien and the Japanese Model*
96. Richard Wich, *Sino-Soviet Crisis Politics: A Study of Political Change and Communication*
97. Lillian M. Li, *China's Silk Trade: Traditional Industry in the Modern World, 1842–1937*
98. R. David Arkush, *Fei Xiaotong and Sociology in Revolutionary China*
*99. Kenneth Alan Grossberg, *Japan's Renaissance: The Politics of the Muromachi Bakufu*
100. James Reeve Pusey, *China and Charles Darwin*
101. Hoyt Cleveland Tillman, *Utilitarian Confucianism: Chen Liang's Challenge to Chu Hsi*
102. Thomas A. Stanley, *Ōsugi Sakae, Anarchist in Taishō Japan: The Creativity of the Ego*
103. Jonathan K. Ocko, *Bureaucratic Reform in Provincial China: Ting Jih-ch'ang in Restoration Kiangsu, 1867–1870*
104. James Reed, *The Missionary Mind and American East Asia Policy, 1911–1915*
105. Neil L. Waters, *Japan's Local Pragmatists: The Transition from Bakumatsu to Meiji in the Kawasaki Region*
106. David C. Cole and Yung Chul Park, *Financial Development in Korea, 1945–1978*
107. Roy Bahl, Chuk Kyo Kim, and Chong Kee Park, *Public Finances During the Korean Modernization Process*
108. William D. Wray, *Mitsubishi and the N.Y.K, 1870–1914: Business Strategy in the Japanese Shipping Industry*
109. Ralph William Huenemann, *The Dragon and the Iron Horse: The Economics of Railroads in China, 1876–1937*
*110. Benjamin A. Elman, *From Philosophy to Philology: Intellectual and Social Aspects of Change in Late Imperial China*

111. Jane Kate Leonard, *Wei Yüan and China's Rediscovery of the Maritime World*
112. Luke S. K. Kwong, *A Mosaic of the Hundred Days: Personalities, Politics, and Ideas of 1898*
*113. John E. Wills, Jr., *Embassies and Illusions: Dutch and Portuguese Envoys to K'ang-hsi, 1666–1687*
114. Joshua A. Fogel, *Politics and Sinology: The Case of Naitō Konan (1866–1934)*
*115. Jeffrey C. Kinkley, ed., *After Mao: Chinese Literature and Society, 1978–1981*
116. C. Andrew Gerstle, *Circles of Fantasy: Convention in the Plays of Chikamatsu*
117. Andrew Gordon, *The Evolution of Labor Relations in Japan: Heavy Industry, 1853–1955*
*118. Daniel K. Gardner, *Chu Hsi and the "Ta Hsueh": Neo-Confucian Reflection on the Confucian Canon*
119. Christine Guth Kanda, *Shinzō: Hachiman Imagery and Its Development*
*120. Robert Borgen, *Sugawara no Michizane and the Early Heian Court*
121. Chang-tai Hung, *Going to the People: Chinese Intellectual and Folk Literature, 1918–1937*
*122. Michael A. Cusumano, *The Japanese Automobile Industry: Technology and Management at Nissan and Toyota*
123. Richard von Glahn, *The Country of Streams and Grottoes: Expansion, Settlement, and the Civilizing of the Sichuan Frontier in Song Times*
124. Steven D. Carter, *The Road to Komatsubara: A Classical Reading of the Renga Hyakuin*
125. Katherine F. Bruner, John K. Fairbank, and Richard T. Smith, *Entering China's Service: Robert Hart's Journals, 1854–1863*
126. Bob Tadashi Wakabayashi, *Anti-Foreignism and Western Learning in Early-Modern Japan: The "New Theses" of 1825*
127. Atsuko Hirai, *Individualism and Socialism: The Life and Thought of Kawai Eijirō (1891–1944)*
128. Ellen Widmer, *The Margins of Utopia: "Shui-hu hou-chuan" and the Literature of Ming Loyalism*
129. R. Kent Guy, *The Emperor's Four Treasuries: Scholars and the State in the Late Chien-lung Era*
130. Peter C. Perdue, *Exhausting the Earth: State and Peasant in Hunan, 1500–1850*
131. Susan Chan Egan, *A Latterday Confucian: Reminiscences of William Hung (1893–1980)*
132. James T. C. Liu, *China Turning Inward: Intellectual-Political Changes in the Early Twelfth Century*
*133. Paul A. Cohen, *Between Tradition and Modernity: Wang T'ao and Reform in Late Ching China*
134. Kate Wildman Nakai, *Shogunal Politics: Arai Hakuseki and the Premises of Tokugawa Rule*
*135. Parks M. Coble, *Facing Japan: Chinese Politics and Japanese Imperialism, 1931–1937*
*136. Jon L. Saari, *Legacies of Childhood: Growing Up Chinese in a Time of Crisis, 1890–1920*
137. Susan Downing Videen, *Tales of Heichū*

138. Heinz Morioka and Miyoko Sasaki, *Rakugo: The Popular Narrative Art of Japan*
139. Joshua A. Fogel, *Nakae Ushikichi in China: The Mourning of Spirit*
140. Alexander Barton Woodside, *Vietnam and the Chinese Model: A Comparative Study of Vietnamese and Chinese Government in the First Half of the Nineteenth Century*
*141. George Elison, *Deus Destroyed: The Image of Christianity in Early Modern Japan*
142. William D. Wray, ed., *Managing Industrial Enterprise: Cases from Japan's Prewar Experience*
*143. T'ung-tsu Ch'ü, *Local Government in China Under the Ching*
144. Marie Anchordoguy, *Computers, Inc.: Japan's Challenge to IBM*
145. Barbara Molony, *Technology and Investment: The Prewar Japanese Chemical Industry*
146. Mary Elizabeth Berry, *Hideyoshi*
147. Laura E. Hein, *Fueling Growth: The Energy Revolution and Economic Policy in Postwar Japan*
148. Wen-hsin Yeh, *The Alienated Academy: Culture and Politics in Republican China, 1919–1937*
149. Dru C. Gladney, *Muslim Chinese: Ethnic Nationalism in the People's Republic*
150. Merle Goldman and Paul A. Cohen, eds., *Ideas Across Cultures: Essays on Chinese Thought in Honor of Benjamin L Schwartz*
151. James M. Polachek, *The Inner Opium War*
152. Gail Lee Bernstein, *Japanese Marxist: A Portrait of Kawakami Hajime, 1879–1946*
*153. Lloyd E. Eastman, *The Abortive Revolution: China Under Nationalist Rule, 1927–1937*
154. Mark Mason, *American Multinationals and Japan: The Political Economy of Japanese Capital Controls, 1899–1980*
155. Richard J. Smith, John K. Fairbank, and Katherine F. Bruner, *Robert Hart and China's Early Modernization: His Journals, 1863–1866*
156. George J. Tanabe, Jr., *Myōe the Dreamkeeper: Fantasy and Knowledge in Kamakura Buddhism*
157. William Wayne Farris, *Heavenly Warriors: The Evolution of Japan's Military, 500–1300*
158. Yu-ming Shaw, *An American Missionary in China: John Leighton Stuart and Chinese-American Relations*
159. James B. Palais, *Politics and Policy in Traditional Korea*
*160. Douglas Reynolds, *China, 1898–1912: The Xinzheng Revolution and Japan*
161. Roger R. Thompson, *China's Local Councils in the Age of Constitutional Reform, 1898–1911*
162. William Johnston, *The Modern Epidemic: History of Tuberculosis in Japan*
163. Constantine Nomikos Vaporis, *Breaking Barriers: Travel and the State in Early Modern Japan*
164. Irmela Hijiya-Kirschnereit, *Rituals of Self-Revelation: Shishōsetsu as Literary Genre and Socio-Cultural Phenomenon*
165. James C. Baxter, *The Meiji Unification Through the Lens of Ishikawa Prefecture*
166. Thomas R. H. Havens, *Architects of Affluence: The Tsutsumi Family and the Seibu-Saison Enterprises in Twentieth-Century Japan*

167. Anthony Hood Chambers, *The Secret Window: Ideal Worlds in Tanizaki's Fiction*
168. Steven J. Ericson, *The Sound of the Whistle: Railroads and the State in Meiji Japan*
169. Andrew Edmund Goble, *Kenmu: Go-Daigo's Revolution*
170. Denise Potrzeba Lett, *In Pursuit of Status: The Making of South Korea's "New" Urban Middle Class*
171. Mimi Hall Yiengpruksawan, *Hiraizumi: Buddhist Art and Regional Politics in Twelfth-Century Japan*
172. Charles Shirō Inouye, *The Similitude of Blossoms: A Critical Biography of Izumi Kyōka (1873–1939), Japanese Novelist and Playwright*
173. Aviad E. Raz, *Riding the Black Ship: Japan and Tokyo Disneyland*
174. Deborah J. Milly, *Poverty, Equality, and Growth: The Politics of Economic Need in Postwar Japan*
175. See Heng Teow, *Japan's Cultural Policy Toward China, 1918–1931: A Comparative Perspective*
176. Michael A. Fuller, *An Introduction to Literary Chinese*
177. Frederick R. Dickinson, *War and National Reinvention: Japan in the Great War, 1914–1919*
178. John Solt, *Shredding the Tapestry of Meaning: The Poetry and Poetics of Kitasono Katue (1902–1978)*
179. Edward Pratt, *Japan's Protoindustrial Elite: The Economic Foundations of the Gōnō*
180. Atsuko Sakaki, *Recontextualizing Texts: Narrative Performance in Modern Japanese Fiction*
181. Soon-Won Park, *Colonial Industrialization and Labor in Korea: The Onoda Cement Factory*
182. JaHyun Kim Haboush and Martina Deuchler, *Culture and the State in Late Chosŏn Korea*
183. John W. Chaffee, *Branches of Heaven: A History of the Imperial Clan of Sung China*
184. Gi-Wook Shin and Michael Robinson, eds., *Colonial Modernity in Korea*
185. Nam-lin Hur, *Prayer and Play in Late Tokugawa Japan: Asakusa Sensōji and Edo Society*
186. Kristin Stapleton, *Civilizing Chengdu: Chinese Urban Reform, 1895–1937*
187. Hyung Il Pai, *Constructing "Korean" Origins: A Critical Review of Archaeology, Historiography, and Racial Myth in Korean State-Formation Theories*
188. Brian D. Ruppert, *Jewel in the Ashes: Buddha Relics and Power in Early Medieval Japan*
189. Susan Daruvala, *Zhou Zuoren and an Alternative Chinese Response to Modernity*
*190. James Z. Lee, *The Political Economy of a Frontier: Southwest China, 1250–1850*
191. Kerry Smith, *A Time of Crisis: Japan, the Great Depression, and Rural Revitalization*
192. Michael Lewis, *Becoming Apart: National Power and Local Politics in Toyama, 1868–1945*
193. William C. Kirby, Man-houng Lin, James Chin Shih, and David A. Pietz, eds., *State and Economy in Republican China: A Handbook for Scholars*
194. Timothy S. George, *Minamata: Pollution and the Struggle for Democracy in Postwar Japan*

195. Billy K. L. So, *Prosperity, Region, and Institutions in Maritime China: The South Fukien Pattern, 946–1368*
196. Yoshihisa Tak Matsusaka, *The Making of Japanese Manchuria, 1904–1932*
197. Maram Epstein, *Competing Discourses: Orthodoxy, Authenticity, and Engendered Meanings in Late Imperial Chinese Fiction*
198. Curtis J. Milhaupt, J. Mark Ramseyer, and Michael K. Young, eds. and comps., *Japanese Law in Context: Readings in Society, the Economy, and Politics*
199. Haruo Iguchi, *Unfinished Business: Ayukawa Yoshisuke and U.S.-Japan Relations, 1937–1952*
200. Scott Pearce, Audrey Spiro, and Patricia Ebrey, *Culture and Power in the Reconstitution of the Chinese Realm, 200–600*
201. Terry Kawashima, *Writing Margins: The Textual Construction of Gender in Heian and Kamakura Japan*
202. Martin W. Huang, *Desire and Fictional Narrative in Late Imperial China*
203. Robert S. Ross and Jiang Changbin, eds., *Re-examining the Cold War: U.S.-China Diplomacy, 1954–1973*
204. Guanhua Wang, *In Search of Justice: The 1905–1906 Chinese Anti-American Boycott*
205. David Schaberg, *A Patterned Past: Form and Thought in Early Chinese Historiography*
206. Christine Yano, *Tears of Longing: Nostalgia and the Nation in Japanese Popular Song*
207. Milena Doleželová-Velingerová and Oldřich Král, with Graham Sanders, eds., *The Appropriation of Cultural Capital: China's May Fourth Project*
208. Robert N. Huey, *The Making of 'Shinkokinshū'*
209. Lee Butler, *Emperor and Aristocracy in Japan, 1467–1680: Resilience and Renewal*
210. Suzanne Ogden, *Inklings of Democracy in China*
211. Kenneth J. Ruoff, *The People's Emperor: Democracy and the Japanese Monarchy, 1945–1995*
212. Haun Saussy, *Great Walls of Discourse and Other Adventures in Cultural China*
213. Aviad E. Raz, *Emotions at Work: Normative Control, Organizations, and Culture in Japan and America*
214. Rebecca E. Karl and Peter Zarrow, eds., *Rethinking the 1898 Reform Period: Political and Cultural Change in Late Qing China*
215. Kevin O'Rourke, *The Book of Korean Shijo*
216. Ezra F. Vogel, ed., *The Golden Age of the U.S.-China-Japan Triangle, 1972–1989*
217. Thomas A. Wilson, ed., *On Sacred Grounds: Culture, Society, Politics, and the Formation of the Cult of Confucius*
218. Donald S. Sutton, *Steps of Perfection: Exorcistic Performers and Chinese Religion in Twentieth-Century Taiwan*
219. Daqing Yang, *Technology of Empire: Telecommunications and Japanese Expansionism in Asia, 1883–1945*
220. Qianshen Bai, *Fu Shan's World: The Transformation of Chinese Calligraphy in the Seventeenth Century*
221. Paul Jakov Smith and Richard von Glahn, eds., *The Song-Yuan-Ming Transition in Chinese History*

222. Rania Huntington, *Alien Kind: Foxes and Late Imperial Chinese Narrative*
223. Jordan Sand, *House and Home in Modern Japan: Architecture, Domestic Space, and Bourgeois Culture, 1880–1930*
224. Karl Gerth, *China Made: Consumer Culture and the Creation of the Nation*
225. Xiaoshan Yang, *Metamorphosis of the Private Sphere: Gardens and Objects in Tang-Song Poetry*
226. Barbara Mittler, *A Newspaper for China? Power, Identity, and Change in Shanghai's News Media, 1872–1912*
227. Joyce A. Madancy, *The Troublesome Legacy of Commissioner Lin: The Opium Trade and Opium Suppression in Fujian Province, 1820s to 1920s*
228. John Makeham, *Transmitters and Creators: Chinese Commentators and Commentaries on the Analects*
229. Elisabeth Köll, *From Cotton Mill to Business Empire: The Emergence of Regional Enterprises in Modern China*
230. Emma Teng, *Taiwan's Imagined Geography: Chinese Colonial Travel Writing and Pictures, 1683–1895*
231. Wilt Idema and Beata Grant, *The Red Brush: Writing Women of Imperial China*
232. Eric C. Rath, *The Ethos of Noh: Actors and Their Art*
233. Elizabeth Remick, *Building Local States: China During the Republican and Post-Mao Eras*
234. Lynn Struve, ed., *The Qing Formation in World-Historical Time*
235. D. Max Moerman, *Localizing Paradise: Kumano Pilgrimage and the Religious Landscape of Premodern Japan*
236. Antonia Finnane, *Speaking of Yangzhou: A Chinese City, 1550–1850*
237. Brian Platt, *Burning and Building: Schooling and State Formation in Japan, 1750–1890*
238. Gail Bernstein, Andrew Gordon, and Kate Wildman Nakai, eds., *Public Spheres, Private Lives in Modern Japan, 1600–1950: Essays in Honor of Albert Craig*
239. Wu Hung and Katherine R. Tsiang, *Body and Face in Chinese Visual Culture*
240. Stephen Dodd, *Writing Home: Representations of the Native Place in Modern Japanese Literature*
241. David Anthony Bello, *Opium and the Limits of Empire: Drug Prohibition in the Chinese Interior, 1729–1850*
242. Hosea Hirata, *Discourses of Seduction: History, Evil, Desire, and Modern Japanese Literature*
243. Kyung Moon Hwang, *Beyond Birth: Social Status in the Emergence of Modern Korea*
244. Brian R. Dott, *Identity Reflections: Pilgrimages to Mount Tai in Late Imperial China*
245. Mark McNally, *Proving the Way: Conflict and Practice in the History of Japanese Nativism*
246. Yongping Wu, *A Political Explanation of Economic Growth: State Survival, Bureaucratic Politics, and Private Enterprises in the Making of Taiwan's Economy, 1950–1985*
247. Kyu Hyun Kim, *The Age of Visions and Arguments: Parliamentarianism and the National Public Sphere in Early Meiji Japan*
248. Zvi Ben-Dor Benite, *The Dao of Muhammad: A Cultural History of Muslims in Late Imperial China*

249. David Der-wei Wang and Shang Wei, eds., *Dynastic Crisis and Cultural Innovation: From the Late Ming to the Late Qing and Beyond*
250. Wilt L. Idema, Wai-yee Li, and Ellen Widmer, eds., *Trauma and Transcendence in Early Qing Literature*
251. Barbara Molony and Kathleen Uno, eds., *Gendering Modern Japanese History*
252. Hiroshi Aoyagi, *Islands of Eight Million Smiles: Idol Performance and Symbolic Production in Contemporary Japan*
253. Wai-yee Li, *The Readability of the Past in Early Chinese Historiography*
254. William C. Kirby, Robert S. Ross, and Gong Li, eds., *Normalization of U.S.-China Relations: An International History*
255. Ellen Gardner Nakamura, *Practical Pursuits: Takano Chōei, Takahashi Keisaku, and Western Medicine in Nineteenth-Century Japan*
256. Jonathan W. Best, *A History of the Early Korean Kingdom of Paekche, together with an annotated translation of* The Paekche Annals *of the* Samguk sagi
257. Liang Pan, *The United Nations in Japan's Foreign and Security Policymaking, 1945–1992: National Security, Party Politics, and International Status*
258. Richard Belsky, *Localities at the Center: Native Place, Space, and Power in Late Imperial Beijing*
259. Zwia Lipkin, *"Useless to the State": "Social Problems" and Social Engineering in Nationalist Nanjing, 1927–1937*
260. William O. Gardner, *Advertising Tower: Japanese Modernism and Modernity in the 1920s*
261. Stephen Owen, *The Making of Early Chinese Classical Poetry*
262. Martin J. Powers, *Pattern and Person: Ornament, Society, and Self in Classical China*
263. Anna M. Shields, *Crafting a Collection: The Cultural Contexts and Poetic Practice of the* Huajian ji 花間集 *(Collection from Among the Flowers)*
264. Stephen Owen, *The Late Tang: Chinese Poetry of the Mid-Ninth Century (827–860)*
265. Sara L. Friedman, *Intimate Politics: Marriage, the Market, and State Power in Southeastern China*
266. Patricia Buckley Ebrey and Maggie Bickford, *Emperor Huizong and Late Northern Song China: The Politics of Culture and the Culture of Politics*
267. Sophie Volpp, *Worldly Stage: Theatricality in Seventeenth-Century China*
268. Ellen Widmer, *The Beauty and the Book: Women and Fiction in Nineteenth-Century China*
269. Steven B. Miles, *The Sea of Learning: Mobility and Identity in Nineteenth-Century Guangzhou*
270. Lin Man-houng, *China Upside Down: Currency, Society, and Ideologies, 1808–1856*
271. Ronald Egan, *The Problem of Beauty: Aesthetic Thought and Pursuits in Northern Song Dynasty China*
272. Mark Halperin, *Out of the Cloister: Literati Perspectives on Buddhism in Sung China, 960–1279*
273. Helen Dunstan, *State or Merchant? Political Economy and Political Process in 1740s China*
274. Sabina Knight, *The Heart of Time: Moral Agency in Twentieth-Century Chinese Fiction*

275. Timothy J. Van Compernolle, *The Uses of Memory: The Critique of Modernity in the Fiction of Higuchi Ichiyō*
276. Paul Rouzer, *A New Practical Primer of Literary Chinese*
277. Jonathan Zwicker, *Practices of the Sentimental Imagination: Melodrama, the Novel, and the Social Imaginary in Nineteenth-Century Japan*
278. Franziska Seraphim, *War Memory and Social Politics in Japan, 1945–2005*
279. Adam L. Kern, *Manga from the Floating World: Comicbook Culture and the* Kibyōshi *of Edo Japan*
280. Cynthia J. Brokaw, *Commerce in Culture: The Sibao Book Trade in the Qing and Republican Periods*
281. Eugene Y. Park, *Between Dreams and Reality: The Military Examination in Late Chosŏn Korea, 1600–1894*
282. Nam-lin Hur, *Death and Social Order in Tokugawa Japan: Buddhism, Anti-Christianity, and the* Danka *System*
283. Patricia M. Thornton, *Disciplining the State: Virtue, Violence, and State-Making in Modern China*
284. Vincent Goossaert, *The Taoists of Peking, 1800–1949: A Social History of Urban Clerics*
285. Peter Nickerson, *Taoism, Bureaucracy, and Popular Religion in Early Medieval China*
286. Charo B. D'Etcheverry, *Love After* The Tale of Genji*: Rewriting the World of the Shining Prince*
287. Michael G. Chang, *A Court on Horseback: Imperial Touring & the Construction of Qing Rule, 1680–1785*
288. Carol Richmond Tsang, *War and Faith:* Ikkō Ikki *in Late Muromachi Japan*
289. Hilde De Weerdt, *Competition over Content: Negotiating Standards for the Civil Service Examinations in Imperial China (1127–1279)*
290. Eve Zimmerman, *Out of the Alleyway: Nakagami Kenji and the Poetics of Outcaste Fiction*
291. Robert Culp, *Articulating Citizenship: Civic Education and Student Politics in Southeastern China, 1912–1940*
292. Richard J. Smethurst, *From Foot Soldier to Finance Minister: Takahashi Korekiyo, Japan's Keynes*
293. John E. Herman, *Amid the Clouds and Mist: China's Colonization of Guizhou, 1200–1700*
294. Tomoko Shiroyama, *China During the Great Depression: Market, State, and the World Economy, 1929–1937*
295. Kirk W. Larsen, *Tradition, Treaties and Trade: Qing Imperialism and Chosŏn Korea, 1850–1910*
296. Gregory Golley, *When Our Eyes No Longer See: Realism, Science, and Ecology in Japanese Literary Modernism*
297. Barbara Ambros, *Emplacing a Pilgrimage: The Ōyama Cult and Regional Religion in Early Modern Japan*
298. Rebecca Suter, *The Japanization of Modernity: Murakami Haruki between Japan and the United States*

299. Yuma Totani, *The Tokyo War Crimes Trial: The Pursuit of Justice in the Wake of World War II*
300. Linda Isako Angst, *In a Dark Time: Memory, Community, and Gendered Nationalism in Postwar Okinawa*
301. David M. Robinson, ed., *Culture, Courtiers, and Competition: The Ming Court (1368–1644)*
302. Calvin Chen, *Some Assembly Required: Work, Community, and Politics in China's Rural Enterprises*
303. Sem Vermeersch, *The Power of the Buddhas: The Politics of Buddhism During the Koryŏ Dynasty* (918–1392)
304. Tina Lu, *Accidental Incest, Filial Cannibalism, and Other Peculiar Encounters in Late Imperial Chinese Literature*
305. Chang Woei Ong, *Men of Letters Within the Passes: Guanzhong Literati in Chinese History, 907–1911*
306. Wendy Swartz, *Reading Tao Yuanming: Shifting Paradigms of Historical Reception (427–1900)*
307. Peter K. Bol, *Neo-Confucianism in History*
308. Carlos Rojas, *The Naked Gaze: Reflections on Chinese Modernity*
309. Kelly H. Chong, *Deliverance and Submission: Evangelical Women and the Negotiation of Patriarchy in South Korea*
310. Rachel DiNitto, *Uchida Hyakken: A Critique of Modernity and Militarism in Prewar Japan*
311. Jeffrey Snyder-Reinke, *Dry Spells: State Rainmaking and Local Governance in Late Imperial China*
312. Jay Dautcher, *Down a Narrow Road: Identity and Masculinity in a Uyghur Community in Xinjiang China*
313. Xun Liu, *Daoist Modern: Innovation, Lay Practice, and the Community of Inner Alchemy in Republican Shanghai*
314. Jacob Eyferth, *Eating Rice from Bamboo Roots: The Social History of a Community of Handicraft Papermakers in Rural Sichuan, 1920–2000*
315. David Johnson, *Spectacle and Sacrifice: The Ritual Foundations of Village Life in North China*
316. James Robson, *Power of Place: The Religious Landscape of the Southern Sacred Peak* (*Nanyue* 南嶽) *in Medieval China*
317. Lori Watt, *When Empire Comes Home: Repatriation and Reintegration in Postwar Japan*
318. James Dorsey, *Critical Aesthetics: Kobayashi Hideo, Modernity, and Wartime Japan*
319. Christopher Bolton, *Sublime Voices: The Fictional Science and Scientific Fiction of Abe Kōbō*
320. Si-yen Fei, *Negotiating Urban Space: Urbanization and Late Ming Nanjing*
321. Christopher Gerteis, *Gender Struggles: Wage-Earning Women and Male-Dominated Unions in Postwar Japan*
322. Rebecca Nedostup, *Superstitious Regimes: Religion and the Politics of Chinese Modernity*
323. Lucien Bianco, *Wretched Rebels: Rural Disturbances on the Eve of the Chinese Revolution*
324. Cathryn H. Clayton, *Sovereignty at the Edge: Macau and the Question of Chineseness*

325. Micah S. Muscolino, *Fishing Wars and Environmental Change in Late Imperial and Modern China*
326. Robert I. Hellyer, *Defining Engagement: Japan and Global Contexts, 1750–1868*
327. Robert Ashmore, *The Transport of Reading: Text and Understanding in the World of Tao Qian (365–427)*
328. Mark A. Jones, *Children as Treasures: Childhood and the Middle Class in Early Twentieth Century Japan*
329. Miryam Sas, *Experimental Arts in Postwar Japan: Moments of Encounter, Engagement, and Imagined Return*
330. H. Mack Horton, *Traversing the Frontier: The* Man'yōshū *Account of a Japanese Mission to Silla in 736–737*
331. Dennis J. Frost, *Seeing Stars: Sports Celebrity, Identity, and Body Culture in Modern Japan*
332. Marnie S. Anderson, *A Place in Public: Women's Rights in Meiji Japan*
333. Peter Mauch, *Sailor Diplomat: Nomura Kichisaburō and the Japanese-American War*
334. Ethan Isaac Segal, *Coins, Trade, and the State: Economic Growth in Early Medieval Japan*
335. David B. Lurie, *Realms of Literacy: Early Japan and the History of Writing*
336. Lillian Lan-ying Tseng, *Picturing Heaven in Early China*
337. Jun Uchida, *Brokers of Empire: Japanese Settler Colonialism in Korea, 1876–1945*
338. Patricia L. Maclachlan, *The People's Post Office: The History and Politics of the Japanese Postal System, 1871–2010*
339. Michael Schiltz, *The Money Doctors from Japan: Finance, Imperialism, and the Building of the Yen Bloc, 1895–1937*
340. Daqing Yang, Jie Liu, Hiroshi Mitani, and Andrew Gordon, eds., *Toward a History Beyond Borders: Contentious Issues in Sino-Japanese Relations*
341. Sonia Ryang, *Reading North Korea: An Ethnological Inquiry*
342. Susan Huang, *Picturing the True Form: Daoist Visual Culture in Traditional China*
343. Barbara Mittler, *A Continuous Revolution: Making Sense of Cultural Revolution Culture*
344. Hwansoo Ilmee Kim, *Empire of the Dharma: Korean and Japanese Buddhism, 1877–1912*
345. Satoru Saito, *Detective Fiction and the Rise of the Japanese Novel, 1880–1930*
346. Jung-Sun N. Han, *An Imperial Path to Modernity: Yoshino Sakuzō and a New Liberal Order in East Asia, 1905–1937*
347. Atsuko Hirai, *Government by Mourning: Death and Political Integration in Japan, 1603–1912*
348. Darryl E. Flaherty, *Public Law, Private Practice: Politics, Profit, and the Legal Profession in Nineteenth-Century Japan*
349. Jeffrey Paul Bayliss, *On the Margins of Empire: Buraku and Korean Identity in Prewar and Wartime Japan*
350. Barry Eichengreen, Dwight H. Perkins, and Kwanho Shin, *From Miracle to Maturity: The Growth of the Korean Economy*
351. Michel Mohr, *Buddhism, Unitarianism, and the Meiji Competition for Universality*

352. J. Keith Vincent, *Two-Timing Modernity: Homosocial Narrative in Modern Japanese Fiction*
353. Suzanne G. O'Brien, *Customizing Daily Life: Representing and Reforming Customs in Nineteenth-Century Japan*
354. Chong-Bum An and Barry Bosworth, *Income Inequality in Korea: An Analysis of Trends, Causes, and Answers*
355. Jamie L. Newhard, *Knowing the Amorous Man: A History of Scholarship on* Tales of Ise
356. Sho Konishi, *Anarchist Modernity: Cooperatism and Japanese-Russian Intellectual Relations in Modern Japan*
357. Christopher P. Hanscom, *The Real Modern: Literary Modernism and the Crisis of Representation in Colonial Korea*
358. Michael Wert, *Remembering Restoration Losers: Oguri Tadamasa, Ii Naosuke, and Tokugawa Supporters*
359. Garret P.S. Olberding, ed., *Facing the Monarch: Modes of Advice in the Early Chinese Court*
360. Xiaojue Wang, *Modernity with a Cold War Face: Reimagining the Nation in Chinese Literature Across the 1949 Divide*
361. David Spafford, *A Sense of Place: The Political Landscape in Late Medieval Japan*